D1595226

THE FUTURE OF THE
DEUTERONOMISTIC HISTORY

BIBLIOTHECA EPHEMERIDUM THEOLOGICARUM LOVANIENSIUM

CXLVII

THE FUTURE OF THE DEUTERONOMISTIC HISTORY

EDITED BY

T. RÖMER

LEUVEN
UNIVERSITY PRESS

UITGEVERIJ PEETERS
LEUVEN

2000

ISBN 90 5867 010 4 (Leuven University Press)
D/2000/1869/60
ISBN 90-429-0858-0 (Peeters Leuven)
D/2000/0602/63
ISBN 2-87723-492-4 (Peeters France)

BS
1286.5
. F87
2000

All rights reserved. Except in those cases expressly determined by law,
no part of this publication may be multiplied,
saved in an automated data file or made public in any way whatsoever
without the express prior written consent of the publishers

Leuven University Press / Presses Universitaires de Louvain
Universitaire Pers Leuven
Blijde-Inkomststraat 5, B-3000 Leuven-Louvain (Belgium)

© 2000, Peeters, Bondgenotenlaan 153, B-3000 Leuven (Belgium)

FOREWORD

WHICH FUTURE FOR THE DEUTERONOMISTIC HISTORY?

Contrary to the Pentateuch, the Prophets and the Writings the so-called "Deuteronomistic History" is a construction of modern research. It is very difficult to know who first invented the term "deuteronomistic". It was certainly "in the air" already in the nineteenth century; this is clear enough in the works of de Wette[1] and many others. All these scholars recognized that texts in the style of Deuterononomy exist both in the historical books and also in the Tetrateuch. Ewald in the middle of the XIXth century had the idea of a double deuteronomistic (Josianic and exilic) edition of the books of Judges through Kings (followed by Wellhausen and others) with the Hexateuch likely having been edited by (another) deuteronomistic redactor[2]. Duhm then found a multiplicity of deuteronomists throughout the book of Jeremiah[3]. Hence, everything was in place when Noth invented the Deuteronomistic History. And even Cross' modification of Noth's hypothesis by locating the first edition of the Deuteronomistic History under Josiah has its roots in the nineteenth century[4].

For a long time the only real problem concerning the Deuteronomistic History was the choice between two alternatives: an original Josianic or a exilic edition. But in the last decade things have become more complicated. The adherents of the Göttingen school are multiplying redactional layers in the Deuteronomistic History, adding new initials such as DtrB, DtrS, DtrÜ and others to DtrH, DtrP, DtrN[5]. This approach makes it

---

1. For more details cf. T. RÖMER et A. DE PURY, *L'Historiographie Deutéronomiste (HD). Histoire de la recherche et enjeux du débat*, in A. DE PURY – T. RÖMER – J.-D. MACCHI (eds.), *Israël construit son histoire. L'historiographie deutéronomiste à la lumière des recherches récentes* (Le Monde de la Bible, 34), Genève, Labor et Fides, 1996, pp. 9-120; English translation : *Israel Constructs Its History. Deuteronomistic Historiography as Understood in Recent Research* (JSOT S, 306), Sheffield, JSOT Press, 2000, pp. 20-138.

2. H. EWALD, *History of Israel,* 6 vol., London 1867-1886.

3. B. DUHM, *Das Buch Jeremia* (HAT, XI), Tübingen – Leipzig, J.C.B. Mohr (Paul Siebeck), 1901.

4. Cross is very close to the view of Wellhausen and others; cf. F.M. CROSS, *The Themes of the Book of Kings and the Structure of the Deuteronomistic History*, in *Canaanite Myth and Hebrew Epic. Essays in the History of the Religion of Israel*, Cambridge, MA – London, Harvard University Press, 1973, pp. 274-289.

5. See for instance J. PAKKALA, *Intolerant Monolatry in the Deuteronomistic History*

more and more difficult to see a coherent ideology in the Deuteronomistic History as did Martin Noth. Other problems also arise. How, for
instance, should we describe the relationship between the Deuteronomistic History and the "deuteronomistic" texts of the Tetrateuch? For
numerous scholars Deuteronomy is not easily understandable as an
introduction to the deuteronomistic opus. Since the exodus is so important for deuteronomistic theology is it not more logical to have the History start with Exodus?[6]

The debate is becoming quite confusing and in recent years more and
more scholars are inclined to deny the existence of a Deuteronomistic
History as elaborated by Noth. They certainly accept the presence of dtr
texts in the Former Prophets, but they argue against any editorial coherence. Westermann[7] for instance goes back to the early critics of Noth
and highlights the different character of each book belonging to the so-
called Deuteronomistic History. In doing so Westermann wants to reha-
bilitate a kind of *Formgeschichte* that highlights the different forms
inside the Deuteronomistic History (lists, accounts, stories etc) in order
to conclude that they have different *Sitze im Leben*, and that they are
indeed closer to the historical events they describe. On the other hand,
more and more scholars consider the stories in the historical books as
late fiction from the Persian or even Hellenistic Period. If one adopts this
view, the intention of the Deuteronomist as described by Martin Noth
does not work any more.

The contributions in this volume reflect the present state of discussion
about the Deuteronomistic History[8]. With one exception, they were
all presented and discussed in three special sessions dedicated to
«Deuteronomism» during the SBL International Meeting in Lausanne
(July 1997). Three topics were treated: «The Future of the Deuteronomistic History», «Identity and Literary Strategies of the Deuteronomists», «Deuteronomism and the Hebrew Bible».

In the first session, well-known scholars in the field of deuteronomistic research tried to evaluate the future of the Deuteronomistic His-

---

(Publications of the Finnish Exegetical Society, 76), Helsinki – Göttingen, Vandenhoeck
& Ruprecht, 1999, pp. 11-14.

6. On this idea see now K. SCHMID, *Erzväter und Exodus. Untersuchungen zur dop-
pelten Begründung der Ursprünge Israels innerhalb der Geschichtsbücher des Alten Testaments* (WMANT, 81), Neukirchen-Vluyn, Neukirchener Verlag, 1999.

7. C. WESTERMANN, *Die Geschichtsbücher des Alten Testaments. Gab es ein
deuteronomistisches Geschichtswerk?* (TB AT, 87), Gütersloh, Kaiser, 1994.

8. A useful complement to the present volume may be found in L.S. SCHEARING &
S.L. MCKENZIE (eds.), *Those Elusive Deuteronomists. The Phenomenon of Pan-
Deuteronomism* (JSOT SS, 268), Sheffield, JSOT Press, 1999.

tory. The contributions of Steven L. McKenzie («The Divided Kingdom in the Deuteronomistic History»), and John Van Seters («The Future of the Deuteronomistic History. Can It Avoid Death by Redaction?») make clear that Noth's hypothesis still offers an attractive solution, even if some of his views need modifications[9]. Van Seters is particularly sceptical about the idea of several deuteronomistic layers that is advocated by Walter Dietrich («Prophetie im Deuteronomistischen Geschichtswerk»). Dietrich defends the triple (exilic) edition of the Deuteronomistic History, whereas Gary Knoppers («Is There a Future For the Deuteronomistic History?»), in what he calls «a moderate defense», highlights the arguments for the compositional unity of the (preexilic?) deuteronomistic work.

The second session dealt with the question of the social location and the literary strategies of the Deuteronomists. Two of the contributions reject the existence of a unified Deuteronomistic History. Hartmut Rösel («Does a Comprehensive "Leitmotiv" exist in the Deuteronomistic History?») concludes that one should abandon Noth's theory since in the historical books central theological motifs appear in different and even contradictory formulations. A. Graeme Auld («Prophets Shared - But Recycled») considers the books of Samuel and Kings as late as the books of Chronicles, since both depend on the same *Vorlage*. Samuel-Kings do not belong, then, to a Deuteronomistic History, which never existed. Rainer Albertz («In Search of the Deuteronomists. A First Solution to a Historical Riddle») postulates a political and theological opposition inside the deuteronomistic party: the left wing of the Deuteronomists edited the book of Jeremiah, while the conservative and nationalistic group took care of the historical books. This opposition is not accepted by Thomas Römer («L'école deutéronomiste et la formation du canon biblique») who, along with Jacques Vermeylen («L'école deutéronomiste à l'origine du canon biblique»), points out the multiple links that exist between the Deuteronomistic History and the book of Jeremiah. Vermeylen makes a strong case for a deuteronomistic origin of the biblical canon, which may have originated inside the *nebi'im*.

The papers presented at the third session were related to the comparison between deuteronomism and what Noth had called the other two «great compilations» («grosse Sammelwerke») in the Hebrew Bible:

---

9. A quite similar point of view is adopted in Christophe NIHAN's paper (*Le(s) récit(s) de l'instauration de la monarchie en 1 Samuel*). This work was not presented during the Meeting but has been included because it deals with a very important question concerning deuteronomistic ideology.

the Pentateuch and the work of the Chronicler. Diana Edelman («The Deuteronomist's David and the Chronicler's David: Competing or Contrasting Ideologies?») addresses the question of Davidic ideology in Samuel-Kings and Chronicles. Her work stands in stark contrast to Auld's conclusions. Félix García López («La muerte de Moisés, la sucesión de Josué y la escritura de la Tôrah [Deuteronomio 31-34]») explores the relationship between the so-called deuteronomistic redaction of the Pentateuch and the Deuteronomistic History, finding support for a late «D-composition» in the Pentateuch. Michaela Bauks («La signification de l'espace et du temps dans l'historiographie sacerdotale») and Ernst Axel Knauf («Die Priesterschrift und die Geschichte der Deuteronomisten») investigate the Priestly tradition, which appears more and more as an ideological counterpart to deuteronomistic theology.

The arrangement of the contributions is simply by alphabetic order since many articles cannot been reduced to one of the three main themes that I have briefly presented. Each article offers a valuable entry into one of the most important discussions of Old Testament scholarship at the end of the twentieth century. Some readers may feel a frustration of sorts at the apparent lack of consensus. Nevertheless, all the papers collected in this volume underline the importance of what we call the deuteronomists[10] for the formation of the Hebrew Bible.

This foreword gives me the opportunity to express my gratitude to Professor F. Neirynck for having accepted this manuscript in the BETL series, to the Publishers Peeters for their careful work, and last but not least to Mr. Christophe Nihan and Mrs. Renée Girardet for their hard work on the indexes.

Thomas C. RÖMER

---

10. Some scholars identify the deuteronomists with the Shafan family. Although the proposal is appealing for its attempt to grant incarnation to this elusive group, it is very hypothetical.

CONTENTS

IN SEARCH OF THE DEUTERONOMISTS
A FIRST SOLUTION TO A HISTORICAL RIDDLE[1]

Lothar Perlitt calls "Deuteronomism" "the slogan of present research"[2]. After Martin Noth had discovered Deuteronomistic History (DtrG) in 1943[3], in more and more biblical books more or less deuteronomistic (dtr.) redaction was acknowledged. Even texts without any dtr. stylistic features were classified as deuteronomistic because of their theological content (e.g. Isa 7 by Otto Kaiser[4]). Thus it would hardly be an exaggeration to say that we are confronted with the danger of "Pandeuteronomism", in which the literary hypothesis goes beyond all bounds.

Considering the optimistic proliferation of the dtr. hypothesis on the literary level, I want to ask the simple historical question of who these enormously productive Deuteronomists (Dtr.) could have been. Such a question seems to be totally out of fashion today, since a scholarly attitude has become prominent in recent Old Testament research: on the one hand, it shows a surprising confidence in the reliability of literary-critical results through the most exacting investigation of the texts but, on the other hand, it demonstrates exaggerated scepticism towards any certainty on the historical level, or even a lack of interest in any historical questions. Anyway, contrary to this modern "scholarly docetism", I want to emphasize the old-fashioned opinion that a literary hypothesis can only be regarded as proved if it is possible to supply it with a plausible basis in real history.

1. Cf. R. ALBERTZ, Le milieu des Deutéronomistes, in A. DE PURY – T. RÖMER – J.-D. MACCHI (eds.), Israël construit son histoire. L'historiographie deutéronomiste à la lumière des recherches récentes (Le monde de la Bible, 34), Genève, Labor et Fides, 1996, pp. 377-407 (translation by T. Römer); ID., Wer waren die Deuteronomisten? Das historische Rätsel einer literarischen Hypothese, in EvT 57 (1997) 319-388. The present version is shortened in the exegetical investigations and more detailed in the historical conclusions.

2. See L. PERLITT, Hebraismus – Deuteronomismus – Judaismus, in G. BRAULIK (ed.), Biblische Theologie und gesellschaftlicher Wandel. FS N. Lohfink, Freiburg – Basel – Wien, Herder, 1993, pp. 279-295, p. 279.

3. See M. NOTH, Überlieferungsgeschichtliche Studien, Darmstadt, Wissenschaftliche Buchgesellschaft, ³1967, pp. 1-110.

4. See O. KAISER, Das Buch des Propheten Jesaja. Kapitel 1-12 (ATD, 17), Göttingen, Vandenhoeck & Ruprecht, ⁵1981, pp. 141ff., more cautious cf. ID., Grundriß der Einleitung in die kanonischen und deuterokanonischen Schriften des Alten Testaments. Bd. II: Die prophetischen Werke, Gütersloh, Gütersloher Verlagshaus, 1994, pp. 35-42.

I. THE RIDDLE OF THE DEUTERONOMISTS

Having asked the question of who the Deuteronomists could have been, one finds the replies given by Old Testament scholars curiously blurred and contradictory. The historical enquiry seems not to be their main interest in this field.

Martin Noth as we know thinks of the Deuteronomist as a single man whom he describes in the following way[5]: he did not belong to the "intellectual sphere of priesthood, he was not rooted in the thoughts of official state-life", he kept his distance from both, "the spirit of the 'written'-prophets" and "the ideology of the so-called national prophets". He did not write "his work on behalf of a single person or a certain group", thus his work did not have "any official character". He was at work after 560 B.C. in Palestine, more specifically in the region of Mizpah-Bethel.

Although we appreciate how Noth tried to characterize, to locate and to date the Deuteronomist as exactly as possible, it must be said that his standing as a reliable historian who dissociated himself from all other groups and was not obliged to anybody, cannot explain why he had such influence on the literary history of the Bible. Noth's lack of interest in situating the author in the Judean society of the exilic period means that Deuteronomism has remained a historical riddle.

Shortly after Noth, a countercurrent appeared which released the author of the DtrG from his splendid isolation: The Deuteronomist became a school or a movement.

The authors of the dtr. literature soon became, for most, those preaching and teaching Levites as portrayed in post exilic times[6], a concept which was already developed by Gerhard von Rad in order to explain the origin of Deuteronomy[7]. Hans Walter Wolff supposed a "levitical-prophetical alliance of opposition"[8], who drove forward the shaping of

---

5. *Überlieferungsgeschichtliche Studien* (see note 3), pp. 109f.
6. Cf. O.H. STECK, *Israel und das gewaltsame Geschick der Propheten. Untersuchungen zur Überlieferung des deuteronomistischen Geschichtsbildes im Alten Testament, Spätjudentum und im Urchristentum* (WMANT, 23), Neukirchen-Vluyn, Neukirchener Verlag, 1967, pp. 196-199; W. ROTH, Art. *Deuteronomistisches Geschichtswerk – Deuteronomistische Schule*, in *TRE VIII* (1981) 543-552, esp. p. 547.
7. Cf. G. VON RAD, *Deuteronomium-Studien* [1947], in *Gesammelte Studien zum Alten Testament II* (TB, 48), München, Kaiser, 1973, pp. 109-153, pp. 143-150; ID., *Das fünfte Buch Mose. Deuteronomium* (ATD, 8), Göttingen, Vandenhoeck & Ruprecht, ²1968, pp. 16ff.; cf. Neh 8,1ff. On the scholarly discussion, cf. H.D. PREUSS, *Deuteronomium* (EdF, 164), Darmstadt, Wissenschaftliche Buchgesellschaft, 1982, pp. 30f.
8. H.W. WOLFF, *Hoseas geistige Heimat* [1956], in *Gesammelte Studien* (TB, 22), München, Kaiser, 1964, pp. 232-250, esp. 150.

the dtn. and dtr. literature from the time of Hosea. He thinks that the authors of the DtrG were from the disciples of Jeremiah[9]. Odil Hannes Steck viewed the dtr. movement as supported by the country-Levites, and lasting even until the Hellenistic era. According to him, Deuteronomism constituted one of the main streams of Israelite literary and theological history in exilic-postexilic times[10]. Others, more intent in dates than in identifying specific groups, like Enno Janssen[11] or Ernest W. Nicholson[12], associated Deuteronomism with the exilic custom of preaching in the emerging synagogues, whether located in Palestine or Babylonia. The assumption of a "dtr. school" enabled Rudolf Smend and his pupils to give enough time for several literary dtr. layers to develop in DtrG, which they believed to be distinguishable in contrast to Noth. Illuminating is a quotation from Smend's Introduction: "The dtr. school – however one may imagine it more exactly – surely existed over generations"[13].

So, how should we characterize the dtr. school or the dtr. movement? Levites, disciples of the prophets, preachers in the synagogues? And what does the statement mean "that" it surely existed over generations? Was it a phenomenon of the exilic period, had it already emerged in pre-exilic times, or did it last into the Persian or even Hellenistic era? As much as we appreciate the attempt to create a wide ranging social basis in accordance with the widespread literary phenomenon, the hypothesis of a dtr. school or movement meant that the historical pinpointing, which was still Martin Noth's interest, was largely given up[14]. The historical riddle of Deuteronomism was not really solved.

---

9. See H.W. WOLFF, *Das Kerygma des Deuteronomistischen Geschichtswerkes* [1956], in *Gesammelte Studien* (TB, 22), München, Kaiser, pp. 308-324, esp. 323.

10. O.H. STECK, *Strömungen theologischer Tradition* [1978], in *Wahrnehmungen Gottes im Alten Testament* (TB, 70), München, Kaiser, 1982, pp. 291-317, esp. 302-315. Cf. his later statement in ID., *Der Abschluß der Prophetie im Alten Testament. Ein Versuch zur Frage der Vorgeschichte des Kanons* (BTSt, 17), Neukirchen-Vluyn, Neukirchener Verlag, 1991, p. 145 n. 313, referring to the late 3rd and early 2nd century B.C.: "in identifying these upholders as 'Levites' I would be more cautious today, but I do not know a better solution".

11. E. JANSSEN, *Juda in der Exilszeit. Ein Beitrag zur Frage der Entstehung des Judentums* (FRLANT, 69), Göttingen, Vandenhoeck & Ruprecht, 1956, p. 123.

12. E.W. NICHOLSON, *Preaching to the Exiles. A Study of the Prose Tradition in the Book of Jeremiah*, Oxford, Blackwell, 1970, p. 134.

13. R. SMEND, *Die Entstehung des Alten Testaments* (TW, 1), Stuttgart, Kohlhammer, ²1984, p. 124.

14. Cf. the legitimate criticism of N. LOHFINK, *Gab es eine deuteronomistische Bewegung?*, in W. GROSS (ed.), *Jeremia und die "deuteronomistische Bewegung"* (BBB, 98), Weinheim, Beltz, 1995, pp. 313-382, esp. 315f.; cf. already my criticism in R. ALBERTZ, *A History of Israelite Religion in the Old Testament Period,* 2 Vol. (OTL), Louisville, MD, Westminster, 1994, pp. 438f.; 469f.

All previously mentioned hypotheses are doubtful in respect to the historical question: The thesis of Levites, put forward by Gerhard von Rad and his followers, suffers from the fact that it projects back into the pre-exilic period, post-exilic conditions, in which the Levites constitute a lower class of priests. Considering the fact that the Levites – apart from some Chronical editing[15] – do not play any role in the DtrG[16], it is entirely unlikely that the Levites could have been the authors of the dtr. literature.

The thesis of prophet's disciples is better founded in so far as the dtr. redactors of prophetic books could naturally be named as disciples of the prophets in a broad sense. However, it remains doubtful whether the thesis can claim validity for the entire dtr. literature since in the DtrG – apart from 2 Kings 18-20, where Isaiah is mentioned as a prophet of salvation – not one of the classical prophets of doom is mentioned at all. The "prophetic silence in the Deuteronomistc History", as Klaus Koch labelled this fact[17], still awaits a plausible explanation[18].

It is difficult to derive the speeches in the DtrG and the dtr. book of Jeremiah (JerD) from the custom of preaching in the synagogue since synagogues are historically attested only in much later times[19]. It cannot

15. So certainly Deut 27,9f.; Josh 3,3; 2 Sam 15,24; 1 Kings 8,4; probably also 1 Sam 6,15; the few remaining occurrences have to do with the Levites proclaiming the curses in Deut 27,14 and with the memory of the "historical" Levites in Judg 17f.; 20,4; Josh 14,3; 18,7; 21.

16. In early times there can be found only "levitical priests" (Deut 27,9f.; 31,9; Josh 3,3; 8,33), in the monarchical period we meet only priests. In the DtrG, in contrast to the Chronicler, not Levites but the priests carry the Ark (Josh 3,6.8.13f.17; 4,3.9-11.16-18; 6,4.6.8f.12; 1 Kings 8,3); the Zadokides are regarded as the elected priesthood (1 Sam 2,35; cf. 1 Kings 12,31). Cf. R. ALBERTZ, *Die Intention und Träger des Deuteronomistischen Geschichtswerks*, in R. ALBERTZ – F.W. GOLKA – J. KEGLER (eds.), *Schöpfung und Befreiung*. FS C. Westermann, Stuttgart, Calwer, 1989, pp. 37-53, esp. 48.

17. K. KOCH, *Das Profetenschweigen des deuteronomistischen Geschichtswerks*, in J. JEREMIAS – L. PERLITT (eds.), *Die Botschaft und die Boten*. FS H.W. Wolff, Neukirchen-Vluyn, Neukirchener Verlag, 1981, pp. 115-128.

18. In my opinion, it does not help to deny this problem as W. Dietrich tried to do, arguing that "books with extensive deuteronomistic redactions (e.g. of the prophets) were at the disposal of the deuteronomistic school. Why should they combine everything?". See W. DIETRICH, *Martin Noth and the Future of the Deuteronomistic History*, in S. L. MCKENZIE – M. P. GRAHAM (eds.), *The History of Israel's Traditions. The Heritage of Martin Noth* (JSOT SS, 182), Sheffield, JSOT Press, 1994, pp. 153-175, esp. 170 n. 4. One may ask him why the authors of the books of Chronicles introduced Jeremiah into their work without any hesitation (2 Chron 35,25; 36,12), although the book of Jeremiah was likewise at their disposal? Why could the authors of the DtrG not proceed in the same way as the Chronists, if they really wished to do so?

19. The first inscription mentioning a προσευχή comes from the 3rd century B.C.; the earliest building, identified as a synagogue was founded on Delos island in the 1st century B.C; the earliest synagogues excavated in Palestine may be from the 1st century A.D. From this time we also have some literary sources (Philo, Josephus, New Testament), cf. L.I.

be excluded that the origins of services based on the word go back into the exilic period, but it is completely uncertain whether sermons would have been a part of it. Admittedly, in some cases, admonishing speeches in the DtrG (1 Kings 8) and in JerD (Jer 7; 26) are located in the temple, but they are not part of the service itself[20]. If they attest anything at all, it is rather a practise of preaching outside the cult[21].

Norbert Lohfink was quite right when pointing out recently how dubious are the ideas about a dtr. school or movement when used unreflectingly[22]. Leaping from dtr. phrasings to conclusions at the social level often causes what he calls "pandeuteronomistic chain reactions"[23], such as: since dtr. texts are spread through many books and over long periods of time, there must exist a similar wide-spread and long-lasting dtr. movement. To counter such assumptions he called for a conscientious historical inquiry with more criteria than stylistic and theological dtr. features[24].

In this context, Lohfink made it clear that movements are not normally defined by their rhetorics, but by their goals[25]. That means it is simplistic to conclude on the basis of common dtr. rhetorics that there exists a uniform dtr. movement or school. It is possible that a group, coming from a different background and thus speaking a different language, can nevertheless be part of the same movement because it fights for the same goals[26]. But more important is the opposite possibility, un-

LEVINE, *Synagogues*, in E. STERN (ed.), *The New Encyclopedia of Archaeological Excavations in the Holy Land*. Vol. IV, Jerusalem, Israel Exploration Society, 1993, pp. 1421-1424, esp. 1422. For more details, see L.L. GRABBE, *Synagogues in the pre-70 Palestine: A Re-Assessment*, in *JTS* 39 (1988) 401-410; ID., *Judaism from Cyrus to Hadrian*, 2 Vol., Minneapolis, MN, Fortress, pp. 541-542.

20. The preaching of Jeremiah in the temple-gate was addressed to the visitors who were coming to take part in the cultic service later; the speech of Solomon in 1 Kings 8,12-21, and even his prayers (8,22-61) were done before the cultic service took place (8,62ff.). This also makes doubtful the thesis that exilic lamentation-services in Mizpah and Bethel should be the historical background of the dtr. movement, as put forward by T. VEIJOLA, *Verheißung in der Krise. Studien zur Literatur und Theologie der Exilszeit anhand des 89. Psalms* (AASF B, 220), Helsinki, Suomalainen Tiedeakatemia, 1982, pp. 190ff.; esp. 205ff.

21. Cf. the speeches of Jeremiah in the city-gate (Jer 17,19ff.) and in the palace-gate (Jer 22,1ff.). That the dtr. "Alternativ-Predigten" in the book of Jeremiah point to a real exilic practice is a thesis advanced by W. THIEL, *Die deuteronomistische Redaktion von Jeremia 1-25* (WMANT, 44), Neukirchen-Vluyn, Neukirchener Verlag, 1973, pp. 290-300. I have followed him, pointing out more precisely that it concerns a non-cultic practice, see R. ALBERTZ, *History of Israelite Religion* (n. 14), pp. 382-387.

22. N. LOHFINK, *Bewegung* (n. 14), pp. 313ff.

23. *Ibid.*, p. 320.

24. *Ibid.*, p. 321.

25. *Ibid.*, p. 324.

26. Lohfink thinks of the authors of the so called "Assyrian-redaction" in the book of Isaiah (*ibid.*, pp. 335-337), who, interpreting the fall of the Assyrian empire in the light of

fortunately overlooked by Lohfink: groups which come from a common background and use the same or similar rhetorics can nevertheless constitute several movements because they fight for different goals[27]. Thus, in order to identify the authors of dtr. literature, the first methodological step should be to analyze the dtr. texts for their *Tendenz* in order to recognize their religious, cultic, political and social interests and, if possible, to distinguish their concepts. In this case alone is there a chance to solve the historical riddle of the Deuteronomists.

II. SHOULD WE RECKON WITH DIFFERENT DEUTERONOMISTIC GROUPS?

If we manage to free ourselves from the *a priori* about Deuteronomists constituting a single group, then the serious differences in the tendency of their works at once become apparent[28]. I will show this by comparing three selected topics from the two most important dtr. works, DtrG and JerD. In doing so, I take for granted the final shape of each work.

1. Jehoiachin and the future of the Davidic kingdom

As is well known, the DtrG ends with the amnesty of Jehoiachin issued by the Babylonian king, Awil-Marduk, in his accession-year

Isaiah's prophecy, likewise supported the reform policy of Josiah. Cf. Isa 9,1-6 and H. BARTH, *Die Jesaja-Worte in der Josiazeit. Israel und Assur als Thema einer produktiven Neuinterpretation der Jesajaüberlieferung* (WMANT, 48), Neukirchen-Vluyn, Neukirchener Verlag, 1977.

27. See my provisional considerations in R. ALBERTZ, *Intentionen* (n. 16), p. 46; ID., *History of Israelite Religion* (see note 14), pp. 382f., and similarly C. HARDMEIER, *Die Propheten Micha und Jesaja im Spiegel von Jeremia XXVI und 2 Regnum XVIII-XX. Zur Prophetie-Rezeption in der nach-joschianischen Zeit*, in *VT* 43 (1991) 172-189; ID., *Prophetie im Streit vor dem Untergang Judas. Erzählkommunikative Studien zur Entstehungssituation der Jesaja- und Jeremiaerzählungen in II Reg 18-20 und Jer 37-40* (BZAW, 187), Berlin-New York, de Gruyter, 1990, pp. 443-468.

28. How strong this prejudice is can be studied in recent scholarly resarch. The assumption that Deuteronomism must constitute a uniform movement forced several scholars to deny any major difference between DtrG and JerD, even when they found some, cf. H.-J. HERMISSON, *Jeremias Wort über Jojachin*, in R. ALBERTZ – H.-P. MÜLLER – H.W. WOLFF – W. ZIMMERLI (eds.), *Werden und Wirken des Alten Testaments*. FS C. Westermann, Göttingen, Vandenhoeck & Ruprecht; Neukirchen-Vluyn, Neukirchener Verlag, 1980, pp. 252-270, esp. 270; W. DIETRICH, *Future* (see note 18), p. 170 n. 3; H.-J. STIPP, *Jeremia im Parteienstreit. Studien zur Textentwicklung von Jer 26, 36-43 und 45 als Beitrag zur Geschichte Jeremias, seines Buches und judäischer Parteien im 6. Jahrhundert* (BBB, 82), Weinheim, Betz, 1992, pp. 8-11; esp. 298f. However, in his later article he is ready to concede that there existed two different branches in the dtr. movement which differ sharply in their "radically opposite attitudes towards Jeremiah", see ID., *Probleme des redaktionsgeschichtlichen Modells der Entstehung des Jeremiabuches*, in W. GROSS (ed.), *Jeremia und die "deuteronomistische Bewegung"* (BBB, 98), Weinheim, Betz, 1995, pp. 225-262, esp. 232.

562 B.C. (2 Kings 25,27-30). The meaning of this strange final scene has been much debated. But however it might be judged, it must be admitted that in the view of the DtrG, Jehoiachin is still a figure of particular interest, even in the late exilic period. When we take into consideration the important role David plays in this history, and how the divine promise given to the Davidic dynasty was manifest in that it could moderate and delay the divine judgement[29], then we may probably conclude that in the view of the authors of the DtrG, Jehoiachin is still a symbol of hope for a better future. His release is an important hint that the divine promise has started to work in history again.

The authors of JerD also dealt with Jehoiachin in detail, as we can see in Jer 22,24-30. In this text they commented on single or already combined sayings of doom proclaimed by Jeremiah about Jehoiachin during the siege of Jerusalem in 598/7 B.C. and during the anti-Babylonian conspiration of 594 B.C. Reconstructed[30], they might have gone as follows:

24 Even if Coniah son of Jehoiakim should be a signet-ring on my right hand, I would pull you off from there
26 and fling you on the ground.
28 "Is Coniah a despised vessel or pot which nobody wants? Why else is he flung on the ground?"
30 Write this man down as childless, as a man who will not have any luck in the days of his life.

Jehoiachin, who thinks he could escape punishment for the risky foreign policy of his father by surrendering the city – so Jeremiah proclaimed in harsh relentlessness –, will be rejected by YHWH. Jehoiachin, on whom the anti-Babylonian nationalists in Judah and Babylonia placed their hopes and whose quick return they expected (Jer 28,3f.), remained rejected, without any heir to the throne, a total failure – so Jeremiah persisted in his proclamation.

The redactors of JerD proved to be faithful disciples of Jeremiah: not only did they comment on this harsh oracle historically, but also prolonged it into their present and sharpened it considerably: Jehoiachin and his mother would never return to Judah (Jer 22,26f.), all the descendants of Jehoiachin were put under the verdict of rejection

29. Cf. 2 Sam 7,14.16; 1 Kings 2,4; 8,25; 9,5; 11,12f.; 15,4; 2 Kings 8,19; 19,34 and more detailed in R. ALBERTZ, *History of Israelite Religion* (n. 14), pp. 392ff.
30. My literary reconstruction largely follows H.-J. HERMISSON, *Jeremias Wort* (n. 28); contrary to his view, I regard v. 30b altogether as a dtr. formation, since the key-word צלח of v. 30a is resumed in v. 30b; the word זרעו in v. 28 represents a dtr. addition as well, and the expression ישׁב על־כסא דוד is testified in JerD (Jer 17,25; 22,2; 29,16), cf. W. THIEL, *Redaktion I* (n. 21), pp. 242-246.

(28bα².30bα), and none of them would ever sit on the throne of David and rule once more in Judah (30bβ). Therefore, this Jehoiachin-oracle represents a sharp contradiction to the hope nourished by the authors of the DtrG in the final note of their work. Whatever the meaning of his release should be, Jehoiachin remained rejected by God. No one of his many children, begotten in Babylonia in spite of Jeremiah's condemnation, would reign in Judah. No divine promise rested on Jehoiachin which could open a better future for Israel. That means that between both dtr. groups of authors there existed total disagreement about the important political question of Israel's future in late-exilic times.

The emphatic call for attention with which the dtr. authors of JerD introduce their concluding judgement about Jehoiachin and all his family shows how explosive was the matter:

> 22,29 O land, land, land, hear the word of YHWH[31]!

Obviously, in their view it was a crucial message for their country.

How important it really was, became clear at a stroke in early post-exilic times: When the Persians appointed the grandson of Jehoiachin, Zerubbabel, as the official to be responsible for the first major return and the reconstruction of the Temple (פחת יהודה, cf. Hag 1,1.14 etc.), whatever their intentions had been, the prophet of salvation Haggai thought it necessary to abolish explicitly in the name of YHWH (Hag 2,20-23) Jeremiah's judgement about Jehoiachin's family. Obviously, he wished to make space for, and legitimate, the great hopes of restoration of the Davidic monarchy which the people placed in Zerubbabel. Thus, nothing less than the political constitution of future Israel was at stake in the controversy between the two dtr. groups.

2. The role of the temple cult in Jerusalem

Contrary to the opinion of Martin Noth and others, the DtrG paid particular attention to the temple of Jerusalem: Construction and destruction of the Solomonic temple were recorded carefully in detail[32]. The period of Solomon's reign was artificially divided into two periods in order to keep the construction of the Jerusalem temple clear from any shadow of apostasy. Besides the Davidic-promise it proves the divine election of Jerusalem, which moderates and delays Judah's punishment

---

31. W. THIEL, *Redaktion I* (n. 21), p. 245, did not know what to do with this verse; he writes: "Äußerst fragwürdig ist Herkunft und Sinn von V. 29". However, he admits that the verse is related to the calls for attention in other dtr. sermons (like Jer 7,2; 17,20; 19,3; 22,2). So an allocation to JerD is most probable.
    32. Cf. 1 Kings 6-8; 2 Kings 24,13f.; 25,13-17.

by YHWH[33]. As Hans-Detlef Hoffmann has pointed out, the detailed report about the cult-reform of king Josiah (2 Kings 22-23), by which all cultic and religious aberrations were eliminated, represents the peak and the highlight of all the DtrG[34]. Even if YHWH's judgement on Judah was irrevocably provoked by the abominable sins of king Manasseh, the state-reformed and state-controlled temple cult in Jerusalem, which Josiah had established, constitutes the cult-political option for the future in the view of the DtrG.

At this point too, the Jeremiah-Deuteronomists hold a different opinion: They also placed Jeremiah's sayings about the temple of Jerusalem at important points in their book (Jer 7; 26)[35]. But following Jeremiah, they castigated confidence in the temple as a lie (7,4). Trusting in the protecting cultic presence of YHWH, in spite of social and religious abuses, had perverted the temple into a robber's cave and caused its destruction by YHWH. A new start for Israel could happen, as the Jeremiah-Deuteronomists explained in their sermon-like redaction (7,3.5-7), only if everybody would "mend their ways and their doings", and that includes not only religious-cultic but also social behaviour. Instead of a monarchic cult reform from above, the Jeremia-Deuteronomists advocated a broad social renewal from below[36].

Again, the importance of this disagreement between the two dtr. groups becomes apparent if we consider the options in the early post-exilic period: Against considerable resistance, the reconstruction of the temple was carried out and – thanks mainly to the the Davidic descendant Zerubbabel – still maintained the traditional state-cultic concept. Again, it was the prophet Haggai who expected the decisive breakthrough to a new era of salvation by means of the reconstruction of the temple (Hag 1,3-11; 2,15-19). This conflicted with the option the Jeremiah-Deuteronomists had fought for, but was in accord with the cultic concept of the DtrG[37].

33. Cf. 1 Kings 8,16; 11,13.32.36; 14,21; 15,4; also 2 Kings 18,34.

34. H.-D. HOFFMANN, *Reform und Reformen. Untersuchungen zu einem Grundthema der deuteronomistischen Geschichtsschreibung* (ATANT, 66), Zürich, Theologischer Verlag, 1980, pp. 223ff.

35. At the head of the collection of Jeremiah's proclamations after the death of Josiah (609 B.C.) and at the head of the collection of Jeremiah-stories.

36. In JerD the reconstructed temple is only a side-effect (see Jer 17,26), not the cause of the new beginnings. Thus it is no accident that in Jer 39,4-10 the destruction of the temple is not mentioned at all, while in the parallel account of 2 Kings 25,1-21 it stands at the center (v. 9.13-17).

37. It is no accident that after the fiasco of national prophecy which accompanied the reconstruction of the temple, the books of Haggai and Zechariah were dtr. reworked (Hag 2,5a; Zech 1,1-6; 6,15b; 7,4-14; 8,14-17,19b). The redaction has a tendency similar to JerD, cf. R. ALBERTZ, *History of Israelite Religion* (n. 14), pp. 454ff.

3. The importance of the social gospel

It is a remarkable fact that the DtrG judges the behaviour of Israel and its kings nearly exclusively according to the religious and cultic commandments and laws of Deuteronomy. The commandments against foreign deities and idols (Deut 5,6-10) constitute the main criterion; and the authors of the DtrG discovered apostasy from YHWH again and again in Israel's history, and denounced it with relentless rigour[38]. However, none of the many dtn. social laws is of any importance in the evaluation of Israelite history[39].

Also at this point there is a clear difference between JerD and DtrG. Like their DtrG colleagues, the dtr. redactors of Jeremiah underlined the religious accusations of the prophet, but they took over his social accusations as well. The conversion they demanded included both the religious-cultic and the social areas, as had already been evident in the temple-sermon, Jer 7,1-15. In their view, the most important duty of the kings should be not cult-reform, but the establishment of law and justice (Jer 22,1-6). So it is no accident that the authors of JerD in distinction from those of DtrG refer to the social legislation of Deut: They stigmatize the way the upperclasses, having released slaves in the days of Zedekiah, soon took them back; it was an explicit violation of the deuteronomic laws of remission and slaves (Jer 34,14; Deut 15,1ff.,12ff.).

Thus one has to say that in the view of the Jeremiah-Deuteronomists, Israel's relationship to God also had its crucial criterion in the realisation of social justice.

III. THE HISTORICAL IDENTIFICATION OF BOTH DEUTERONOMISTIC GROUPS

If the authors or redactors of the two literary works qualified as "deuteronomistic" pursued such different aims on three central points at issue, which could easily be multiplied[40], then it is obviously wrong to imagine the Deuteronomists as a uniform movement. "Deuteronomism" is not to be defined as a movement or school but as "a theological cur-

38. Cf. Josh 23,7f.; Judg 2,11ff. *passim*; 1 Kings 9,6.9; 11,7f.; 14,8f.; 16,30f.; 2 Kings 21,3-7 etc.
39. 1 Kings 12,1-18 and 21,1-19 seem to be exceptions at first glance. But they represent older traditions which the authors of the DtrG were forced to include in their work for several reasons (e.g. the Naboth-theme was already connected with the story of the Jehu revolution which was of crucial importance for the Deuteronomists, cf. 2 Kings 9,25f.). But in both cases the original social conflicts were interpreted by them along theological lines as apostasy, cf. 1 Kings 11,1-12; 12,33ff.; 21,26.
40. I mention only the totally different evaluation of the brothers in the North (cf. 2 Kings 17,24-34a.[34b-41] with Jer 3,6ff.; 30,1ff. and 31,31-34).

rent of the time"[41], typical of the 6th century B.C. In spite of common rhetorics and similiar theological topics, it comprised very different groups.

Taking for granted Lohfink's methodological demand that the authors of particular dtr. literature cannot simply be postulated on the basis of linguistic indications, but have to be reconstructed on the basis of particular historical investigations, it is no longer possible to project a single anonymous group into a dark historical sphere; instead, we have to find a place for them in the spectrum of groups which texts document as living in the 6th century B.C.

Of course, for the time of the exile in a narrow sense (587-539 B.C.), our sources are extremely limited, but for the late pre-exilic and early post-exilic decades, our knowledge about groups and their quarrels is much better (see 2 Kings 22-25; Jer 20-45; Hag; Zech; Ezra 1-6). In the scenery of the quarreling groups or parties of that time, both named dtr. groups of authors can be identified with some degree of probability.

1. Identifying the Jeremiah-Deuteronomists

Only a short outline of my historical reconstruction of the era under discussion can be presented here[42]: Important for the later dtr. development is the fact that the Josianic reform (622 B.C.) was supported by a broad coalition of different groups and persons[43]. According to the account of 2 Kings 22-23, which got its final shape only 60 years after the events, and cannot be totally invented, the following persons and groups were concerned: Members of the royal family (Josiah, later Jehoahaz), influental sections of the priesthood of Jerusalem headed by the mainpriest Hilkiah, important parts of the officials around the scribe Shaphan, the majority of the nobility of Judah (עם הארץ), and prophets like Hulda and the young Jeremiah[44]. Upholders of a common movement, all these

---

41. So R. ALBERTZ, *History of Israelite Religion* (n. 14), p. 382; in German "eine theologische Zeitströmung". C. HARDMEIER, *Prophetie im Streit* (n. 27), p. 467, speaks of a "Epochenphänomen".

42. For more details of my historical reconstruction, see R. ALBERTZ, *History of Israelite Religion* (n. 14), pp. 198-206 and 231-242.

43. Cf. the similar view already taken by F. CRÜSEMANN, *"...damit er dich segne in allem Tun deiner Hand..." (Dtn 14,29). Die Produktionsverhältnisse der späten Königszeit, dargestellt am Ostrakon von Meṣad Ḥashavjahu, und die Sozialgesetzgebung des Deuteronomiums*, in L. and W. SCHOTTROFF (eds.), *Mitarbeiter der Schöpfung. Bibel und Arbeitswelt*, München, Kaiser, 1983, pp. 72-103, esp. 99-102; see now also ID., *Die Tora. Theologie und Sozialgeschichte des alttestamentlichen Gesetzes*, München, Kaiser, 1992, pp. 311-314.

44. N. LOHFINK, *Bewegung* (n. 14), pp. 352-358, regards Crüsemann's and my reconstruction as convincing in the main.

groups regarded deuteronomic theology as their basis. But after the sudden death of Josiah in 609 B.C., this coalition broke up into different and competing parties.

One party tried to carry on the reform work and felt an obligation not only to the cultic and religious message but also to the social message of the reform. It protected Jeremiah even after he had become a prophet of doom; in foreign politics it advocated a pro-Babylonian position. The nucleus of the party was constituted by the Shaphanide family who came to oppose king Jehoiakim (Ahikam, Gemariah, Gedaliah; see Jer 26; 36; 40ff.). It can be named the "reform party".

The other party was satisfied with the realization of most of the cult-political message of the reform, especially with the centralization of the cult in Jerusalem and the purification of YHWH's worship. It advocated a national, anti-Babylonian policy and was supported by king Jehoiakim and other groups of officials, priests like Pashhur (Jer 20,1-6) and cult-prophets like Hananiah (Jer 28). It fought fierely against Jeremiah (Jer 20; 26; 28f.; 37ff.) and was able to draw the Babylonian vassal-king Zedekiah onto its side (Jer 37f.). This party was probably headed by the Hilkiah-family, the family of the chief priests (Seraiah). It can be called the "nationalistic party".

If we now consider the definite pro-Shaphanides tradition in JerD (cf. esp. Jer 26; 29; 36), which was not only collected but even strengthened by the dtr. redactors[45], then it is highly probable that the Jeremiah-Deuteronomists can be identified with the successors of the reform party around the Shaphanides. The Shaphan family rose to the highest rank after the fall of Jerusalem, when the Babylonians appointed Shaphan's grandson Gedaliah their governor (Jer 40ff.). It is probable that the Shaphanides did not completely lose their leading position when

---

45. For the exegetical details I must here refer to R. ALBERTZ, *Milieu* (n. 1), pp. 394-401 and R. ALBERTZ, *Deuteronomisten* (see note 1), pp. 330-333. I will only mention the frame of the most detailed pro-Shaphanide material (Jer 36 and 45) which the Dtr shaped and placed around the Jeremiah-narrative (Jer 37-43;[44]). The personal consolation oracle for Baruch at the end of JerD testifies that the Jeremiah-Deuteronomists understood themselves as followers of this companion of Jeremiah, who was an official associated very closely with the Shaphanide family (cf. Jer 36,10ff.; 44,3 and the seal that can be attributed to him [N. AVIGAD, *Baruch the Scribe and Jerahmeel the King's Son*, in *IEJ* 28 (1978) 52-56]). Also the fact stressed by E.W. NICHOLSON, *Preaching* (n. 12), pp. 10ff., that the "prose material", containing the pro-Shaphanide Jeremiah stories and the dtr. redaction cannot be sharply divided, points to a continuity in literary tradition between the Shaphanides and the Jeremiah-Deuteronomists. – The thesis of H.-J. STIPP, *Jeremia* (n. 28), p. 298 etc., that the the dtr. redactors condemned the Shaphanide officials and that most of the pro-Shaphanide texts belong to a post-dtr. redaction is not convincing, even on a literary-critical basis. Apart from this, he is not able to reconstruct any historical scenario in the early post-exilic period in which the proposed struggle of the Shaphanides fits.

Gedaliah was murdered by a nationalist[46]: the Babylonians must have been interested in supporting further their most loyal subjects, so that many of the disloyal elements preferred to flee from Judah (Jer 41,17ff.) or may have been deported (Jer 52,30).

Thus there is also historical ground for believing that the leading Shaphan family was still responsible for reworking and editing the Jeremiah traditions in the later exilic time, around 550 B.C[47]. They wished to write a book to teach the people, in line with the heritage of that prophet who had once stood closest to the reform party. And they wished to legitimize themselves by demonstrating that the nationalistic party, but not their forefathers, were to blame for the catastrophe of 587/6 B.C. (cf. Jer 36).

Probably the successors of the reform party still lived in Palestine, more precisely in the area of Mizpah, where already Gedaliah had had his residence (Jer 40,12). The area north of Jerusalem escaped the Babylonian destructions as can be seen by archeology[48]. Thus the thesis of Norbert Lohfink[49], that there must be an interrelation between the Shaphan family and the Deuteronomists is basically correct, but it must be restricted to the editors of JerD.

2. Identifying the Deuteronomists of the historical work

With regard to DtrG there is almost no external evidence which can be used for the reconstruction of its origin and for the identification of its authors. However, if we study the *Tendenz* of this work which, as we have seen, clashes with that of JerD at crucial points, there is some degree of probability that the authors of DtrG have to be associated with the successors of the nationalistic party around the Hilkiades.

---

46. The date of Gedaliah's death is uncertain. In Jer 41,1 only the seventh month but no year is mentioned; it is often assumed that the reign of Gedaliah therefore lasted only 2 months after the destruction of Jerusalem (cf. 2 Kings 25,8). But that seems to be very short for all the events recorded in Jer 40,6ff. Therefore it is more reasonable to take the year 582 B.C. as the date of the murder, when another Judean deportation is attested (cf. Jer 52,30).

47. For the date of JerD, cf. W. THIEL, *Die deuteronomistische Redaktion von Jeremia 26-45* (WMANT, 52), Neukirchen – Vluyn, Neukirchener Verlag, 1981, p. 114.

48. Cf. E. STERN, *The New Encyclopedia* (n. 19), pp. 194; 1101-1103. M. NOTH had already looked upon this region as DtrG's place of origin, see *Überlieferungsgeschichtliche Studien* (n. 3), pp. 97; 110, but his reasons are not convincing. If W. DIETRICH, *Future* (n. 18), pp. 169f., wants to support this location by referring to the data in the book of Jeremiah, he does so by taking for granted that there must exist one uniform dtr. group.

49. N. LOHFINK, *Die Gattung der "Historischen Kurzgeschichte" in den letzten Jahren von Juda und in der Zeit des Babylonischen Exils*, in ZAW 90 (1978) 319-347, p. 342; ID., *Bewegung* (n. 14), pp. 359ff.

Of course, DtrG does not represent in full scale the nationalistic position in pre-exilic times which had centered on Zion and kingship theology besides its common dtn. foundation. After the disaster of nationalistic politics in 587/6 B.C. the survivors of the nationalists had to learn their lesson: the eternal promises concerning Jerusalem and the Davidic dynasty were made conditional on obedience to the dtn. law (1 Sam 12; 1 Kings 9). However, if we consider that the authors of the DtrG still regarded the temple of Jerusalem and the Davidic monarchy as important gifts of salvation[50], it becomes apparent that they wanted to hold to the faith of their fathers which constituted the theological basis of the former nationalistic party.

Corresponding to this, DtrG praised the anti-Assyrian rebellion of king Hezekiah and regarded it as an example of confidence in God (2 Kings 18,5ff.). It is no accident that the authors of DtrG took over the Hezekiah-Isaiah story (2 Kings 18,9–19,7.32aβ-34.8-9a.36aβ-37), which has been shown by Christof Hardmeier to be a propaganda story of the nationalistic party from the days of the Babylonian siege of Jerusalem (588 B.C.)[51]. It is no accident either that this story mentioned a certain Eliakim, a forefather of the Hilkiah-family, as a shining example (2 Kings 18,18ff.). And finally, we can now understand why the DtrG ignored Jeremiah and any other prophet of doom with silence: they had been the enemies of their fathers and were still much too radical in their view.

What can we learn about the further fate of the nationalistic party? Distinct traces point to Babylonia: there is absolutely no doubt that the Babylonians punished severely and deported especially the members and the fellow travellers of the nationalistic party already for reasons of political security (cf. 2 Kings 25,18-21). For its leading family, the Hilkiades, this is explicitly attested: The chief priest Seraiah was executed (2 Kings 25,18), his son Jehozadak was exiled (1 Chron 5,41). Regarding the fact that just a grandson of Jehoiachin, Zerubbabel, and just a son of Jehozadak, the high priest Joshua, were leading the first main group who returned home from the Babylonian exile, we can conclude that the Davidic and the Hilkiah family (that is the symbol and the head of the nationalistic party) kept their leadership among the Babylonian exiles during the whole exilic period.

50. For the exegetical basis of this interpretation, see R. ALBERTZ, *Intentionen* (n. 16), pp. 40ff., and ID., *History of Israelite Religion* (n. 14), pp. 388ff.

51. Cf. C. HARDMEIER, *Prophetie im Streit* (n. 27), pp. 287ff.; he pointed out convincingly that the arguments of Jeremiah and Ezekiel against the risky nationalistic enterprise are put in the mouth of the Assyrian chief officer (2 Kings 18,21.29ff.; cf. Ezek 29,6; Jer 37,3.9; 38,3.17f.) in order to denounce it as propaganda of the enemy.

In addition, we hear about nationalistic hopes for a quick return of the exiles arising in the year 594 (cf. Jer 29,21ff.), shortly after the first deportation in 597 B.C. And when we learn from Zech 6,9-15 that after 539, a silver-and-gold donation was collected by the Babylonian exiles in order to make possible a coronation of Zerubbabel and Jeshua and thus to restore the Davidic monarchy in Judah, it becomes obvious that the national position was still popular within the Babylonian exiles even in the early post-exilic period.

Thus, everything points to the fact that the DtrG was written in Babylonia, probably in the vicinity of both leading families, the Davidides and the Hilkiades, who probably lived in the capital Babylon next to the royal court[52]. In light of these considerations older arguments in support of a Babylonian origin for the DtrG[53], stressed by Ernest W. Nicholson and others[54], are strengthened. We also get a much better un-

---

52. That Jehoiachin, accompanied by a group of Judeans, did not live together with the biggest Judean colony in the Nippur region but at the court of Nebuchadnezzar in Babylon is attested by the so-called Weidner Tablets which numerate many persons getting oil rations from the royal court, cf. *TGI*, pp. 78f.; *ANET*, p. 308. One of the four tablets which mention Jehoiachin is dated in the year 592 B.C.; the other three are not datable. The whole archive is said to contain tablets from the years 595-570 B.C. Therefore, we cannot say exactly how long this royal provision took place. The Weidner tablets seems to testify that Jehoiachin was treated with honour like other royal hostages in Babylon. The account in 2 Kings 25,27-30 speaks about his release from prison and a preferential treatment in the midst of the other royal hostages (vv. 27f.). If both testimonies are to be taken seriously, then we are forced to assume that Jehoiahin lost his previous honoured status by a special punishment in-between. We cannot say exactly why and when Jehoiachin fell out of favour with Nebuchadnezzar; it might be the anti-Babylonian revolt of Zedekiah which resulted in the destruction of Jerusalem in 587/6 B.C. But that is a little bit too early because it started already in 594 B.C. So in my opinion, the better solution is the date of the third deportation, attested by Jer 52,30 for the year 582 B.C., especially if we associate it with the murder of Gedaliah (n. 46). Ishmael, who murdered Gedaliah, was a member of the royal family (Jer 41,1); therefore Nebuchadnezzar could hold Jehoiachin personally responsible for this cruel deed. It is perfectly possible that he was accused by Nebuchadnezzar of not preventing or of having caused this revolt against the Babylonian government in Judah. This would mean that Jehoiachin disappeared for about 20 years into the royal prison until he had the chance to come back to court and be seen in public.

53. Cf. prayer in the direction of Jerusalem (1 Kings 8,48), the concept that the whole people was exiled from Israel and Judah (2 Kings 17,6.23; 25,21) and the release of Jehoiachin (25,27-30) which echoes neo-Babylonian language; for the latter see E. ZENGER, *Die deuteronomistische Interpretation der Rehabilitierung Jojachins*, in *BZ* 12 (1968) 16-30, pp. 18f.

54. See E.W. NICHOLSON, *Preaching* (n. 12), pp. 116ff.; J.A. SOGGIN, *Der Entstehungsort des Deuteronomistischen Geschichtswerkes. Ein Beitrag zur Geschichte desselben*, in *TLZ* 100 (1975) 3-8, p. 6; cf. already P.R. ACKROYD, *Exile and Restoration. A Study of Hebrew Thought of the Sixth Century BC* (OTL), London, SCM, 1968=1994, pp. 65-68, without making any decision. The arguments of both against Noth's position were taken up by K.-F. POHLMANN, *Erwägungen zum Schlußkapitel des deuteronomistischen Geschichtswerkes. Oder: Warum wird der Prophet Jeremia in 2 Kön 22-25*

derstanding of why the authors attached so much importance to the release of Jehoiachin: he represented a symbolic figure of their own party.
His rehabilitation in 562 B.C. seems to mark a turning point in the foreign policy of the Babylonian empire[55] and thus was the starting signal
for writing the official Israelite history.

Such an identification of both dtr. groups fits in the early post-exilic
Israelite history very well. When in agreement with the tendency of the
DtrG, Zerubbabel and Joshua, as the leaders of the returning exiles, put
through the reconstruction of the temple as the start of a new beginning,
it becomes apparent that, again, the successors of the nationalistic party
claimed the leadership in Judah as their forerunners had done in the late
pre-exilic period. But this time they failed: their project to restore the
Davidic monarchy under Persian rule[56] ended disastrously because the

---

nicht erwähnt?, in A.H.J. GUNNEWEG – O. KAISER (eds.), *Textgemäß. Aufsätze zur
Hermeneutik des Alten Testaments*. FS E. Würthwein, Göttingen, Vandenhoeck &
Ruprecht, 1979, pp. 94-109, esp. 102-105.

55. It is difficult to evaluate precisely the policies of Awil-Marduk. There are extremely different judgements about him in the Babylonian tradition, and he did not get the
time to develop his policy, because he was murdered by Neriglissar after only two and a
half years of reign. Having in mind that Neriglissar stressed an aggressive imperial
policy, it is very possible that Awil-Marduk planned a break with the imperial policy of
his father Nebuchadnezzar who exploited the provinces in favour of the Babylonian
center and was not concerned about their development. Perhaps Awil-Marduk intended to
reestablish Jehoiachin or one of his sons as his vassal king in Judah such as Nabonidus
probably did later with the exiled royal family of Tyre (cf. Josephus, *Contra Apionem*,
I.158 and H.J. KATZENSTEIN, *The History of Tyre. From the Beginning of the Second
Millenium B.C.E. until the Fall of the Neo-Babylonian Empire in 538 B.C.E.*, Jerusalem,
Schocken Institute for Jewish research, 1973, pp. 324f.). But Awil-Marduk was not able
to carry through his new policy against the resistance of the Babylonian nobility who had
profited from his father's policy. A similar attempt to overcome the one-sided imperial
policy was probably done by Nabonidus when he proposed to rebuild the Sin tempel in
the border region of Harran using the means of the whole empire. But this enterprise provoked a serious revolt of nearly all of the Babylonian cities and failed finally because of
the resistance of the Marduk priests in the capital. Aparently, the Persians were the first to
succeed in keeping the balance between both the imperial claims of the center and the local rights of the provinces. Considering these two competing political options tried out
after the death of Nebuchadnezzar, we must admit that the hopes of the dtr. historians that
the release of Jehoiachin would open a new chance for Judah and the Judean exiles were
not unfounded, even if they were realized not by the Babylonians but by the Persians 23
years later. For more details see R. ALBERTZ, *Die Exilszeit* (Biblische Enzyklopädie,
Bd. 7), Stuttgart, Kohlhammer, forthcoming.

56. As we can see in Cyprus and elsewhere, the Persians were generally willing to accept vassal monarchies in their empire. Normally they retained the political system which
already existed. In Judah the political system was not so clear because it seemed to be
controlled by the Samarian governor at the end of the Babylonic era. But the decision of
the Persians to appoint Zerubbabel as the official of the Judean returnees points to the
assumption that they would be willing to accept him as vassal king later if he was able to
found a loyal Judean state. Therefore, the project of the nationalistic groups was not completely unfounded but a perfectly possible political option.

building of the temple and the projected coronation of Zerubabbel inflamed heated nationalistic hopes among the people. The Persian government, which had just succeeded in pacifying the empire, must have been afraid of a new revolt in Judah and removed Zerubbabel from the political stage[57]. After this second disaster of the nationalistic Judean politics, a non-monarchical policy system was founded in post-exilic Judah, consisting of two councils, one of the elders and one of the priests, which were assisted by the people's assembly[58]. This political organization, which consciously gave up the Davidic monarchy in order to get more freedom and self-determination for the Judean nobility, corresponded more to the interests of the Jeremiah-Deuteronomists according to whom the Jehoiachin-family remained condemned by YHWH.

Thus the dispute between the two dtr. groups in the DtrG and JerD proves to be a quarrel between the two leading families, the Hilkiades, the leading family of the Babylonian exiles, and the Shaphanides, the leading family of the Judean population which remained in the land, about their predominance and the political and religious options for Israel's future.

Evangelisch Theologische Fakultät   Rainer ALBERTZ
der Westfälischen Wilhelms-Universität Münster
Universitätsstrasse 13-17
D-48143 Münster

---

57. Cf. the intervention of the Persian governor Tattenai (Ezra 5) and the fact that Zerubbabel, Haggai and Zechariah did not take part in the consecration of the temple (Ezra 6).
58. Cf. R. ALBERTZ, *History of Israelite Religion* (n. 14), pp. 443-450.

PROPHETS SHARED – BUT RECYCLED

Kings without Privilege used Solomon and Manasseh as main worked examples; and argued that what was common to Samuel-Kings and Chronicles was also the shared source text which both traditions had adjusted and extended[1]. They shared a story of David's house from the death of Saul to the fall of Jerusalem and of Yahweh's house in Jerusalem from David's entry to that city till his last successor's departure – a story in which the period of David and Solomon took up one half of the space and all of their successors together the other. I suggested that neither Samuel-Kings nor Chronicles had been as free with the shared material they developed as the Chronicler is widely understood to have been with Samuel-Kings (147-150).

Worship at 'high places' [במות] causing Yahweh 'provocation' [הכעיס], removing קדשים and גלולים from the land, 'burning incense' [קטר] are some of the most frequently expressed concerns in both Samuel-Kings and Chronicles. *Kings without Privilege* noted that they do not often appear at the same place in both synoptic texts: when they do, there appears to be an extra ring of authenticity (87-103). This paper offers shared and diverse prophetic materials as fresh examples to test the integrity of my reconstructed Book of Two Houses further – as also to demonstrate how difficult it is to reconstruct it precisely.

Samuel-Kings and Chronicles are both very interested in the phenomenon of prophecy. This paper will review four of the only six or seven stories of divine intermediaries which they actually share. The reports in 1 Kings 22 and 2 Chron 18 of Micaiah consulted by the two Kings are virtually identical but for the different opening verses. The mission from the court of Josiah to Huldah is again reported very similarly in 2 Kings 22 and 2 Chron 34. On Nathan's dynastic oracle, the text preserved in 2 Sam 7 is significantly fuller than that in 1 Chron 17. The stories of David's census in 2 Sam 24 and 1 Chron 21 diverge still more, with significant pluses in both versions, but again a fuller text in Samuel. (Ahijah, Shemaiah, and Isaiah also appear in both books.) The first and last of these stories deal with divine deception; the second and third with promise and threat for David and Jerusalem. Even granted the regular view that Chron has rewritten Sam-Kings, it is strange to find Rofé

---

1. A.G. AULD, *Kings without Privilege*, Edinburgh, T&T Clark, 1994, pp. 12-34, 73-86.

recording surprise that 'this alone (i.e., 1 Kings 22) of all the prophetic
stories is included in the Book of Chronicles'[2].

1. The Prophet called 'Grant' [Nathan]

In both Samuel and Chronicles, the setting of the chapter reporting
Nathan's oracle and David's prayer is the same: it follows the arrival of
the ark in Jerusalem, and precedes a series of successful military exploits
by David among the surrounding peoples. In Chronicles, the intimate
link with the ark story is particularly obvious. The last verse of 1 Chron
16 tells of all the people going to their houses, and David to his to bless
it; and 1 Chron 17 opens with David in his house but the divine ark
without a house, and closes with a prayer for the divine blessing of
David's house. In Samuel the development of the theme of blessing
David's house is interrupted – but also focussed – by the plus in 2 Sam
6,20b-23 reporting the altercation between David and Michal. A synoptic presentation of 2 Sam 7 and 1 Chron 17 makes it immediately obvious that we are dealing with the same text only slightly altered in each.
Sam offers a fuller text than Chron, and Sam [MT] even fuller than Sam
[LXX].

A particularly interesting divergence is between כון [establish] in
2 Sam 7,24 and נתן [grant/put] in 1 Chron 17,2 [and note the links with
the Micaiah story]. As we pose the question whether it is possible to
settle on the original readings of the Book of Two Houses, the incidence
of נתן with divine subject within the text shared by Sam-Kings and
Chron sets the context instructively.

God 'gives' most of what he gives within the Solomon stories: wisdom in 1 Kings 3,5.12; 10,24 // 2 Chron 1,7.10; 9,23 and commands in
1 Kings 9,6 // 2 Chron 7,19; riches in 1 Kings 3,13 // 2 Chron 1,12 and
also rain in 1 Kings 8,36 // 2 Chron 6,27; a son in 1 Kings 5,21 //
2 Chron 2,11 and Solomon on the throne in 1 Kings 10,9 // 2 Chron 9,8;
land to fathers in 1 Kings 8,34.36.40.48; 9,7 // 2 Chron 6,25.27.30.38;
7,20; just deserts in 1 Kings 8,32.39 // 2 Chron 6,23.30 and his people to
the enemy in 1 Kings 8,46 // 2 Chron 6,36.

There is a correspondingly loud silence over the verb give/ נתן with a
divine subject throughout the similarly extensive shared text on David
(1 Sam 31; 2 Sam 5-8; 10; 11-12*; 21,18-22; 23,8-39; 24 // 1 Chron
10-11; 13-15; 17-21). There it is used in just two contexts: of David's
oracular enquiry whether he should move against the Philistines (2 Sam

---

2. A. ROFÉ, *The Prophetical Stories. The Narratives about the Prophets in the Hebrew Bible, Their Literary Types and History*, Jerusalem, Magnes, 1988, p. 142.

5,19 // 1 Chron 14,10); and of the sending of the plague after the census
(24,15 // 21,14) – ironically just after David had spoken with 'Lucky'
his seer.

Then after Solomon it is found in just three contexts, two of them
within the Micaiah story. The prophetic enquiry whether Ramoth would
be 'given' into the hands of the two kings (1 Kings 22,6.12.15.23 // 2
Chron 18,5.11.14.22) resumes David's oracular question about the
Philistines. Yahweh 'gave'/put a lying spirit into the mouth of the
prophets to make a fool of Ahab (1 Kings 22,23 // 2 Chron 18,22). And
his contrasting commitment to the Davidic house [cf 1.1.3 above] is re-
stated in 2 Kings 8,19 // 2 Chron 21,7 in terms of the gift of a ניר.

The textual choice is between ותתן at the end of the Chronicler's version of a chapter in which many things are provided for David and his
people, but the common word 'give' used only once; and ותכונן in the
Samuel version, so that only the name of the prophet mutely states the
main theme – like the names of the three children in Isaiah 7-8. (נתן does
govern [an implied] עמך towards the end of Solomon's prayer – כונן
never.)

2. 'Lucky' [Gad] and David's Census

The biggest single difference between the two texts is the complete
absence in 1 Chron 21 of any material corresponding to the route taken
by Joab and the army commanders described in 2 Sam 24,4b-8a. Quite
apart from the much shorter or longer pluses, it is clear that elements of
the inherited text in Sam or Chron or both have been rewritten. And
some differences within the synoptic portions obviously form part of
wider patterns within these biblical books. There can of course be no
doubt that David – like Ahab in the Micaiah story – was deliberately
deceived by God. The key issue, when it comes to reconstructing the
opening of the shorter more original story, is whether the deity was assisted by an agent [the שטן] in the incitement to number the people, as he
was [by the מלאך] in inflicting the plague.

A helpful way of reminding ourselves of significant points in the
shared tradition is to review the several links between the earlier story
and the prologue to Job. There is a unique clustering of significant
shared terms.

Both David and Job are described by the deity as 'my servant'. חנם (2
Sam 24,24 // 1 Chron 21,24) is also used in Job (1,9; 2,3). Job offers
holocausts at the beginning, and David at the end. 1 Chron 21 uses
הסית (v. 1), שטן (v. 1), and התהלך (v. 4) and 2 Sam 24 הסית (v. 1) and שוט

(v. 2.8), while Job 1-2 uses all four words (1,7; 2,2.3 and *passim*). Just as Israel is counted and the 'number' brought to David (2 Sam 24,9 // 1 Chron 21,5), and just as the number of the fallen is reported, so the reckoning of Job's family and flocks and herds is very precisely given – and Job organises his sacrifices exactly according to their מספר (1,5). Job's family fall to four successive divine blows, two each from humans and from above. David faces a choice between three divine blows, one from a human foe, two from above. Job's family is lost, but he himself must not be touched. Much of Israel is lost, but Jerusalem and David are spared. The behaviour of both Job and David is evaluated in terms of 'sin'. In all of Job's response to the Satan he did not sin (1,22; 2,10) – in fact his scrupulous sacrificial practice was observed just in case one of his family might have sinned (1,5). David's counting of the people was sin (24,10 // 21,8) – his sin alone (24,17 // 21,17). (Might Job 1,5 be ironic, because Job's scrupulous counting was in fact his sin?) The several details of the correspondence and the increased likelihood that the assonant שוט and הסית remain in 2 Sam 24 as allusions to an original 'Satan' warn against the widespread view that the Chronicler introduced this divine agent into his reworking of 2 Sam 24 under the influence of Job 1-2 and Zech 3,1-2. More likely Zech 3 represents another allusion to our story.

David's חטאתי in this story has very significant resonance within the whole Shared Text – חטא is used elsewhere only in Solomon's prayer, the Mosaic rule cited in 2 Kings 14,6, and the evaluation of Manasseh. After Moses' teaching [everyone shall die for his own sin], and David's protest [it was not the nation, but I and my family who sinned], and Solomon's hope [if a sinner prays to this place], what do we expect to result from Manasseh's sin? The interplay between these four texts in the story of David's house allows for much more subtle musing about the entail of sin than is possible for the reader of the more familiar Books of Kings. 'The sins of Jeroboam which he made Israel to sin' again and again and again make us deaf to delicate suggestion.

The whole story of the census functions as a parable/משל, the relevance of which is probed in a series of episodes, each in turn involving prophetic interpretation: The division of the kingdom (1 Kings 12,15 // 2 Chron 10,15 [Ahijah]) involves the loss of much of Israel by the Davidic house – but not Judah or Jerusalem. The Assyrian invasion under Sennacherib led to the occupation of much of Judah – but Jerusalem and King Hezekiah remained safe (2 Kings 19,24-32 // 2 Chron 32,20-22 [Isaiah]). Huldah warned Josiah of the threat to 'this place and its inhabitants' – 'but the king of Judah … will not see' (2 Kings 22,15-20 // 2 Chron 34,23-28). When that house was finally deported, …

3. The picture of Micaiah ben Imlah with Jehoshaphat and Ahab *is painted almost identically in 1 Kings 22,4-35a and 2 Chron 18,3-34, but set by both in a different narrative frame.*

Each time the king of Israel makes his proposal for joint action in Chronicles (vv. 5.14), he says: 'Shall we go up … or shall I desist [אחדל]?' The implication of the singular subject of the second verb must be: shall I desist from pressing [on you?] my scheme? In the second instance, 1 Kings 22,15 (MT, but not LXX) offers the plural 'shall we desist?', now implicating Jehoshaphat in responsibility for the scheme. The double use of 'desist' by the king of Israel, as indeed the presence within the story of Judah's kings of a substantial story about a king of Israel warring with Syria over lost territory, is nicely anticipated in the Book of Two Houses by the report of Baasha of Israel, who 'desists' (1 Kings 15,21 // 2 Chron 16,5) from building Ramah to put pressure on nearby Jerusalem and Asa king of Judah, when Asa buys help from the king of Syria (who promptly annexes cities close to his border with Israel). The original story, as still the version in 2 Chron 18, had been told within and had been part of the story of Jehoshaphat: a part which showed him succumbing to an invitation from the king of Israel. It was not, as widely argued, an originally separate prophetic story which made its way into Kings *via* a hypothetical prophetic collection related to the house of Omri.

In the main body of the story about Micaiah and the two kings, where the texts of Kings and Chronicles hardly diverge, Jehoshaphat's royal partner is referred to consistently as simply 'the king of Israel', except in 1 Kings 22,20 // 2 Chron 18,19 where Yahweh seeks someone 'to seduce Ahab'. With פתה here, compare Jer 20 and Ezek 14,1-11[3]. This unique mention of Ahab in the main body of the shared text (whether simply that name on its own, as in Kings MT, or 'Ahab king of Israel', as in Kings LXX and Chr), and at the very middle of the story, will be especially significant. It may suggest that the divine deception is of Ahab the man, rather than of the king of Israel. It is very hard to restore the original beginning to the story. The opening verses of 1 Kings 22 also talk of 'the king of Israel' (vv. 2.3), while he is 'Ahab' three times in 2 Chron 18,1.2 and 'Ahab king of Israel' in 18,3.

Micaiah's second utterance before the two kings begins 'I saw all Israel scattered upon the mountains, as sheep that have no shepherd'. 'All Israel' and 'shepherd' are both sufficiently rare in the Shared Text for

3. J.J.M. Roberts, *Does God Lie? Divine Deceit as a Theological Problem in Israelite Prophetic Literature*, in J.A. Emerton (ed.), *Congress Volume Jerusalem 1986*, Leiden etc., Brill, 1988, pp. 211-220.

the echoes in this account to tell their own story. 'All Israel' is what David rules over (2 Sam 8,15 // 1 Chron 18,14) and Solomon too (1 Kings 11,42 // 2 Chron 9,30); what David leads out (also) against the Syrians (!) (2 Sam 10,17 // 1 Chron 19,17) and Solomon presides over at the great feast (1 Kings 8,65 // 2 Chron 7,8). And David is shepherd of Yahweh's people (2 Sam 5,2 // 1 Chron 11,2) – a role he inherits from earlier 'judges' (שפטים) (2 Sam 7,7 // 1 Chron 17,6). The armies gathered under Jehoshaphat and Ahab represent 'all Israel' for the first time since the division of the kingdom (*NB* textual problems in 1 Kings 12 – 'all Israel' attested in vv. 1.16,18, but the alternative LXX text attests 'the tribes of Israel' in v. 1, 'all the people' in v. 16, and does not reflect v. 18), yet neither Ahab nor even Jehoshaphat (יהו-שפט) justifies the title 'shepherd'.

4. The report of the mission to Huldah the prophetess *is part of the synoptic report (2 Kings 22,12-20//2 Chron 34,20-28) on Josiah's reign before Kings and Chronicles diverge: Kings to concentrate on details of the reforms, and Chronicles on the passover.*

There are not many differences between the versions of the royal mission. In some instances Kings attests one word or short phrase and Chron an alternative, and it is hard to prefer one or the other. The shift from שמע (22,13) to שמר (34,21), or *vice versa*, could be a simple copying slip or adjustment, similar to alterations in proper names like Micah (22,12) and Micaiah (34,20). As with the names, there is no precise parallel. Both verbs are very rare with 'fathers' as subject: שמע only in Jer 34,14 and Zech 1,4 (both followed by 'to me'), and שמר in Judg 2,22 (with 'Yahweh's way(s)' as object). Then Esther 5,5 offers the only parallel to לעשות with דבר as direct object in 34,31, while הקים takes דבר as object 10x in Sam-Kings (1 Sam 1,23; 15,11.13; 2 Sam 7,25 [not 1 Chron 17,23]; 1 Kings 2,4; 6,12; 8,20; 12,15; 2 Kings 23,3.24) Jer 28,6; 29,10; 33,14; 34,18; 2 Chron 6,10; 10,15 (// 1 Kings 8,20; 12,15); Dan 9,12; Neh 5,13; 9,8. The two instances repeated from the Shared Text, together with the other certainly late instances in Daniel and Nehemiah, demonstrate that the construction is not unacceptable to Chronicles. On the other hand, it is normally the deity who 'establishes' his word or oath or covenant – not a human who demonstrates its efficacy by obeying its terms. Again there is another significant difference in David's prayer, where 2 Sam 7,25 [MT] has imperative הקם but 1 Chron 17,23 the jussive יאמן and 1 Kings 6,12 is an MT plus. It seems to me that in most of the alternative readings a decision is 'too close to call'. In no case has a commoner expression been substituted for a rarer one; nor are we dealing with terms obviously more at home whether in Kings or Chronicles.

A number of expressions are used only here in the Book of Two Houses. Four examples: Josiah is the only person – let alone king – reported as 'weeping' (2 Kings 22,19 // 2 Chron 34,27) in all of Chronicles (this gives extra poignancy to the few pluses in earlier parts of Sam-Kings). נאם יהוה too is never found again in Chronicles. 'This place' is followed by 'and its inhabitants' only in Huldah's two responses (2 Kings 22,16.19 // 2 Chron 34,24.27) and in Jer 19,12. And the only other person in Kings reported as 'being submissive' is Ahab in the significant plus 1 Kings 21,29 (נכנע is much commoner in Chron).

Within the text shared by Sam-Kings and Chron, there are significant links between Huldah's responses and earlier reports. Indeed I might helpfully anticipate a conclusion at this point, and note how economical is the linguistic architecture of the Book of Two Houses. Very many of its most significant words are used in just two contexts: to compare or contrast the kings in question; or else they are used many times in connection with David or Solomon and then just once elsewhere. This simple yet effective usage is often completely obscured in the extended versions of the story we now read in Samuel-Kings and in Chronicles.

There are three unique links between Huldah's words and Solomon's second vision: Yahweh threatens to 'bring evil' (1 Kings 9,9 // 2 Chron 7,22 and 2 Kings 22,16 // 2 Chron 34,24), as often in Sam-Kings and Jer but nowhere else in Chron. 'Other gods' are condemned (1 Kings 9,6.9 // 2 Chron 7,19.22 and 2 Kings 22,17 // 2 Chron 34,25) – with one plus in 2 Chron 28,25 and many in Sam-Kings. Yahweh is 'forsaken' by his people in 1 Kings 9,9 // 2 Chron 7,22 and 2 Kings 22,17 // 2 Chron 34,25 – and in many pluses in both Kings and Chr. Each of Huldah's responses is in the name of 'Yahweh, God of Israel' – and 'God of Israel' has been absent from the Book of Two Houses since the prayer of David (2 Sam 7,27 // 1 Chron 17,24) and the first part of Solomon's prayer (6x in 1 Kings 8,15-26 // 2 Chron 6,4-17). (This helps to point up the significance of Elijah's opening claim in 1 Kings 17,1. It is prophets who plot the contemporary position relative to the ancient ideal.) And there are links with three other earlier stories: Only Athaliah (11,14 // 23,13) and Josiah (22,11.19 // 34,19.27) 'rend clothes' – but *NB* pluses in 2 Sam 1,2.11; 3,31; 13,31; 1 Kings 21,27; 2 Kings 2,12; 5,7.8; 6,30; 11,14; 18,37; 19,1. Only of Ahaz has the piel of קטר earlier been used of 'burning incense' (Auld 1994:96). Only Manasseh's behaviour has been termed 'provocation' of Yahweh to anger (85).

5. Language of Divine Intermediation

It is worth pausing to note the range of 'prophetic' terminology shared by the four passages just reviewed. Micaiah is produced as a further 'prophet of Yahweh' [נביא ליהוה]. Nathan is titled 'the prophet' and Huldah 'the prophetess'. Both available themes of the verb נבא [*niphal* 1x and *hithpael* 3x] are used in the Micaiah story. Gad is titled 'David's seer', and Nathan's speech is followed by the unusually formal 'As all these words and as all this vision, so spoke Nathan to David.' Under challenge, Micaiah cites a vision of Yahweh's court starting with 'I saw' and including 'the spirit' as a principal character. And Huldah cites Yahweh's oracle [נאם יהוה]. Both Jehoshaphat and Josiah call for Yahweh to be 'consulted' [דרש]. David also takes the initiative in speaking to Nathan the prophet; and Gad's title 'David's seer' suggests a role of expected consultation.

There are a number of very striking features about this short listing. One is that these four stories deploy between them virtually the complete biblical range of technical terms for intermediation. The brief report of Shemaiah (1 Kings 12,22-24 // 2 Chron 11,2-4, cf. p. 19 above) allows us to add 'the man of God' to the list. Another is that several of these terms are used within the synoptic portions of Samuel-Kings and Chronicles only in these few stories. And even that understates the unique status of some of this usage. Samuel-Kings and Chronicles, for all their additional interest in intermediation, in fact each deploy in their very many pluses a much narrower range of the available terminology.

A further point is that the opening story programmatically suggests the difference between David consulting the prophet Nathan and obtaining his opinion (2 Sam 7,2-3 // 1 Chron 17,1b-2) and receiving *via* that prophet the divine word (7,4ff // 17,3ff). Micaiah discusses with his escort, with the king, and with his rival the distinction between what prophets say and what Yahweh says (1 Kings 22,13-28 // 2 Chron 18,12-27). And the final story returns to the issue: 'Tell the man who sent you to me (2 Kings 22,15 // 2 Chron 34,23)... as to the king of Judah who sent you to enquire of Yahweh...' (22,18 // 34,26).

6. Separate Ways

Divine intermediaries are cited in relation to most of the nineteen kings of Judah within Chronicles. The reign of Jehoshaphat is covered by Micaiah and Jehu ben Hanani; and of Jehoram by Elijah's letter. It is by a priest that Uzziah is rebuked for usurping priestly functions; however, Isaiah the prophet the son of Amoz is cited for further information

(26,22). Apart from the following Jotham (27), it is only to the ironically named Ahaziah that no prophet speaks – his counsellor in wrong is his mother Athaliah of the family of Omri. Yet all of the names mentioned only in Chronicles, Iddo (Solomon, Rehoboam, Abijah), (Azariah ben) Oded (Asa), and Oded (Ahaz), are related to or sound as if they are related to the verb העיד, used of the testimony of prophets in 24,19. The immediately following 24,20-22 depicts a priest as clothed with the divine spirit, but stoned for his warning to the court. This verb is used once only in Kings, in a significant summary of divine rebuke delivered 'by every prophet and every seer' – also the sole instance in Kings of the term 'seer'. Has Chron borrowed העיד from 2 Kings 17,13, adapted it in 2 Chron 24,19, and built the names Iddo and Oded from it? Or has 2 Kings 17,13, which seems to interrupt an otherwise smooth transition from v.12 to v.14, drafted its added note in language from Chronicles? Note too that the last words of v.14, 'who did not believe in Yahweh their God', are also reminiscent of 2 Chron 20,20 – using the same language as Isaiah 7,9?

Chronicles has an interesting double relationship with Samuel-Kings: In their synoptic portions they share the same groundwork of an account of the house of David: either each book has preserved a remarkably faithful transcript of a shared source, or Chron has worked from an earlier version of Sam-Kings than we now possess.

Their non-synoptic portions also exhibit a variety of inter-connections. It is widely held that the Chronicler, while excising the story of Samuel and Saul and of the houses of Jeroboam and those which followed in northern Israel, except in so far as details had already been given in the basic story of David's house, retained and reworked many motifs from the account he excised. However, two other models for their relationship should be probed, and not necessarily as either/or.

Chronicles, although it only transcribes in detail the story of David's house, is familiar with much other [now biblical] material. What we have to ask is whether its familiarity with non-synoptic Sam-Kings is greater or less than its familiarity with, say, Isaiah or Jeremiah? It clearly worked from a text of an account that stretched from Saul's fall to the fall of Jerusalem. But how many other texts were in the Chronicler's library? Only quite general awareness of the Jeremiah story is demonstrated by a prophet in the stocks (with 2 Chron 16,10, compare Jer 20,2.3; 29,26) or a seventy-year sabbath for Jerusalem (with 2 Chron 36,21, compare Jer 25,11.12; 29,10) – or of Isaiah in calls to 'lean on' or 'believe in' Yahweh, or to 'seek him while he may be found' (with 2 Chron 16,7.8; 20,20; 32,15; 15,2.4.15, compare Isa 10,20; 7,9; 55,6).

Does mention of Saul consulting a medium (with 1 Chron 10,13, compare 1 Sam 28) or Jehu ben Hanani prophesying soon after the division in the kingdom (with 2 Chron 19,2, compare 1 Kings 16,1.7) presuppose possession of a text of the Books of Samuel or Kings?

Sam-Kings and Chron – or at least their prototypes – may have been subject to similar influences and to mutual influence. Chronicles demonstrates heightened prophetic interest both by supplying prophetic advice or critique for almost every king of Judah who did not already have it, and by having several of these kings give encouraging orations like prophets. Samuel-Kings extended the role of Nathan and Isaiah in relation to the succession to David and the deliverance of Jerusalem. But its larger extensions concentrate on the giants who criticised rivals of the house of David: Samuel on Saul, and – in even greater detail – Elijah and Elisha on the house of Omri and Ahab. When it concentrates on Ahab throughout 1 Kings 17-2 Kings 10, Kings is building on a theme of the Shared Text on the house of David. The prior scoundrel of the piece – Jeroboam – is vilified partly by formulaic repetition, and partly by the unnamed 'man of God' from Judah.

University of Edinburgh   A. Graeme AULD

LA SIGNIFICATION DE L'ESPACE ET DU TEMPS DANS «L'HISTORIOGRAPHIE SACERDOTALE»[*]

Cet exposé qui traite de la signification de l'espace et du temps dans la dite historiographie sacerdotale[1] procède de l'intention suivante. Je voudrais démontrer que le terme *historiographie* suscite des malentendus à plusieurs niveaux: 1. Il n'est pas évident que toutes les œuvres littéraires assemblées dans le Pentateuque soient autant focalisées sur l'histoire de la prise de possession du pays que ne l'est l'historiographie deutéronomiste par rapport à l'étiologie de la perte de ce pays[2]. 2. La composition sacerdotale ne se soucie pas du pays et de sa ré-acquisition. Elle traite le thème de l'histoire de la révélation divine envers son peuple. 3. Les catégories de temps et d'espace, certes importantes pour un projet historiographique, ont une autre connotation dans l'écrit sacerdotal, à savoir une connotation cultuelle.

Ces trois thèses principales correspondent à la structure de mon exposé.

I. L'ÉCRIT SACERDOTAL
EN RAPPORT AVEC LES AUTRES HISTORIOGRAPHIES BIBLIQUES

Selon J. Van Seters[3] «le fait d'écrire l'histoire» est défini par les cinq critères suivants: 1. L'historiographie est une forme littéraire intention-

---

* Dédié à Monsieur le professeur Manfred Weippert pour son 60e anniversaire, de qui j'ai beaucoup appris sur l'histoire, l'historiographie et Fernand Braudel.

1. G. VON RAD, *Der Anfang der Geschichtsschreibung im Alten Israel* (1944), in *Gesammelte Studien zum Alten Testament* (TB, 8), München, C. Kaiser, 1958, pp. 148-188, qui cherche le début de l'historiographie à l'époque salomonienne, le *siècle des lumières* en Israël; ID., *Die Theologie der Priesterschrift* (1934), in *Gesammelte Studien zum Alten Testament* Bd. II (TB, 48), München, C. Kaiser, 1973, pp. 165-188, où il caractérise l'historiographie sacerdotale en tant que conception d'une histoire révélatrice du salut qui se base sur trois cycles narratifs: celui du monde, celui des Noachites et celui des Abrahamites qui aboutissent dans le livre de Josué; plus réticent in *La théologie de l'Ancien Testament*, vol. I (Nouvelle série théologique, 12), Genève, Labor & Fides, 1963, pp. 259, 260 avec note 2.

2. Cf. déjà M. WEIPPERT, *Fragen des israelitischen Geschichtsbewußtseins*, in *VT* 23 (1973) 415-442, p. 441: «Ich habe versucht, den Komplex der historischen Überlieferungen Israels in den Büchern Genesis – Könige (...) als zwei große Ätiologien zu interpretieren: die des Landbesitzes und die des Landverlustes. Beide sind in Krisenzeiten entstanden und in der entscheidenden Existenzkrise Israels nach 586 zu *einem* großen Geschichtswerk vereinigt worden». L'écrit sacerdotal obtient cependant selon Weippert une position différente: Il n'est intégré que tardivement dans cette conception historiographique (432s.).

3. J. VAN SETERS, *In Search of History. Historiography in the Ancient World and the*

nelle et non accidentelle. 2. L'historiographie n'est pas seulement une description objective du passé, mais comprend aussi l'évaluation et l'interprétation des événements historiques. 3. L'historiographie antique considère les conditions actuelles avec leur causalité morale. 4. L'histo-riographie est créée par une nation ou un groupe ethnique défini. 5. L'historiographie appartient aux traditions littéraires d'un peuple et forme son identité nationale.

Selon Van Seters, l'Historiographie deutéronomiste répond pour la première fois à ces critères[4]. Racontant l'histoire du peuple élu depuis Moïse jusqu'à la fin du royaume de Juda, elle a pris un peu plus tard un prologue sous la forme de l'Historiographie yahwiste ou pré-sacerdo-tale[5]. Ce prologue traite des origines de l'humanité et des ancêtres du peuple d'Israël.

Je ne souhaite pas discuter ce modèle historiographique. Je me de-mande plutôt si les critères cités plus haut sont valables pour caractériser l'écrit sacerdotal en tant qu'historiographie. Nous reviendrons à cette question dans la 3e partie de mon exposé.

II. La composition de l'écrit sacerdotal[6]

Avec David Carr[7], je considère l'écrit sacerdotal comme une œuvre littéraire de l'époque exilique / post-exilique qui est formulée en opposi-

---

Origins of Biblical History, New Haven, CT-London, Yale University Press, 1983, p. 4. Dernièrement pour la discussion autour de l'historiographie, cf. C. Conrad et M. Kessel (eds.), *Geschichte schreiben in der Postmoderne. Beiträge zur aktuellen Diskussion*, Stuttgart, Reclam, 1994, dont l'introduction indique déjà comment la définition d'un genre historiographique est difficile.

4. Même ce pilier de la recherche vétérotestamentaire n'est plus stable; cf. récemment E.A. Knauf, *L'historiographie Deutéronomiste (DTRG) existe-t-elle?*, in: A. de Pury – T. Römer – J.-D. Macchi (éds.), *Israël construit son histoire. L'historiographie deutéronomiste à la lumière des recherches récentes* (Le Monde de la Bible, 34), Genève, Labor & Fides, 1996, pp. 411-418.

5. J. Van Seters, *Prologue to History. The Yahwist as Historian in Genesis*, Zürich, Theologischer Verlag, 1992, p. 328.

6. Pour un dernier survol de l'état de la recherche, cf. T. Pola, *Die ursprüngliche Priesterschrift. Beobachtungen zur Literarkritik und Traditionsgeschichte von P^g* (WMANT, 70), Neukirchen-Vluyn, Neukirchener Verlag, pp. 17-50; E. Otto, *For-schungen zur Priesterschrift*, in *TR* 62 (1997) 1-50.

7. D.M. Carr, *Reading the Fractures of Genesis. Historical and Literary Ap-proaches*, Louisville, KY, Westminster, John Knox Press, 1996, pp. 129-140, 312s., qui a développé la conception de E. Blum (*Studien zur Komposition des Pentateuch* [BZAW, 189], Berlin-New York, NY, de Gruyter, 1990, pp. 221-228; 287-332) à la faveur d'une hypothèse documentaire; cf. aussi J.-L. Ska, *Quelques remarques sur P^g et la dernière rédaction du Pentateuque*, in A. de Pury (éd.), *Le Pentateuque en question* (Le Monde de la Bible, 19), Genève, Labor et Fides, 1989, pp. 106s., 115, 124s., qui considère P^g comme un auteur, interprétant les sources anciennes, et comme rédacteur final.

tion avec la littérature pré-exilique, que Carr a désignée comme *non-P*. Ces deux œuvres littéraires figureront plus tard dans le livre de la Genèse après avoir obtenu une révision de style deutéronomiste. Au moins pour l'écrit sacerdotal, Carr présente une esquisse globale débutant en Gn 1 et se terminant en Dt 34. Cet écrit comprend, à côté des narrations, des parties rédactionnelles. Ce sont des textes d'origine pré-sacerdotale que P a incorporés dans son œuvre. Par exemple, on peut citer le livre des *toledôt*, qui est même devenu un élément structurant de haute importance pour la composition de P[8].

À cause de la forme cohérente et bien structurée et à cause de la suite narrative qui constitue une trame continue, il faut le considérer comme une œuvre littéraire indépendante.

Selon Carr, l'écrit sacerdotal comprend trois blocs thématiques[9]: 1. le récit de la *création* qui forme le *programme théologique* de toute l'œuvre; 2. une *généalogie élargie* commençant par Gn 5,1 et se terminant en Gn 50 qui raconte sur le plan des récits patriarcaux comment Israël devient peuple; 3. Contrairement à Carr qui a intitulé le 3e bloc *the Mose's Life Work Story*, je préfère le caractériser par le titre *Histoire de la révélation divine*. Cette révélation se produit par étapes et trouve son apogée non pas en Dt 34,7-9 avec la mort de Moïse, comme Carr l'a proposé, mais dans la péricope du Sinaï. Nous lisons en Ex 40,33s:

וַיְכַל מֹשֶׁה אֶת־הַמְּלָאכָה: 34 וַיְכַס הֶעָנָן אֶת־אֹהֶל מוֹעֵד
וּכְבוֹד יְהֹוָה מָלֵא אֶת־הַמִּשְׁכָּן:

Moïse acheva son œuvre[10]. La nuée couvrit la tente de la rencontre et la gloire de YHWH remplit la demeure.

Ex 40,33bs. forme l'apogée de l'écrit sacerdotal. J'avance encore un peu plus loin: Ex 40,33bs. est aussi la fin de la narration sacerdotale. Cette thèse n'est pas nouvelle. Récemment, T. Pola a présenté une étude qui examine aussi les réflexions compositionnelles sur le plan de la critique littéraire. Son étude correspond curieusement à certaines observations méthodologiques que Carr a faites dans sa lecture beaucoup plus intégrale de la Genèse: c'est le fait de se préoccuper des fractures par lesquelles le sens du texte se produit. Pour Pola, ce sont surtout les *leitmotive* sémantiques qui permettent de distinguer les différentes couches

---

8. D.M. CARR, *Reading the Fractures*, pp. 68-77, et récemment ID., βίβλος γενέσεως *Revisited. A Synchronic Analysis of Patterns in Genesis as Part of the Torah (Part I and II)* in ZAW 110 (1998) 159-172; 327-347.

9. *Ibid.*, pp. 120-125.

10. Pour POLA (*Priesterschrift*, pp. 295s.), le texte primitif de Pᵍ se termine en Ex 40,33b. Cf. la suite.

qui se trouvent aussi à l'intérieur de l'écrit sacerdotal. Si les textes compilés comme celui du déluge montrent des ajouts rédactionnels pour réunir les deux grandes œuvres littéraires pré-sacerdotale et sacerdotale, la structure se complique encore dans la péricope du Sinaï: les récits sacerdotaux, qui sont écrits pour ré-interpréter, corriger et remplacer l'œuvre pré-sacerdotale sur le plan théologique, ont connu eux-mêmes plusieurs révisions tardives. Pola a démontré qu'il ne s'agissait pas seulement de la fameuse distinction en P^g et P^s. Mais P^g avait déjà subi de petites révisions et des ajouts bien manifestes sur le plan sémantique avant que les ajouts plus systématisés, que nous appelons P^s, ne soient insérés (p. ex. les termes pour désigner le sanctuaire: אֹהֶל מוֹעֵד – מִשְׁכָּן – מִקְדָּשׁ)[11].

Pola a développé son esquisse compositionnelle[12] selon trois critères différents: 1. sur le plan de l'histoire des traditions en comparaison avec la conception préfigurée chez Ezéchiel; 2. sur le plan formel en examinant l'usage de certaines formules; 3. sur le plan terminologique par l'étude des désignations du sanctuaire. Je m'appuie dans ce contexte bien limité sur les deux derniers critères. Son étude de formules utilisées en P est concentrée sur celles qui constatent la réalisation d'un ordre divin donné depuis Gn 6,22 à Noé, Abraham ou Moïse. Ces formules sont construites avec צוה pi. + יהוה ou, lorsque JHWH même est l'acteur, avec דבר pi.[13]. Pola démontre que la formule connaît plusieurs variantes, dont seuls les passages avec la formule complète appartiennent à P^g[14] et ont une fonction structurante dans l'ensemble de l'écrit. Les autres formules, sous des formes modifiées et abrégées, sont des ajouts rédactionnels[15]. Un deuxième critère pour vérifier la critique littéraire du texte de P^g est celui de l'usage terminologique pour désigner le sanctuaire[16]. Contrairement aux résultats courants de la recherche, Pola a suggéré que la tente de la rencontre (אֹהֶל מוֹעֵד) n'appartenait pas encore à P^g[17], mais représente une spécification tardive de la demeure divine (מִשְׁכָּן) qui a remplacé l'institution originelle du sanctuaire (מִקְדָּשׁ), exclusivement utilisé en Ex 25,8. Pola constate que ce dernier terme ne joue plus aucun rôle dans la péricope du Sinaï[18] et l'attribue à un type préliminaire de la théologie de la *shekina*, de la présence divine au milieu du peuple.

11. T. POLA, *Priesterschrift*, pp. 229ss. E. ZENGER a récemment réaffirmé que la reconstruction définitive du texte primitif de P^g resterait un problème (*Priesterschrift*, in *TRE* 27 [1996] 435-447, p. 437): Les difficultés s'accumulent à la fin d'Ex 40. Cf. le discours suivant.

12. T. POLA, *Priesterschrift*, p. 298, qui englobe dans la péricope du Sinaï seulement les versets suivants: 19,1;24,15b.16s.18a; 25,1.8a.9; 29,45s.; 40,16.17a.33b.

13. T. POLA, *Priesterschrift*, pp. 122-124.

14. Gn 6,22+7,6; Ex 7,6;12,28+40; 39,32.43; 40,16+17a; T. POLA, *Priesterschrift*, pp. 125, 227s. Ces passages sont toujours suivis d'une indication chronologique.

15. Pour la critique littéraire cf. T. POLA, *Priesterschrift*, pp. 125-134.

16. *Ibid.*, pp. 229-256.

17. C'est une observation qui a des conséquences p. ex. pour la critique littéraire d'Ex 40,34a.

18. T. POLA, *Priesterschrift*, p. 254.

Il faut compter sur un modèle mixte qui comprend des rédactions et des révisions d'un récit primitif. Ces rédactions évoluent souvent selon le principe de l'intersection: le langage de type P^g sert de base pour insérer des termes nouveaux qui englobent des précisions sémantiques souvent d'une manière corrective. La distinction entre écrit de base et écrit supplémentaire se manifeste à partir de la cohérence compositionnelle et thématique de la narration. Il faut poser la question: Comment peut-on vérifier l'extension textuelle et l'intention théologique du corpus sacerdotal sur le plan compositionnel?

Trois points en particulier sont contestables dans l'argumentation pour la fin de P^g en Dt 34,1a.7-9[19]:

1. Pourrait-on compter un 3e bloc thématique traitant *the Mose's Life Work Story*, comme Carr l'a proposé? On a souvent souligné que les détails concernant la biographie de Moïse sont presque absents dans l'écrit sacerdotal[20]. Contrairement au corpus non-P ou pré-sacerdotal, une narration de la naissance et de l'enfance de Moïse est absente. En Ex 6,1 Moïse entre en action sans exposition. En Dt 34,7 le lecteur n'apprend sa mort que par une petite notice de son âge au moment de sa mort.

2. Il n'est pas certain que le thème du pays promis, c'est-à-dire le territoire national, joue un rôle éminent en P^g. T. Pola a proposé d'interpréter les passages concernant le don du pays en Gn 17,8 et en Ex 6,4.8 dans le sens d'une conception où-topique de P^g. La place du sanctuaire non précisée présente une allusion au Sion-Sinaï abstrait. Si l'on suit sa proposition selon laquelle la fin du récit se trouve déjà en Ex 40,33b, passage qui souligne l'accomplissement de l'œuvre par Moïse et non pas l'entrée de YHWH dans sa demeure (v. 34b), le récit reste inachevé[21]. Je préférerais voir la fin du récit en Ex 40,34b[22]. Il semble évident que la

---

19. Sur les différentes propositions concernant la fin de P^g cf. T. POLA, *Priesterschrift*, pp. 44-108.

20. Cf. T. POLA, *Priesterschrift*, pp. 103, 106-110. Certaines réflexions concernant ce fait se trouvent dans l'article de J.-L. SKA, *De la relative independance de l'écrit sacerdotal*, in Bib 76 (1995) 396-415, pp. 399s. avec note 15, qui compte sur l'état fragmentaire de P^g (p. 404). Cf. aussi L. PERLITT, *Priesterschrift im Deuteronomium?* (1988), in ID., *Deuteronomium-Studien* (FAT, 8), Tübingen, J.C.B. Mohr (Paul Siebeck), 1994, pp. 123-143, esp. 133-141. Pour la fin en Dt 34,8b s'est prononcé récemment C. FREVEL, *Mit Blick auf das Land die Schöpfung erinnern. Zum Ende der Priestergrundschrift* (HBS, 23), Freiburg, Herder, 2000, pp. 348ss.

21. T. POLA, *Priesterschrift*, pp. 270ss., esp. 275: «Obwohl Ex 29,45f die Erfüllung der Landgabe im Rahmen der Volksgeschichte vorführt, so bleibt in Ex 29,45f die Ankündigung der Einwohnung Jahwes (V. 45a.46aγ) offen. Ihre Erfüllung findet sich hier nicht berichtet, sondern erst in Ex 40,34f.; Lev 1,1, bzw. in Lev 9. Doch scheinen diese Texte nur Weiterbildungen von P^g zu sein».

22. Sur le plan littéraire il serait possible de considérer la mention de la tente de la rencontre aux v. 34a.35 une comme conjecture (cf. T. POLA, *Priesterschrift*, pp. 275s., 291-298), mais Ex 40,34b(.35?) serait l'apogée thématique (cf. B. JANOWSKI, *Tempel und*

signification du pays au milieu des promesses est beaucoup moins importante[23] que celle de la formation d'un grand peuple ou de la révélation de YHWH en tant que Dieu de ce peuple. Étant le négatif théologique de l'esquisse pré-exilique, il est bien compréhensible que P[g] n'a pu
que modifier sa présentation des espoirs historiques et théologiques:
l'espoir du retour en Israël réhabilité faisait partie du programme, mais
l'intérêt primordial se basait sur la continuité de l'identité du peuple
dans sa religion. Selon ces présuppositions, l'écrit sacerdotal serait ciblé
sur un programme cultuel au lieu d'un programme politique.

3. La conception développée par Karl Elliger de la fin ouverte de
P[g][24] est une hypothèse trop vague sur le plan méthodologique. De
même, le modèle d'une histoire de la rédaction finale qui compte sur la
suppression d'une certaine quantité de récits me semble difficile à vérifier. Les deux conceptions sont d'autant plus douteuses que la base textuelle peut être reconstruite d'une façon assez intégrale sur le plan
compositionnel. Les inclusions thématiques, sémantiques et théologiques entre Gn 1 et la fin du livre de l'Exode sont évidentes[25], tandis que
le schéma compositionnel de la suite narrative se présente comme beaucoup plus lacunaire[26].

Schöpfung [1990], in ID., *Gottes Gegenwart in Israel. Beiträge zur Theologie des Alten
Testaments*, Neukirchen-Vluyn, Neukirchener Verlag, 1993, pp. 214-246, esp. 224-232).
Cf. ci-dessous.

23. M. KÖCKERT (*Das Land in der priesterlichen Komposition des Pentateuch*, in D.
VIEWEGER – E.-J. WASCHKE [eds.], *Von Gott reden. Beiträge zur Theologie und Exegese
des AT*. FS S. Wagner, Neukirchen-Vluyn, Neukirchener Verlag, 1996, pp. 147-162, esp.
151s.) souligne le double sens de אֶרֶץ terre / pays depuis Gn 9,1: «Die priesterliche
Schule nimmt dabei die ältere Vorstellung auf, in der Volk und Land zusammengehören,
und schreibt sie in die Konditionen des Menschseins nach der Flut ein. (…) Die
Gliederung der Menschheit auf Erden in differenzierte Völker und Länder ist das Produkt
der um der Sünde willen erfolgten Revision der Schöpfungsordnung». L'installation dans
le pays en Gen 17, qui présente la *berît* valable pour les patriarches, serait encadrée par la
promesse de la présence permanente de Dieu au milieu de son peuple. Gn 9 manifestait
l'auto-restriction divine, Gn 17 l'auto-révélation divine. Par l'interdépendance du don du
pays et de la relation Dieu-Homme, l'exode se présente sous la forme d'un retour au point
de départ («Heraufführung als Heimführung»).

24. Cf. aussi E. ZENGER, *Priesterschrift* (n. 11), p. 440: «Daß die Zusage, die für
Israel Rettung aus dem Tod (Ex 1-14*), Gabe des Lebens (Ex 16*), soziale Gemeinschaft
(Ex 19-40*) und Gemeinschaft mit Gott (Lev 9) bedeutet, durch die Sünde Israels nicht
hinfällig wird, ist der offene Schluß mit dem P[g] ihre zweifelnden Zeitgenossen zum
Aufbruch in das Land des Lebens (vgl. Gen 17,8; Ex 6,4.8) aufrufen will».

25. B. RENAUD (*La formation de Ex 19-40*, in P. HAUDÉBERT [éd.], *Le Pentateuque.
Débats et recherches* [LD, 151], Paris, Cerf, 1992, pp. 101-133, esp. 103-110) a récemment souligné les parallèles entre Ex 24 (la demeure de la gloire de YHWH sur le Sinaï)
et Ex 40 (la demeure de la gloire de YHWH dans le sanctuaire). Ce parallèle thématique
et structurel mettrait la fin de P[g] en Ex 40,38 avec la fin du livre, qui est suivie d'une
reprise rédactionelle à partir de Lv 1,1 faisant référence à Ex 24,18; 25,15. C'est alors
que la rédaction insère le motif de la pratique cultuelle. Cf. la suite.

26. N. LOHFINK (*Priesterschrift und Geschichte*, in *VT* 29 [1978] 189-225) a proposé
d'attribuer Jos 18,1 à l'écrit sacerdotal en tant que formule d'inclusion qui atteste l'ac-

Il faut noter que Janowski et surtout Zenger ont proposé de voir la fin de Pg en Lv 9,24 avec les arguments suivants: à partir de ce texte la quantité de versets appartenant à Pg diminue. Sur le plan thématique les instructions aux prêtres en Lv 8 suivies du récit du premier sacrifice réalisé par Aaron dans la tente de la rencontre correspondent bien au langage et aux thèmes attribués généralement à P. Les références structurelles et thématiques de Lv 9 s'étendent à travers Ex 16; 24,15-18aα jusqu'en Ex 40,34s. Cependant il me semble plus prudent de chercher une composition plus compacte qui se termine à la fin du livre de l'Exode[27]. En s'appuyant sur différentes rédactions et révisions sacerdotales («Fortschreibungen»), on retrouve des références sémantiques jusqu'en Jos 18,1;19,51[28]. Cependant un tel volume me fait plutôt croire à un travail rédactionnel[29]. Ne peut-on penser que Pg a présenté une conception exilique qui considère le sanctuaire comme lieu de la présence divine, tandis que ses successeurs ont insisté sur le sanctuaire comme étant aussi le lieu du sacrifice? En Ps le théologoumène de la théophanie est ré-utilisé pour légitimer la liturgie sacrificielle[30].

> En général on attribue la fin du livre de l'Exode à Pg et à Ps: Ex 40,34-35 parle de la présence statique de Dieu demeurant dans son sanctuaire, tandis que dans les vv. 35-38 elle «se fait dynamique, accompagnatrice d'Israël dans tous ses déplacements»[31]. B. Janowski[32] nous a présenté un schéma de composition qui reprend des observations de K. Koch[33]. Selon eux Ex 40,33b.34s. ne se continue pas par 40,36-38, mais – en correspondance avec Ex 24,15bss.; 25,1 – par Lv 1,1. Les vv. 36-38 sont secondaires et forment un rapport étroit avec Nb 9,15-23[34].

complissement de Gn 1,28 (כבש + ארץ) pour éviter au moins les lacunes thématiques du type «fin ouverte». Cependant il ne réussit pas à expliquer les lacunes narratives à partir d'Ex 40. Cf. dans ce volume la contribution d'E.A. Knauf pour compléter l'argumentation de Lohfink.

27. E. OTTO a même proposé de chercher la fin de Pg déjà en Ex 29,42b-46 (*Forschungen*, p. 36).

28. N. LOHFINK, *Les traditions du Pentateuque autour de l'exil* (CE, 97), Paris, Cerf, 1996, p. 14. Cf. ID., *Die Schichten des Pentateuch und der Krieg*, in ID., *Studien zum Pentateuch* (SBAAT, 4), Stuttgart, Katholisches Bibelwerk, 1988, pp. 255-315, esp. 284s. Pour toute la discussion, cf. récemment ZENGER, *Priesterschrift*, pp. 438s.

29. Cf. dernièrement J. VERMEYLEN, *Théophanie, Purification et Liturgie*, in R. KUNTZMANN (éd.), *Ce Dieu qui vient. Mélanges offerts à Bernard Renaud* (LD, 159), Paris, Cerf, 1996, pp. 113-130, esp. 114 avec note 3.

30. Cf. dans ce contexte B. RENAUD, *Formation*, pp. 106s.

31. B. RENAUD, *Formation*, p. 104. Cf. note 25.

32. *Sühne als Heilsgeschehen. Studien zur Sühnetheologie der Priesterschrift und zur Wurzel KPR im Alten Orient und im Alten Testament* (WMANT, 55), Neukirchen-Vluyn, Neukirchener Verlag, 1982, pp. 313s.

33. *Die Priesterschrift von Ex 25 bis Lev 16. Eine überlieferungsgeschichtliche und literarkritische Untersuchung* (FRLANT, 71), Göttingen, Vandenhoeck & Ruprecht, 1959, p. 99.

34. Ainsi T. POLA, *Priesterschrift*, p. 217 avec note 13 et E. BLUM, *Komposition*, pp. 302 note 55; 313 et note 97; autrement Renaud (cf. note 25).

Ex 40,33b-Lv 1,1
Moïse acheva ainsi tous les travaux. La nuée couvrit la tente de la rencontre et la gloire de YHWH remplit la demeure. Moïse ne pouvait pas entrer dans la tente de la rencontre, car la nuée y demeurait et la gloire de YHWH remplissait la demeure. Quand la nuée s'élevait au-dessus de la demeure, les fils d'Israël prenaient le départ pour chacune de leurs étapes. Mais si la nuée ne s'élevait pas, ils ne partaient pas avant le jour où elle s'élevait de nouveau. Car la nuée de YHWH était sur la demeure pendant le jour mais, pendant la nuit, il y avait en elle du feu, aux yeux de toute la maison d'Israël, à toutes leurs étapes.
YHWH appela Moïse et, de la tente de la rencontre, lui adressa la parole:…

וַיְכַל מֹשֶׁה אֶת־הַמְּלָאכָה׃ פ

34 וַיְכַס הֶעָנָן אֶת־אֹהֶל מוֹעֵד וּכְבוֹד יְהוָה מָלֵא אֶת־הַמִּשְׁכָּן׃

35 וְלֹא־יָכֹל מֹשֶׁה לָבוֹא אֶל־אֹהֶל מוֹעֵד כִּי־שָׁכַן עָלָיו הֶעָנָן וּכְבוֹד יְהוָה מָלֵא אֶת־הַמִּשְׁכָּן׃

36 וּבְהֵעָלוֹת הֶעָנָן מֵעַל הַמִּשְׁכָּן יִסְעוּ בְּנֵי יִשְׂרָאֵל בְּכֹל מַסְעֵיהֶם׃

37 וְאִם־לֹא יֵעָלֶה הֶעָנָן וְלֹא יִסְעוּ עַד־יוֹם הֵעָלֹתוֹ׃ 38 כִּי עֲנַן יְהוָה עַל־הַמִּשְׁכָּן יוֹמָם וְאֵשׁ תִּהְיֶה לַיְלָה בּוֹ לְעֵינֵי כָל־בֵּית־יִשְׂרָאֵל בְּכָל־מַסְעֵיהֶם׃

1:1 וַיִּקְרָא אֶל־מֹשֶׁה וַיְדַבֵּר יְהוָה אֵלָיו מֵאֹהֶל מוֹעֵד לֵאמֹר׃

Selon Janowski, les mots-clés, appartenant à Pᵍ, sont כְּבוֹד יְהוָה et הֶעָנָן et sont disposés en chiasme aux vv. 34a et 35aβ (הֶעָנָן) et aux vv. 34b et 35b (כְּבוֹד יְהוָה). La voix divine en Lv 1,1 depuis la tente de la rencontre comprend déjà dans le texte primitif une référence à la constatation au v. 35aα que Moïse ne pouvait pas entrer dans la tente, puisque le nuage l'a remplie. Le v. 35b est une reprise mot à mot du v. 34b. En ce qui concerne les vv. 36-38, les opinions semblent presque unanimes: ces versets appartiennent à une rédaction sacerdotale tardive. Concernant Ex 40,34s il existe deux modèles différents d'explication: pour les deux options la correspondance entre Ex 40,34s et Lv 1,1 est évidente. L'observation amène cependant deux conclusions différentes: Pola émet l'hypothèse que l'écrit de base de Pᵍ se termine déjà avec le v. 33b par l'achèvement de l'œuvre par Moïse, et que les vv. 34ss. figurent dans un ajout secondaire. Autrement dit: l'entrée divine (*shekina*) n'est pas explicitement racontée. Cette hypothèse me semble peu convaincante: Pola sous-entend un autre modèle de «fin ouverte», mais il court le danger de supprimer l'intention théologique primordiale, la demeure divine au milieu de son peuple. Par la fin du récit au v. 33b l'accent serait mis sur l'achèvement de la création / de l'œuvre par Moïse et non pas sur la sentence théologique formulant une théologie de la *shekina*. La seconde option, présentée par Janowski, se base sur la continuité de P^g jusqu'en Lv 9,23s. (ou même Dt 34)[35]. Pour lui la péricope du Sinaï commence déjà en Ex 16,10 à cause de la première notion de la כְּבוֹד יְהוָה au lieu qu'elle commence en Ex 19,1. Cette inclusion s'achève en Lv 9,23s. Cette conception insiste sur la gravité du culte ainsi que sur la tente de la rencontre dans le récit primitif de P. Je voudrais proposer une troisième hypothèse: Lorsqu'on prend les observations méthodologiques de Pola au sérieux, il faut compter sur un grand nombre de rédacteurs qui ont inséré des explications et précisions dans le style du récit de base (P^g)[36]: on pourrait en conclure que la fin de P^g se trouve en Ex 40,33b.34b[37] et que le v. 35 serait un ajout du type P^ge, qui prépare l'annexe secondaire concernant la pratique cultuelle, qui se termine probablement en Lv 9,23s., avant d'intégrer tous ces textes que nous résumons sous le nom de P^s.

Ce schéma plein de répétitions et d'inclusions peut être interprété comme la suite de plusieurs ajouts (vv. 34a.35a) et reprises (v. 35b), qui donne le témoignage d'un travail rédactionnel bien élaboré. Le nuage qui remplit le sanctuaire peut être compris comme un retardement dans le «drame» de la révélation divine, ajouté plus tard pour souligner que le sanctuaire sans culte ne correspond pas encore à l'ordre divin. Ce thème se présente comme une bonne motivation pour tout ce qui suit en Lv 1,1 – 9,23, une dernière apogée qui culmine dans l'apparition de la כְּבוֹד יְהוָה au terme du premier sacrifice célébré dans le sanctuaire. C'est le moment où le lieu saint où-topique s'est transformé en un temple, le nouveau temple à Jérusalem.

Continuons alors avec une reconstruction de l'écrit sacerdotal (P^g) en détail.

III. LA VALEUR DES CATÉGORIES TEMPS ET ESPACE DANS L'ÉCRIT SACERDOTAL

Le critère le plus caractéristique d'une historiographie est celui d'une présentation du passé avec une évaluation des événements historiques concentrée sur un groupe national.

Comment cette présentation est-elle réalisée?
1. par la définition du groupe habitant un territoire fixe
2. par la présentation de leur histoire sur un axe chronologique.

Le premier point intègre la catégorie de l'espace autant que le second inclut celle du temps.

35. Cf. B. JANOWSKI, *Tempel und Schöpfung*, pp. 224ss.
36. Cf. T. POLA, *Priesterschrift*, p. 222; pour le principe cf. D.M. CARR, *Reading the Fractures*, pp. 38s.; 57ss.; 75-77; 112-118.
37. Concernant le v. 34a cf. ci-dessus p. 32 avec note 17.

1. La catégorie de l'espace pour définir le groupe ethnique considéré en P^g

En P^g l'espace joue un rôle à trois niveaux:

1. Il y a les itinéraires et les notions de lieux. Le fait d'observer que l'arrivée au terminus Canaan ne figure pas dans les narrations sacerdotales, a poussé p. ex. Karl Elliger[38] ou plus récemment Peter Weimar[39] à présenter une conception de P^g se terminant par une *fin ouverte* qui laisse sous-entendre l'installation dans le pays au-delà de Dt 34. Ils ont promulgué que les histoires patriarcales comprennent déjà une prolepse de l'installation dans le pays de Canaan, qui se manifeste dans l'acquisition de territoire familial pour enterrer les ancêtres. À cause de cela toute l'historiographie sacerdotale serait ciblée sur la conquête pacifique du pays promis – après l'exil[40].

2. L'espace joue un certain rôle dans le récit de la création. Dans les trois œuvres de la séparation, Dieu crée le temps et l'espace dans sa verticalité et dans son horizontalité. Face aux sept versets qui y sont consacrés, l'aménagement de ces deux catégories occupe presque un volume double (17 versets), avant d'aboutir dans la sphère sacro-sainte du septième jour.

3. Dans un tout autre contexte on rencontre la notion d'espace à travers des généalogies. Parmi les trois types de généalogies dans la Genèse, ce sont les *toledôt* qui ont une valeur structurante en P^g. Elles sont suivies des généalogies narratives concernant Noé, Abraham, Isaac et Jacob. Ces dernières sont interrompues par des généalogies énumératives pour des lignées collatérales et secondaires dans la table des nations et dans les généalogies d'Ésaü et d'Ismaël.

Ces systèmes généalogiques ont une double fonction: d'abord ils présentent *l'ampleur universelle* de la bénédiction de Gn 1,28, qui s'est explicitement manifestée dans la table des nations en Gn 10,1ss. À partir de ce texte se produit comme deuxième principe celui de la *sélection* d'une branche, l'Israël futur.

38. *Sinn und Ursprung der priesterschriftlichen Geschichtserzählung* [1952], in ID., *Kleine Schriften zum Alten Testament* (TB, 32), H. GESE – O. KAISER eds., München, Kaiser, 1966, pp. 174-198, ici 189: «Es ist die… Verheißung…, die… auf die Verleihung des uneingeschränkten Besitzes des heiligen Landes hindrängt. Aber der endgültige Aufstieg zum letzten Ziel auf den alles überragenden Gipfel bleibt aus».
39. *Struktur und Komposition der priesterschriftlichen Geschichtsdarstellung*, in *BN* 23 (1984) 81-134; BN 24 (1984) 138-162, p. 161 note 200: La fin ouverte serait un moyen stylistique pour démontrer que le processus achevé sur le plan littéraire ne serait pas encore accompli pour les destinataires du récit; cf. ZENGER (citation en note 24).
40. Cf. dernièrement D.M. CARR, *Reading the Fractures*, pp. 122s.

R. Lux[41] a précisé cette double fonction de l'ampleur universelle et de la sélection par des aspects de verticalité et d'horizontalité. Le caractère horizontal d'une généalogie s'exprime dans l'extension des familles, des lignées et des peuples. Il correspond tout à fait à une connotation spatiale. Cependant le caractère vertical d'une généalogie souligne l'aspect de la temporalité. Ces généalogies décrivent la lignée principale dans la suite de plusieurs générations qui mène à la formation du peuple Israël. Il semble que par ce type de généalogie une certaine historicité soit créée. À vrai dire, ce type de généalogie ne traite pas du temps linéaire, mais du temps dans sa circularité: les généalogies verticales sont des preuves pour la continuité dans l'histoire.

Par le genre des généalogies, les catégories spatiale et temporelle sont confondues. Je me tourne maintenant vers les catégories proprement temporelles.

2. La catégorie du temps en rapport avec une présentation de l'histoire d'Israël

Bien sûr, P^g présente aussi une étape de l'histoire d'Israël qu'on résume en général sous le titre de «proto-histoire». Mais, cette époque est-elle d'un intérêt historique? Quelle notion de temps est envisagée lorsque P^g en parle?

Il est frappant de constater que le récit de P^g en Gn 1 commence par la création du temps. Premièrement, le temps signifie l'alternance de jour et de nuit (v. 4), suivie de l'alternance des mois (vv. 14ss.). La base pour une chronologie historique semble établie. Mais le fait que tout le récit de la création se déroule en une semaine introduit un autre aspect: le septième jour est caractérisé par l'arrêt de l'œuvre divine, un phénomène qu'on a toujours mis en rapport avec la justification du Shabbat, comme elle est prononcée dans le décalogue en Ex 20,11 (P^s) et préfigurée en Ex 16 (P^s)[42]. Par le respect du Shabbat, Israël appartient au temps sacré qu'au commencement Dieu avait réservé à lui-même[43].

---

41. *Die Genealogie als Strukturprinzip des Pluralismus im Alten Testament*, in J. MEHLHAUSEN (ed.), *Pluralismus und Identität*, Gütersloh, Kaiser, pp. 242-258, esp. 245s., 249.

42. Pour la critique littéraire d'Ex 16, cf. T. POLA, *Priesterschrift*, pp. 134-143, qui attribue le texte à une couche supplémentaire, tandis que K. GRÜNWALDT (*Exil und Identität. Beschneidung, Passa und Sabbat in der Priesterschrift* [BBB, 85], Frankfurt/M, Anton Hain, 1992) le considère comme P^g.

43. V. FRITZ, Das *Geschichtsverständnis der Priesterschrift*, in ZTK 84 (1987) 426-439, p. 431.

La notion du temps figure aussi dans les chronologies absolues qui parcourent l'écrit sacerdotal. La recurrence du schéma des 7 jours (Ex 16,26 [Pˢ]; Ex 24,16 [Pᵍ]) ainsi que la référence au 1er jour du 1er mois, le jour du Nouvel An (Gn 7,6; 8,13; Ex 12,41; 40,17 [Pᵍ]), font allusion à un calendrier cultuel. Le temps n'est pas traité dans le sens d'une chronique, mais d'un temps liturgique. Les événements historiques se déroulent selon le schéma de l'ordre divin[44].

Résumons les observations concernant l'espace et le temps dans l'écrit sacerdotal: Les deux catégories de temps et d'espace se trouvent dans une relation d'interdépendance. Déjà l'emploi du terme אֶרֶץ[45] en Pᵍ démontre les enjeux entre universalité (terre) et sélection (pays de Canaan). Aussi les généalogies suivent le même principe à coté de leur caractère mono- et multi-linéaire: par leur multi-linéarité, les généalogies énumératives manifestent l'ampleur universelle. Dans leur mono-linéarité les *toledôt* et les généalogies narratives présentent la sélection d'une branche particulière à travers le temps en insistant surtout sur l'aspect de la continuité. Les deux aspects ne sont pas vraiment distincts l'un de l'autre.

> Je voudrais formuler la thèse que le cercle de l'humanité (Steck[46] parle du «Welt-/Menschen-Kreis») et le cercle d'Israël (selon Steck: «Israel-Kreis») se trouvent dans un rapport d'interdépendance qui manifeste une révélation continue. Le noyau de cette révélation avec le parcours qu'elle effectue se trouve déjà en Gn 1. Le parcours est repris dans les deux autres parties de l'écrit sacerdotal Pᵍ, dans la généalogie élargie et l'installation divine au milieu de son peuple au Sinaï.

À la fin de nos observations, il faut se poser la question de savoir dans quelle perspective la conception pseudo-historique figure en Pᵍ.

3. Le thème de la révélation en étapes et la conception ritualisée de l'histoire

Retournons à la triple structure théologique de Pᵍ:

Le programme théologique en Gn 1 est suivi d'une généalogie élargie commençant en Gn 5,1 et se terminant en Gn 50, juste avant l'accom-

---

44. S.E. MCEVENUE, *The Narrative Style of the Priestly Writer* (AnBib, 50), Rome, Pontifical Institute, 1971; JANOWSKI, *Tempel und Schöpfung*, pp. 224-232 (cf. note 22); V. FRITZ *Geschichtsverständnis der Priesterschrift*, p. 428: «Geschichte wird nicht als Aneinanderreihung von Ereignissen verstanden, vielmehr erhält die Chronologie ihr eigenes Gewicht. Die genauen Angaben für jedes Ereignis sind also mehr als ein bloßes Datum, der Zeitverlauf ist Ausdruck der göttlichen Ordnung der Welt. Die geschichtlichen Ereignisse verlaufen im Rahmen dieses Ordnungsschemas. Die chronologischen Angaben entspringen somit dem priesterschriftlichen Verständnis des Geschichtsablaufes im Rahmen der von Gott gegebenen Zeit.»

45. Autrement M. KÖCKERT, *Land*, pp. 149-151.

46. *Aufbauprobleme der Priesterschrift*, in D.R. DANIELS – U. GLESSMER – M. RÖSEL (eds.), *Ernten, was man sät.* FS K. Koch, Neukirchen-Vluyn, Neukirchener Verlag, 1991, pp. 287-308, esp. 305s.

plissement de la bénédiction prononcée en Gn 1,28, qui se trouve en Ex 1,7.

Par ce verset est introduite une troisième partie qui traite de la sortie de l'esclavage en Égypte et de la révélation divine au Sinaï.

Quels sont les rapports des parties II et III avec le texte programmatique en Gn 1? Quels sont les mots-clés? Quels sont les enjeux théologiques et littéraires?

J'ai choisi deux thèmes théologiques pour démontrer comment le programme se poursuit depuis Gn 1 jusqu'en Ex 40,34b (cf. schéma page 42).

1. Je commence par le thème de la révélation introduit en Gn 1,2 par le terme רוּחַ אלהים qui connaîtra à travers le récit la modification en כְּבוֹד יְהוָה.

Dans ma thèse de doctorat[47]. j'ai proposé une lecture de la רוּחַ אֱלֹהִים, terme oscillant signifiant vent, souffle et esprit, qui décrit la présence divine dans une description négative du monde, dont l'installation n'est présentée qu'à partir du verset 3. Cette description négative suit le plan d'une description contrastive d'un monde qui est imaginé comme existant dans les versets suivants. Le Dieu créateur qui entre en action par la mise en ordre d'éléments différents est présent en silence dans le v. 2 du premier chapitre. Grâce à lui le monde, après avoir été établi, a obtenu la capacité d'une auto-reproduction considérable (cf. Gn 5,1ss.). La révélation divine ne se produit pas par un acte primordial, mais par des gestes permanents. La notion de l'alliance avec Noé et ses descendants est caractérisée par son universalité, comme elle se manifeste dans la table des nations en Gn 10. Comparée à la table des nations, la généalogie de Térach et Abraham, à la fin du chapitre 11, introduit l'aspect d'exclusivité et de sélection. Ce changement de perspective du monde envers le fondateur d'Israël semble être un peu rélativisé en Gn 17. Par le fait que dans le deuxième récit d'alliance, Abraham est en même temps présenté comme père des nations futures, nous constatons de nouveau un certain universalisme à côté de la notion d'exclusivité. Aussi la condition de cette alliance, la circoncision, inclut plutôt l'aspect d'une confession que d'une appartenance générale à une nation/peuple particulier[48]. Théoriquement le signe de distinction est transmissible à tous ceux qui veulent

---

47. M. BAUKS, *Die Welt am Anfang: Zum Verhältnis von Vorwelt und Weltentstehung in Gen 1 und in der altorientalischen Literatur* (WMANT, 74), Neukirchen-Vluyn, Neukirchener Verlag, 1997, esp. pp. 136-141.

48. T. POLA, (*Priesterschrift*, pp. 168s.) souligne que le signe de *berît*, la circoncision, ne se présente pas comme signe de distinction ethnique. L'ordre est donné à tous les membres de la maison d'Abraham, ceux qui y sont nés comme les autres, d'être circoncis pour être intégrés dans le peuple divin. Il s'agit d'une mesure bien compréhensible dans le contexte exilique.

s'intégrer dans la communauté de ce dieu qui s'est révélé sous le nom El Shaddaj.

Ce dieu se revèle en Ex 6 à Moïse sous un autre nom, le Tetragramme. Le changement du nom est accompagné par le changement de la qualité de la révélation. À partir d'ici aussi, une nouvelle étape de l'histoire de la révélation est introduite: la promesse de la descendance et de la formation du peuple est largement accomplie (Ex 1,7). Un nouveau thème est introduit à côté de celui de la présence divine au milieu de son peuple: c'est celui de la servitude, de la dépendance d'un régime politique qui est entré en controverse avec l'ordre de vie présupposé jusqu'ici. Dans ce contexte, la notion de pays promis acquiert son sens profond: grâce à la libération du régime opprimant, le peuple de YHWH peut être en accord avec l'ordre divin.

Il s'agit d'une conception qui nécessite peu d'imagination pour être placée

• révélation

Gn 1,2	רוח אלהים	«vent/souffle/esprit divin»	ne-pas-encore de la révélation
Gn 1,3	ויאמר אלהים	parole divine	entrée en action de Dieu
Gn 17,1 וירא יהוה (nif)		YHWH se montre	révélation sous le nom אל שדי pour קום (hif) ברית עולם (v. 7)
Ex 6,2 אני יהוה		«Je suis YHWH»	révélation sous le nom de YHWH
Ex 6,7		- Israël mon peuple - YHWH son Dieu - sortie d'Égypte pour le faire	venir (בוא hif) dans le pays (ארץ)
[Ex 16,10 (Pˢ) כבוד יהוה נראה]		apparition de la gloire de YHWH	avant la découverte du Shabbat]
Ex 24,16 וישכן כבוד יהוה		la gloire de YHWH demeure sur	le mont Sinaï
Ex 29,45-46	וְשָׁכַנְתִּי בְּתוֹךְ בְּנֵי יִשְׂרָאֵל וְהָיִיתִי לָהֶם לֵאלֹהִים׃		Je demeurerai parmi les fils d'Israël et, pour eux, je serai Dieu
	וְיָדְעוּ כִּי אֲנִי יְהוָה אֱלֹהֵיהֶם אֲשֶׁר הוֹצֵאתִי אֹתָם		Ils reconnaîtront que c'est moi, YHWH, qui suis leur Dieu, moi qui
	מֵאֶרֶץ מִצְרַיִם לְשָׁכְנִי בְתוֹכָם		les ai fait sortir du pays d'Égypte pour demeurer parmi eux
	אֲנִי יְהוָה אֱלֹהֵיהֶם׃		C'est moi YHWH, qui suis leur Dieu
Ex 40,34b	וּכְבוֹד יְהוָה מָלֵא אֶת־הַמִּשְׁכָּן		La gloire de YHWH remplit la demeure

dans la situation historique de l'écrit sacerdotal avec le souvenir des cultes imposés par des oppresseurs assyriens à Jérusalem. Cette pensée est présentée d'ailleurs explicitement dans le récit de non-P en Ex 5: au lieu de laisser partir le peuple pour célébrer une fête pour YHWH dans le désert, les Égyptiens renforcent leur oppression.

Les histoires de plaies impressionnent parce qu'elles ont introduit la notion d'une double révélation: envers Pharaon et les Égyptiens et envers les Israélites. D'une certaine manière l'universalisme se manifeste une dernière fois pour aboutir dans l'exode et l'arrivée au Sinaï, le terme de la révélation divine envers son peuple.

Déjà sur le plan sémantique, l'inclusion avec Gn 1 est parfaite comme P. Weimar et B. Janowski l'ont démontré. La reprise de la structure des six jours suivis d'un septième où Moïse obtient les consignes de construction du sanctuaire (מִשְׁכָּן en Ex 24,15ss.; 29,43ss.) rappelle beaucoup Gn 1. Au moment de l'exécution des consignes de construction, la promesse de la présence divine se réalise: c'est l'apparition du כְּבוֹד יְהוָה, qui se manifeste dans le sanctuaire. Le sanctuaire devient la manifestation concrète du septième jour: l'espace temporel qui est réservé à Dieu dans le récit de création, devient dans le récit du Sinaï le lieu de rencontre entre créateur et créature.

2. Le second thème est celui de la bénédiction et de la sanctification.

Le thème de la bénédiction est inséré dans plusieurs contextes thématiques, que j'ai mentionnés dans le schéma suivant sous les termes *installation*, *révision*, *sélection* et *accomplissement*. Le motif de la bénédiction (ברך pi) est utilisé pour manifester la capacité de la création à se perpétuer par une re-production autonome. L'extension et la multitude sont constatées à la fin de l'histoire patriarcale en Ex 1,7. Ce verset résume que la généalogie élargie a trouvé son apogée dans la formation du peuple Israël. Cependant le terme de la sanctification (en hébreu les radicales קדש) est beaucoup plus rare. En Pᵍ il ne se rencontre qu'en Gn 2,2, dans le contexte du septième jour et en Ex 25,8, dans celui des consignes de construction du sanctuaire. Dans les ajouts de Pˢ le terme קוֹדֶשׁ a remplacé le terme courant en Pᵍ מִשְׁכָּן. C'est seulement en Ex 25,8 que nous trouvons comme terme alternatif מִקְדָשׁ, qui sera le terme employé pour la demeure future au milieu des Israélites.

L'usage du terme מִשְׁכָּן en Ex 40,34 remplaçant מִקְדָשׁ dans les consignes pour la construction du sanctuaire (en Ex 25,8) indique peut-être le décalage entre le projet et sa réalisation: au temps de Pᵍ la rencontre entre Dieu et son peuple ne se passe pas encore dans le temple reconstruit. Ce temple reste un projet. Mais indépendamment de sa réalisation, la présence divine est donnée.

En Ex 29,43 nous retrouvons le verbe קדש au nif: le sanctuaire sera consacré par le כְּבוֹד יְהוָה autant que les Aaronites seront consacrés pour leur sacerdoce, mais l'attribution de ces versets est à rediscuter[49].

---

49. Il faut noter que POLA n'intègre pas ces versets généralement attribués à Pᵍ (JANOWSKI, BLUM, RENAUD, cf. ci-dessus) pour des raisons syntaxiques et contextuelles assez intéressantes (*Priesterschrift*, pp. 234-236).

On ne sait dans quelle mesure ce sanctuaire s'est présenté concrètement. On ne peut répondre avec certitude à la question de savoir si P^g avait déjà en vue le second temple de l'époque post-exilique. Les jeux de mots que les textes comprennent autour de la terminologie de ce sanctuaire peuvent faire imaginer un travail théologique successif de différents courants sacerdotaux, dont la première conception n'a contenu que la notion d'un lieu dans le temps, le Shabbat, au lieu d'un bâtiment concret. Cette conception évolue, soit sous la forme d'une tente du désert, soit sous la forme d'un nouveau temple à Jerusalem.

Selon notre schéma de composition, l'aspect de la sanctification du septième jour semble aboutir dans la construction du sanctuaire[50]. Ce sanctuaire représente la demeure divine au milieu de son peuple dans laquelle s'installe son כָּבוֹד[51].

• Bénédiction et sanctification

installation	Gn 1,22	bénédiction des animaux du ciel et de l'eau
(sous garantie de	Gn 1,28	bénédiction des hommes
continuité)	Gn 2,3	bénédiction (ברך pi) et sanctification (קדש) du septième jour
révision	Gn 9,1	bénédiction de Noé et de ses fils
	Gn 9,8s.	alliance avec hommes et animaux pour garantir la continuité
sélection	Gn 17,2.7	alliance avec Abraham et sa descendance (multitude, présence divine, promesse du pays)
	Gn 17,19.21	exclusivité de l'alliance pour la lignée d'Isaac
	Gn 17,20	bénédiction d'Ismaël (cf. Gn 28,3; Gn 39,9ss.; Gn 48,3-4
accomplissement	Ex 1,7	accomplissement de la bénédiction prononcée en Gn 1,28
	Ex 25,8	accomplissement de la sanctification prononcée en Gn 2,3: suit l'ordre de la construction d'une מקדש pour que Dieu puisse demeurer (שכן) dans le sanctuaire (en général משכן en P^g), qui est consacré (קדש nif) par la gloire de YHWH

Une dernière remarque pour évaluer les observations faites pour la discussion autour des historiographies bibliques: l'idée directrice de l'histoire de la révélation dans l'écrit sacerdotal se résume dans la nécessité de la rencontre permanente entre Dieu et son peuple. Envisagée dès

---

50. Ce jour appartient à la sphère divine; cf. B. JANOWSKI, *Tempel und Schöpfung*; B. RENAUD, *Théophanie du Sinaï*, pp. 191s.
51. H. RINGGREN, in *TWAT* 6, 1989, cc. 1190s.

la création, cette rencontre se reproduit au travers de plusieurs événements jusqu'à la fin de l'écrit. Elle se termine par l'établissement de la demeure permanente de Dieu au milieu de son peuple. Depuis la présence divine sous la forme du רוּחַ dans le pré-état du monde (Gn 1,2), en passant par son activité depuis Gn 1,3 jusqu'à l'accomplissement de son œuvre en Gn 2,1 nous continuons le parcours d'étapes qui se reproduisent dans les histoires que P^g décrit: la présence divine dans le déluge se dirige vers la création du peuple Israël pour aboutir dans la présence de sa כָּבוֹד au milieu de son peuple. Cette gradation à travers une narration pleine de ruptures et de recommencements devrait comprendre la fonction consolatrice la plus forte qu'une conception théologique puisse comprendre. Au-delà de l'espoir d'une reconstitution de l'identité nationale et territoriale, Dieu annonce sa présence au milieu de son peuple indépendemment de la situation historique[52]. C'est le message que P^g a développé par sa composition bien close.

Il devrait être évident qu'une telle conception est bien loin d'un genre littéraire que nous appelons en général *historiographie*. Ce genre se rencontre dans les inscriptions royales assyriennes et sous forme restreinte dans l'historiographie deutéronomiste à travers les chroniques des rois d'Israël et de Juda. Une telle conception est cependant perdue de vue dans l'écrit sacerdotal.

Montpellier   Michaela BAUKS

---

52. O.H. STECK (*Aufbauprobleme*, pp. 304s.) aboutit à des resultats similaires: la comparaison sémantique d'Ez 7-9 avec l'annonce du tribunal suite à la culpabilité des actants en Gn 6,11-13 nous révèle comment P^g a intégré le motif de la culpablilité d'Israël dans un contexte primordial de son histoire. Par ce moyen stylistique il souligne le fait que «politische Wechselfälle und geschichtliche Einbrüche wie die Exilszeit bis hin zu dem nicht gegebenene Besitz des Landes die Identität des Gottesvolkes nicht in Frage stellen». La punition s'est passée avant tout temps, suivi de la promesse divine que la «fin» ne viendrait plus (Gn 6,13 et 9,15).

PROPHETIE IM DEUTERONOMISTISCHEN GESCHICHTSWERK

Die Deuteronomismusforschung ist wie kaum eine andere Sparte der alttestamentlichen Wissenschaft vom Sisyphus-Syndrom geprägt. Martin Noth hat 1943 den ersten grossen Stein ins Rollen gebracht[1]. Nach seiner Auffassung sind die Bücher von Deuteronomium bis 2 Könige ein zusammenhängendes, von einem einzigen Verfasser planvoll gestaltetes, zur Exilszeit entstandenes Werk über die Geschichte Israels von der Landnahme bis zum Landverlust. Seither haben viele Deuteronomismusforscher seine Theorie zu untermauern oder zu variieren, z.T. auch zu widerlegen versucht, indem sie näherhin nach den Quellen, der Einheitlichkeit, dem Ort und der Intention des Geschichtswerkes fragten. Einen Wissensstein nach dem anderen wälzten sie bergwärts, doch allzu oft rollten diese, ehe sie auf der Höhe gesicherter Erkenntnis deponiert waren, wieder talwärts in die Gefilde ungesicherter und umstrittener Vermutungen – wo noch genug andere, schwergewichtige und schwer zu fassende Brocken darauf warten, nach oben geschafft zu werden[2].

I. DIE PROPHETISCHE DIMENSION IN DER DEUTERONOMISTISCHEN GESCHICHTSSCHREIBUNG

1971 hatte Rudolf Smend[3] anhand von Texten des Josua- und Richterbuches Noths »Dtr« aufgeteilt in den exilischen Grundverfasser des Geschichtswerkes und eine jüngere, nomistisch profilierte Bearbeitungs-

---

1. M. NOTH, *Überlieferungsgeschichtliche Studien. Die sammelnden und bearbeitenden Geschichtswerke im Alten Testament*, Darmstadt, Wissenschaftliche Buchgesellschaft, 1943, ³1967.
2. Einen Eindruck von diesem Ringen geben mehrere neuere Berichte über die Deuteronomismusforschung: G.N. KNOPPERS, *Two Nations Under God. The Deuteronomistic History of Solomon and the Dual Monarchies. Vol. 1* (HSM, 52), Atlanta, Scholars Press, 1993, pp. 1-56; H.D. PREUSS, *Zum deuteronomistischen Geschichtswerk*, in *TR* 58 (1993) 229-264; 341-395; H. WEIPPERT, *Das deuteronomistische Geschichtswerk. Sein Ziel und Ende in der neueren Forschung*, in *TR* 50 (1985) 213-249. Noch umfassender orientiert der äusserst verdienstvolle, von S.L. MCKENZIE und M.P. GRAHAM edierte Band, *The History of Israel's Traditions. The Heritage of Martin Noth*, (JSOT SS, 182) Sheffield, Sheffield Academic Press, 1994.
3. R. SMEND, *Das Gesetz und die Völker*. FS G. von Rad, München, Kaiser, 1971, pp. 494-509; wieder abgedruckt in R. SMEND, *Die Mitte des Alten Testaments. Gesammelte Studien 1* (BEvT, 99), München, Kaiser, pp. 124-137.

und Ergänzungsschicht. In meiner 1972 veröffentlichten Dissertation[4] meinte ich speziell in den Königsbüchern neben diesen beiden einen dritten, prophetisch gesinnten Deuteronomisten ausmachen zu können, dem eine Reihe selbstverfasster, auffallend stereotyp formulierter Prophetenreden sowie einige ältere, von ihm aufgenommene Propheten-überlieferungen zuzuweisen waren. Timo Veijola wandte die Theorie einer dreifachen dtr Redaktion auf die Samuelbücher an[5]. Damit war die sog. Göttinger Hypothese von den drei dtr Redaktionen DtrH, DtrP und DtrN kreiert, die vor allem in der deutschsprachigen Exegese beträchtlichen Widerhall und auch bereits Aufnahme in Überblicksartikel[6] und Lehrbücher[7] gefunden hat.

Zu glauben, damit seien drei grosse Steine auf den Berg des Wissens gerollt und dort fest verankert worden, ist eine Täuschung. Andere, vorwiegend amerikanische Exegeten wälzten nämlich von einer anderen Seite her andere Steine auf den gleichen Berg, wo sie mit den Göttinger Steinen kollidieren mussten – eine besonders heimtückische Variante des Sisyphus-Syndroms. Gemäss dem sog. Blockmodell gab es bereits unter Joschija ein dtr Geschichtswerk, das in exilischer Zeit nur noch den neuen, traurigen Umständen angepasst wurde[8].

Wer zwischen den beiden redaktionsgeschichtlichen Modellen einen Kompromiss anstrebt, wird ungefähr so verfahren, wie es G. Braulik in der neuesten »Einleitung in das Alte Testament« getan hat: Er wird DtrH in die joschijanische und DtrN in die exilische Zeit ansetzen und zu zeigen versuchen, dass sich der dazwischen störende »DtrP erübrigen«[9] lässt. R. Smend selber scheint dazu Hand zu bieten, indem er un-

4. *Prophetie und Geschichte. Eine redaktionsgeschichtliche Untersuchung zum deuteronomistischen Geschichtswerk* (FRLANT, 108), Göttingen, Vandenhoeck & Ruprecht, 1972.

5. T. VEIJOLA, *Die ewige Dynastie* (AASF B, 193), Helsinki, Suomalainen Tiedeakatemia, 1975; ID., *Das Königtum in der Beurteilung der deuteronomistischen Historiographie* (AASF B, 198), Helsinki, Suomalainen Tiedeakatemia, 1977.

6. W. ROTH, *Deuteronomistisches Geschichtswerk / Deuteronomistische Schule*, in *TRE* 8 (1981) 543-552.

7. R. SMEND, *Die Entstehung des Alten Testaments* (TW, 1), Stuttgart, Kohlhammer, 1978, [4]1989, §19; O. KAISER, *Einleitung in das Alte Testament*, Gütersloh, Gerd Mohn, [5]1984, §16 (dort p. 176 das Urteil, das Dreischichtenmodell stelle »bei allen noch verbliebenen Unsicherheiten und Lücken in der Analyse einen echten Fortschritt der Erkenntnis« dar).

8. Grundgelegt von F.M. CROSS, *Canaanite Myth and Hebrew Epic*, Cambridge, MA, Harvard University Press, 1973, pp. 274-289, ausgebaut durch R.N. NELSON, *The Double Redaction of the Deuteronomistic History*, (JSOT SS, 18) Sheffield, Sheffield Academic Press, 1981.

9. So G. BRAULIK in: E. ZENGER *et al.*, *Einleitung in das Alte Testament* (ST, Bd. 1,1), Stuttgart, Kohlhammer, 1995, p. 130; [3]1998, p. 187. Schon die Monographie von M.A. O'BRIEN, *The Deuteronomistic History Hypothesis. A Reassessment* (OBO, 92), Freiburg, Universitätsverlag; Göttingen, Vandenhoeck & Ruprecht, 1989, läuft auf einen ähnlichen Kompromiss hinaus.

terschiedliche Sicherheitsgrade in der Göttinger Hypothesenbildung andeutet: »Als eigene lit[erarische] Grössen sind DtrH und DtrN mit Sicherheit, DtrP, bei dem die Textbasis am schmalsten ist, mit hinlänglicher Wahrscheinlichkeit greifbar«[10].

Nun soll es im Folgenden keineswegs darum gehen, eine einmal aufgestellte These mit allen Mitteln zu verteidigen. Es ist, wie gesagt, schon mancher deuteronomistische Stein wieder zu Tale gerollt. Immerhin aber hat es doch diverse Versuche gegeben, die DtrP zuzuschreibende Textbasis zu sichern und auszuweiten. Veijola[11] schrieb ihr u.a. die Abschnitte 1.Sam 3,11-14; 28,17-19aα; 2 Sam 7,22-24; 22,22-25 zu, Foresti[12] die Grundschicht von 1 Sam 15, Werner[13] Passagen in 2 Sam 11 und 16, Würthwein[14] – freilich von DtrP-»Kreisen« redend – die Einfügung des Kranzes von Elija-Erzählungen 1 Kön 17–19 sowie die Einführung Elischas in die Jehugeschichte, 2 Kön 9,1-10.

Besonders beachtenswert indes und methodisch bestechend ist m. E. die redaktionskritische Analyse von Ludger Camp zu den Jesajalegenden[15]. Er schreibt dem dtr Grundwerk (DtrH) als Bericht über Hiskija lediglich die knappen, annalistischen und von ihm mit religiösen Bewertungen versehenen Notizen 2 Kön 18,1-4.7b.8.13b-16 sowie 20,21 zu. Erst eine dtr-prophetische Redaktion (DtrP) habe die ältere der beiden Sanherib-Jesaja-Legenden eingebaut (*18,17–19,9a)[16] und daran die i.w. selbstformulierte Erzählung über einen Zusammenstoss zwischen Jesaja und Hiskija angehängt (20,12-17)[17]. Durch diese Erweiterung wird die ursprüngliche dtr Geschichtserzählung tiefgreifend verändert: Ein Prophet übernimmt die Führungsrolle in der Politik, wogegen der – doch eben noch als Kultreformer gelobte (18,4) – König eine eher klägliche Rolle spielt. Um ein Haar hätte Jerusalem schon 701 das Schicksal des soeben untergegangenen Samaria erlitten. Dass die Haupt-

10. R. SMEND, *Die Entstehung des Alten Testaments* (n. 7), p. 123.

11. T. VEIJOLA, *Die ewige Dynastie* (n. 4).

12. F. FORESTI, *The Rejection of Saul in the Perspective of the Deuteronomistic School. A Study of 1 Sm 15 and Related Texts* (Studia theologica, 5), Roma, Ed. del Teresianum, 1984.

13. W. WERNER, *Studien zur alttestamentlichen Vorstellung vom Plan Jahwes* (BZAW, 173), Berlin - New York, NY, de Gruyter, 1988.

14. E. WÜRTHWEIN, *Das erste Buch der Könige, Kap. 1-16* (ATD, 11/1) Göttingen, Vandenhoeck & Ruprecht, ²1985; *Die Bücher der Könige. 1. Kön 17–2. Kön 25* (ATD, 11/2), Göttingen, Vandenhoeck & Ruprecht, 1984.

15. L. CAMP, *Hiskija und Hiskijabild. Analyse und Interpretation von 2. Kön 18–20* (MtA, 9), Altenberge, Telos Verlag, 1990.

16. Dazu habe DtrP selber v.a. 18,20b-22.25.29f; 19,3f beigesteuert.

17. Dazu habe er sich der knappen Vorlage 20,12a.13 bedient. – Später dann habe DtrN die kurz zuvor entstandene zweiteVersion der Sanherib-Jesaja-Legende (19,*9b-20; 20,32f.35.36aβ) sowie die Passagen 18,5-7a.9-12.22; 19,34; *20,1-7 hinzugefügt, während 18,5bβ; 18,*13 (das Datum).33-35; 19,11-13.21-31 nach-dtr seien.

stadt Judas Sanherib nicht in die Hände gefallen ist, verdankt sich nicht dem Kalkül bzw. der Unterwürfigkeit der Politiker und Militärs, sondern dem Einsatz Jesajas und dem Eingreifen Jhwhs. Mit der Schlusserzählung indes, in der die Babylonier auftauchen und Hiskija eine leichtfertig-protzige Haltung zeigt, rückt deutlich genug bereits die Katastrophe von 587 in den Blick.

Dieser Grundstock der Jesajalegenden fügt sich, sowohl im engeren wie im weiteren historischen Kontext, ausgezeichnet zu den Grundanliegen der prophetisch-dtr Redaktion, wie sie auch anderswo im Geschichtswerk in Erscheinung treten: Die Geschichte wird in erster Linie durch das prophetische Wort und Wirken – im tiefsten natürlich: durch Gott selber – gelenkt. Die Propheten decken vollmächtig das jeweilige Gottesverhältnis Israels bzw. Judas auf und benennen dessen innerweltliche Folgen: Verlässt sich das Gottesvolk auf Jhwh (wie in der assyrischen Krise dank Jesaja), wird es gerettet; verlässt es sich auf die vermeintlich stärkeren Bataillone (wie in der babylonischen Krise), ist es verloren. Sehr sorgfältig wird das Ende der assyrischen Belagerung und des assyrischen Königs in genauer Entsprechung zu der Heilsweissagung Jesajas (vgl. 2 Kön 19,36f mit 19,7), und wird die abschliessende Unheilsweissagung Jesajas deutlich mit Blick auf die Vorgänge bei der ersten Eroberung Jerusalems formuliert (vgl. 20,17f mit 24,13-15). Leicht hätten in beiden Fällen Erfüllungsvermerke der bekannten Art eingesetzt werden können: »… (und das geschah) gemäss dem Wort, das Jhwh durch den Propheten Jesaja geredet hatte«; die Redaktion hat darauf im Vertrauen auf die Aufmerksamkeit der Leserschaft verzichtet[18].

Wichtiger jedoch als redaktionskritische Schichtungshypothesen ist die grundlegende Tatsache, dass die Dimension des Prophetischen in die dtr Geschichtsschreibung Eingang gefunden hat. Die Bedeutung dieses Vorgangs kann kaum hoch genug veranschlagt werden[19]. Da wird fast jede wichtige Geschichtszäsur in dtr-prophetischem Stil angekündigt und dadurch als Auswirkung göttlicher Geschichtslenkung gedeutet, da

---

18. Analog unterliess es DtrP auch, die zweite Eroberung und Zerstörung Jerusalems als Erfüllung der (gut dtr!) Weissagungen der »Knechte Jhwhs, der Propheten« und namentlich der Prophetin Hulda (2 Kön 21,10-15; 22,16f) zu deklarieren.

19. Gar zu prätentiös ist m.E. die These von E. BEN ZVI (*The Account of the Reign of Manasseh in II Reg 21,1-18 and the Redactional History of the Book of Kings*, in ZAW 103 [1991] 355-374), das in Dtn 18,21f grundgelegte und in den Königsbüchern immer wieder durchgeführte Schema Weissagung-Erfüllung diene nicht der Erhöhung, sondern gerade der Bestreitung prophetischer Autorität, indem deren Beglaubigung in die Zukunft verlegt und damit der Leserschaft zu ihrer Zeit verweigert werde. Man kann genauso umgekehrt argumentieren: Die Bewahrheitung des Prophetenwortes in der Vergangenheit demonstriert dessen Bedeutsamkeit auch in der Gegenwart.

wird die deuteronomisch-deuteronomistische und die prophetische Denk-
und Sprachwelt zusammengeführt, da wird ein ums andere Mal in pro-
phetischem Geist eine dezidiert staats- und königs-, sogar davidkritische
Position[20] markiert.

Nur wer das prophetische Element in der dtr Geschichtsschreibung
verkennt, kann die dtr Bewegung aufspalten in eine kritisch-prophetische
Linie einerseits, wie sie sich angeblich in der Redaktion des Jeremiabuches zu Wort meldet, und eine »national-religiös eingestellte« andererseits, die auch nach 587 noch unverdrossen an der Zions- und Davids-
ideologie festgehalten habe und die im dtr Geschichtswerk die Feder
führe. Diese Klassifizierung durch Albertz[21] hat eine längere Vorgeschichte: etwa in der Behauptung Crüsemanns, in 2 Kön 14,27 werde
deuteronomistische »Kritik an Amos« geübt[22]; ferner in der Vermutung
Kochs, das »Profetenschweigen des deuteronomistischen Geschichtswerks« rühre daher, dass in dessen Theologie die Unbedingtheit der prophetischen Gerichtsankündigung nicht passe[23]. Hinzu kommt die immer
wieder gemachte Beobachtung, dass zwar Jesaja im Geschichtswerk auf-
tritt, dass er hier aber weitgehend[24] die Züge eines Heilspropheten trägt
– ein Bild, das seit der grossen Arbeit Hardmeiers im Verdacht steht,
just von national-religiösen Kreisen in der Zidkija-Zeit als chauvinisti-
sches Gegenbild zu Jeremia entworfen worden zu sein[25].

Gegen die Einteilung in gute und in schlechte Deuteronomisten, in pro-
phetisch-selbstkritische und in historisch-chauvinistische, spricht vielerlei.

Setzt man mit Noth die dtr Geschichtsschreibung in der Exilszeit und
später (nicht aber schon in der Joschijazeit!) an, dann bietet sie eine

---

20. Vgl. 2 Sam 12,7-10, einen klar dtr erweiterten Passus (s. DIETRICH, *Prophetie und
Geschichte* [n. 4], pp. 127-131), sowie die durch dtr Hand verursachte Wendung Natans
gegen Davids Tempelbauplan 2 Sam 7,1ff (vgl. W. DIETRICH, *David, Saul und die Propheten* [BWANT, 122], Stuttgart, Kohlhammer, ²1992, pp. 132-136).

21. R. ALBERTZ, *Religionsgeschichte Israels in alttestamentlicher Zeit* (GAT, 8/2),
Göttingen, Vandenhoeck & Ruprecht, 1992, pp. 387ff, bes. 399. Vgl. auch die noch
plakativere Darstellung in ID., *Die Intentionen und die Träger des Deuteronomistischen
Geschichtswerks*, in R. ALBERTZ, F.W. GOLKA, J. KEGLER (eds.), *Schöpfung und Befreiung. FS C. Westermann*, Stuttgart, Calwer, 1989, pp. 37-53; sowie ID., *Wer waren die
Deuteronomisten? Das historische Rätsel einer literarischen Hypothese*, in EvT 57
(1997) 319-333.

22. F. CRÜSEMANN, *Kritik an Amos im deuteronomistischen Geschichtswerk*, in H.W.
WOLFF (ed.), *Probleme biblischer Theologie. FS G. von Rad*, München, Kaiser, 1971,
pp. 57-63.

23. K. KOCH, *Das Profetenschweigen des deuteronomistischen Geschichtswerks*, in L.
PERLITT (ed.), *Die Botschaft und die Boten. FS H.W. Wolff*, Neukirchen-Vluyn,
Neukirchener Verlag, 1981, pp. 115-128, bes. 127f.

24. Allerdings nicht vollkommen: In 2 Kön 20 blitzt plötzlich Unheilsprophetie auf!

25. C. HARDMEIER, *Prophetie im Streit vor dem Untergang Judas. Erzählkommunikative Studien zur Entstehungssituation der Jesaja- und Jeremiaerzählungen in II Reg 18-*

Ätiologie, sogar eine Doxologie für das Ende der Staatlichkeit und des Königtums. Wer dies tut, ist aber schwerlich des Chauvinismus verdächtig. Dass die Deuteronomisten in einer düsteren Gegenwart nicht nur nach Schatten, sondern auch nach Licht in der Vergangenheit Ausschau halten, ist nicht nur begreiflich, sondern überlebensnotwendig. Eine gewisse Hochschätzung zumal des davidischen Königtums ist von daher nur zu erwarten. Gerade die prophetisch-deuteronomistische Redaktion indes ist äusserst kritisch gegen das Missverständnis von Staat und Königtum als Heilsgütern. Ihr Hauptanliegen ist es gerade, über die Königshäuser und den Staat Unheil ansagen zu werden zu lassen – fast noch unerbittlicher, als die sog. Unheilspropheten dies getan haben.

Es muss nicht mehr betont werden, dass es reine Unheilspropheten unter den sog. Schriftpropheten wohl nicht gibt. Alle hofften sie, in unterschiedlichen Graden und Formen, trotz andringenden Unheils auf Heil für ihr Volk. *Wenn* 2 Kön 14,27 dtr ist und auf Amos anspielt – was nicht ausgeschlossen ist –, dann handelt es sich nicht um abwehrende Kritik, sondern um eine ernsthafte und durchaus vertretbare Interpretation der Amosbotschaft: »Jhwh hatte nicht angekündigt, den Namen [nach einem Teil der griechischen Texttradition: den Samen] Israels auszutilgen unter dem Himmel«; in der Tat hat Amos kaum das Ende des *Volkes*, sondern des *Staates* Israel und seiner Führungselite erwartet[26]; und er oder einer seiner Schüler hat den Umkehrwilligen in Israel das berühmte »Vielleicht« zugerufen (Am 5,15). Was Jesaja anlangt, hat dieser Prophet den an ihn ergangenen, äusserst erschreckenden Verstockungsauftrag – das Wort sei gewagt – *verraten*, indem er ihn nämlich seinen Mitbürgern mitgeteilt und ihnen dadurch die Möglichkeit der Umkehr und Rettung eröffnet hat (Jes 6,9f)[27]. Wohl hat er über

20 *und Jer 37-40* (BZAW, 187), Berlin, de Gruyter, 1990.
    26. Diesem Nachweis gilt das ganze Bemühen von H. REIMER, *Richtet auf das Recht. Studien zur Botschaft des Amos* (SBS, 149), Stuttgart, Katholisches Bibelwerk, 1992; das Ergebnis ist insgesamt überzeugend, pièce de résistance aber ist Am 8,1f. Zum Strophengedicht Am 1f und speziell zu der den *Staat* bedrohenden Israelstrophe 2,6-16 vgl. W. DIETRICH, *JHWH, Israel und die Völker beim Propheten Amos*, in TZ 48 (1992) 315-328. Zum Problem im ganzen siehe O. KEEL, *Rechttun oder Annahme des drohenden Gerichts?* in BZ (NF) 21 (1977) 200-218, sowie E. ZENGER, *Die eigentliche Botschaft des Amos*, in FS J.B. Metz, Mainz, Matthias Grünewald Verlag 1988, pp. 394-406.
    27. Vgl. A. SCHENKER, *Gerichtsverkündigung und Verblendung bei den vorexilischen Propheten* [1986=]: ID., *Text und Sinn im Alten Testament. Textgeschichtliche und bibeltheologische Studien* (OBO, 103), Freiburg, Universitätsverlag; Göttingen, Vandenhoeck & Ruprecht, 1991, pp. 217-234. Nach U. BECKER (*Jesaja - von der Botschaft zum Buch* [FRLANT, 178] Göttingen, Vandenhoeck & Ruprecht, 1997, pp. 61 ff.) birgt der Verstockungsauftrag zwar reines Unheil, stammt aber aus nachexilischer Zeit, während der 'echte' Jesaja reiner Heilsprophet war! Eine konventionellere Sicht bietet J. BARTHEL, *Prophetenwort und Geschichte. Die Jesajaüberlieferung in Jes 6-8 und 28-31* (FAT, 19), Tübingen, Mohr Siebeck, 1997.

Jerusalem schweres Gericht angesagt, doch mit der Aussicht auf endliche Läuterung der verderbten Stadt und auf ihre Restituierung als »Stadt der Gerechtigkeit und feste Burg« (Jes 1,26). In der syrisch-efraimitischen und später in der assyrischen Krise hat er zwar am Ende jeweils das Schlimmste befürchtet, sich anfangs aber immer wieder für den Willen Jhwhs verbürgt, sein Volk vor den Feinden zu schützen (z.B. Jes 7,1-9; 10,5-15)[28]. So ist der Jesaja der Legenden nicht einfach ein Anti-Jesaja. Er ist auch kein Anti-Jeremia. Wenn Jeremia immer wieder zur Unterwerfung unter Babylon geraten hat, dann nicht in der Absicht, sein Volk der Vernichtung preiszugeben, sondern es im Gegenteil vor ihr zu bewahren. Auch er erhoffte Heil, freilich erst für eine Zeit nach dem nicht mehr abwendbaren Unheil; deshalb lag ihm am äusseren und inneren Überleben der ersten Gola (Jer 29), deshalb wollte er mitten im Krieg einen Acker kaufen (Jer 32), deshalb schloss er sich nach dem Sieg Babylons der Gruppe um Gedalja an, die sich um die Konsolidierung einer jüdischen Gemeinschaft unter babylonischer Herrschaft bemühte (Jer 39f). Nach wohlbegründeter Vermutung wirkten übrigens die dtr Geschichtsschreiber, zumindest anfangs, in Mizpa[29] – eben dem Residenzort Gedaljas. Ist es dann ein Zufall, dass die dtr-prophetische Textschicht im Geschichtswerk am nachhaltigsten von Jeremia beeinflusst ist?[30] Dass Jeremia, Amos, Micha im Geschichtswerk nicht persönlich in Erscheinung treten, mag einerseits daran liegen, dass die Redaktion überzeugt war, in ihrem Geist zu wirken, andererseits daran, dass sie andere dtr Gruppen mit der Bearbeitung der prophetischen Literatur beschäftigt wusste (oder gar sah)[31]. Jesaja wiederum gelangte, in der Darstellungsform, in der er den Deuteronomisten greifbar war, wohl deshalb ins Geschichtswerk, weil die authentische Jesajaüberlieferung ihnen gerade *nicht* greifbar war[32], sondern ihren Weg über die babylonische Gola nahm, wie ihre Neuinterpretation in den Kreisen um Deuterojesaja zeigt.

28. Vgl. W. DIETRICH, *Jesaja und die Politik* (BEvT, 74), München, Kaiser, 1976.
29. So schon Noth (n. 1), mit breiter Begründung T. VEIJOLA (*Verheissung in der Krise. Studien zur Literatur und Theologie der Exilszeit anhand des 89. Psalms* [AASF B, 220], Helsinki, Suomalainen Tiedeakatemia, 1982, pp. 176-210) mit Blick auf DtrH (und DtrP?), während er DtrN im nahegelegenen Betel zu situieren versucht.
30. W. DIETRICH (n. 4), pp. 70-81.
31. Die in der Exegese längst geäusserte Vermutung (vgl. J. WELLHAUSEN, *Die Composition des Hexateuchs und der historischen Bücher des Alten Testaments* [1885, ³1899 =] Berlin, de Gruyter, ⁴1963, pp. 277f.), hinter dem in Nordisrael, speziell in Betel wirkenden jüdischen Propheten von 1 Kön 13 verberge sich ein popularisierter Amos, könnte durchaus DtrP dazu veranlasst haben, das Kapitel ins Geschichtswerk einzubauen.
32. Mit L. PERLITT (*Jesaja und die Deuteronomisten*, in V. FRITZ, K.-F. POHLMANN, H.-C. SCHMITT (eds.), *Prophet und Prophetenbuch. FS O. Kaiser* [BZAW, 185], Berlin, de Gruyter, 1989, pp. 133-149) kann ich das Jes-Buch nicht als dtr bearbeitet ansehen.

In 2 Kön 21,10-15 redet die prophetisch-dtr Redaktion von den
»Knechten Jhwhs, den Propheten«, die zur Zeit Manasses den damals
grassierenden Synkretismus angegriffen und Jerusalem und Juda Unheil
angedroht hätten. Es scheint, als werde hier die Botschaft mehrerer
Schriftpropheten und prophetischer Tradentenkreise zusammengefasst.
Zur Zeit des Manasse bzw. des jungen Joschija haben sich die Propheten
Nahum, Habakuk und Zefanja gegen die politische und religiöse Unterwürfigkeit der herrschenden Clique in Jerusalem gegenüber der assyrischen Vormacht und auch gegen diese selber gewandt, indem sie das
Eingreifen Jhwhs bzw. der von Jhwh herbeigerufenen Babylonier gegen
die Assyrer und ihre judäischen Lakaien ankündigten[33]. Ferner wurde,
nach plausibler Hypothese[34], in der ausgehenden Assyrerzeit die Jesajaüberlieferung durch eine antiassyrisch ausgerichtete Redaktion bearbeitet, dabei erheblich erweitert und zu einem neuen Ganzen geformt. Zu
jener Zeit könnte auch, wie ich zu erwägen gegeben habe[35], in prophetischen Oppositionskreisen ein »Buch der Prophetengeschichten« entstanden sein, in dem paradigmatische Erzählungen über das – durchwegs kritische – Verhältnis zwischen Propheten und Königen zusam-
mengestellt waren; von ihnen hätte die dtr Redaktion (genauer: DtrP)
einige aufgenommen und an passender Stelle ins Geschichtswerk eingefügt.

Die Kriterien, nach denen die Redaktion prophetische Überlieferung
teils übernommen, teils nicht übernommen hat, scheinen weniger inhalt-
lich-theologischer als formal-pragmatischer Art gewesen zu sein. Offenbar hat die Redaktion nur prophetische *Prosatexte* aufgenommen, und
zwar mit Vorrang solche, die vom Verhältnis der Propheten zu den Königen, also zur Staatsmacht, handeln und die nicht schon – wie etwa Erzählungen über Amos (Am 7), oder Jeremia (die sog. Leidensgeschich-
te) – Eingang in Prophetenbücher gefunden hatten. Immerhin aber hat
sie auf diese Weise eine ganz eigene Dimension des israelitischen
Prophetismus der Nachwelt überliefert und, angelehnt daran, eine ganz

---

33. Vgl. W. DIETRICH, *Der Eine Gott als Symbol politischen Widerstands. Religion
und Politik im Juda des 7. Jahrhunderts*, in W. DIETRICH – M.A. KLOPFENSTEIN (eds.),
Ein Gott allein? JHWH-Verehrung und biblischer Monotheismus (OBO, 139), Freiburg
(Schweiz), Universitätsverlag; Göttingen, Vandenhoeck & Ruprecht, 1994, pp. 463-490;
ID., *Habakuk – ein Jesajaschüler*, in H.M. NIEMANN (ed.), *Nachdenken über Israel, Bibel
und Theologie*. FS K.-D. Schunck, (BEAT, 37), Frankfurt /M., Lang, 1994, pp. 197-215;
ID., *Die Kontexte des Zefanjabuches*, in W. DIETRICH – M. SCHWANTES (eds.), *Der Tag
wird kommen. Ein interkontextuelles Gespräch über das Buch des Propheten Zefanja*
(SBS, 170), Stuttgart, Katholisches Bibelwerk, 1996, pp. 19-37.
34. H. BARTH, *Die Jesaja-Worte in der Josiazeit. Israel und Assur als Thema einer
produktiven Neuinterpretation der Jesajaüberlieferung* (WMANT, 48), Neukirchen-
Vluyn, Neukirchener Verlag, 1977.
35. W. DIETRICH, *David, Saul und die Propheten* (n. 20).

eigene Linie in die israelitische Historiographie eingetragen: die des göttlichen Wortes, das Geschichte macht.

II. Ein prophetisches Erzählwerk
aus vordeuteronomistischer Zeit

Die beiden Dimensionen Prophetie und Geschichte sind auf der dtr Textebene nicht das erste Mal zusammengetroffen. Vielmehr hat die dtr Redaktion auf weite Strecken nur nachvollzogen bzw. ihrer exilisch-nachexilischen Leserschaft weitergegeben, was schon vorexilische Geschichtsschreibung über Propheten zu berichten gewusst hatte.

Es ist verschiedentlich behauptet worden, prophetische Kreise hätten lange vor der dtr Ära erste grössere Geschichtsdarstellungen über die israelitische Königszeit hervorgebracht. Mildenberger[36] postulierte eine »nebiistische« Bearbeitung, welche einen älteren Grundstock von David-Saul-Überlieferungen zur Aufstiegsgeschichte Davids in 1 Sam 13 – 2 Sam 7 ausgebaut habe. McCarter[37] bezeichnet eine Bearbeitung der Thronfolgegeschichte als »prophetic«[38]. McKenzie[39] rechnet mit einer prophetischen Geschichtsschreibung, welche im 8. Jahrhundert entstanden und dann viel später in die Königsbücher integriert worden sei. Campbell[40] postuliert ein grosses prophetisches Geschichtswerk vom Ende des 9. Jahrhunderts, welches die gesamte Textmasse von 1 Sam 1 bis 2 Kön 10 umfasst habe.

Nun gibt es in den Samuelbüchern mancherlei Erzählungen, die von Propheten und speziell von prophetischer Einflussnahme auf die Könige und die Politik berichten; man denke nur an die drei grossen Auftritte des Natan: zur Übermittlung der Dynastieverheissung (2 Sam 7), zum Bussruf an David nach dem Batscheba-Urija-Skandal (2 Sam 12) und zur Inaugurierung des Machtwechsels von David auf Salomo (1 Kön 1). Dennoch weist m.E. der grosse Abschnitt 1 Sam 1 – 1 Kön 11 nicht genügend Indizien für die Annahme einer vordeuteronomistisch-propheti-

---

36. F. Mildenberger, *Die vordeuteronomistische Saul-Davidüberlieferung*, Diss. ev. theol., Tübingen, 1962.

37. P.K. McCarter, *II Samuel* (AB, 9), Garden City, NY, Doubleday, 1984, pp. 13f.

38. Zu diesem und ähnlichen Versuchen vgl. W. Dietrich – T. Naumann, *Die Samuelbücher* (EdF, 287), Darmstadt, Wissenschaftliche Buchgesellschaft, 1995, pp. 69-72; 199-206.

39. S.L. McKenzie, *The Prophetic History and the Redaction of Kings*, in *HAR* 9 (1985) 203-220.

40. A.F. Campbell, *Of Prophets and Kings. A Late Ninth-Century Document (1Samuel 1 – 2 Kings 10)* (CBQ MS, 17), Washington, DC, Catholic Biblical Association of America, 1986.

schen Gesamtredaktion auf (wohl aber einer vordeuteronomistisch-höfischen, doch ist dies hier nicht das Thema[41]). Der Abschnitt 1 Kön 17 – 2 Kön 10 hingegen ist durch umfangreiche, zusammenhängende und kaum dtr gefärbte prophetische Überlieferungen geprägt. Dieser Umstand rechtfertigt die – nachfolgend zu begründende – Hypothese, es sei in diesem Textbereich ein grosses, vor-dtr prophetisches Erzählwerk erhalten.

Obwohl das postulierte Werk sichtlich aus verschiedenen, ursprünglich selbständigen Zyklen und Novellen zusammengesetzt ist, weist es in sich eine bemerkenswerte Kohärenz auf. In dem ersten uns erhaltenen Satz[42] kündigt der Prophet Elija dem König Ahab das Kommen einer Dürrezeit an (1 Kön 17,1). Damit wird einerseits ein Erzählbogen eröffnet, der (vorerst) bis 1 Kön 18,41ff reicht, wo vom Wiederkommen des Regen erzählt wird, andererseits eine Grundthematik, die sich bis zum Ende des Erzählwerkes durchhält: der Kampf zwischen Jhwh und Baal um die Zuständigkeit für Naturphänomene wie Regen und Fruchtbarkeit – und darin um die Seele Israels. Der Jhwh-Prophet Elija erweist sich während der Trockenzeit als gottbehütet und wunderkräftig (1 Kön 17), der zu Baal neigende König Ahab als rat- und hilflos (1 Kön 18,1-18). Im Götterwettstreit auf dem Karmel (1 Kön 18,19-40) demonstrieren Jhwh und Elija ihre souveräne Überlegenheit über Baal und dessen Propheten; danach kann es wieder regnen. Der eben glanzvoll bestätigte Jhwh-Verehrer Elija muss dann freilich vor der Wut der Baal-Verehrerin Isebel zum Horeb (= Sinai) fliehen, erfährt dort aber die Nähe Jhwhs und wird ermutigt zum weiteren Kampf gegen Baal, der noch lange andauern werde. In Elischa soll er einen Nachfolger finden, und auch (aussen-)politisch kommt in Gestalt der Usurpatoren Hasaël in Damaskus und Jehu in Israel ein Wechsel in Sicht (1 Kön 19). Damit ist wiederum ein Bogen eröffnet, der bis 2 Kön 8–10 reicht.

Die Elija- und die Elischageschichten werden durch mannigfache weitere Klammern zusammengebunden. Beide Propheten bezeichnen sich als »vor Jhwh stehend« (1 Kön 17,1; 18,15; 2 Kön 3,14; 5,16), beide tragen die Ehrentitel »Streitwagenkorps Israels und seine Gespan-

41. Vgl. dazu W. DIETRICH, *Die frühe Königszeit in Israel. 10. Jahrhundert v.Chr.* (Biblische Enzyklopädie, Bd. 3), Suttgart, Kohlhammer, 1997, pp. 259-273.

42. Der ursprüngliche Anfang des Werkes scheint nicht mehr erhalten, sondern zugunsten der von DtrH formulierten (und vielleicht von DtrP vervollständigten?) Vorstellung des Königs Ahab weggefallen zu sein (1 Kön 16,29-34). Informationen wie die in 16,31f gegebenen, wonach Ahab eine sidonische Prinzessin namens Isebel geheiratet und in Samaria einen Baalstempel errichtet habe, werden im Fortgang der Erzählung vorausgesetzt.

ne« (2 Kön 2,12; 13,14) sowie »Mann Gottes« (1 Kön 17,18.24; 2 Kön 1,9ff; 4,7.21f; 5,8 u.ö.), beide sind zu Wundertaten – beide sogar zu der gleichen: der Erweckung eines toten Knaben – fähig (1 Kön 17; 2 Kön 4–6), beide haben mit Dürre und Hungersnot zu tun (1 Kön 17; 2 Kön 8,1), beide kümmern sich um die sozialen Belange von in Not geratenen oder ungerecht behandelten Menschen (1 Kön 17,10-16; 21; 2 Kön 4,1-7; 8,1-6); vor allem aber: beide führen als Propheten Jhwhs den Streit gegen Baal in Israel an (1 Kön 18; 2 Kön 1; 9f).

Die Propheten unseres Erzählwerkes pflegen zu den Königen ein ambivalentes Verhältnis. Mit den Nordreichskönigen – auch den Omriden! – können sie kooperieren (1 Kön 18,41ff; 20,1-34; 2 Kön 3; 6–8; 13,14-19), häufiger aber liegen sie mit ihnen – speziell den Omriden! – im Streit (1 Kön 17,1; 20,35ff; 21; 22; 2 Kön 1; 9). Ein völlig ungebrochenes Verhältnis zu den Omriden haben nur falsche Propheten (1 Kön 18; 22). Die wahren Propheten bringen zwar dem Davididen Joschafat Respekt entgegen (1 Kön 22; 2 Kön 3), sehen aber anscheinend ohne Bedauern dessen Sohn und Nachfolger Ahasja mit einem Grossteil seiner männlichen Verwandtschaft dem Putsch Jehus zum Opfer fallen (2 Kön 9,27-29; 10,12-14). Anscheinend identifizieren sie ihn und das Davidshaus jener Zeit mit dem omridischen Königsgeschlecht.

Durchgehendes Thema des Erzählwerkes ist der Kampf zwischen Jhwh und Baal. Jhwh verlangt von Israel als einziger Gott anerkannt und verehrt zu werden. Mag es andere Götter geben – bei den Aramäern, Philistern, Moabitern –: sie können sich mit Jhwh nicht messen. Noch am gefährlichsten ist Baal, weil er sich in Israel (und Juda) breitmacht, wo doch auf Israel (und Juda) Jhwh allein Anspruch hat! Nicht ein förmlicher Monotheismus wird hier vertreten, wohl aber in geradezu militanter Weise die Jhwh-Monolatrie propagiert. Sehr gezielt steht am Ende – und wurde womöglich erst auf der Stufe der Gesamtredaktion hier angefügt – die Nachricht, man habe nach Jehus Massaker unter den Baalsverehrern auch deren Kultstätte verwüstet und zu Aborten gemacht »bis heute«; und damit habe man »den Baal ausgerottet aus Israel« (2 Kön 10,27f). Kaum verhohlen signalisiert der Erzähler seine Zustimmung.

Mit dieser Einstellung führt das Erzählwerk nahe an die Schwelle, die durch das *Sch^ema-Jisrael* in Dtn 6,4 markiert ist. Deuteronomisch oder gar deuteronomistisch ist es indes (noch) nicht, weil es nicht auf die Tora und den Jerusalemer Tempel zentriert ist. Dass die Prophetie als Vorreiter im Kampf gegen den Baalismus geschildert wird, spiegelt mindestens ebensosehr die Gegebenheiten in Juda wie in Nordisrael –

freilich erst im 7. Jahrhundert. Damals wurde die Prophetie tatsächlich
zu einem der wichtigsten Träger des Widerstandes gegen die politische
und religiöse Selbstauslieferung an die assyrische Fremdherrschaft. Namen wie Nahum, Habakuk, Zefanja sind hier zu nennen[43]. Die prophetischen Kreise sahen sich nach Ausweis unseres Erzählwerkes in der
Nachfolge der alten, nordisraelitischen Prophetie und ihres Kampfes gegen Baal.

Zu der Ansetzung des Erzählwerkes ins 7. Jahrhundert führen nicht
nur religions-, sondern auch literargeschichtliche Gründe. Die mehrfa-
che Erweiterung, Bearbeitung und schliessliche Verschmelzung etwa
des Elija- und des Elischa-Zyklus benötigen eine erhebliche Zeitspanne.
Dass speziell das 'leise' Kapitel 1 Kön 19 auf die Komposition 1 Kön
17f folgt und sanft gegen die tatsächlichen und vorgeblichen Grausam-
keiten Jehus und Elijas protestiert, setzt zumindest die hoseanische Re-
flexion (Hos 1,4f) voraus. Die Aufnahme und Weiterführung nord-
israelitischer Tradition in Juda ist kaum vor 722 v.Chr. zu erwarten. Be-
merkenswert ist auch der Gebrauch der gehäuft erst ab Jeremia und in
der dtr Literatur auftretenden Wortereignisformel (1 Kön 17,2.8; 18,1).

So spricht vieles dafür, dass unser Erzählwerk zwar von Geschehnis-
sen im 9. Jahrhundert berichtet, in Wahrheit aber auf die Situation des 7.
Jahrhunderts zielt. Im Spiegelbild der Omriden wird das Regime des
Mannes sichtbar, den die Bibel als den Ketzerkönig schlechthin zeich-
net: Manasse (696-641 v.Chr.). Ihn noch deutlicher zu porträtieren, gar
beim Namen zu nennen, wäre damals vermutlich nicht opportun gewesen. Doch auch so bot das Erzählwerk seiner Leserschaft deutliche Ori-
entierung in den aktuellen Auseinandersetzungen und bereitete sie auf
den Umschwung unter Joschija vor. Gewiss nicht von ungefähr wird
Manasse in 2 Kön 21,3 vorgeworfen, er habe Baalsdienst betrieben und
die Aschera verehrt, und in 2 Kön 23,4.6f dem Joschija nachgerühmt, er
habe dem Baalsdienst und der Aschera-Verehrung ein Ende gemacht.
Auch oder gerade wenn unter den Chiffren Baal und Aschera das assyrische Götterpaar Aschur und Ischtar verborgen sein sollte[44], wäre die
Aktualisierung der alten, ursprünglich nordisraelitischen Überlieferungen vom Kampf Jhwhs gegen Baal – und Aschera?[45] – im Juda der
Manassezeit wohlbegreiflich.

---

43. Vgl. W. DIETRICH (n. 33).
44. So H. SPIECKERMANN, *Juda unter Assur in der Sargonidenzeit* (FRLANT, 129),
Göttingen, Vandenhoeck & Ruprecht, 1982, pp. 200-221.
45. 1 Kön 14,15; 16,33; 18,19; 2 Kön 13,6 – freilich in jeweils jungem literarischem
Zusammenhang.

III. Der Einbau des prophetischen Erzählwerks
ins deuteronomistische Geschichtswerk

Neuerdings mehren sich die Stimmen, die das starke prophetische Element innerhalb des dtr Geschichtswerkes nicht für primär, sondern für sekundär eingetragen halten. Speziell der Elischa-Zyklus soll ein Zuwachs erst aus nach-dtr Zeit sein[46]. Diese Lösung, für die sich durchaus Gründe geltend machen lassen, ist beides: zu radikal und zu wenig radikal. Die gesamte prophetische Überlieferung zwischen 1 Kön 17 und 2 Kön 10 bildet, wie gezeigt, einen integralen Zusammenhang, und sie ist integral ins dtr Geschichtswerk aufgenommen worden – freilich nicht auf dessen erster, sondern auf einer zweiten Redaktionsstufe.

Das grosse »Prophetische Erzählwerk« in das gerade im Bereich von 1 Kön 16 bis 2 Kön 11 recht knappe Vorgängerwerk von DtrH[47] einzubauen, gleicht dem Versuch, einen Elefanten in einen Handwagen zu verfrachten. DtrP ist dieses Kunststück in staunenswerter Weise gelungen. Dass er den Erzählkranz 1 Kön 17–19 an die Einführungsformel für Ahab anschloss und so in dessen Regierungszeit situierte, lag auf der Hand[48]. Dann aber sprengte er die Prophetenerzählungen 1 Kön 20+22 – die in der Septuaginta noch oder wieder beieinander stehen – auf und setzte die Nabotgeschichte 1 Kön 21 zwischenhinein. Dadurch erreichte er, dass zwei Ahab schwer belastende Erzählungen ans Ende des Abschnittes über diesen König gelangten und dessen gewaltsames Ende begründeten. Freilich: mit diesem Schluss geriet er in Gegensatz zur Schlussformel von DtrH, die ein friedliches Ableben Ahabs voraussetzt (1 Kön 22,40). DtrP entschloss sich, die prophetische und die geschicht-

---

46. So S.L. McKenzie (*The Books of Kings in the Deuteronomistic History*, in Id. – M.P. Graham [n. 2], pp. 281-307, esp. 295) in Anlehnung an H.-J. Stipp (*Elischa – Propheten – Gottesmänner* [ATSAT, 24], St. Ottilien, EOS, 1987) und A. Rofé (*The Prophetical Stories. The Narratives about the Prophets in the Hebrew Bible. Their Literary Types and History*, Jerusalem, Magnes Press, 1988).

47. Vgl. die Wiedergabe des vermutlichen DtrH-Textes zwischen 2 Kön 3 und 10 unten im Anhang. Würthwein hat in seinem Kommentar (ATD, 11/2, 1984; cf. n. 14) anhangsweise »Die deuteronomistische Grundschrift des Königsbuches« in Übersetzung abgedruckt; was den hier zur Debatte stehenden Abschnitt anlangt (pp. 508-510), kann ich dem weitgehend zustimmen. Zum Passus über Ahab (1 Kön 16,29-33) allerdings würde ich fragen, ob die Notiz über die Heirat Isebels (V. 31bα) nicht – wie auch die über die Errichtung eines Baalstempels und -altars in Samaria (V. 32) – der Einfügung des prophetischen Erzählwerkes gedient haben könnte (vgl. Isebels negative Sonderrolle in 1 Kön 18f; 21; 2 Kön 9f sowie die Szene von der Zerstörung des Baalstempels 2 Kön 10,18-27), und ob nicht umgekehrt (und gegen Würthwein) der Vorwurf des Dienstes für Baal und Aschera (1 Kön 16,31bβ.33) schon von DtrH erhoben worden sein muss.

48. Die dtr Bearbeitungsspuren etwa in 1 Kön 18,18.36f; 19,9b-11*aα dürften somit von DtrP stammen.

liche Überlieferung nebeneinander stehen zu lassen und der Leserschaft die Spannung zwischen beiden zuzumuten.

Die Episode von der Orakelanfrage eines – usprünglich nicht beim Namen genannten – verunglückten israelitischen Königs (2 Kön 1) bezog DtrP auf Ahasja, von dem er im Werk des DtrH las, er habe nur zwei Jahre regiert. Das Erzählwerk war an dieser Story besonders deswegen interessiert, weil sich der König an den *Baal* von Ekron wendet und dafür von einem Jhwh-Propheten zur Rechenschaft gezogen wird. DtrP dürfte mindestens ebenso der Schlusssatz der Erzählung beeindruckt haben: »Und er starb gemäss dem Wort [Jhwhs], welches Elija geredet hatte« (2 Kön 1,17)[49]. Die genaue und ausdrücklich konstatierte Entsprechung von Weissagung und Erfüllung war (oder wurde) bestimmend für sein eigenes theologisches Denken.

Die Erzählung von der Entrückung Elijas und dem Einrücken Elischas in seine Position 2 Kön 2 steht zwischen der Schlussformel für Ahasja (2 Kön 1,18) und der Einführungsformel für dessen Nachfolger Joram (2 Kön 3,1-3[50]), also ausserhalb des Königsrahmens. Sie ist deshalb keineswegs ein Nachtrag, sondern von DtrP wohl bewusst transzendent zur Historie positioniert worden: Himmelfahrten passen in kein geschichtliches Schema. Zudem war bei DtrH die Einführungsformel für Joram unmittelbar von der Nachricht über den Abfall der Moabiter gefolgt (2 Kön 3,4f), die DtrP als Auftakt zur Erzählung vom Moabiterfeldzug 2 Kön 3,6ff gut gebrauchen konnte.

Von 2 Kön 3,6 an bis 2 Kön 8,15 bleibt der von DtrH gesetzte Rahmen im Hintergrund stehen, denkt sich also DtrP den Judäer *Joschafat* und den Israeliten *Joram* als regierende Könige; wo diese Namen in den Elischa-Erzählungen fallen – namentlich in 2 Kön 3 – können sie also genauso gut von DtrP eingetragen wie ursprünglich sein. Wenn dann aber in 2 Kön 8,7-15 das Erzählwerk von der Machtübernahme Hasaëls in Damaskus berichtet, ist dies für DtrP das Signal, mit Hilfe der Angaben von DtrH die judäische Königsliste nachzuführen: von Joschafat über (den Judäer!) Joram auf *Ahasja* (2 Kön 8,16-27); denn der Name des Aramäerkönigs Hasaël ist mit dem Putsch des Jehu verknüpft (2 Kön 8,28; 9,14), und bei diesem Putsch kommt neben dem Israeliten *Joram* der Judäer *Ahasja* ums Leben (2 Kön 9,27-29).

---

49. Ohne diesen Satz fehlte der Erzählung der Abschluss, also ist er nicht erst von DtrP formuliert. Allenfalls könnte er das Tetragramm eingefügt haben, so das Elija-Wort ausdrücklich als Jhwh-Wort deklarierend.

50. Die sich mit 2 Kön 3,1 stossende Nachricht von der Inthronisation Jorams in 2 Kön 1,17 fehlt in LXX und mag sekundär sein (so WÜRTHWEIN, in ATD, 267).

Das prophetische Erzählwerk selbst musste solche Rücksichten nicht nehmen. Hier schloss an die Designierung Hasaëls durch Elischa (2 Kön 8,7-15) unmittelbar die Designierung Jehus durch einen Elischaschüler (2 Kön 9,1-5.*6.10b) an[51]. Diese Drei, der Prophet und die beiden Usurpatoren, werden den Kampf gegen Baal führen – genau wie es Elija auf dem Horeb angekündigt worden ist (1 Kön 19,17). Die Rolle, welche der Aramäer dabei spielt, deutet sich in der Mitteilung an, dass die Salbung und Akklamation Jehus im Armeelager zu Ramot-Gilead, d.h. im Grenzgebiet zu Aram, stattgefunden habe (2 Kön 9,11-13). Jehu macht sich danach unverzüglich auf den Weg nach Jesreel, »wo Joram lag« und wohin »Ahasja hinabgestiegen war, um Joram zu besuchen« (2 Kön 9,15b.16). Offenbar ist hier nicht an eine Teilnahme der beiden Könige an den Aramäerkämpfen gedacht, sondern an eine Erkrankung des Israeliten in seiner Residenz und an einen Krankenbesuch des Judäers bei ihm. Der schaurige Fortgang der Dinge ist bekannt.

DtrH bot, gestützt auf die höfischen Annalen und ohne Berücksichtigung des prophetischen Erzählwerks, eine andere Version des Geschehens. An die Eingangsformel und sein religiöses Urteil über Ahasja (2 Kön 8,25-27) schloss er aus dem 'Tagebuch der Könige von Juda' die Notiz an: »Und er (Ahasja) zog mit Joram, dem Sohn Ahabs, in den Kampf mit Hasaël, dem König von Aram, in Ramot-Gilead« (2 Kön 8,28a). Darauf muss eine kurze Nachricht über Ahasjas Tod gefolgt sein, die jetzt durch die farbige Darstellung der Jehu-Novelle ersetzt ist; denn in deren Fortgang findet sich plötzlich der charakteristische Annalen-Satz: »Und seine Diener brachten ihn mit dem Wagen nach Jerusalem und begruben ihn in seiner Grabstätte« (2 Kön 9,28)[52].

Aus dem 'Tagebuch der Könige von Israel' hatte DtrH die Formel: »Und es verschwor sich Jehu ben Jehoschafat ben Nimschi gegen Joram« (2 Kön 9,14a). Solche Formeln waren in den Annalen immer ein wenig näher verumständet; so auch in diesem Fall: »Joram hielt gerade

---

51. Selbst der überaus (literar-) kritische Y. MINOKAMI (*Die Revolution des Jehu* [GTA, 38], Göttingen, Vandenhoeck & Ruprecht, 1989) geht nicht so weit wie E. WÜRTHWEIN (ATD z.St.) die gesamte Prophetenszene in 2 Kön 9,1-10 für dtr zu erklären.

52. Vgl. 2 Kön 23,30 über Joschija nach seinem Tod bei Megiddo: »Und seine Diener brachten ihn mit dem Wagen tot von Megiddo und führten ihn nach Jerusalem und begruben ihn in seiner Grabstätte«. Der in 2 Kön 9,28 noch folgende Passus »bei seinen Vätern in der Davidstadt« fehlt teilweise in der LXX und könnte in Angleichung an Schlussformeln für *friedlich verstorbene* judäische Könige (vgl. z.B. 1 Kön 15,8; 2 Kön 12,11) von DtrP angefügt worden sein; DtrH wäre diese leise Verwechslung der Formeln vermutlich nicht unterlaufen. – Woher die Notiz 2 Kön 9,29 mit ihrem von 2 Kön 8,25 leicht abweichenden Synchronismus stammt (Thronbesteigung Ahasjas im 11. statt im 12. Jahr Jorams), ist unerfindlich.

Wacht in Ramot-Gilead, er und ganz Israel, gegen Hasaël, den König von Aram« (2 Kön 9,14b). Dieser Passus, der jetzt ein wenig störend inmitten der Jehu-Novelle steht, dürfte unmittelbar an die Einführungsformel für Joram und die Nachricht vom damaligen Abfall der Moabiter in 2 Kön 3,1-5 angeschlossen haben; auf jeden Fall ist ihm, wie immer in solchen Fällen, die Notiz gefolgt: »Und Jehu erschlug den Joram und wurde König an seiner Statt«[53] – ein Satz, der wiederum von DtrP zugunsten der grossen Revolutionserzählung weggelassen worden ist. Von der Eingangsformel für Jehu fehlt der Synchronismus mit den Davididen, während die Angabe über die Regierungsdauer (2 Kön 10,36) sowie die religiöse Bewertung durch DtrH (2 Kön 10,28f) erhalten sind[54] – wenn auch einigermassen versprengt, hinter dem Abschluss der Jehu-Novelle.

Die literarhistorischen Beobachtungen sind möglicherweise nicht ohne historische Folgen, hat es doch den Anschein, als habe den Annalen bzw. DtrH zufolge der (doppelte) Königsmord Jehus in *Ramot*, also im Grenzgebiet zu Aram stattgefunden; das vereinbart sich gut mit der neu gefundenen Inschrift aus Dan[55], in der sich Hasaël rühmt, den israelitischen und den judäischen König beiseitegeräumt zu haben: Betrachtete (oder benutzte) er Jehu etwa als sein Werkzeug? Nach der Jehu-Novelle bzw. nach dem Prophetischen Erzählwerk kam es demgegenüber in Ramot lediglich zur Salbung und Akklamation Jehus, während sich die Königsmorde bei *Jesreel* ereigneten: vermutlich, weil mit diesem Ortsnamen die Erinnerung an einen Justizmord verbunden war, für den das omridische Königshaus büssen musste[56]. DtrP hat den geographischen Hiat überbrückt, indem er Joram von den Aramäern vor Ramot verwunden werden und von dort nach Jesreel zurückkehren liess – und das gleich zweimal: mit Blick auf den ihn besuchenden Ahasja vor Beginn der Jehu-Geschichte (2 Kön 8,29)[57], mit Blick auf Joram selbst vor Jehus Aufbruch nach Jesreel (2 Kön 9,15).

Diejenigen Mitteilungen über Ahasja, Joram und Jehu, die DtrH geboten hatte und die über die Angaben des Erzählwerkes hinausgingen, hat DtrP in dieses an geeigneten Stellen eingeschoben. Offenbar wollte er seine beiden Quellen möglichst treu bewahren – so wie er ihnen auch nur möglichst wenig Eigenes hinzufügte. Nur an einer Stelle hat er relativ ausführlich das Wort ergriffen bzw. einer Erzählfigur seine Gedanken in den Mund gelegt: Der Prophetenjünger, der im Auftrag Elischas

53. Vgl. 2 Kön 15,10 und 14 über Schallum und Menahem.
54. 2 Kön 10,30f ist spät-dtr Zufügung, vgl. DIETRICH (n. 4), p. 34.
55. Vgl. W. DIETRICH, *dāwīd, dôd und bytdwd*, in TZ 53 (1997) 17-32.
56. Vgl. 2 Kön 9,25 und, in anderer und ausführlicherer Version, 1 Kön 21.
57. Die Nachricht vom Krankenbesuch in 8,29b hat DtrP aus der Novelle (9,16b) vorweggenommen.

Jehu zu salben und diesen Akt eigentlich nur ganz knapp zu deuten und
dann das Weite zu suchen hatte (2 Kön 9,1-3), hält jetzt eine grosse,
deutlich von DtrP inspirierte Gerichtsrede gegen das »Haus Ahabs« (2
Kön 9,*6b[58].7-10a). Auf diese Weise werden die nachfolgenden, bluti-
gen Ereignisse als gottgewolltes Strafgericht über das durch und durch
baalistisch verseuchte omridische Königtum interpretiert.

In 2 Kön 10,12-14 wird erzählt, Jehu habe auf dem Weg von Jesreel
nach Samaria 42 Männer getroffen, die sich als »die Brüder Ahasjas« zu
erkennen gaben und sagten, sie »gingen in freundschaftlicher Absicht zu
den Söhnen des [israelitischen] Königs und den Söhnen der Königs-
mutter [d.h. Isebels] hinab«; Jehu liess sie, als Freunde und Verwandte
des verhassten omridischen Königshauses, allesamt abschlachten. In 2
Kön 11,1 aber lesen wir: »Als Atalja, die Mutter des Ahasja, sah, dass
ihr Sohn [i.e. Ahasja] tot war, machte sie sich daran, die gesamte königliche Nachkommenschaft auszurotten.« Beide Nachrichten vertragen
sich nicht gut miteinander. Offenbar haben wir zwei Versionen des gleichen Ereignisses vor uns: eines Massenmordes an Mitgliedern des
Davidhauses – einmal vollbracht von Jehu, einmal von Atalja. Die erste
Version ist diejenige der Jehu-Novelle bzw. des Prophetischen Erzählwerkes, die zweite diejenige des 'Tagebuchs der Könige von Israel'
bzw. des DtrH[59]. Wieder hat DtrP getreulich beide Varianten nebeneinander stehen lassen.

Zwischen 2 Kön 11 und 2 Kön 17 hat DtrP das Werk des DtrH nur an
wenigen Stellen aus seiner spezifisch prophetischen Sicht erweitert oder
kommentiert[60], ehe er in 2 Kön *18-20 anhand ihm zugänglichen Materials über Jesaja wieder ausführlicher das Wort ergriff. Davon und von
seinen Kommentaren zu dem Ketzerkönig Manasse und dem Reform-
könig Joschija muss jetzt nicht noch einmal die Rede sein.

Mit diesen Erwägungen ist wieder ein kleines Stück deuteronomistischer
Sisyphus-Arbeit geleistet. Was davon plausibel ist und Bestand haben
kann, wird der Fortgang der Forschung erweisen.

* *

*

---

58. Die formelhaften Appositionen in 2 Kön 9,6b »Gott Israels« (zu Jhwh) und
»Volk Jhwhs« (zu Israel) dürften von DtrP zugefügt sein, vgl. die entsprechend kürzere
Fassung in 9,12.

59. Vgl. die – manchmal vielleicht gar zu artifizielle, im Grundsatz aber überzeugen-
de – Analyse von C. LEVIN, *Der Sturz der Königin Atalja. Ein Kapitel zur Geschichte Judas im 9. Jahrhundert v.Chr.* (SBS, 105), Stuttgart, Katholisches Bibelwerk, 1982.

60. Laut meiner Untersuchung von 1972 (Anm. 4) war das in 2 Kön 14,25 und 2 Kön
17,21-23 der Fall.

Zur Verdeutlichung – speziell für nicht-deutschsprachige Leserinnen und Leser
– sei der Inhalt der vorstehenden Ausführungen noch einmal in einer Thesen-
reihe zusammengefasst und in einer Rekonstruktion des mutmasslichen DtrH-
Textes in 2 Kön 3–10 veranschaulicht. Ich danke Steven L. McKenzie für
sprachliche Unterstützung in diesem Passus.

A. Thesis

I. The prophetic dimension of deuteronomistic history writing

1. The 'Schichtenmodell' and the 'Blockmodell' in dtr scholarship are opposed
   to each other. In the former the DtrP layer appears to be the least certain.
2. Among others the redaction critical analysis of the Isaiah legends by Ludger
   Camp offers a noteworthy support of the hypothesis of a specific DtrP
   redaction.
3. More important than redaction critical theories is the perception of the
   prophetic dimension in dtr history writing.
4. The prophetic element in the dtr history is not fundamentally different from
   that of the prophetic books.
5. Seen from this perspective the division of the dtr movement into a (self-)
   critical branch (Jer) and a chauvinistic branch (Jos-Kgs) is improper.

II. A prophetic narrative work from pre-deuteronomistic times

1. For the material from 1 Sam 1 to 1 Kgs 11 the theory of a pre-dtr prophetic
   redaction is less plausible.
2. The section from 1 Kgs 17 to 2 Kgs 10, on the other hand, preserves a pre-
   dtr prophetic narrative work.
3. Originally independent and individually developed sections have been bound
   together into a comprehensive narrative work .
4. The narrative work deals essentially with the opposition of prophets and
   kings and is especially concerned with the exclusive worship of Yhwh.
5. The narrative work, like other prophetic opposition literature, probably arose
   in the 7th century at the time of Manasseh.

III. The insertion of the prophetic narrative work into the deuteronomistic history

1. On the one hand, the prophetic narrative work was not part of the
   composition of DtrH; on the other hand, it is not a post-dtr addition.
2. DtrP incorporated the narrative work into the framework built by DtrH on
   the basis of the 'books of the days of the Israelite and Judahite kings'.
3. Especially in the section on Jehu, DtrP had to smooth out the differences
   between historical details in the Jehu novela and those given by DtrH.
4. Altogether DtrP played the role of an 'honest broker' (Martin Noth) between
   the prophetic and the historiographic traditions.
5. DtrP combined the dtr idea of exclusive worship of Yhwh with the prophetic
   ideas of opposition to governmental power and absolute reliability of the
   divine word.

B. The Text of DtrH in 2 Kgs 3–10

(Reconstructed passages in cursive letters)

On Judah:

(8,25) In the 12th year of Joram son of Ahab king of Israel **Ahaziah** son of Joram king of Judah became king. (8,26) Ahaziah was 22 years old when he became king and he reigned 8 years in Jerusalem. And the name of his mother was Athaliah, the (grand-) daughter of Omri king of Israel. (8,27) And he walked in the way of the house of Ahab and did what was evil in the eyes of Yhwh as the house of Ahab, because he was a son-in-law to the house of Ahab. (8,28a) And he accompanied Joram son of Ahab in battle against Hazael king of Aram at Ramoth Gilead. *Death notice...* (9,28) And his servants brought him by chariot to Jerusalem and buried him in his tomb. *The rest of the acts of Ahaziah, are they not written in the book of the days of the kings of Judah?* (11,1) But when **Athaliah** mother of Ahaziah saw that her son was dead she arose to annihilate all the royal line...

On Israel:

(3,1) And **Joram** son of Ahab became king of Israel in Samaria in the 18th year of Jehoshaphat king of Judah and he reigned 12 years. (3,2) And he did what was evil in the eyes of Yhwh but not as his father and his mother, rather he removed the Baal stela that his father had made. (3,3) But still he continued in the sins of Jeroboam son of Nebat which he made Israel sin and he did not turn aside from them. (3,4) And Mesha king of Moab was a sheep breeder and had to pay to the king of Israel the wool of 100000 lambs and 100000 rams. (3,5) But when Ahab died the king of Moab rebelled against the king of Israel. (9,14) And Jehu son of Jehoshaphat son of Nimshi conspired against Joram. And Joram was keeping watch in Ramoth Gilead he and all Israel against Hazael king of Aram. *And Jehu slew Joram and became king in his place. The rest of the acts of Joram, are they not written in the book of the days of the kings of Israel? In the x year of y king of Judah* **Jehu** *became king and* (10,36) reigned over Israel 18 years in Samaria. (10,28) Jehu wiped out Baal from Israel. (10,29a) But he did not turn aside from the sins of Jeroboam son of Nebat which he made Israel sin. (10,32) At that time Yhwh began to trim off parts of Israel. Hazael defeated them in the whole boundary of Israel: (10,33) from the Jordan eastward all the land of Gilead, Gad, Reuben, and Manasseh from Aroer by the wadi Arnon, Gilead and Bashan. (10,34) The rest of the acts of Jehu and all that he did and all his heroism are they not written in the book of the days of the kings of Israel? (10,35) And Jehu slept with his fathers and they buried him in Samaria.

Universität Bern   Walter DIETRICH

THE DEUTERONOMIST'S DAVID AND
THE CHRONICLER'S DAVID

COMPETING OR CONTRASTING IDEOLOGIES?

Recently, A.G. Auld has raised anew the question of the relationship between the so-called Deuteronomistic History and the so-called Chronistic History[1]. Specifically, is Chronicles written from an early form of the books of Samuel and Kings, as a midrash or as an expression of a contrasting ideology to the one expressed in the earlier work, or are both based on an earlier source and written perhaps almost contemporaneously, reflecting competing ideologies, both of which came to be accepted eventually? A third option also needs consideration: that Samuel and Kings were based on an earlier source and that Chronicles was written later, as a reaction to the ideology in Samuel and Kings, using Samuel and Kings as sources or possibly these books and, in addition, the earlier source. How can and should we go about choosing among the available options?

Since neither narrative can be dated with any type of precision, chronological order is not a possible criterion upon which to base a choice. There seems to be a general acceptance that Chronicles is written later than Samuel and Kings and that its Hebrew reflects a later stage of development, but this impression is not supportable by clear documentation. There are not enough extrabiblical writing samples currently available to allow the dating of changes in the Hebrew language with confidence. An argument that the two could have been roughly contemporaneous in their composition does not seem impossible, based on our current, limited knowledge[2].

The fact that Chronicles tends to follow the order of events as they appear in Samuel and Kings also cannot be of help in arguing for a dependence on Samuel and Kings. Both Chronicles and Samuel and Kings

---

1. *Kings without Privilege*, Edinburgh, T. & T. Clark, 1994. A. Rainey has also recently reexamined the issue of the Chronicler's sources and seems to conclude that the Deuteronomistic Historian and the Chronicler independently drew from at least one common source, the Book of the Chronicles of the Kings of Judah, which was a composition built up from historical essays by prophets in the kingdom of Judah (*The Chronicler and His Sources – Historical and Geographical*, in M.P. Graham, *et al.* [eds.], *The Chronicler as Historian* [JSOT SS, 238], Sheffield, Academic Press, 1997, pp. 30-72, esp. 30-38).

2. Auld, *Kings*, pp. 9-10, argues the same point, as does P.R. Davies (*In Search of 'Ancient Israel'* [JSOT SS, 148], Sheffield, Academic Press, 1992, pp. 97-101).

could have derived their order of events from a common, underlying source. Even where the order differs, it is uncertain whether one has followed an underlying source and the other has altered the order in the underlying source for ideological purposes, or whether the Chronicler simply rearranged the order of the events in 1 Samuel and 1 Kings for his own purposes.

Before tackling the main issue of trying to establish some sort of criteria for choosing among the three options given above for the relationship between Chronicles and Samuel and Kings, it would be useful to sketch the differences between the two works. This might provide some further insight that can help on the theoretical level. There are five categories of variations that can be examined: 1) differences between the Hebrew and Greek texts of each book, as a way to explore possible later expansions within a given narrative; 2) texts that are found in Samuel and Kings but which are not present in Chronicles; 3) texts that are present in Chronicles but not found in Samuel or Kings; 4) texts that are common to both but which have differences in detail; and 5) differences in the order of events between the two accounts. In the present article, I will begin a small part of the monumental task of contrasting the Chronicler's account of Israel's past with that produced by the Deuteronomistic Historian by focusing on the last four of these categories as they apply to the accounts of the career of David as king over Israel and Judah. The two accounts to be compared and contrasted are 2 Samuel 5-24 on the one hand, and 1 Chronicles 11-24 on the other. Differences between the Hebrew and Greek texts of each book will not be systematically examined at present, even though they are important. This task has been undertaken already in a number of studies. Instead, a consideration of variant readings will be limited to specific examples that are discussed from the fourth category, texts common to both that have differences in detail.

Texts in the 2 Samuel narrative that are absent in 1 Chronicles include the following: the regnal accession formula for David's reign (5,4); the portion of the account of the capture of Jerusalem that makes reference to sayings involving the blind and the lame (5,6; 5,8); the discovery of the existence of Mephiboshet and his placing under house arrest (9); the Bathsheba incident, including the birth and death of the first child (11-12); the rape of Tamar (13); the wise woman of Tekoa (14); Absalom's bid for power, his revolt, David's abandoning of Jerusalem, Absalom's subsequent death and David's return to Jerusalem (15-20); the sacrifice of the seven Saulides (21,1-14); the psalm of deliverance (22); and the last words of David (23). What is particularly noteworthy is that most of the narrative that recounts David's personal family dealings, from

Bathsheba through Absalom's revolt, is not found in Chronicles: 2 Sam 11-20. Yet parts of the so-called appendix after this chunk of narrative in 2 Sam 21-24 are found. Thus, it is not easy to conclude that the Chronicler simply did not know this material when he wrote, unless one wants to argue that it was inserted in its present location at a later date by disrupting the original narrative in which 2 Sam 21 immediately succeeded 2 Sam 10. This is not likely, however, since the tradition about the sacrifice of the seven Saulides makes the most narrative sense if placed prior to the Mephiboshet incident in 2 Sam 9. Then David's question, "Is there anyone still left in the house of Saul to whom I can show loyalty for the sake of Jonathan?", makes good sense. As it stands, it comes out of the blue, with no introduction.

As noted by R.A. Carlson[3], 2 Sam 11-20 tend to represent David "under the curse" as a balance to his earlier career, which began as early as 1 Sam 16, where he is depicted as being "under the blessing". For this reason, many have concluded that the Chronicler has deliberately excised from his account any negative traditions about David because he wanted to idealize the founder of the Judahite monarchy. This seems like a reasonable suggestion, although it needs to be qualified, because some of the traditions found in Samuel but not in Chronicles are neutral or place David in a positive light. Explanations for their removal need to be provided as well.

The accession formula is essentially neutral information, so why has it been omitted? Two possibilities come to mind. First, it mentions that David established Hebron as the first capital of Judah, before Jerusalem, and the Chronicler may not have wanted there ever to have been a precursor or rival to Jerusalem as the political and religious capital. Alternatively, it mentions that David was king over Judah for seven and a half years before becoming king over Israel as well, and the Chronicler may not have wanted this historical situation to be known. He has not included any information in his account of David's career from 2 Sam 1-4, where David's crowning by Judah and his long war with the house of Saul before his assumption of the throne of Israel is recounted. Instead, he focuses on "all Israel", including Judah, working together.

The second possible explanation for the omission of the regnal formula is consistent with the further omission of the traditions involving David's dealings with the house of Saul: the sacrifice of the seven

---

3. *David the Chosen King: A Traditio-Historical Approach to the Second Book of Samuel* (translated from Swedish by E.J. Sharpe and S. Rudman), Uppsala, Almqvist & Wicksell, 1964, pp. 24-25. He defines the boundaries of the curse section as 2 Sam 13-24, thus beginning it later than I would, and he also includes the appendix section within the curse section.

Saulides, any reference to the covenant between David and Jonathan, and the incidents involving Mephiboshet, Jonathan's alleged son and the surviving Saulide heir to the throne. As presented, all of these narrative segments place David in a positive light, as upholder of his covenant with Jonathan and respectful of the Saulide family, ensuring its burial together in the ancestral family tomb. Their omission cannot simply be attributed to their casting David in a negative light, then, like the bulk of the rest of the traditions in 2 Sam 11-20. Rather, it seems as though the Chronicler has not wanted to recount anything about how David came to supplant the Saulides on the throne of Israel. He summarizes events in 1 Sam 16 – 2 Sam 4 by stating simply that YHWH caused Saul to die for the sins he committed against Him, and then He caused the kingdom to be turned over to David, son of Jesse (10,13-14)[4].

The Chronicler is familiar with some of these Saulide traditions. In 10,1-12 he relates the death of Saul and his sons at Mt. Gilboa in language that parallels 1 Sam 31,1-13 almost verbatim. Also, in 1 Chron 12, in a narrative segment unique to the Chronicles account, he refers to David's being at Ziklag while hiding from Saul and seems to allude to his attack against the Amalekites to retrieve families and goods that had been taken when he had gone to the Philistine troop muster for the battle at Gilboa. Thus, he is familiar with events that currently are narrated in 1 Sam 27-31 or which were part of an underlying source that he chose not to repeat in full but merely to allude to in passing[5].

The Chronicler seems to want to avoid focus on David's early career prior to his becoming king, just as he has said almost nothing about Saul's career. He does not suppress this information altogether, but he omits most detail and passes over it quickly so he can move on to what

---

4. A similar view is taken by e.g. T.-S. IM, *Das Davidbild in den Chronikbüchern* (EurHS, 263), New York, NY, – Frankfurt am Main, Peter Lang, 1985, pp. 43-44. Contrast the view of S.L. McKENZIE that David is not the central focus of 2 Sam 1-4, that the events take place before David's capture of Jerusalem and by implication, are expendable, since the Chronicler wants to recount the capture of the future cultic site as quickly as possible, and that their omission fits well with the Chronicler's pan-Israelite interest (*The Chronicler's Use of the Deuteronomistic History* [HSM, 33], Atlanta, GA, Scholars Press, 1984, p. 36). A.C. WELCH has observed that the Chronicler omitted all mention of the kingdom of Eshbaal because according to his theological perspective, there could be no successor to the doomed house of Israel (*The Work of the Chronicler: Its Purpose and Its Date* [Schweich Lectures, 1938], London, Oxford University, 1939, p. 12). F. MI-CHAELI has drawn similar conclusions (*Les livres des Chroniques, d'Esdras et de Néhémie* [CAT, XVI], Neuchâtel, Delachaux & Niestlé, 1967, pp. 76-77). Welch's subsequent tying of the omission of the reference to David's temporary reign in Hebron to the same motive is less convincing (*Work of Chronicler*, p. 12).

5. None of these events is mentioned in the headings to various psalms that have been connected to events in David's life, so it cannot be argued that the Chronicler derived them from the Psalter.

he wants his audience to understand was most important about David's career: his serving as an able king over both Israel and Judah, as a successful commander-in-chief, and as founder of Jerusalem and its administrative and cultic practices. He may be concerned that readers could infer from the extant tradition that David might have usurped the throne from Saul, which would cast him in a negative light. But it seems as though his readers knew something of this tradition anyway, since he alludes to it, especially in 1 Chron 12. Rather than try to whitewash the implied usurpation by recounting it and adding additional explanations for David's behavior, he appears to have decided to minimize it by ignoring it for the most part, giving it only a passing reference[6].

Material that is unique to the Chronicles narrative includes the listing of all of David's supporters from the twelve tribes who gathered to him while he was still a Philistine mercenary at Ziklag (12); expansions of the stories pertaining to the Ark to include a reason why it had been neglected under Saul; an emphasis on the role of the priests and levites, and the addition of two psalms (15-16); and the final eight chapters of the book, which focus on David's instrumental role in stockpiling supplies for the building of the temple in Jerusalem and his establishment of a royal administration that covered both the civil and religious spheres (22-29). The listing of supporters seems designed to emphasize that David was made king at Hebron by both Judah and Israel simultaneously. This seems to be a deliberate counter to the tradition in 2 Sam 1-5 that states that he was made king in Hebron by Judah alone and ruled over Judah for seven and a half years before being made king over Israel as well. In this instance, the Chronicler seems bent on providing an alternate understanding of David's accession. Since he alludes to other portions of the narrative now found in 1 Sam 27-31, it seems likely that he is opposing the view that is presented in the ensuing portion of that narrative, in 2 Sam 1-5. Whether this same view was part of an earlier source and simply copied by the author of the books of Samuel is not clear, however.

6. It is generally recognized that the Chronicler presupposes his audience's knowledge of stories in older presentations and that by allusion, brief summary and comment he suggests a new understanding in many cases. See e.g. MICHAELI, *Chroniques*, pp. 76-77; T. WILLI, *Die Chronik als Auslegung* (FRLANT, 106), Göttingen, Vandenhoeck & Ruprecht, 1972, pp. 63-68; R.J. COGGINS, *The First and Second Books of Chronicles* (CBEB), New York, NY, Cambridge University, 1976, pp. 10-11; MCKENZIE, *Chronicler's Use*, pp. 72-73; IM, *Davidbild*, pp. 35-36; P.R. ACKROYD, *The Chronicler in His Age* (JSOT SS, 101), Sheffield, Academic Press, 1991, p. 276; G. JONES, *1 & 2 Chronicles* (OTG), Sheffield, Academic Press, 1993, p. 72; M.Z. BRETTLER, *The Creation of History in Ancient Israel*, New York, NY, Routledge, 1995, pp. 21-22.

The emphasis on the role of the priests and the levites is found in the additions to the ark narrative as well as in the final chapters, where their divisions or genealogies are presented together with the work with which they were entrusted. An emphasis on the Aaronites as the most important priestly line is consistent with views expressed in Ezek 40-48, indicating at least an exilic date for the development of the supremacy of this priestly line, but a more specific date is not able to be pinpointed. In addition, once the Aaronites were established in power, any material subsequently composed would need to reflect their status, and Aaronite supremacy may have lasted centuries, meaning that there could be hundreds of years between the composition of these two works. The focus on cultic administration seems to reflect practices in the second temple in particular, but that would allow a date from ca. 515 BC-70 CE, which is too broad to be helpful.

It can also be noted that the Chronicler knows that Solomon was young when he succeeded to the throne (22,5), which suggests that he was familiar with some traditions about him that are now found in 2 Samuel. While he has chosen not to relate anything about Solomon's birth or Absalom's revolt or Amnon's rape of Tamar, he clearly is aware of the unusual situation of a young son succeeding to the throne. In addition, while he has omitted the list of sons born to David in Hebron that is found in 2 Sam 3,2-5, in 14,4 he has included the list of children born to David at Jerusalem, in which Solomon is the fourth-born son. This would allow his hearers to know that there were elder sons ahead of Solomon who had a rightful claim to the throne by birth and lead them to wonder perhaps what happened to the older brothers. Again, the Chronicler has taken the approach that he will not suppress known traditions but will pass over them quickly as a way to downplay or ignore them, thereby suggesting they are not relevant to what needs to be known about Solomon as a great and memorable ruler. It is not how he came to the throne but what he did in office, which counts. At the same time, his elimination of the reference to sons being born in Hebron avoids the implication that this city was Jerusalem's precursor as capital of Judah, which was the alternate possible reason for his omitting of the accession formula. This could mean, then, that the Chronicler is consciously trying to eliminate traditions that imply Hebron's status as the first capital of Judah as well as all traditions about how David came to occupy the Saulide throne of Israel.

It can be noted that the narrative segment in 1 Chron 22–29 substitutes for the material in 2 Sam 11–20 about David's family dealings. Instead of portraying the problems David encountered within his family, or "David under the curse", it focuses on David as founder and organizer of the temple hierarchy, civil administration, and as the moving force behind the building or refurbishing of the first temple. It portrays the founder of Jerusalem and Judah as an ideal figure. Thus, it either was a deliberate alternate ending to an already established tradition, or it was simply one of two competing depictions of David's career that were developed from an underlying source.

Space precludes the enumeration of all the differences in details in texts that are common to 2 Samuel and 1 Chronicles. I would like to concentrate, however, on a small group that seem to be more significant, which go beyond mere paraphrase or a change from passive to active voice. In 1 Chron 11,7-9 in the MT, Joab is said to have "preserved alive" the rest of Jerusalem that lay beyond the city of David and the Millo, which David is to have built or fortified, while in 2 Sam 5,9 David is credited with fortifying the area surrounding the city of David from the Millo inward only and there is no reference to Joab "preserving" the rest of the city. The verb used to describe Joab's activity is unusual: the imperfect of the verb חיה, "to live". If parsed as a *piel* rather than a *qal*, it could be construed to mean "preserved alive". Only in Neh 3,34 is חיה possibly used in the *qal* to convey the sense "to rebuild", and in that context, a meaning of "revive" is equally plausible. The standard translation, "rebuilt", would presume some form of the verb בנה, which is not present, and seems to be made on the basis of an assumed parallel between David's building activity in the acropolis and Joab's activity in the rest of the city. Why, however, would the army general be responsible for building activities? Corvee labor, not the army, would normally have been used for such building or repair. By understanding חיה to mean "preserved alive", better sense can be made of the situation: the acropolis was captured and its population decimated, but the rest of the city and its population was left more or less intact[7].

The LXX wording of 1 Chron 11,7-8 does not mention Joab at all, but instead reads "he [i.e. David] sat in the stronghold; therefore he called it the city of David, and he fortified the city round about". The last two thirds of v. 8 in the MT are missing in the LXX. The entire phrase about Joab is also lacking in Samuel; instead, that verse ends with the phrase "and his house/palace" as the last element in the list of things that David built/fortified. Under the circumstances, the evidence for the mention of

---

7. This understanding of the text represents a minority view among various rabbis cited in the Talmud (so I.W. SLOTKI, *Chronicles*, London, Soncino, 1971, pp. 63-64). It also is favored by e.g. W. RUDOLPH, *Chronikbücher* (HAT, I,21), Tübingen, J. Mohr, 1955, p. 94; P.R. ACKROYD, *I & II Chronicles, Ezra, Nehemiah* (Torch Bible Commentaries), Gateshead, SCM, 1973, p. 52.

Joab as an original detail in any underlying source is weak. Its presence in the MT version of Chronicles apparently should be seen as a change within the Hebrew tradition[8] that blamed Joab for a mixed population within the city of Jerusalem, leaving David's reputation intact[9].

In 1 Chron 18,12, Abshai son of Zeruiah, David's nephew, is credited with the military victory in the Valley of Salt, while in 2 Sam 8,13, there is no mention of him, but instead, the text states that "David made a name" when he returned from defeating Edom in the Valley of Salt. There is a strong implication in the Samuel wording that David was responsible for the victory, although his "making a name" and being credited with the defeat need not mean that he personally risked his life and led the army. This is clear from the narrative about Joab's capture of Rabbat Ammon in 2 Sam 12,26-31, where Joab warns David that he had better put in an appearance at the battle or the name of Joab will be associated with the deed.

---

8. An alternative view suggests the possibility that this material was part of the underlying Vorlage but was lost in the developing Palestinian tradition and only restored in the Lucianic version to make it conform to the proto-MT text. So e.g. MCKENZIE, who notes the lack of a good explanation for how the initial haplography would have occurred, however. At the same time, he is troubled by the need to posit a revision of the OG text toward the proto MT prior to Lucian if one adopts the position espoused here and does not commit to either explanation in the end (*Chronicler's Use*, p. 43). L.C. ALLEN, quoting a doctoral dissertation by V.M. Rogers, has suggested that the initial haplography in the Greek tradition may have been motivated by a desire to give David the sole glory of capturing Jerusalem (*The Greek Chronicles: The Relation of the Septuagint of I and II Chronicles to the Massoretic Text* [SVT, 25], Leiden, Brill, 1974, p. 130). He goes on to argue, however, that the LXX reading appears to be based on a poor ms. version of the MT, where ויואב was misread as ויארב and יחיה was misread as וחיה, with שאר then omitted as superfluous (*ibid.*).

9. E. BERTHEAU thinks that the account giving Joab credit is an old alternate to the one that gave David credit and that the Chronicler has combined the two here (*Die Bücher der Chronik* [KHAT, 15], Leipzig, S. Hirzel, 1873, pp. 112-113). In contrast, E.L. CURTIS and A.A. MADSEN propose that the legend concerning Joab may have arisen from the prominence of his family in postexilic Israel, citing 1 Chron 4,14 and Ezra 2,6; 8,9 in support (*The Books of Chronicles* [ICC, 11], Edinburgh, T. & T. Clark, 1910, p. 186), while J.M. MYERS concludes that "The reference to Joab's activities is doubtless another attempt to glorify him since it is missing in II Samuel" (*I Chronicles* [AB, 12], New York, NY, Doubleday, 1965, p. 85). IM proposes that Joab's introduction is the result of the Chronicler wanting to place Joab at the head of the list of heroes that ensues in 11,10 – 12,41 because he did not appear in the latter list yet was the commander-in-chief of the entire Israelite army (*Davidbild*, pp. 50-51). P. WELTEN credits the Chronicler with the introduction of Joab but gives no motivation (*Geschichte und Geschichtsdarstellung in den Chronikbüchern* [WMANT, 42], Neukirchen-Vluyn, Neukirchener Verlag, 1973, pp. 34-35), while R. MOSIS suggests that the Chronicler has introduced Joab and his building activity here from Joab's initial mention in 1 Chron 11,6 (*Untersuchungen zur Theologie des chronistischen Geschichtswerkes* [FTSt, 92], Freiburg, Herder, 1973, pp. 45-46). ACKROYD suggests that the passage reflects a tradition in which Joab showed himself to be a magnanimous conqueror (*I & II Chronicles*, p. 52).

A minority view holds that the reading in Chronicles has resulted from a copyist's error. It acknowledges that the Chronicler deliberately omitted the initial phrase found in 2 Sam 8,13: ויעש דוד שם, "David made a name," although it provides no rationale for such a move. It then proposes that the ensuing phrase, בשבו, "when he returned," was originally written in the underlying manuscript with *the plene* spelling בשובו, which was inadvertently corrupted by a copyist into אבשי בן, with Zeruiah added to complete the identification[10]. The consistency in the order of the consonants in the original phrase and the proposed corruption is noteworthy, although the need to presume a *plene* spelling to allow for one of the two changes is a potential weakness in the argument. In addition, *waw* and *yod* are often confused in manuscripts and *waw* and final *nun* could easily be confused in square script written by a careless hand, making the proposed changes plausible. Nevertheless, the proposed corruption lacks cogency because it fails to explain why the initial phrase, "David made a name", would have been omitted by the Chronicler. The statement is consistent with the glorification of David as a military leader and so would not have been objectionable to the Chronicler; to the contrary, it would have served his aims admirably.

It is also noteworthy that Ps 60,2 credits another son of Zeruiah, Joab, Abshai's brother, with the victory in the Vally of Salt. The psalm provides independent testimony that the hero of this particular battle was someone other than David, but a relative, a son of Zeruiah. 1 Chron 8,12 and Ps 60,2 would appear to be variant traditions that were handed down about which son of Zeruiah was responsible for the victory over the Edomites in the Valley of Salt.

In light of the tendency in 2 Samuel to portray David as human and lacking in good judgment after chap. 12, it is plausible to argue that the more original reading of the tradition names Abshai as the victor, which is preserved in Chronicles. The author of 2 Samuel would have altered the tradition to credit David with this victory because he placed the incident in the segment of his narrative illustrating "David under the blessing"[11]. Had the event been placed in the narrative flow anywhere after 2

10. So e.g. I. BENZINGER, *Die Bücher der Chronik* (KHAT, 20), Tübingen, J. Mohr, 1901, pp. 58-59; R. KITTEL, *Die Bücher der Chronik* (HAT, 1.6. pt. 1), Göttingen, Vandenhoeck & Ruprecht, 1902, p. 76; CURTIS and MADSEN, *Books of Chronicles*, p. 236; M. REHM, *Textkritische Untersuchungen zu den Parallelstellen der Samuel-Königsbücher und der Chronik* (Alttestamentliche Abhandlungen, XIII, 3), Münster, Aschendorffsche Verlagsbuchhandlung, 1937, p. 117; RUDOLPH, *Chronikbücher*, p. 135; MICHAELI, *Chroniques*, p. 103; WILLI, *Chronik*, pp. 74-75. Not all of the above scholars insist on the *plene* spelling for בשבו.

11. Contrast, for example, T.-S. IM, who suggests that for some reason, the Chronicler wanted the fame for the conquests of the state not just to be associated with David, but with

Sam 12 in the segment illustrating "David under the curse", the writer of Samuel would have left Abshai as the victor. In this way, he could have reinforced his negative portrait of David by implying that he was no longer able to lead his army successfully but had to rely on others to do so.

In the present instance, it seems likely that the Chronicler was using an underlying source that the author of Samuel also accessed for information. There is a less ready explanation for why the Chronicler would have altered an underlying text that credited David with the victory in the Valley of Salt to attribute it to his nephew instead, especially when he seems to want to demonstrate David's ability as military leader as one of his admirable characteristics as founder of the Davidic dynasty centered in Jerusalem. In general, deeds migrate from lesser known figures to more famous ones, which would favor the Abshai version as the older form of the tradition.

Finally, in 1 Chron 18,17, David's sons are made "first ministers" to the king, while in the MT of 2 Sam 8,18 they are made priests and in the LXX, "chiefs of the court". The phrase in Chronicles is הראשנים ליד מלך, "the first ones beside the king", vs. כהנים in the MT and *aularchai* in the LXX. If one accepts the MT reading of "priests" to be more original than the LXX's "chiefs of the court", the less objectionable idea between "priests" and first ministers" would be the latter, especially in the second temple period, when membership in the priesthood was strictly regulated by lineage and genealogy. The Davidic line was not of priestly descent, even if the king in theory were the "high priest" of his kingdom and may have officiated at certain religious occasions in the preexilic period. Thus, the reading in Chronicles is consistent with postexilic cultic practice and could be seen to be a deliberate change in wording from any underlying source that reflected monarchic practices[12].

It is worth considering, however, whether the reading in which David appoints his sons to be priests in the MT text of 2 Samuel might not be a

---

Joab (1 Chron 20,2) and with Abshai (1 Chron 18,12) (*Davidbild*, p. 53), and R. BRAUN, who lists this passage as one of five that are "probably (or at least possibly) dependent upon the unique views of the writer" (i.e. the Chronicler) (*1 Chronicles* [WBC, 14], Waco, TX, Word Books, 1986, pp. 204-205). Most commentators note the difference in the named leaders of the battle but fail to suggest a reason for the discrepancy.

12. It is commonly thought that the Chronicler has altered his underlying source, whether it be 2 Samuel or a common source used also by the DtrH. See e.g. BERTHEAU, *Bücher der Chronik*, p. 167; BENZINGER, *Bücher der Chronik*, p. 59; CURTIS and MADSEN, *Books of Chronicles*, p. 237; MYERS, *1 Chronicles*, p. 139; MICHAELI, *Chroniques*, p. 103; SLOTKI, *Chronicles*, p. 108; WILLI, *Chronik*, p. 127; COGGINS, *Chronicles*, p. 100; J. BECKER, *1 Chronik* (KAT, 18), Würzburg, Echter Verlag, 1986, p. 81; BRAUN, *1 Chronicles*, pp. 204-205.

secondary change to reflect a postexilic ideology that wanted to push for the union of the office of high priest and Davidic kingship into a single unit. In anticipation of the restoration of a Davidic ruler, there may have been a move among one circle of the intelligentsia of Yehud or Judaea to create a precedent that would allow a Davidic descendant also to serve as high priest, simultaneously. The more obvious answer that would see "priests" rather than "first ministers" to be the original reading is not the only possible option and caution needs to be exercised in drawing firm conclusions in this instance.

F. Hitzig[13], T.K. Cheyne[14], M. Rehm[15] and G.J. Wenham[16] have argued, however, that the LXX preserves the more original reading over the MT in 2 Sam 8,18 and that there never was a reference to David's sons being priests in the underlying text. They all suggest that *aularchai* renders the Hebrew term, סכנים, "stewards", which is used in Isa 22,15. The corruption found in the MT would have occurred as *heh* and *samek* were confused in the old script, followed by the metathesis of the first and second consonants. Wenham, in particular, offers four arguments to support the originality of the reading סכנים: 1) corruption to a more familiar term is more likely than from a familiar one to a lesser known one, 2) there is already a corruption in the first half of the verse, making a mistake in the second half plausible as well, 3) priests have already been enumerated two verses earlier in the list of officials and it is unlikely that another sets of priests would be listed with no distinction drawn, and 4) in Solomon's cabinet, there is an office called "over the house" that would seem to correspond with the function envisioned for David's sons[17]. It appears likely, then, that the Chronicler paraphrased the original text סכנים with his expression הראשנים ליד מלך and that the MT reading of כהנים is a later, secondary reading that arose through scribal error. Perhaps the title סכן no longer existed in the Chronicler's time, even if the duties associated with the office were still carried out

13. *Die Psalmen II*, Leipzig, C.F. Winter, 1865, p. 318.
14. *The Priesthood of David's Sons,* in *The Expositor* 9 (1899) 453-457, esp. p. 454.
15. *Textkritische Untersuchungen*, p. 75.
16. *Were David's Sons Priests?*, in ZAW 87 (1975) 79-82.
17. *Ibid.*, p. 81. A. CODY has also argued that *aularchai* translates סכנים but has concluded that MT's כהנים is the more original reading and that the LXX's *aularchai,* as well as the Chronicler's phrase "first ministers", was a deliberate correction to avoid the reference to David's sons being priests when they were not members of an official priestly line (*A History of Old Testament Priesthood* [AnBib, 35], Rome, Pontifical Biblical Institute, 1969, pp. 103-105). As Wenham notes, however, the Chronicler has no theological objection to portraying David in a priestly role, wearing the linen ephod, offering sacrifices and blessing the people (1 Chron 16,2-3) so it is not obvious that he would have objected to David's sons being appointed as priests (p. 80).

under a different title, leading to the paraphrase or supplying of a roughly equivalent job description.

To summarize the results of looking at three changes in detail, the first, 1 Chron 11,8, which credits Joab with preserving alive the non-acropolis area of Jerusalem after its capture, seems to be an inner development in the MT tradition and so does not shed any light on the issue of the Chronicler's source(s). The second, 1 Chron 18,12, which credits Abshai rather than David with the victory in the Valley of Salt, seems best attributed to an underlying source different from the book of 2 Samuel. The last, 1 Chron 18,17, which makes David's sons first ministers rather than priests, is inconclusive. While it normally is taken to be a deliberate change of 2 Samuel by the Chronicler to reflect the genealogical restrictions on the priesthood that applied in the second temple period, an argument can be made that the reading in 2 Samuel is a deliberate change by a faction that sought to unite the Davidic and priestly lines into a single office. In addition, it seems likely that the LXX's presumed "stewards" preserves the better reading over the MT's "priests" and that the Chronicler has simply paraphrased his received text rather than repeat an obsolete title. In the first and third instances, the reading could have been derived from an underlying source or from 2 Samuel; in the second instance, the reading would have been derived from an underlying source other than 2 Samuel.

The final category of comparison to be examined is the order of events in David's career in 1 Chronicles and 2 Samuel. While they tend to agree in general outline, there are some notable exceptions. The tradition about David's heroes found in the appendix section of 2 Samuel in 23,8-39 occurs in the Chronicles account immediately after the story of the capture and rebuilding of Jerusalem in 11,10-12,41. Although there are differences in consonants in some of the names and the stories of Eleazer and Shammah have been conflated in Chronicles, both seem to reflect the same underlying tradition, whether that comes from an earlier narrative, from an independent source used by the author of Samuel to create 2 Samuel, or from the author of Samuel himself. It needs to be noted, however, that the conflation may be deliberate rather than an accident. The story about Eleazer that is missing from 1 Chronicles is precisely the part that is a *non-sequitur* in 2 Samuel: he was one of the three warriors with David when they defied the Philistines gathered there for battle – where? There is no antecedent for "there", implying that the tradition is not in its original context in 2 Samuel. It would have followed immediately after the account of one of David's battles against the Philistines.

Yet it does not make sense to argue that Chronicles preserves the original narrative location of the list of David's mighty men and their military exploits either, even though there is a certain logic in placing it immediately after the account of the capture of Jerusalem. An account of a battle with the Philistines is demanded as an antecedent. The segment detailing David's heroes and their exploits would have a generic connection with the accounts in 2 Sam 21,15-22 of incidents in David's wars against the Philistines, and if the intervening psalms in 2 Sam 22 and last words of David in 23,1-7 are removed, the segment about David's heroes that is introduced by the story of Eleazar's exploit at an unspecified battle and the preceding accounts of exploits accomplished during wars with the Philistines would have formed a single unit. Even so, in that sequence, there still would not be a clear antecedent for the "there".

The Chronicler recounts the incidents in 2 Sam 21,18-22 much later in 1 Chron 20,4-8, immediately after his account of the defeat of Rabbat Ammon. In 2 Samuel, this battle is narrated early, in 2 Sam 11-12, as the framework to the Bathsheba incident. The Chronicler has omitted all reference to the Bathsheba episode but has chosen to include in his narrative the report of David's defeat and humiliation of Rabbat Ammon because it illustrates David's accomplishments as an able commander-in-chief.

The Chronicler interrupts his version of the story about the transfer of the Ark to Jerusalem with material that occurs in 2 Samuel in 5,11-25, prior to the Deuteronomistic version of the transfer of the Ark that is narrated in 2 Sam 6. The intervening material includes the report of envoys Hiram sent to help David build his palace, the children born to David at Jerusalem, and the two Philistine wars that took place in the Valley of Rephaim. The Chronicler's version seems designed to drive home the point that three months time passed before there was another attempt to deal with the Ark by providing a narrative interlude before returning to the story of the Ark. This interlude serves to heighten interest in what will happen when the story resumes again[18].

---

18. Many do not comment on the literary function of the interlude; instead, they tend to stress merely that the Chronicler takes the opportunity to showcase David's personal courage, prowess, fame or greatness after the reference to the gap in time. So e.g. RUDOLPH, *Chronikbücher*, p. 113; MICHAELI, *Chroniques*, pp. 88-89; ACKROYD, *I & II Chronicles*, p. 58; COGGINS, *Chronicles*, p. 81; BECKER, *1 Chronik*, p. 65. Two alternate rationales are suggested for the interlude: 1) it shows how busy and preoccupied David was during this period (W.H. BENNETT, *Books of Chronicles* [The Expositor's Bible], New York, Armstrong and Son, 1894, p. 153) so that he was too busy with affairs of state to prepare a place for the Ark (BRETTLER, *Creation of History*, pp. 44-45), and 2) it demonstrates that David's achievements in vv. 1-17 were the result of his prior action of seeking out the Ark and God's blessing in reward for David's faithfulness (IM, *Davidbilder*,

After the recounting of the transfer of the Ark, the two narratives parallel one another and present events in exactly the same order for three chapters, except for the material on Mephiboshet that the Chronicler omits (1 Chron 17-19 = 2 Sam 7-10). As already noted, the mirroring ends in 1 Chron 20. Although the Bathsheba incident is omitted (2 Sam 11-12), the defeat of Rabbat Ammon is maintained and appears in parallel order, as expected. It is then followed immediately by the material about Philistine wars that currently occurs in 2 Sam 21,18-22. It should be noted that while the ten-chapter gap between the two incidents in 2 Samuel seems enormous, these are the very chapters that the Chronicler does not include in his account of David's reign. Essentially then, the Philistine war material is the next block of neutral material that has not yet been used that one would find if one were moving through the book of Samuel as a source or if one were using an underlying source whose order of events has been preserved intact in Samuel.

It is worth considering whether in some underlying source or in an earlier form of the book of Samuel, the Philistine war material originally followed the account of the capture of Rabbat Ammon. The appendix section in 2 Samuel does not seem to be original but contains material that either has been moved from somewhere earlier in the book, added as a supplement from one or more sources, or both. Since the war material has nothing to do with David's family woes, it is not likely that it was part of 2 Sam 12-20. It has a different feeling than the narrative about the capture of Rabbat-Ammon, even if the parts of the narrative that deal with the Bathsheba incident are removed. The tradition about Rabbat-Ammon portrays David as a potentially weak commander-in-chief since he is not present at the siege himself, while David personally leads both battles in the Valley of Rephaim.

It is interesting to note that the Chronicler places Sibbecai's slaying of Sippai during a battle at Gezer, and the second battle against the Philistines in 2 Sam 2,22-25 ends with David routing the Philstines from Geba to Gezer. Gezer could have been a common thread that led to the stringing together of a number of accounts dealing with wars against the Philistines into a loose collection. Thus, it is plausible to suggest that originally, all the traditions about the Philistine wars were consecutive

p. 82; JONES, *1 & 2 Chronicles*, pp. 36-37). IM notes further that its focus on the kingdom is part of a larger pattern that alternates segments dealing with the cult and segments dealing with the kingdom. The account of the transfer of the Ark that chap. 14 interrupts constitutes two units dealing with the cult (*Davidbilder*, pp. 180-81). R.K. DUKE endorses IM's proposed patterning (*The Persuasive Appeal of the Chronicler* [JSOT SS, 88; Bible and Literature Series, 25], Sheffield, Almond, 1990, p. 59). MOSIS connects the interlude to the theme of David's concern for the Ark (*Untersuchungen*, p. 60).

and that their current division in 2 Sam 5,17-25 and 21,18-22 and in 1 Chron 14,8-17 and 20,4-8 is secondary in each case. In 2 Sam 21,18, the location of the slaying of Sibbecai is placed at Gob or Nob, as is the incident featuring Elhanan and Goliath; Gob could be a corruption of Gezer, with the *waw* being mistaken for a *zayin* and the *beth* a mistaken *resh*.

Should this single collection have been part of an underlying, common source used by the author of 2 Samuel and the Chronicler, it seems logical to suggest that the block of material would have been located relatively early in the narrative flow of events, since in 2 Samuel it is linked to the Philistine reaction to David's crowning over Israel. We cannot be certain whether this is an original or secondary linkage, however. Alternatively, it is possible that the collection was an independent source accessed by both the author of Samuel and the Chronicler, which would explain why the material has been placed in different locations by each author. Since it was not part of a fixed order of events, it could be split up and used in a way that best enhanced each writer's portrait.

Finally, 1 Chron 21,1-26 presents a variant account of David's census that is found in 2 Sam 24, continuing the paralleling of incidents by skipping over the psalm and the last words of David in the appendix section. The Chronicles version makes Satan responsible for inciting David to undertake the census, and the story is used primarily as a bridge to the unique account of how the first king gathered together materials for the building of the temple and charged his young son with its subsequent building in 1 Chron 22,1-16. It appears to have been taken up by the Chronicler because of its ending, which relates how David bought the site of the future temple from Ornan[19]. The figure of "the adversary" appears to be a late development theologically and its presence here is consistent with the Chronicler's use of only positive material in his portrait of the founder of the Davidic dynasty[20]. By having Satan incite David to number Israel, David's guilt is mollified; the king did not formulate the

---

19. So also e.g. WELCH, *Work of the Chronicler*, pp. 23-24; MICHAELI, *Chroniques*, p. 112; ACKROYD, *I & II Chronicles*, p. 73; MCKENZIE, *Chronicler's Use*, p. 39; IM, *Davidbild*, p. 146; BRAUN, *1 Chronicles*, p. xxx; DUKE, *Persuasive Appeal*, p. 60; JONES, *1 & 2 Chronicles*, 39. COGGINS argues that the tradition's emphasis on David's repentance had as much influence over Chronicler's decision to it in his account as its account of how David purchased the site of the future temple (*Chronicles*, p. 107).

20. So also, e.g. RUDOLPH, *Chronikbücher*, p. 143. A number of scholars argue that this tradition portrays David in a negative light in Chronicles as well as in Samuel. So e.g. MYERS, *I Chronicles*, p. 146; COGGINS, *Chronicles*, p. 107; DUKE, *Persuasive Appeal*, p. 60. Some even claim that David's responsibility for the abortive census is magnified in the version in Chronicles; so, e.g. MOSIS, *Untersuchungen*, p. 108; BRAUN, *1 Chronicles*, xxxiii; JONES, *1 & 2 Chronicles*, p. 39.

plan on his own but was driven to it by Satan. He was a pawn in a larger struggle. The author of 2 Samuel, on the other hand, uses the account as a further example of "David under the curse", who must follow the directions of the prophet Gad in order to end the divinely sent plague by building an altar on the future site of the temple. It is separated from the account of Solomon's building of the temple by two chapters that relate the last days of David, but it is possible that in an underlying source, it originally served as an introduction to the temple-building account.

SUMMARY

The examination of four of five categories of differences between the account of the career of David in 2 Samuel and 1 Chronicles has provided some preliminary results that can be applied to the issue of whether these two works represent competing or contrasting ideologies. Texts unique to 2 Samuel tend to place David in a negative light, illustrating "David under the curse". The Chronicler alludes to events now recorded in 1 Sam 27-31 but chooses not to narrate them in full; he seems to want to avoid recounting how David came to supplant the Saulides on the throne of Israel. He also seems to want to avoid any indication that Hebron served as the religious precursor to Jerusalem. It is not clear whether the material unique to 2 Samuel was part of an underlying source that the Chronicler deliberately chose not to include or was material added to an underlying source by the author of 2 Samuel.

Texts unique to the Chronicler emphasize the role of priests and levites in the temple cult and focus on David as founder and organizer of the temple hierarchy, civil administration, and as the moving force behind the building or refurbishing of the first temple. They portray the founder of Jerusalem and Judah as an ideal figure. It is not clear if any of this material was part of an underlying source that the author of 2 Samuel deliberately chose not to include, or was material added to an underlying source by the Chronicler.

Three texts common to 2 Samuel and 1 Chronicles that have differences in detail have yielded mixed results. The one in 1 Chron 11,8 that credits Joab with sparing alive the population of Jerusalem outside of the acropolis is probably an inner development in the MT and does not shed light on the source question. The text in 1 Chron 18,17 that makes David's sons to be first ministers rather than priests is also not able to help resolve the source question, since there are two possible ways to understand how the changed reading came about. The text in 1 Chron 18,12 that names Abshai rather than David as the person responsible for the victory in the Valley of Salt, on the other hand, seems to point to the Chronicler's dependence on an underlying source other than 2 Samuel. There is no apparent reason why the Chronicler would deliberately alter a text that attributed a victory to David and credit that victory to another; it is inconsistent with his idealization of David.

Finally, differences in the order of events in 2 Samuel and 1 Chronicles might be taken to indicate that the material that talks about deeds accomplished by David and his mighty men in connection with wars against the Philistines may once have been a single unit and that the author of 2 Samuel and the Chronicler have each chosen to split this material up and place it at different points in their narratives: 2 Sam 5,17-25 and 21,18-22, on the one hand, and 1 Chron 14,8-17 and 20,4-8, on the other. Given this situation, it is uncertain whether the original block of material belonged to a common underlying source used by both authors or whether it might have been derived from a separate source but one that was used by both authors. In the first instance, its original location in the narrative cannot be determined but should probably be placed early; in the second case, a logical reason for why the material was split up and placed at different points in the common narrative thread is provided.

Do the accounts of the career of David in 2 Samuel and 1 Chronicles represent competing or contrasting ideologies? A definitive answer cannot be given. The foregoing considerations provide only a single instance that points strongly to the use of a common underlying source that each writer supplemented in his own way: Abshai's victory in the Valley of Salt. It would be premature, however, to conclude that the two are competing ideologies based on this single detail. A systematic comparison of other narratives in 1 and 2 Kings vs. 1 and 2 Chronicles might provide a longer list of such examples that could make the existence of such an underlying source more probable. Even so, it is going to be extremely difficult to prove that the Chronicler knew only the underlying source and was not familiar with forms of the books of Samuel and Kings. He could well have had access to both, in which case his account would constitute a contrasting ideology, even if it were written within a few years of the Deuteronomistic version. Only more detailed work in the future will allow the complexity of this issue to be more fully grasped and understood.

University of Sheffield   Diana EDELMAN

LA MUERTE DE MOISÉS, LA SUCESIÓN DE JOSUÉ Y LA ESCRITURA DE LA TÔRAH (DEUTERONOMIO 31-34)

I. UN TRIÁNGULO TENAZ

La muerte de Moisés, la sucesión de Josué y la escritura de la Tôrah aparecen en Dt 31-34 como tres acontecimientos trabados en un triángulo tenaz. Los tres poseen una importancia singular en el libro del Deuteronomio, en el canon de las Escrituras y en la historia de Israel.

Con la muerte de Moisés no sólo culmina el libro del Deuteronomio sino también todo el Pentateuco, a la par que llega a su término el período fundante de la historia de Israel. Moisés contribuyó de modo decisivo al nacimiento del pueblo de Israel, al que acompañó y guió desde la salida de Egipto hasta la entrada en la tierra de Canaán. La talla extraordinaria de este personaje ha quedado muy bien reflejada en Dt 34,10-12.

Pero el Deuteronomio no marca el final de la historia de Israel. Tan sólo señala el término de un período, al mismo tiempo que prepara el camino para el período sucesivo. Josué, *mešaret mošeh* / «servidor (ayudante) de Moisés» (Ex 24,13; 32,11; Num 11,28; Jos 1,1) y persona de su total confianza (así se trasluce en el título de *mešaret*: cf. 1Cr 27,1; 28,1), será el sucesor de Moisés y el jefe del pueblo en la nueva etapa de la historia de Israel. A lo largo de toda la marcha a través del desierto, Josué mostró reiteradamente sus dotes de liderazgo (cf. Ex 17,8-16; Num 14,6-9; etc.), acreditándose como digno sucesor de Moisés (cf. Num 27,18-23; 32,38; 34,17; Dt 31,7-8.23; 34,9; Jos 1,1ss).

Con la mirada puesta en el tiempo posterior a su muerte, Moisés escribe la *tôrah*. En ella se trazan las directrices fundamentales que deben guiar la vida de Israel en la tierra prometida. A partir de Dt 31,9ss, la *tôrah* aparece como la enseñanza codificada por Moisés en un documento que se leerá al pueblo y se conservará junto al arca de la alianza. Será una enseñanza autoritativa y normativa para Israel, a la par que servirá de testimonio contra él (cf. 31,9-13.24-27; 32,45-47).

En los apartados que siguen pondré de relieve estos tres aspectos, tratando de mostrar su valor para la comprensión de Dt 31-34 en sí mismos, en su relación con el Deuteronomio y con la Historia Deuteronomista.

II. LA MUERTE DE MOISÉS, CLAVE DE BÓVEDA

Tal como se relatan los acontecimientos en Dt 31-34, la sucesión de Josué y la escritura de la *tôrah* se hallan determinados por la cercanía o inminencia de la muerte de Moisés.

Desde el punto de vista literario, el libro del Deuteronomio es una narración. Se inicia con la voz del narrador, que inmediatamente cede el paso a Moisés, quien llevará la voz cantante a lo largo del libro. En realidad, el Deuteronomio aparece formalmente configurado como el relato de un discurso de Moisés en los umbrales de la tierra prometida: *'lh hdbrym 'šr dbr mšh 'l-kl yśr'l b'br hyrdn* (Dt 1,1a). A juzgar sólo por este título, no se puede decir que el Deuteronomio sea realmente el discurso de despedida o el testamento de Moisés. El narrador lo presenta sencillamente como las «palabras que Moisés dirigió a todo Israel al otro lado del Jordán...». En la perspectiva de los primeros compases del libro, tampoco se puede afirmar sin más que Moisés pronunciase este discurso poco antes de su muerte.

En realidad, de la muerte de Moisés no se habla hasta el final del libro, concretamente hasta Dt 31-34. Aunque de algún modo pueda verse insinuada en Dt 1,37 y 3,27-29, en sentido estricto las primeras referencias claras en el libro del Deuteronomio a la muerte de Moisés no aparecen hasta el cap. 31.

Ahora bien, Dt 31 se presenta como un discurso de Moisés, en términos que recuerdan el título del libro: *wylk mšh wydbr 't-hdbrym h'lh 'l-kl-yśr'l* (31,1a). Efectivamente, el narrador introduce con el verbo *dbr* y la expresión *hdbrym h'lh* (invertida, respecto de Dt 1,1a) un discurso de Moisés que tiene como destinatario a «todo Israel». Si la introducción del narrador nos remite al comienzo del libro, las primeras palabras de Moisés nos llevan más bien al final del mismo: *bn-m'h w'śrym šnh 'nky hywm* (31,2; cf. 34,7: *wmšh bn-m'h w'śrym šnh bmtw*).

La indicación de la edad de Moisés, en Dt 34,7 (cf. Gen 6,3), va directamente asociada a su muerte (*bmtw*); en 31,2, sólo indirectamente: «tengo 120 años hoy y no puedo salir ni entrar». En sentido estricto, en 31,2, Moisés se refiere únicamente a su mal estado de salud, aunque, en sentido amplio, aluda también a la cercanía de su muerte. Esta apreciación contrasta con la del narrador (cf. 34,7) que sostiene que no se había debilitado el vigor de Moisés cuando murió.

Entre 31,2 y 34,7 se menciona repetidas veces la muerte de Moisés (31,14.16.27-29; 32,48-52; 33,1; 34,5). A la luz de estas citas, Dt 31-34 reviste el carácter de «discurso de despedida» o de «últimas disposiciones» de Moisés. «Última disposición» o «última voluntad» son expresiones sinónimas de «testamento» o manifestación hecha por alguien de lo que desea que se haga después de su muerte. Esta concepción, característica de Dt 31-34, se extenderá a todo el libro del Deuteronomio, cuando es presentado como un solo discurso de Moisés.

Las referencias reiteradas a la muerte de Moisés y la serie de disposiciones por él tomadas en Dt 31-34 dan a estos textos un tenor distinto de los precedentes. Mientras que los cap. 29-30 gravitan en torno al momento presente en el que se concluye la alianza (baste ver la repetición de *hywm* en 29,9.11.12.14.17; 30,11.15.16.18.19.20 y el uso frecuente del participio, sobre todo en 29,9-14 y 30,11-14), los cap. 31-34 están orientados más bien hacia el tiempo que sigue a la muerte de Moisés. Esta observación viene a reforzar la necesidad de establecer una cesura entre Dt 29-30 y 31-32, avalando así la delimitación que hemos propuesto en otro estudio sobre Dt 31[1].

Aunque se parta del sistema de títulos - como hacen Kleinert y otros autores, al proponer una división general del Deuteronomio[2] - y se admita que en Dt 28,69 comienza una nueva sección[3], es obligado reconocer que los cap. 29-30 forman una unidad retórica y que los cap. 31-32 constituyen otra unidad. En este sentido, no parece muy acertado titular Dt 28,69-32,52 como «las últimas disposiciones de Moisés»[4], puesto que la idea de últimas disposiciones arranca realmente de las referencias a la muerte de Moisés, esto es, de los capítulos 31 y siguientes.

En coherencia con el sistema de títulos propuesto por Kleinert, sería preferible titular esta sección con las palabras de 28,69: '*lh dbry hbryt /* «Estas son las palabras de la alianza»[5], aunque es muy discutible que el motivo de la alianza abarque hasta Dt 31-32. Fundándose en la idea de que la sucesión al soberano forma parte de los tratados de vasallaje y del rito de conclusión de la alianza, algunos autores sostienen que la

---

1. Cf. F. GARCÍA LÓPEZ, *Deuteronomio 31, el Pentateuco y la Historia Deuteronomista*, en M. VERVENNE - J. LUST (eds.), *Deuteronomy and Deuteronomic Literature*. FS. C. H. W. Brekelmans (BETL, 133), Leuven, University Press - Peeters, 1997, pp. 71-85, esp. 73-75.
2. Cf. E. TALSTRA, *Deuteronomy 31: Confusion or Conclusion? The Story of Moses' Threefold Succession*, en M. VERVENNE - J. LUST (eds.), *Deuteronomy and Deuteronomic Literature* (n. 1), pp. 87-110, esp. 92.
3. Siguen las discrepancias, a este respecto, entre los exégetas. Ver, a modo de ejemplo, los dos Comentarios más recientes: E. NIELSEN, *Deuteronomium* (HAT, I/6), Tübingen, Mohr, 1995, p. 261; y J.H. TIGAY, *Deuteronomy* (The JPS Commentary), Philadelphia, PA - Jerusalem, The Jewish Publication Society, 1996, p. 274.
4. Cf. G. BRAULIK, *Deuteronomium II 16,18-34,12* (NEB, 28), Würzburg, Echter Verlag, 1992, p. 211.
5. Cf. D.T. OLSON, *Deuteronomy and the Death of Moses. A Theological Reading*, (Overtures to Biblical Theology), Minneapolis MN, Fortress Press, 1994, p. 126.

sucesión de Josué a Moisés (Dt 31,2-8.14-15.23) constituye parte
integrante de la misma «unidad» que 28,69 y 29-30. Sus razones, sin
embargo, no parecen demasiado convincentes[6]. Por de pronto, ni Moisés
ni Josué son los soberanos que proveen a la sucesión; en Israel, el único
soberano es Yahvé.

Además, el hecho de que en Dt 31-32 aparezcan algunos elementos
dispersos de alianza no es razón suficiente para sostener que estos
capítulos hayan sido estructurados siguiendo el modelo de los tratados
de vasallaje. Tal es el caso de Dt 31,9-13, coincidente en cierto sentido
con la cláusula -usual en los tratados de alianza- de depositar un
documento escrito en el santuario y de leerlo periódicamente para
recordar los compromisos entre el soberano y el vasallo[7]. Dt 31,9-13
refleja una práctica común, sin que ello signifique necesariamente que
ha sido modelado siguiendo la forma de los tratados de alianza[8].

Por otro lado, si bien es cierto que existen algunas conexiones entre
Dt 31-34 y los tratados de alianza no es menos cierto que se pueden
apreciar puntos de contacto significativos entre estos capítulos y otros
géneros literarios, entre los que hay que destacar las últimas enseñanzas
de un moribundo[9] y el género literario de los discursos de despedida[10].

Dejando aparte estas consideraciones formales, de lo que no cabe
duda es que en estos textos conclusivos del Deuteronomio la muerte de
Moisés ocupa un lugar preeminente y de que se halla estrechamente
relacionada con sus últimas disposiciones. Presintiendo cercana su
muerte, Moisés desea dejar solucionado un problema de capital importancia para el futuro de Israel. Se trata de un problema con dos
dimensiones, que expresan los siguientes interrogantes: ¿quién guiará a
Israel hasta Canaán? y ¿cómo se guiará Israel en Canaán? A la primera
cuestión, responde la investidura de Josué y a la segunda, la escritura de
la *tôrah*. Ambos aspectos serán objeto de estudio en los próximos
apartados.

6. Cf. K. BALTZER, *Das Bundesformular* (WMANT, 4), Neukirchen-Vluyn, Neukirchener Verlag, 1964[2] (1960[1]), pp. 76-79; N. LOHFINK, *Der Bundesschluss im Land
Moab. Redaktionsgeschichtliches zu Dt 28,69-32,47*, en *BZ* 6 (1962) 32-56, pp. 45-54; G.
BRAULIK, *Deuteronomium II* (ver n. 4), pp. 211-236.
7. Cf. K. BALTZER, *Das Bundesformular* (n. 6), pp. 91-95; L. PERLITT, *Bundestheologie im Alten Testament* (WMANT, 36), Neukirchen-Vluyn, Neukirchener Verlag,
1969, pp. 115-28.
8. Cf. J. W. WATTS, *Public Readings and Pentateuchal Law*, en *VT* 45 (1995) 540-57.
9. Cf. S. WEITZMAN, *Lessons from the Dying: The Role of Deuteronomy 32 in its Narrative Setting*, en *HTR* 87 (1994) 377-93; ID., *Allusion, Artifice, and Exile in the Hymn of
Tobit*, en *JBL* 115 (1996) 49-61.
10. Cf. E. CORTÉS, *Los discursos de adiós de Gn 49 a Jn 13-17*, Barcelona, Herder,
1976; E. VON NORDHEIM, *Die Lehre der Alten. II. Das Testament als Literaturgattung im
Alten Testament und im alten Vorderen Orient* (Arbeiten zur Literatur und Geschichte des
hellenistischen Judentums, 18), Leiden, Brill, 1985, esp. pp. 18-72.

III. LA SUCESIÓN DE JOSUÉ

La figura de Josué ocupa un lugar relevante en los cap. 31-34, con especial incidencia en el tema de la sucesión. La primera mención ocurre en un discurso de Yahvé, citado por Moisés: *yhwsʿ hwʾ ʿbr lpnyk* (Dt 31,3b). La afirmación del v. 3b, referida a Josué, se corresponde al pie de la letra con la del v. 3a, referida a Yahvé: *yhwh ʾlhyk hwʾ ʿbr lpnyk*. Ambas contrastan con la del v. 2b, referida a Moisés: *lʾ tʿbr ʾt-hyrdn hzh*. Elemento común a las tres es el verbo *ʿbr*, capital en la frase.

A juzgar por los vv. 2b-3, parece claro que Moisés no pasará el Jordán (v. 2b), pero no está tan claro quién pasará el Jordán al frente del pueblo: ¿Yahvé o Josué? Mientras que unos autores, como Levenson, descartan el v. 3a como secundario[11], otros, como Schäfer-Lichtenberger, consideran secundario el v. 3b[12].

Si atendemos a la fórmula *kʾšr dbr yhwh* (v. 3b), que reenvía a Dt 3,27-28, podemos comprobar que allí se hace referencia únicamente a Moisés y a Josué: éste pasará el Jordán, aquél no. En esta perspectiva, el v. 3b parecería la secuencia lógica del v. 2b; el v. 3a habría sido interpolado, anteponiéndolo al v. 3b, para enfatizar teológicamente el papel de Yahvé: es tanto como decir que el paso del Jordán se debe en realidad a Yahvé - sólo Él es el Soberano de Israel - y no a Josué. En los vv. 7-8 y 14-15.23 se ofrecen otras variantes de este mismo tema.

A primera vista, Dt 31,23 podría parecer un doble de 31,7-8, pero, bien mirado, son dos textos diferentes, cada uno con su propia función en el conjunto de la narración. Mientras que en 31,7-8 el discurso se pone en boca de Moisés, en 31,23 se pone en boca de Yahvé, subrayando la iniciativa divina. Yahvé avala, con su autoridad, la misión de Josué.

Por otro lado, la función de Josué adquiere nuevas connotaciones en 31,14-23 respecto de 31,1-8. La interrupción entre los vv. 14-15 y 23 (las «órdenes» / *ṣwh*[13] que Yahvé va a dar a Josué) sirve para que Josué escuche, en la tienda del encuentro, el discurso de Yahvé acerca de la

---

11. «Vv. 3a and 3b are parallel, the former being a pious editor's attribution to YHWH of the action the latter attributes to Joshua with, of course, divine help. In this sense, v. 3a is a subtle anticipation of v. 8»: J. D. LEVENSON, *Who Inserted the Book of the Torah?*, en *HTR* 68 (1975) 203-233, p. 209.

12. Cf. C. SCHÄFER-LICHTENBERGER, *Joshua und Salomo. Eine Studie zu Autorität und Legitimität des Nachfolgers im Alten Testament* (SVT, 58), Leiden - New York, NY - Köln, Brill, 1995, pp. 181-184.

13. Acerca del significado de *ṣwh* en el Antiguo Testamento y, de modo particular, en relación con la misión de Josué, cf. F. GARCÍA LÓPEZ, *ṣwh*, en H.-J. FABRY - H. RINGGREN (eds.), *TWAT*, VI, Stuttgart - Berlin - Köln, Kohlhammer, 1989, cc. 936-959; ID., *Deuteronomio 31* (n. 1), p. 79.

futura apostasía de Israel (vv. 16-21). A la luz del mismo, Josué tomará conciencia del pecado del pueblo al que tendrá que guiar. Esto repercutirá, lógicamente, en el modo de comprender y abordar su misión.

Con la ruptura de la alianza y la apostasía de Israel en el horizonte, la presencia de Yahvé en medio de Israel y su asistencia a Josué adquieren también un valor añadido. Las circunstancias en que Josué guiará a Israel son equiparables a las de Moisés cuando tuvo que guiar a Israel tras la apostasía del Horeb (Ex 32). Así lo confirma una comparación entre Ex 33,1-17 y Dt 31,14-23: en ambos pasajes no sólo está en juego la presencia divina en medio del pueblo, debido al pecado de éste (cf. Ex 33,1-6 y Dt 31,16-17), sino también la asistencia de Yahvé a Moisés y a Josué (cf. Ex 33,14 y Dt 31,23)[14]. La fórmula *w'nky 'hyh 'mk*, mediante la que Yahvé promete su personal asistencia a Josué (cf. Dt 31,23), evoca la empleada en el relato de la vocación de Moisés (cf. Ex 3,12; 4,12.15)[15].

Según Dt 31,14-23, Josué posee el mismo rango que Moisés, no así según 31,1-8. Desde el relato de su vocación hasta el final de su vida, Moisés aparece investido como jefe y profeta a la vez (cf. Ex 3,10.16; Dt 34,10-12)[16]. La suya es una misión especial, que hace de él «un fondé de pouvoir». Los textos que mejor explican su singularidad pertenecen fundamentalmente a las tradiciones nórdicas: Os 12, los ciclos de Elías y Eliseo, el Deuteronomio y Jeremías. En cuanto a Josué, el modelo seguido para su investidura es el de la vocación de Eliseo, sucesor de Elías en el oficio profético. Josué es el primer profeta semejante a Moisés y juega un papel similar al suyo. En la investidura de Josué se dejan entrever, asimismo, los rasgos de jefe y profeta[17].

A lo dicho a propósito de Dt 31,14-23, hay que añadir el testimonio de Dt 34,9: «Josué, hijo de Nun, estaba lleno del espíritu de sabiduría» (*rwḥ ḥkmh*). Dicho espíritu es un don divino para el gobierno de Israel. Isaías anuncia un futuro rey sobre el que reposará el «espíritu de sabiduría...» / *rwḥ ḥkmh*... (Is 11,2). Cuando Salomón sucede en el trono a su padre David, pide a Dios el don de la sabiduría para gobernar la nación. La petición agrada a Dios, que le concede un «corazón sabio»

---

14. Para otros detalles sobre estos textos, ver mi artículo sobre, *Deuteronomio 31* (n. 1), pp. 77-79.

15. Sobre la relación de Dt 31 y Ex 32, cf. E.H. MERRILL, *Deuteronomy* (NAC, 4), Nashville, TN, Broadman & Holman, 1994, p. 401, n. 11.

16. Cf. F. GARCÍA LÓPEZ, *El Moisés histórico y el Moisés de la fe*, en *Salmanticensis* 36 (1989) 5-21; ID., *Deut. 34, Dtr History and the Pentateuch*, en F. GARCÍA MARTÍNEZ - A. HILHORST *et al.* (eds.), *Studies in Deuteronomy in Honour of C. J. Labuschagne* (SVT, 53), Leiden - New York, NY, - Köln, Brill, 1994, pp. 47-61.

17. Cf. B. RENAUD, *La figure prophétique de Moïse en Exode 3,1-4,17*, en *RB* 93 (1986) 510-534; F. GARCÍA LÓPEZ, *Deuteronomio 31* (n. 1), pp. 78-82.

/ *lb ḥkm* (1 Re 3,7-12; cf. 4,29; 5,12; 7,14). A las semejanzas formales y temáticas entre los relatos de los últimos momentos de Moisés y de David (comparar Dt 31,14-16 con 1 Re 2,1-10*)[18], hay que añadir las semejanzas entre los primeros momentos de liderazgo de Josué y Salomón, sucesores respectivamente de Moisés y de David. Ambos estarán dotados de un espíritu / corazón sabio para el gobierno de Israel.

Tanto Josué como Salomón deberán, además, seguir fielmente la «enseñanza» (*tôrah*) de Yahvé / Moisés. Esta es una cualidad que, según el Deuteronomio y la Historia Deuteronomista, ha de caracterizar a los jefes / reyes de Israel (cf. § V).

IV. LA ESCRITURA DE LA TÔRAH

1. La muerte inminente de Moisés ocasiona el nacimiento de la *tôrah* escrita. La primera referencia en el Deuteronomio a la escritura de la *tôrah* se enmarca precisamente en el contexto de la muerte de Moisés. En Dt 31,9, se dice que 'Moisés escribió la *tôrah*': *wyktb mšh 't-htwrh hz't*. A continuación se prescribe leerla periódicamente ante todo Israel (*mqṣ šbˤ šnym ... tqrʾ 't-htwrh hz't ngd kl-yśrʾl bʾznyhm*: 31,10-11*) Éste la escuchará y observará, aprendiendo así a respetar a Yahvé: ... *lmˤn yšmˤw wlmˤn ylmdw wyrʾw 't-yhwh 'lhykm wšmrw lˤswt 't-kl-dbry htwrh hz't* (31,12b).

Las alusiones a la *tôrah* se continúan en los vv. 24-27, tras la interrupción de los vv. 14-23, referentes a la investidura de Josué y al Cántico de Moisés. El narrador, después de decir que «Moisés escribió este cántico y lo enseñó a los israelitas» (31,22), añade que, cuando Moisés acabó de escribir completamente las palabras de esta *tôrah*, dio orden a los levitas de que tomaran el libro de la *tôrah* y lo colocaran junto al arca de la alianza como testimonio contra Israel: *wyhy kklwt mšh lktb 't-dbry htwrh-hz't 'l-spr ˤd tmm wyṣw mšh 't-hlwym... lʾmr lqḥ 't spr htwrh hzh wśmtm 'tw mṣd 'rwn bryt-yhwh 'lhykm whyh-šm bk lˤd* (31,24-25*).

Al final de la sección, en Dt 32,46, aún sonará una vez más el término *tôrah* en una invitación apremiante de Moisés a todo Israel para que grabe en su corazón todas las palabras con las que testimonia contra ellos y mande a sus hijos que cumplan cuidadosamente todos los términos de esta *tôrah*: *śymw lbbkm lkl hdbrym 'šr 'nky mˤyd bkm hywm 'šr tṣwm 't -bnykm lšmr lˤśwt 't-kl-dbry htwrh hz't*.

Después de la serie de referencias que acabamos de reseñar, es obligado reconocer que la *tôrah* reviste una importancia singular en los

---

18. Consultar mi artículo sobre *Deuteronomio 31* (n. 1), p. 77.

últimos capítulos del Deuteronomio. No se trata, ciertamente, de una «ley» o «enseñanza» cualquiera, sino de un documento bien delimitado y preciso - el libro de la *tôrah* o libro del Deuteronomio - que servirá de contraseña, tras la muerte de Moisés, para todos los israelitas.

Con la *tôrah-Deuteronomio* comienzan a sentarse las bases de lo que será luego la *tôrah-Pentateuco*. La *tôrah* transmitida primero oralmente y luego por escrito por Moisés, se convertirá en normativa para todo Israel. Este paso es de tal envergadura para la vida de la comunidad, que merece ser analizado más detalladamente. Para ello, tomamos como punto de partida los textos de Dt 31-34, pero extenderemos el análisis a todo el Deuteronomio y a la Historia Deuteronomista.

2. En el Deuteronomio se encuentra uno de los núcleos más consistentes y significativos del Antiguo Testamento sobre la *tôrah*. Su radio de acción no se limita a este libro, sino que se extiende al menos a toda la Historia Deuteronomista (Josué-Reyes) y a la Historia Cronista (Esdras, Nehemías y Crónicas).

En el libro del Deuteronomio se acuñan dos expresiones nuevas para referirse a la *tôrah*: *spr htwrh* y *dbry htwrh*; ambas reaparecerán en las Historias Deuteronomista y Cronista. La primera, *spr htwrh* / «el libro de la *tôrah*», se halla estrechamente relacionada con las afirmaciones de Dt 31,9-12, relativas a la escritura de la *tôrah*. Todas las alusiones a la *tôrah* en Dt 31,1-32,47 se refieren directa o indirectamente al libro del Deuteronomio, entendido como *tôrah*. En 31,9ss, se presupone el libro del Deuteronomio como un todo fijo y conocido; no sólo resalta la importancia de la *tôrah*, sino también el hecho de que ésta se escriba y permanezca, se lea y se observe.

Una enseñanza o ley de esta naturaleza, fijada por escrito y designada como «libro de la *tôrah*», corresponde a los últimos estadios de la redacción del Deuteronomio, más concretamente a la redacción deuteronomista. A esta misma redacción se deben también las referencias al arca de la alianza, junto a la cual se ha de custodiar el libro de la *tôrah* (Dt 31,25).

Las diferentes expresiones del Deuteronomio sobre la *tôrah* remiten, por regla general, a la serie de normas, leyes, instrucciones, etc., dadas por Yahvé a Israel mediante Moisés. Aunque en el Deuteronomio nunca se emplean las fórmulas *twrt mšh* o *twrt yhwh*, por el tenor de todo el libro queda claro que las palabras de la *tôrah* son proclamadas por Moisés y que remontan, en última instancia, a Yahvé.

La *tôrah*, en esta perspectiva, aparece como el conjunto codificado de todas estas enseñanzas y directrices divino-mosaicas. En la misma dirección apuntan también las restantes expresiones de la Historia

Deuteronomista. En ésta, la *tôrah* suele asociarse explícitamente con Moisés (cf. Jos 1,7; 8,32; 22,5; 1 Re 2,3; 2 Re 21,8; 23,25) o con Yahvé (cf. 2 Re 10,31; 17,13.34.37).

Para el Deuteronomista, «el libro de la *tôrah*» (de Yahvé o de Moisés) designa el Deuteronomio, libro que se halla colocado en cabeza de la Historia Deuteronomista como prólogo y espejo de cuanto sigue. Es el libro encontrado en el templo de Jerusalén en tiempos de Josías (cf. 2 Re 22-23). Otra se le denomina el «libro de la *tôrah*» otra el «libro de la *berît*» (cf. 2 Re 22,8.11; 23,2.3.21.24)[19]. En cualquiera de las denominaciones, aparece como un documento escrito, cuyo contenido exacto no es fácil precisar, si bien todos los indicios invitan a pensar que se trata substancialmente de una versión primitiva del libro del Deuteronomio.

La importancia atribuida a este libro en 2 Re 22-23 es tal que da la impresión de que todas las medidas adoptadas por el rey arrancan de dicho libro. Por primera vez en la historia de la monarquía - si damos crédito a 2 Re 23,1-3 - todo el pueblo se comprometió a observar las obligaciones contenidas en ese documento. Es la primera ocasión en que un libro, el *spr htwrh* (= *spr hbryt*), es considerado como la base constitutiva y normativa de la comunidad judía[20].

La segunda expresión, *dbry htwrh*, aunque diferente de la anteriormente comentada, se halla próxima a ella en varios particulares. Ante todo, hay que subrayar que es típica del Deuteronomio: de las 12 veces que ocurre en Deuteronomio-Reyes, 9 pertenecen al Deuteronomio. En Dt 17,9; 27,3.8; 28,58; 29,28; 31,12; 32,46 y en Jos 8,13, dicha expresión va precedida de *kl*, dando a entender que no se trata de palabras aisladas, sino de un todo.

En la mayoría de los textos que acabamos de citar se hace referencia expresa a «palabras *escritas*». Se remite, por tanto, a un documento o escrito del mismo tenor que el reflejado en la fórmula *spr htwrh*. Además, en 2 Re 22,11 se emplea la fórmula compuesta *dbry spr htwrh*; análogamente, en Dt 31,24 y 2 Re 23,24, donde falta el *kl*, la expresión *dbry htwrh* se refiere a un libro. Ahora bien, si las *dbry htwrh* de Dt 31,24 no son otras que las de 2 Re 23,24, el *spr htwrh* de Dt 31,25 es, consiguientemente, el mismo de 2 Re 22,8ss. En este sentido, la expresión *dbry htwrh*, por cuanto a su significado y alcance se refiere, se aproxima mucho a la expresión *spr htwrh*.

19. Cf. F. GARCÍA LÓPEZ, *Le Deutéronome. Une loi prêchée* (CE, 63), Paris, Cerf, 1988, pp. 5,16.

20. Cf. M. COGAN - H. TADMOR, *II Kings* (AB, 11), New York, NY, Doubleday, 1988, p. 296; Y. KAUFMAN, *The Religion of Israel: From Its Beginnings to the Babylonian Exile*, Chicago, IL, University of Chicago Press, 1960, p. 175.

Por otro lado, si se prescinde del término que denota totalidad (kl) y de los textos en que se habla específicamente de escribir (ktb), la expresión dbry htwrh invita a pensar asimismo en los artículos concretos de la ley, en plural e individualmente considerados[21], que muy bien pudieran tener su origen en la tradición oral. Conviene recordar, a este respecto, que el Deuteronomio se presenta como un discurso de Moisés, bajo el título 'lh hdbrym.

Aparte de las dos expresiones que acabamos de comentar, en Dt 31,1-32,47 y en otros textos del Deuteronomio se usa una tercera: htwrh hz't (cf. 1,5; 4,8; 31,9.11). La concreción hz't tiene por función determinar el libro del Deuteronomio como punto de referencia de la tôrah. De este modo, se está poniendo de manifiesto el carácter sintetizador y globalizante de esta expresión. En Dt 17,18-19, además de htwrh hz't (v. 18), se emplea con idéntico sentido la expresión kl-dbry-htwrh hz't (v. 19). El rey, cuando se siente en el trono, deberá escribir una copia de esta tôrah en un libro: wktb lw 't-mšnh htwrh 'l-hspr (cf. Jos 8,32). La expresión htwrh hz't posee, por consiguiente, un significado equivalente al de las otras dos expresiones: spr htwrh y dbry htwrh.

3. En el Deuteronomio, como acabamos de mostrar, han cristalizado diversas formulaciones sobre la tôrah. En ellas se puede sentir el eco de las diferentes corrientes que confluyen en el libro. El Deuteronomio es una encrucijada: a él llegan las tradiciones primitivas del Tetrateuco y de él parten las redacciones deuteronomistas. Las vías del Deuteronomio, además, se cruzan con las de la literatura profética y sapiencial.

a) La expresión dbry htwrh -típica del Deuteronomio- guarda cierta conexión con la tôrah en los profetas[22]. Por de pronto, el término dabar, característico de los profetas (cf. Jer 18,18), tiene gran peso en el Deuteronomio. Aparece ya en el mismo título del libro: 'lh hdbrym 'šr dbr mšh (1,1a). Por otro lado, Moisés es presentado como el más grande profeta (Dt 34,10-12) y como prototipo de una serie de profetas que vendrán tras él (Dt 18,15-22). En este último texto, precisamente en relación con la actividad profética, se hace hincapié en el término dabar, estableciéndose además una conexión con el Horeb (cf. Dt 5). En Dt 18,15ss y 5,5.22, se presenta a Moisés como el gran mediador entre Dios y el pueblo: Moisés escucha a Yahvé y comunica al pueblo cuanto Él le dice o manda.

---

21. Cf. L. MONSENGWO PASINYA, La notion de nomos dans le Pentateuque grec (AnBib, 52), Rome, Biblical Institute Press, 1973, pp. 84-85.

22. Acerca de la tôrah en los profetas, cf. F. GARCÍA LÓPEZ, tôrah, en H.-J. FABRY & H. RINGGREN (eds.), TWAT, VIII, Stuttgart - Berlin - Köln, Kohlhammer 1995, cc. 597-637 (611-18).

La expresión *dbry htwrh*, en la perspectiva anteriormente señalada, representa la síntesis de las palabras y órdenes de Yahvé. No se trata simplemente de «leyes», sino del conjunto de la voluntad de Dios: su punto de arranque está en el Horeb y su plena manifestación en los mandamientos y enseñanzas que de allí dimanan. Lo mismo que en Ex 18,15ss los oráculos divinos se traducen en una serie de preceptos y *tôrôt*, que Moisés transmite al pueblo, en el Deuteronomio los *dbry htwrh* son la manifestación de la voluntad divina, que llega al pueblo por medio de Moisés. En la expresión *dbry htwrh* se puede percibir el eco de la enseñanza *oral* de Moisés.

b) Por el contrario, en la expresión *spr htwrh* se refleja la enseñanza *escrita*. Las expresiones *dbry htwrh* y *spr htwrh* evocan momentos diferentes en la tradición, lo que podría justificar - al menos en parte - su variación en el libro del Deuteronomio. De los *dbry htwrh*, además, se dice en algunos textos que han sido consignados por escrito (cf. § 2). Estamos, por tanto, ante un tipo de enseñanza que, si bien en un determinado momento pudo haber sido oral, ahora se presenta codificada por escrito. Se logra así la síntesis de una concepción y de una práctica parcialmente preexistentes.

Efectivamente, en Is 8,16 y Os 8,12 se establece ya cierta conexión entre una forma oral de la enseñanza / *tôrah* profética y su forma escrita[23]. Posiblemente se encuentran aquí los primeros testimonios de una escritura canónica codificada. Un documento-*tôrah* que invita a pensar en otros documentos del género, como los mencionados en 2 Re 22-23. Asimismo en Ex 24,7 se hace referencia a un *spr hbryt*, expresión coincidente con la utilizada en 2 Re 23,2-21, de cuya intercambiabilidad con la expresión *spr htwrh* ya hemos hablado en el § 2.

Además, las fórmulas de Deuteronomio-Reyes referentes a un *spr htwrh* - particularmente las que especifican *spr twrt yhwh* / *'lhym*- cuentan con claros antecedentes en la literatura profética (ver Is 1,10[24]; Os 4,6; Jer 8,8; etc.). El paso de las fórmulas proféticas a las deuteronómico-deuteronomistas se realiza mediante la expresión *bspr*. Consiguientemente, la fórmula *bspr twrt x* del Deuteronomio y de la Historia Deuteronomista tiene un valor sintetizador y globalizante, mientras que las de los profetas aparecen más bien como enseñanzas individuales y concretas.

---

23. Cabe señalar aquí la conexión que se establece en Is 8,16.20 entre la «enseñanza» / *tôrah* y el «testimonio» / *t'wdh* del profeta, comparable, en cierto modo, a la de Dt 31,26.28.

24. Sobre las conexiones de este texto con Dt 31, ver mi artículo *Deuteronomio 31* (n. 1), p. 83.

c) En la *tôrah*, tal como ocurre en el Deuteronomio, se reflejan algunos rasgos didáctico-sapienciales importantes (aparte de los legales y proféticos). Según Foresti, la elección de la *tôrah* para designar la instrucción mosaica se debe a una comprensión sapiencial del último ministerio de Moisés. Un punto de apoyo para esta afirmación se encuentra en Dt 1,5; 4,44; 31,9.11, textos particularmente afines con el uso y significado de *tôrah* en los discursos didácticos de Prov 1-9[25].

Conviene notar que, en los cuatro pasajes del Deuteronomio que acabamos de citar, el término *tôrah* va acompañado únicamente de *hz't*, sin formar parte de una relación constructa con *dbry* o *spr*. La fórmula de Dt 1,5 (*...hw'yl mšh b'r 't-htwrh hz't*) ofrece la imagen de un Moisés-escriba que, preocupado por la transmisión de 'su enseñanza', redacta una primera copia de la misma[26]. El verbo *b'r*, comúnmente traducido por «explicar» o «interpretar», no puede separarse de la idea de «escribir» o «grabar» (ver Dt 27,8; Hab 2,2), de modo que Moisés aparece aquí como si estuviera haciendo un borrador de su enseñanza. Este versículo, difícil de encuadrar en estrato alguno del Deuteronomio o de la Historia Deuteronomista[27], posiblemente se inspire en Dt 1,1a; 27,8 y trate de corregir la concepción según la cual la forma escrita de la ley apareció después del asentamiento de Israel en la tierra. De aquí que se presente a Moisés como un escriba y no como un orador. Esta concepción se expone sin paliativos en Dt 31,9ss, donde se afirma que Moisés escribió esta *tôrah* y la entregó a los sacerdotes levitas.

En la perspectiva señalada, la *tôrah* se revela como la última y la más genérica de todas las expresiones para indicar lo que escribió Moisés[28]. Dt 1,5, colocado en cabeza del libro, y 4,44, con una función semejante, muestran claramente el deseo de redefinir todo el Deuteronomio como *tôrah*. Pero en 1,5 el término *tôrah* precede inmediatamente a una síntesis histórica y en 4,44 antecede a otro título en el que se dan cita los términos *ḥqym wmšptym* (4,45), con los que se caracterizará el cuerpo legal deuteronómico (cf. 12,1). Entre 4,44-45 y 12,1, por otro lado, se encuentra una serie de amonestaciones, exhortaciones, etc., de distinto tenor que las leyes del código legal deuteronómico. Finalmente, en 31,9.11 se sintetiza todo lo que precede.

25. Cf. F. Foresti, *Il Deuteronomio: nascita della Torah come proposta di sapienza*, in A. Fanuli (ed.), *Spienza e Torah. Atti della XXIX Settimana Biblica*, Bologna, 1987, pp. 17-30, esp. 22-23.
26. Cf. S. Mittmann, *Deuteronomium 1,1–6,3 literarkritisch und traditionsgeschichtlich untersucht* (BZAW, 139), Berlin - New York, NY, de Gruyter, 1975, pp. 13-14; A.D.H. Mayes, *Deuteronomy* (NCeB), Grand Rapids, MI, Eerdmans; London: Marshall, Morgan & Scott, 1979, p. 116.
27. Cf. S. Mittmann, *Deuteronomium 1,1–6,3* (n. 26), pp. 13-15,184.
28. Cf. L. Perlitt, *Bundestheologie* (n. 7), p. 117.

A la luz de estos datos, parece evidente que el término *tôrah* - si con él se pretende redefinir y sintetizar todo el Deuteronomio (= *htwrh hz't* / *wz't htwrh*) - ha de tener un significado suficientemente amplio y comprensivo. Traducir *tôrah* por «ley» sería, a juzgar por lo dicho, insuficiente. «Enseñanza» podría ser más exacto, pero sin excluir otros términos que, al menos en determinados casos, pueden definirla mejor. Las conexiones de Dt 1,5; 4,44 y 31,9.11 con la actividad escribal y con los discursos didácticos de Prov 1-9 nos ayudarán a precisar el sentido y el alcance de la *tôrah*.

Según Driver, en hebreo hay que distinguir dos verbos *yrh*: uno relacionado con el etíope *warawa* (arrojar) y el otro con el acádico *(w)aru* / ugarítico *yr(y)* (ir), que en su forma causativa significa «hacer ir», «guiar», «liderar»[29]. De aquí, McKane deduce que el verbo *yrh* - y el substantivo que de él deriva: *tôrah* - en el libro de los Proverbios tiene el sentido de «guide»: «...where the Instruction is presented as a way of life, it is admirably described as *tora*, and the word has appeared in such contexts (1,8; 3,1). If *miswa* is to be correlated with the imperious form of the Instruction and *musar* with its character as a educational discipline, *tora* can be associated with the presentation of Instructions as a way of life; it contains directions for the road of a mandatory kind, that is, directives»[30].

El Deuteronomio se presenta, en primer lugar, como un discurso de Moisés en los umbrales de la tierra prometida (1,1-4). Su redefinición como *tôrah* (1,5; 4,44) significa que, según los editores, en este discurso programático se trazan las directrices para vivir en la tierra. Moisés aparece como un maestro, sabio y experimentado, mostrando a los israelitas el camino que conduce a la vida. Desde este ángulo de mira, la *tôrah* es una enseñanza sobre el modo de vivir en la tierra. Enseñanza autoritativa, en la que se contienen normas de vida, leyes que tienen su origen en el Horeb (*dbry htwrh*). Vienen de Dios a través de la mediación de Moisés, el más grande profeta y legislador. Enseñanza que ha sido recogida en un documento, codificada en un libro (*bspr htwrh*).

Un libro que ha de ser leído y estudiado por todo el pueblo, desde el rey hasta el último israelita. En él aprenderán a temer a Yahvé y a poner en práctica todas las palabras de la *tôrah* (cf. Dt 17,18-19; 31,12). Un libro o documento que ha de ser conservado junto al arca de la alianza, para que sirva de testimonio contra Israel (Dt 31,24-29), de modo que no pueda alegar ignorancia de los caminos de Dios. Testimonio, en fin, para

---

29. Cf. G. R. DRIVER, *Hebrew Notes*, en *VT* 1 (1951) 241-250, pp. 249-250.
30. Cf. W. MCKANE, *Proverbs. A New Approach* (OTL), London, SCM Press, 1980, p. 308.

que todos los israelitas observen las palabras de la *tôrah* (32,46). Palabras de gran importancia, pues de ellas depende la vida de Israel, la prolongación de sus días sobre la tierra que, una vez pasado el Jordán, van a tomar en posesión (Dt 32,47).

V. Moisés, Josué, los Reyes de Israel y la Tôrah

Al principio y al final de la Historia Deuteronomista descuellan respectivamente las figuras de *Moisés* y de *Josías*. Si del primero se afirma que «no surgió en Israel otro profeta como Moisés» (Dt 34,10), del último se dice que 'no hubo otro rey como Josías' (2 Re 23,25). Ambos mostraron un mismo celo respecto de la *tôrah*: Moisés mandó que se leyera «a los oídos de Israel» (Dt 31,11) y Josías la leyó 'a oídos de todo Israel' (2 Re 23,2).

Entre ambos extremos de la Historia Deuteronomista destacan otras figuras, cuya misión respecto de la *tôrah*, no pasa inadvertida a los redactores deuteronomistas. Hay que mencionar, en primer lugar, a *Josué*, sucesor y continuador de la obra de Moisés a la par que predecesor y prototipo de los reyes de Israel (cf. Jos 1,7-8 y 1 Re 2,1-4). El Deuteronomista parece impaciente por mostrar a Josué poniendo en práctica, al pie de la letra, las instrucciones de Moisés sobre el cumplimiento y la proclamación de la *tôrah* (Jos 8,30-35). La colocación de Dt 31,14-23 entre 31,9-13 y 24-27, separando las referencias que en éstos se hace a la *tôrah*, da a entender que Josué tiene que liderar al pueblo en el marco de la *tôrah*. Más aún, el mismo Josué -presente con Moisés en el encuentro teofánico- recibe el encargo de contribuir a escribir / completar la *tôrah*: *w'th ktbw lkm hšrh hz't* (Dt 31,19; ver 31,24).

El Historiador Deuteronomista, a su vez, enfatiza la importancia que tiene para Josué la obediencia personal a la *tôrah* de Moisés (Jos 1,7-8). Si importante es el papel público y oficial del rey respecto de la *tôrah*, no menos lo es el personal y privado. Esta misma concepción late en los otros textos deuteronomistas. En efecto, la *tôrah* escrita ocupa un lugar central en la teología deuteronomista, convirtiéndose en el criterio de valoración de los reyes de Israel (cf. 1 Re 2,3; 2 Re 10,31; 14,6; 21,8; 23,24-25). Este criterio es extensible también a Josué (Jos 1,7-8) y al pueblo (Jos 8,31; 22,5; 23,6; 2 Re 17,13.34.37)[31].

1 Re 2,1-4, al transmitir el encargo de *David* a *Salomón*, evoca Dt 17,18-20 y Jos 1,7-9 (cf. Jos 8,30-35; 23-24). Las mismas expectativas

---

31. Cf. G. von Rad, *Theologie des Alten Testaments. I. Die Theologie der geschichtlichen Überlieferungen Israels* (Einführung in die evangelische Theologie, 1), München, Kaiser, ⁵1966, pp. 351-352.

puestas antes en Josué, respecto de la *tôrah*, se trasfieren ahora a Salomón y más tarde a Josías. Todos ellos han de cumplir su misión en conformidad con la *tôrah*. De la obediencia a ésta depende su éxito y el de todo el pueblo.

Como contraprueba, cabe recordar otras figuras especialmente significativas en la Historia Deuteronomista. *Jeroboán* y *Manasés* representan el lado opuesto de Josué y Josías. Ambos tenían que guiar al pueblo a la obediencia a la *tôrah*, a la fidelidad a la *berît*. Pero ni Jeroboán ni Manasés lo hicieron así, siendo responsables, en última instancia, del pecado de los reinos de Israel y de Judá respectivamente (cf. 2 Re 17,7-23, de modo especial el v. 13, y 2 Re 21,2-8, particularmente el v. 8).

En conclusión, los textos deuteronomistas sobre la *tôrah* ponen de relieve no sólo la importancia que ésta tiene en sí, sino también la trascendencia de su aceptación o rechazo por parte de los responsables del pueblo. Sobre esta *tôrah*, como norma fija, se asentará la vida del pueblo, pasando a ser uno de los pilares de la comunidad israelítico-judía. En ella se encuentran las directrices para vivir en la tierra, tras la muerte de Moisés. Josué será el primero en seguirlas.

Universidad Pontificia   Félix García López
Compañía, 5
E-37002 Salamanca

DIE PRIESTERSCHRIFT
UND DIE GESCHICHTEN DER DEUTERONOMISTEN

Man kann den Gegensatz zwischen P-Tradition und D-Tradition nicht scharf genug fassen[1]. Jedenfalls waren die zelotischen Nachfahren der Deuteronomisten dieser Meinung, als sie die sadduzäischen Erben der Priesterschrift mit den Argument der schärferen Schwerter widerlegten[2].

1. Die Entstehung der Tora als Corpus »öffentlichen Rechts« ist historisch nur verständlich unter den Bedingungen der persischen Innen- und Religionspolitik: Jerusalem wurde innenpolitische Autonomie und Selbstverwaltung angeboten unter der Voraussetzung, daß die »väterlichen Gesetze und Bräuche« der Zentralregierung schriftlich vorgelegt wurden, um auf ihre Verträglichkeit mit dem Bestand und dem inneren Frieden des Imperiums überprüft und vom Großkönig als Reichsrecht für die betreffende Körperschaft in Kraft gesetzt zu werden. Die literarische und theologische Spannung zwischen P und D reflektiert also einen politischen Konflikt zwischen zwei »Religionsparteien«, die Tora in ihrer Endgestalt einen gemeinsamen Verfassungsentwurf, der im kontroversen Gespräch als Kompromiß ausgehandelt wurde; vgl. P. FREI, *Zentralgewalt und Lokalautonomie im Achämenidenreich*, in P. FREI – K. KOCH (eds.), *Reichsidee und Reichsorganisation im Perserreich* (OBO, 55), Freiburg/Schweiz, Göttingen, Universitätsverlag, Vandenhoeck & Ruprecht, ²1996, pp. 5-131; R. ALBERTZ, *Religionsgeschichte Israels in alttestamentlicher Zeit II* (GAT, 8/2), Göttingen, Vandenhoeck & Ruprecht, 1992, pp. 497-504; E.A. KNAUF, *Die Umwelt des Alten Testament* (NSKAT, 29), Stuttgart, Katholisches Bibelwerk, 1994, pp. 171-175. Das Ausmaß wirtschaftlicher, rechtlicher und religiöser Autonomie, das die Zentralregierung zu gewähren pflegte, ist an nichts anderem so gut abzulesen wie an den Münzen, die im Achämenidenreich geprägt wurden; cf. L. MILDENBERG, *Vestigia Leonis* (NTOA, 36), Freiburg/Schweiz, Göttingen, Universitätsverlag, Vandenhoeck & Ruprecht, 1998, pp. 3-97 und 127-135. Was an der Berücksichtigung »sozialgeschichtlicher Entwicklungen theologisch«-»soziologisch innerjüdischer und vor allem rechtlich«-»persischer Provenienz« »einseitig« sein soll (so T. POLA, *Die ursprüngliche Priesterschrift. Beobachtungen zur Literarkritik und Traditionsgeschichte von Pg* [WMANT, 70], Neukirchen-Vluyn, Neukirchener Verlag, 1995, p. 48 Anm. 164), leuchtet nicht ein; der Vorwurf der Einseitigkeit trifft wohl eher die Suche nach »textinterne«(»n«) »Gründe«(»n«) »theologischer Art«, »die zur Zusammenarbeit nötigten« (*ibid.*). Hätte P die modern-theologische Berührungsangst vor Wirtschaft, Gesellschaft und Politik geteilt, hätte er gar nicht erst geschrieben. Über sein altorientalisches Erbe hinaus, in dem eine gottlose Welt undenkbar war, hat er das orientalische und biblische Verständnis eines die Welt nicht nur geschaffen habenden, sondern auch fürderhin beanspruchenden Gottes in neue Tiefen geführt (s.u. zu Gen 9). Christliche, von der Menschwerdung Gottes her denkende Theologie vollzieht sich schon gar nicht im luftleeren, »textinternen« Raum.
2. Damit soll keineswegs eine mehrhundertjährige Geschichte der »deuteronomistischen Bewegung« impliziert sein, die nach N. LOHFINK, *Gab es eine deuteronomistische Bewegung?* in W. GROSS (ed.), *Jeremia und die deuteronomistische Beurgung* (BBB, 98), Weinheim, Beltz, 1995, pp. 313-382; = ID., *Studien zum Deuteronomium und zur deuteronomistischen Literatur III* (SBAAT, 20) Stuttgart, Katholisches Bibelwerk, 1995, pp. 65-142, so nicht existiert hat. Hinzuweisen ist aber auf ein oft verdrängtes Moment der Wirkungs- und Rezeptionsgeschichte des Deuteronomismus. Über Lohfink hinaus wird man diejenigen Elemente des dtr Geschichtsbildes (wie Landnahme, Jhwh-Krieg, ewige Erwählung der Dynastie Davids und des Zion) für gruppenspezifisch halten und

Den Gegensatz so deutlich wie möglich zu fassen, dient der präziseren Beschreibung des theologischen Profils von P wie von D. Letztlich geht es bei ihrem Streit um Fragen, die alles andere als akademisch sind: Auf welche Weise ist der Gott Israels zugleich Gott der ganzen Welt? Wie verhält sich der Gott, der sich den Vätern offenbart hat, zum Gott, den auch die Philosophen bei rechtem Gebrauch ihrer Vernunft erkennen könnten – oder können sie es nicht? Was verlangt dieser Gott von seinem Volk mehr als jenes ethische Verhalten, das von allen Menschen immer und überall zu erwarten ist – oder verlangt er darüber hinaus nichts?

Ich beginne den folgenden knappen Überblick über das Verhältnis von P zu D mit (1) der grundlegenden priesterlichen Absage an den deuteronomistischen Gott in Gen 9,1-17; fahre fort mit (2) der Ansicht von P, wie man Geschichte schreiben soll; komme dann (3) zu P im Josua-Buch und schließe mit (4) dem Verhältnis von P zu Königen.

1. Genesis 9,1-17 oder: Gott hängt seine Rolle als Gott, der Assurs und Israels Kriege führte, an den Nagel und schließt eine ברית *mit aller Welt*

Der Widerspruch von P gegenüber dem deuteronomistischen Denken konzentriert sich in Gen 9. Er äußert sich in folgenden Punkten, die allesamt im Ganzen von P und D nicht marginal sind:

(a) Die ברית von D ist ein Vasallitätsvertrag, in dem Jhwh dem Volk Israel ein Land verleiht mit der Gegenleistung, sein Gesetz zu halten. Israel kann seinen Teil des Vertrages brechen und dadurch des Landes verlustig gehen.

Die ברית ist bei P eine einseitige Setzung Gottes allein aus Gnaden, zu der eine menschliche Mitwirkung weder nötig noch überhaupt möglich ist und die darum auch vom Menschen aus nicht infrage gestellt werden kann. Das leuchtet bei der Noach-Berit in Gen 9 unmittelbar ein und liegt strukturell auch der Abraham-Berit in Gen 17 zugrunde: daß Abraham in Gen 17 »Nein« sagen könnte, wird nicht einmal erwogen. Weil »Israel« bei P jedoch nicht auf natürlichen Weg aus dem Schöpfungssegen (Gen 1,28; 5*; 9,1.7; 10*) hervorgeht wie alle anderen Völker, sondern aus einer Setzung Gottes wider alle Natur (Gen 17,1.15-21)[3], bedarf die Zugehörigkeit zu Israel des menschlichen Nachvollzugs, der Beschneidung. Insofern hat der Einzelne durchaus die

---

insofern wechselnde Trägergruppen dtr Gedankengutes identifizieren dürfen, in Abgrenzung zu Stimmen oder Kreisen, die solche Überzeugungen noch nicht oder nicht mehr teilten.

3. Deswegen gibt es auch keine תולדת אברם.

Möglichkeit, diesen Nachvollzug zu verweigern und dann nicht zu Israel zu gehören (Gen 17,14). Ungehorsam ist im Schöpfungsordnungs-Denken von P keine Option; er ist weiter mit keinen Sanktionen bedroht, weil er *per se* unmittelbar zum Tode führt[4].

(b) Die ברית von D ergeht an Israel als Staatsvolk nach Analogie der assyrischen Vasallitätsverträge, die ihr als Vorbild gedient haben[5]. Israel muß sich seine staatlich-nationale Existenz durch Einhaltung dieses Vertrages je und je verdienen[6].

Die Gnaden-ברית von P ergeht in Gen 9 an die ganze Menschheit als Garantie des Bestandes der Welt und in Gen 17 an Abraham als Garantie des Bestandes des Gottesvolkes in der Welt[7]. Sie ergeht jeweils zu einer Zeit und in einer Situation, in der weder Israel noch die Menschheit sich diese Zusage verdienen oder sie gefährden können.

Die ברית von D ergeht am Horeb, zwischen dem Auszug aus Ägypten und dem Einzug ins Verheißene Land. Von diesen drei Momenten, die das dtr Israel konstituieren, ist sie das zentralste.

Die Gnaden-ברית von P ergeht am Ende der Schöpfung der Welt und am Anfang der Schöpfung Israels[8]. Sie ist grundlegend, aber nicht zen-

---

4. Der Ungehorsam der Sintflut-Generation (und zwar von Mensch wie Tier) gegen die Schöpfungsordnung Gen 1,29-30, der sich als »Gewalttat« äußert, ist aus Gen 6,11-13; 9,2-6 zu rekonstruieren, der unterdrückerische Ungehorsam Pharaos (kann man Ex 1,13f als Verstoß gegen Gen 1,26f verstehen?) führt ihn ins Rote Meer und nicht wieder heraus. Daß Pharao durch die »Prophetie« (Moses und) Aarons die Möglichkeit hätte, von seinem Irrtum abzulassen und es dennoch nicht tut, muß geschichtstheologisch erklärt werden (Ex 7,1-5; 14,4) – derart unverständlich ist Uneinsichtigkeit einem theologischen Rationalisten wie P. Nur der Ungehorsam Israels hat eine andere Qualität und wird sanktioniert: Num 14,27-29.35-37 (dazu N. LOHFINK, *Die Ursünden in der priesterlichen Geschichtserzählung*, in G. BORNKAMM & K. RAHNER [eds.], *Die Zeit Jesu. FS H. Schlier*, Freiburg, Herder, 1970, pp. 38-57 = ID., *Studien zum Pentateuch* [SBAAT, 4], Stuttgart, Katholisches Bibelwerk, 1988, pp. 169-189, esp. 184-186).
   5. N. LOHFINK, *Das Deuteronomium*, in ID., *Studien zum Deuteronomium und zur deuteronomistischen Literatur II* (SBAAT, 12), Stuttgart, Katholisches Bibelwerk, 1991, p. 221; KNAUF, *Umwelt*, pp. 132-135,
   6. Wo Texte der D-Tradition zum *sola gratia* vorstoßen (wie Gen 15; Dtn 9,4-6 u.ö), liegt die Annahme nach-priesterlicher dtr Texte nahe (D[P]); cf. zu Gen 15 C. LEVIN, *Der Jahwist* (FRLANT, 157), Göttingen, Vandenhoeck & Ruprecht, 1993, p. 151; T. RÖMER, *Genèse 15 et les tensions de la communauté juive postexilique dans le cycle d'Abraham*, Transeuphratène 7 (1994) 107-121. N. LOHFINK spricht im Falle von Dtn 7-9 von der »wechselseitigen Anpassung der noch getrennt existierenden Pentateuchquellen« (*Gewalt und Gewaltlosigkeit im Alten Testament* [QD, 96], Freiburg, Herder, pp. 94-96; = ID., *Studien zum Pentateuch* (SBAAT, 4), Stuttgart, Katholisches Bibelwerk, 1988, pp. 298-299).
   7. Der Landbesitz (Gen 17,8a; 35,12; 48,4; Ex 6,4.8; Num 13,2; 27,12; Jos 18,1) ist für die Existenz dieses wie jedes anderen Volkes (Gen 10,5.20.31; 36,9) mit Ausnahme der beduinischen Ismaeliter (Gen 25,16b) konstitutiv; was bei P »Gottesvolk« heißt, wird unter (e) präzisiert.
   8. Vgl. zu Gen 9,1-17 als Ende der Schöpfung die Rückverweise 9,1.7 → 1,28a-e; 9,2 → 1,28f-g; 9,3 → 1,29; 9,6b → 1,26-27; 9,10 → 8,18-19; 9,11 → 6,17. In Gen 9,1-17

tral. Zentral und damit am Sinai situiert ist bei P die Wohnsitznahme Gottes in Israel (Ex 29,43-46; 40,34-35), für P das Ziel von Schöpfung wie Geschichte.

(c) Bei D erhält Israel sein Land als נחלה »Lehen«[9] und kann es darum im Ungehorsams-Fall wieder verlieren. Bei P ist das Land אחזה »Eigentum« (Gen 17,8a) und kann insofern von Gott nicht mehr zurückgenommen werden[10].

(d) Bei D ist das Halten eines Gesetzes mit privatrechtlichen, öffentlich-rechtlichen, staatsrechtlichen und kirchenrechtlichen Bestimmungen Inhalt der ברית.

Bei P(g) hingegen gibt es mit zweieinhalb[11] Ausnahmen keinerlei »Gesetz« und sofern doch, eher als »Naturgesetz« denn als »Sittengesetz«. Der Sabbat etwa wird nirgends geboten, sondern als letztes »Werk« (oder eben Nicht-Werk) der Schöpfung gestiftet (Gen 2,2-3) und von Israel in der Wüste (Ex 16) entdeckt. Bei P gibt es keinen Gegensatz zwischen göttlichen Anweisungen, die sich auf die Natur beziehen (wie Gen 1,3.6.9.11.14.20.24; Ex 14,16) und solchen, die menschliches Verhalten (wie Gen 1,29; Ex 14,16) regeln.

Die beiden »Gesetze« im landläufigen Sinn, die bei P ergehen, stehen außerhalb einer ברית: das in Gen 9,3 abrogierte Gebot von Gen 1,29, Korn- und Baumfrucht zu essen, und das Verbot von Blutgenuß und Mord in Gen 9,4-6[12]. Praktisch ist das Verbot, zu morden, das einzige

---

redet Gott zum letztenmal zu einem Menschen, ohne dazu erscheinen zu müssen (anders dann 17,1; 35,9; Ex 2,25b [txt. em. ויודע אלהים למשה als Einleitung zu 6,2]).

9. Vgl. ugaritisch *nḥlt* »Lehen« und sabäisch *nḥl* (G und H) »verpachten«, »ausleihen«.

10. Anders im »Heiligkeitsgesetz« Lev 25,23, das ebenso eine Neubearbeitung des dtn Gesetzes seitens der P-Schule wie die Rezeption dtr Theologumena seitens dieser Schule darstellt; cf. N. LOHFINK, *Die Schichten des Pentateuch und der Krieg* (QD, 96), Freiburg, Herder, 1983, pp. 51-110; = ID., *Studien zum Pentateuch*, pp. 255-315, esp. 298f.

11. Die halbe Ausnahme ist die Beschneidungsforderung in Gen 17,10-14, die sich kaum als »Gesetz« verstehen läßt (s.o. unter [a]). – Gegen N. LOHFINK, *Die Priesterschrift und die Geschichte* (SVT, 29), Leiden, Brill, 1979, pp. 189-225; = ID., *Studien zum Pentateuch*, pp. 213-253, bes. 222 Anm. 29 gehören die »Tafeln des Zeugnisses« Ex 31,18; 34,29b nicht zu P^g, in dessen Kontext sie funktionslos sind. Ex 29,43-46 ist ein, wenn nicht der zentrale Text der Priesterschrift. Nach 29,46d bleibt Mose nur noch, vom Sinai herabzusteigen, was er in 34,29a tut. Weder die Tafeln noch eine Lakune gehören zwischenein. 34,29b gibt sich durch die Wiederholung des »Herabsteigens« als Glosse zu 34,29a zu erkennen. Man kann an Zusätze zu P im dtr Geiste denken im Zuge der wechselseitigen Angleichung der Positionen während der Pentateuch-Kompositions-Diskussion – P^D (vgl. Anm. 6).

12. Gegen LOHFINK, *Geschichte*, p. 222 Anm. 29 u.v.a.m. und mit O.H. STECK, *Der Mensch und die Todesstrafe. Exegetisches zur Übersetzung der Präposition Beth in Gen 9,6a*, in *TZ* 53 (1997) 118-130, sind diese Verse keineswegs sekundär: das Blut-Tabu

ethisch und politisch relevante »Gesetz« in P. An einem weiter spezifi-zierten göttlichen Gebot besteht nach P menschlicherseits offenbar kein Bedarf. Der Rückgriff auf die »Gottesstandbildhaftigkeit des Men-schen« in Gen 9,6b dient gleichermaßen der Berechtigung des autono-men, aber nicht souveränen Sachwalters Gottes auf Erden, sich weitere Gesetze selber zu geben, wie als Angabe des Grundprinzips, aus dem heraus diese zu erschließen wären. Der Gott und seine Schöpfung recht erkennende Mensch hat nach P von sich aus, ohne Kenntnis der dtr Ge-bote und Verbote, die Möglichkeit, wie Henoch תמים »integer« zu sein (Gen 5,22) oder es wie Abraham (Gen 17,1)[13] sein zu sollen.

Während man תורה im D-Komplex durchaus zutreffend mit »Gesetz« übersetzen kann, bezeichnet תורה auf P und den von ihr dominierten Pentateuch angewandt »Lehre« im umfassendsten Sinn: *cognitio Dei et hominis*.

(e) Während das Gesetz von D Israel als »Gottesstaat« konstituiert, gilt das »Gesetz« von P universal. Das Mord-Verbot ist die Form, in der P den Staat begründet und legitimiert[14]. Gegenüber dem noch in der D-Tradition rezipierten sakralen Königtum der Davididen[15] wird der Staat ganz utilitaristisch eingeführt, oder gerade nicht eingeführt: er ist eine sinnvolle Ordnung, um einen göttlichen Auftrag zu erfüllen, aber er ist eine menschliche Ordnung ohne unmittelbare göttliche Legitimation. Die königliche Rolle der Stellvertretung Gottes auf Erden kommt jedem Menschen zu[16]. Der Staat ist eine abgeleitete Institution, aus der »Gottesstandbildhaftigkeit« eines jeden Menschen abgeleitet. Nicht als »Staat«, sondern als »Kirche« ist Israel eine Institution unmittelbar göttlichen Ursprungs: aus dem Verhältnis von Gen 9,1-17 zu Gen 17 resultiert die Zwei-Reiche-Lehre von P. Wie der Mensch ist auch der Staat autonom, d.h. er erfüllt die ihm übertragenen Aufgaben aus eige-

folgt nicht aus der kultischen Verwendung des Blutes, sondern die Kult-Praxis setzt die materielle »Heiligkeit« des Blutes konzeptionell voraus.

13. Vor- und außerhalb der ברית! Die jeweilige Vorschaltung der »Imperative« Gen 9,2-6; Gen 17,1 vor die »Indikative« Gen 9,8-17 und 17,2-21 kann nicht als Kondition verstanden werden, da die göttlichen Zusagen auf keine Bedingung zurückgreifen und die Imperative unabhängig von den folgenden »Verheißungen« gelten.

14. Vgl. zur Blutrache (die in Gen 9,4-6 mit-, aber nicht ausschließlich gemeint ist) als Rechtssystem staatlicher wie vorstaatlicher Gesellschaften T. KRÜGER, *»Du sollst nicht töten!«: »Ehrfurcht vor dem Leben« in Ethik und Recht des Alten Testaments*, in ZEE 38 (1994) 17-30; = ID., *Kritische Weisheit. Studien zur weisheitlichen Traditions-kritik im Alten Testament*, Zürich, 1997, pp. 23-39, 28-32.

15. Dazu R. ALBERTZ, *Religionsgeschichte*, I, pp. 174-185; II, pp. 397-413.

16. M. GÖRG, *Das Menschenbild der Priesterschrift*, in BiKi 42 (1987) 21-29; = ID., *Studien zur biblisch-ägyptischen Religionsgeschichte* (SBAAT, 14), Stuttgart, Katholi-sches Bibelwerk, 1992, pp. 137-151, bes. 143-147.

nen Kräften und nach eigenem Ermessen, aber er ist nicht souverän: er kann das in der Schöpfungsordnung implizite Recht nur erfüllen, nicht setzen. Der Staat darf nach P sowenig wie der einzelne Mensch morden, er soll aber illegitimer Gewalt mit legitimer Gewalt entgegentreten[17]. Zugleich erlaubt die Entsakralisierung des Staates, das »fremde« Imperium der Achämeniden als legitim zu akzeptieren und sich in seinem Rahmen autonom zu organisieren.

Israel ist bei P kein Staat und soll es auch nicht mehr werden, sondern mehr als ein Staat: das Gottesvolk als Kirche. Mit Gen 9,4-6 ist das Problem der »Staatlichkeit« für P abgehandelt und kommt nur noch einmal als Negativbeispiel vor in Gestalt der Ägypter als Symbol des sich selbst überhebenden Staates, aus dem Israel auszieht. Daß die Autonomie der Jerusalemer Tempel-Gemeinde den Schutzraum des Imperiums voraussetzte, wußten die Verfasser von P zweifellos. Ihr weitgehendes »Staatsschweigen« darf darum nicht als atavistischer Traum von der Wiederherstellung »vorstaatlicher« Zustände in Israel ausgelegt werden[18], sondern als Hinweis, daß Israels Proprium auf einer anderen Ebene zu suchen ist[19].

(f) Für die D-Tradition ist Jhwh der Gott Israels, indem er dessen staatliche Existenz garantiert [vgl.(e)] und Israels Kriege führt[20].

---

17. Das hier vom Staat im Singular zu reden ist, ergibt sich aus den zeitgeschichtlichen Verhältnissen: im 5. Jh. v.Chr. war die zivilisierte Welt, die Ökumene, im Perserreich geeint, an dessen Rändern es wohl noch den einen oder anderen Barbaren-Stamm gab (wie das Chaos am Rande des Kosmos), aber keinen gleichwertigen Gegner. So könnte der »Pazifismus« von P (dazu unten) aus der Anschauung geboren sein, daß Krieg nicht mehr nötig ist, weil niemand mehr da war, gegen den er zu führen gewesen wäre. »Internationale Polizeiaktionen« wie gegen Skythen oder Griechen damals, im Irak oder in Bosnien heute, bleiben im Rahmen von Gen 9,4-6 und fallen dann nicht unter das Kriegs- und Agressionsverbot.
Tu regere imperio populos, Romane, memento
Hae tibi erunt artes, pacique imponere morem
Parcere subiectis et debellare superbos
(*Aen.* VI 851-853). Die ächemenidischen Königsinschriften sagen mit anderen Worten dasselbe.
18. So LOHFINK, *Krieg*, pp. 294-297. Bei der Beurteilung dieser Frage spielt eine Rolle, ob man Pg (spät-)exilisch oder nachexilisch ansetzt und ob man die sekundär-priesterschriftliche Theorie des Opfers schon in der Grundschicht angelegt findet oder aufgrund der o. mit Anm. 4 behandelten Beobachtung eher nicht.
19. Die DP, d.h. ein nach-priesterschriftlicher Deuteronomist, in Ex 19,4-6 gut auf den Punkt gebracht hat.
20. Ex 13-14 D; 23,22.27-28 u.ö.; M. WEIPPERT, *»Heiliger Krieg« in Israel und Assyrien. Kritische Anmerkungen zu Gerhard von Rads Konzept des »Heiligen Krieges« im Alten Israel*, in ZAW 84 (1972) 460-493. Dem Versuch von R. ALBERTZ (*Religionsgeschichte I*, pp. 122-127) u.a., das in der altorientalischen Staatstheologie verankerte dtr Theologumenon im »vorstaatlichen Israel« historisch zu verankern, steht entgegen, daß ein derartiges »Israel« seinerseits ein theologisches Konstrukt der Exilszeit sein dürfte.

In P hängt Jhwh den Bogen, den er als Kriegs- und Nationalgott einst geführt hat[21], in die Wolken und damit an den Nagel (Gen 9,13a). Gott garantiert der ganzen Menschheit, daß er künftig gegen sie nicht mehr Krieg führen wird. Insofern die Sintflut mit einen Zitat der Prophetie Israels von Amos bis Ezechiel eingeleitet wird (Gen 6,13b)[22], wird der alte Flut-Mythos zum Gleichnis der Gewaltsamkeit wie der Katastrophenerfahrung des assyrisch-babylonischen Zeitalters, das für P mit dem Regierungsantritt des Kyros bzw. Dareios überwunden und vergangen ist[23]. Damit wird die Prophetie, aber auch die von den Deuteronomisten dargestellte Geschichte zur Vergangenheit, die keine Zukunft und keine Gültigkeit mehr hat. Die Prophetie ist mit dem assyrisch-babylonischen Gericht und der achämenidischen Wiederherstellung Israels erfüllt.

So wie P keine Staaten mehr kennt – außer dem in Gen 10* implizit vorausgesetzten Perserreich[24] – gibt es auch keine Kriege mehr[25]. P ist gegenüber D akzentuiert pazifistisch. Konflikte aus der P vorliegenden Tradition werden unterdrückt[26], entschärft[27] oder wenigstens entmilitari-

---

21. Hab 3,9.13-14 und vgl. die vorige Anm. Jhwh's Anfänge als Wettergott mögen P durchaus noch bewußt geworden sein, doch steht seit der Eisen-I-Zeit beim »bogenschießenden Gott« der politische, nicht der kosmisch-metereologische Aspekt im Vordergrund; cf. O. KEEL – C. UEHLINGER, *Göttinnen, Götter und Gottessymbole. Neue Erkenntnisse zur Religionsgeschichte Kanaans und Israels aufgrund bislang unerschlossener ikonographischer Quellen* (QD, 134), Freiburg-Basel-Wien, Herder, 1992, pp. 129-138; 147f.

22. Ob P hier an Am 8,2 oder an Ez 7,2-3.6 dachte (für letzteres: O.H. STECK, *Aufbauprobleme der Priesterschrift*, in D.R. DANIELS [ed.], *Ernten, was man sät*. FS K. Koch, Neukirchen-Vluyn, Neukirchener Verlag, 1991, pp. 287-308, 297-302), muß nicht unbedingt zu Ungunsten einer der beiden Möglichkeiten entschieden werden (cf. C. LEVIN, *Das Amosbuch der Anawim*, in ZTK 94 [1997] 407-436, pp. 407f). Repräsentierten Am* und Ez* für P das jeweils älteste bzw. jüngste Prophetenbuch?

23. Cf. zum zeitgeschichtlichen Hintergrund der Flutgeschichte bei P schon GÖRG, *Menschenbild*, p. 141.

24. C. UEHLINGER, *Weltreich und »eine Rede«. Eine neue Deutung der sogenannten Turmbauerzählung (Gen 11,1-9)* (OBO, 101), Freiburg/Schweiz, Göttingen, Universitätsverlag, Vandenhoeck & Ruprecht, 1990, pp. 576-583.

25. Diese Erkenntnis von (S.E. McEVENUE und) N. LOHFINK, *Geschichte*, pp. 223-224 Anm. 30; 239 m. Anm. 65; = ID., *Krieg*, pp. 279-297, ist für die Opposition von P und D grundlegend: es geht beim Streit der beiden Schulen keineswegs um Nuancen. Die P-Version von Num 13-14 ist wohl noch pazifistischer, als LOHFINK, *Geschichte*, p. 238; *Ursünden*, p. 185 annimmt, da Num 13,32e.f schwerlich der Grundschicht angehört – diese hatte mit 13,32c alles gesagt (vor allem auch, was mit den »Hethitern« von Gen 23 mittlerweile geschehen war) – sondern zu 13,33 D überleitet.

26. Vgl. etwa die Bearbeitung der Abraham-Lot- und der Abraham-Sara-Hagar-Ismael-Geschichte durch P in Gen 12,4-5; 13,6.12ab; 19,29a und Gen 16,3.15-16; 17,18-21; 25,9.12-17 und zur Jakobsgeschichte LOHFINK, *Krieg*, p. 280.

27. Vgl. etwa die »Nacherzählung« der Josefs-Geschichte durch P, die so kurz ist, daß meistens (aber zu Unrecht) ein Textausfall angenommen wird. Da P in diesem Fall den Konflikt zwischen Josef und seinen Brüdern schlechterdings nicht entschärfen kann, erzählt er ihn gar nicht erst, sondern verläßt sich darauf, daß sein Auditorium deren Ver-

siert[28]. Wo Gott die durch menschliche Gewaltsamkeit bedrohte Ordnung der Schöpfung wiederherstellt, handelt er nicht als Kriegs- und Gewittergott in der Geschichte, sondern als Schöpfergott: führt Jhwh in der vorpriesterlichen Flutgeschichte[29] die Sintflut durch einen Dauerregen herbei (Gen 7,4.12; 8,2b), was zweifellos innerhalb der Kompetenzen des alten Gewittergottes lag[30], so hebt der priesterschriftliche Gott die Trennung zwischen den Wassern über und unter dem Firmament auf, macht also eine der grundlegendsten Unterscheidungen des werdenden Kosmos zunichte (Gen 1,6b-7d). Der Gegensatz wird besonders deutlich in der Meerwunder-Erzählung: handelt es sich im D-Bericht um eine Jhwh-Kriegserzählung[31], so bei P um eine temporäre Modifikation der Schöpfungsordnung[32].

lauf kennt. Aus Josefs »Verleumdung« resultiert seine Trennung von der Familie und sein persönlicher »Verlust des Landes Kanaan« (vgl. Num 13,32a; 14,36d.37), also 41,46a. 46,6-7 hebt Jakob die Trennung der Familie auf, indem er sich nach Ägypten begibt. Im Rahmen der Lakonik von P ist das bereits eine »Geschichte«.

28. Dies wird besonders deutlich am Vergleich der P- und D-Versionen von Ex 13-14, Num 13-14 und Jos 1-18 (s. dazu u. Abschnitt 3).

29. Gegen T. KRÜGER, *Das menschliche Herz und die Weisung Gottes. Elemente einer Diskussion über Möglichkeit und Grenzen der Tora-Rezeption im Alten Testament*, in R.G. KRATZ & T. KRÜGER (eds.), *Rezeption und Auslegung im Alten Testament und in seinem Umfeld. Ein Symposion aus Anlass des 60. Geburtstages von Odil Hannes Steck* (OBO, 153), Freiburg/Schweiz, Universitätsverlag, Göttingen, Vandenhoeck & Ruprecht, 1997, pp. 65-92, esp. 73-76, rechne ich weiterhin mit einer vor-priesterlichen Sintflutgeschichte im Rahmen einer »Judäischen Atrahasis«-»Geschichte«(»AJ«) in Gen 2,4b-8,22*, die vermutlich aus dem 7. Jh. v. Chr. stammt. Gen 4,25-26 und selbst 4,20-22 sind eher sekundär als 6-8*; mit »Wortstatistik« kann man – statistisch signifikant – nichts beweisen: daß ein »urgeschichtlicher«, kosmologisch-anthropologischer Text in der weisheitlichen und exegetischen Literatur des AT (Qoh, Chr) nachwirkt bzw. mit dieser Vokabular teilt, ist nicht verwunderlich; eine nachpriesterliche Überarbeitung von Gen 6,5-8 ist wahrscheinlicher als der nachpriesterliche Charakter des ganzen Textes, in dem 6,7b R und »das Vieh«, »das Kriechgetier und die Vögel des Himmels« keineswegs fest verankert sind; Beziehungen von Gen 6,5-8 zu Ex 32-34 sprechen nicht zwingend für die Abhängigkeit der Gen-Perikope; und das abschließende Opfer, das den Gebrauch von Opferterminologie erfordert, hat AJ eher aus seinen mesopotamischen Vorlagen denn aus P. In diesem Fall scheint mir der Nachweis eines nachpriesterlichen Pentateuch-Bestandes für einmal nicht gelungen. Krüger wird freilich sekundiert von E. OTTO, *Die Paradieserzählung Genesis 2-3: eine nachpriesterschriftliche Lehrerzählung in ihrem religionshistorischen Kontext*, in A.A. DIESEL et al. (eds.), *»Jedes Ding hat seine Zeit ...« Studien zur israelitischen und altorientalischen Weisheit. Diethelm Michel zum 65. Geburtstag* (BZAW, 241), Berlin - New York, NY, de Gruyter, 1996, pp. 167-192.

30. Cf. zur Geschichte Jhwhs O. KEEL, *Eine Kurzbiographie der Frühzeit des Gottes Israels – im Ausgang von Ausgrabungsbefunden im syro-palästinischen Raum*, in *Bulletin. Europäische Gesellschaft für Katholische Theologie* 5 (1994) 158-175, p. 168.

31. P. WEIMAR, *Die Jahwekriegserzählungen in Exodus 14, Josua 10, Richter 4 und 1Samuel 7*, in *Bib* 57 (1976) 38-73.

32. Wer durch sein Wort ein Firmament zwischen den Chaos-Wassern entstehen lassen kann, vermag zweifellos, auch irdischen Wassern eine feste Grenze zu ziehen. – Auch die Auseinandersetzung mit Ägypten in Ex 2-14 P reflektiert Jhwh's Haltung gegenüber

(g) Für D erschöpft sich Jhwh's Gottsein für Israel im wesentlichen in der Rolle, die im alten Orient jeder Nationalgott spielte. Die Auseinandersetzung mit dem assyrischen Imperialismus, die zur Formulierung der D-Theologie führte, hat im deuteronomistischen Jhwh Züge des Gottes Assur hinterlassen[33].

Für P ist Gott dreifach Gott Israels: als Elohim ist er der Gott der ganzen Welt (damit auch Israels) und trägt als solcher Züge des persischen Reichsgottes Ahuramazda[34]. Als El Schaddai ist er der Gott aller Nachfahren Abrahams (damit auch Israels) und trägt Züge eines Sippen- oder Stammesgottes von Völkerschaften am Rande der Zivilisation[35]. Soweit bei P überhaupt ein »Nationalgott« vorkommt, spielt El Schaddai diese Rolle, aber nicht nur für Israel. Nur als Jhwh, also unter seinem Eigennamen, ist er ausschließlich der Gott Israels, aber in keiner anderen Weise, als daß er beschließt, inmitten seines Volkes auf Erden anwesend und (kultisch) ansprechbar zu sein (Gen 17,7.8b; Ex 6,7ab; 25,8-9; 29,42-46; 40,34-35). Da Jhwh kein anderer als Elohim und El Schaddai ist, ist er in Israel zugleich für alle Welt in der Welt, ein »Licht für die Heiden« ebenso wie »zur Ehre seines Volkes Israel«. Bei P vollendet die Erwählung des Gottesvolkes die Schöpfung, bei D läuft der Erwählungsgedanke Gefahr, Israel vom Rest der Welt zu isolieren (Dtn 4,5-8.32-40; 7).

---

der Anmaßung staatlicher Gewaltsamkeit nach dem Vorbild Assurs; cf. LOHFINK, *Krieg*, p. 280.

33. KNAUF, *Umwelt*, pp. 133-134; vgl. B. BRECHT, »*An die Nachgeborenen*«: *Dabei wissen wir doch: / Auch der Haß gegen die Niedrigkeit / Verzerrt die Züge. / Auch der Zorn über das Unrecht / Macht die Stimme heiser. Ach wir / Die den Boden bereiten wollten für Freundlichkeit / Konnten selber nicht freundlich sein.*
Radikaler sagt es E. FRIED (»Bibelfest«, in *Ges. Werke* [Berlin, Wagenbach 1993] 545f): *Seit Moses / gilt es als gut / daß Ägypter / sterben // Ihr Tod / soll gerechte / Strafe / der Krieg gegen sie // soll anders / sein / als alle / anderen Kriege // Das alte / Buch / wird ein Freibrief / für neue Taten // ...*
34. Besonders nach Gen 9,4-6 und Gen 10 P; cf. K. KOCH, *Weltordnung und Reichsidee im alten Iran und ihre Auswirkungen auf die Provinz Jehud*, in FREI - KOCH, *Reichsordnung*, pp. 133-337, 143f; 149-153; KNAUF, *Umwelt*, pp. 173-174. Natürlich ist der Elohim der Priesterschrift auch der eine »Gott der Philosophen« und hat als solcher eine Vorgeschichte, die bis ins 2. Jahrtausend v. Chr. zurückreicht (KNAUF, *Umwelt*, pp. 266-268).
35. Wieviel von der Vorgeschichte dieses ursprünglichen Appellativs (dazu E.A. KNAUF, *Shadday*, in K. VAN DER TORN - B. BECKING - P.W. VAN DER KARST (eds.), *Dictionary of Deities and Demons in the Bible*, Leiden, Brill, 1995, pp. 1416-1423) P noch bekannt war, ist schwer zu sagen – seine Heimat am Rand oder sogar außerhalb der Zivilisation und seine »Internationalität« vielleicht schon; theologisch wichtig ist der produktive Gebrauch, den P von diesem Überlieferungselement gemacht hat.

2. Wie P aus den Geschichten der Deuteronomisten Geschichtsschrei-
bung macht

Auch wer, wie der Verfasser, bestreitet, daß es ein »Deuteronomistisches Geschichtswerk« je gegeben hat[36], muß nach dem Befund in Gen
9,1-17 damit rechnen, daß P einen Grundbestand[37] der Vorderen wie
Hinteren Propheten sowie Teile[38] der D-Komposition des Pentateuch ge-
kannt und sich damit auseinandergesetzt hat. Abgesehen von 1-2 Kön
handelt es sich dabei jedoch nicht um »Geschichtsschreibung«, ge-
schweige denn um ein »Geschichtswerk«, sondern um überlieferte Geschichten, die im 6./5. Jh. v. Chr. bereits zum Bildungsgut gehört haben
mögen. Weder von P, was hier zu zeigen ist, noch im Kanon der Hebräischen Bibel wurden diese Geschichten aber als »Geschichtsschreibung«
akzeptiert; »Geschichtsbücher« gibt es (kaum zufällig) erst in der griechischen und lateinischen Bibel.

Über die Frage, was »eigentlich« Geschichtsschreibung sei und wann
sie beginne, läßt sich trefflich und endlos streiten: schon Herodot oder
erst Thukydides? schon Voltaire oder doch erst Ranke? weder Ranke
noch Droysen, sondern überhaupt erst Braudel? Verstehen wir unter
Geschichtsschreibung, herauszufinden und darzustellen, was wirklich
geschah und warum, müßte der ganze Orient einschließlich des Alten
Testaments zum Thema schweigen; man konnte das Überlieferte auf
seine Wahrheit befragen[39], aber nicht auf seine Wirklichkeit.

Fragt man umgekehrt, ob es eine Gattung »Historiographie« im Alten
Orient gegeben habe, wird man hingegen fündig: sie existiert in Form
der babylonischen und assyrischen Chroniken und der assyrischen Annalen[40], sie hat auch in Israel, Juda und Moab existiert nach Aufweis der

---

36. *L'»Historiographie Deutéronomiste« (DtrG) existe-t-elle?* in A. DE PURY –
T. RÖMER – J.D. MACCHI (eds.), *Israël construit son histoire. L'historiographie deuté-*
ronomiste à la lumière des recherches récentes (Le Monde de la Bible, 34), Genève,
Labor & Fides, 1996, pp. 411-418.

37. Deren »Endgestalt« ist freilich nachpriesterlich. Vgl. in den Königsbüchern die
Glossen im P-Stil (C. LEVIN, *Der Sturz der Königin Athalja. Ein Kapitel zur Geschichte*
Judas im 9. Jahrhundert v. Chr [SBS, 105], Stuttgart, Katholisches Bibelwerk, 1982,
pp. 29-57), zu Jes und XII, E. BOSSHARD-NEPUSTIL, *Rezeptionen von Jesaja 1-39 im*
Zwölfprophetenbuch. Untersuchungen zur literarischen Verbindung von Propheten-
büchern in babylonischer und persischer Zeit (OBO, 154), Freiburg/Schweiz, Universitätsverlag; Göttingen, Vandenhoeck & Ruprecht, 1997, pp. 253-267; 415-431.

38. Ob diese Teile schon ein durchkomponiertes Ganzes von der Schöpfung bis zum
Tod des Mose gebildet haben, ist durchaus fraglich. Über E. BLUM, *Studien zur Komposi-*
tion des Pentateuch (BZAW, 189), Berlin – New York, NY, de Gruyter, 1990, pp. 361-
378 und LEVIN, *Jahwist*, hinaus ist mit weitaus größeren nachpriesterlichen Erweiterun-
gen in der D-Komposition in Gen und besonders in Num zu rechnen.

39. Vgl. z. B. Ps 44,2-4.10-23.

40. Die sich immerhin auf ihr Verhältnis zum berichteten Geschehen und ihren doku-

in den Königsbüchern und in der Mescha-Inschrift erhaltenen Annalen-
exzerpte. Unter formal-gattungskritischen Gesichtspunkten sind also weder vorpriesterliche Schöpfungs[41]-, Väter- und Exodusgeschichte, noch
Jos, Ri, 1-2 Sam und 1-2 Kön (in ihrer vorliegenden Form) Geschichtsschreibung – darum sah sich P (und später Chr[42]) herausgefordert, aus
diesen Quellen Geschichtsschreibung zu machen. Indem P die Offenbarung von Ort, Art und Weise der Anwesenheit Gottes in der Welt (und
damit den Sinn der Geschichte Israels) unter Mose mit einer chronogra-
phischen Einleitung von der Schöpfung her versah, folgt sie einem auch
altorientalisch belegten Aufriß einer »historischen Monographie«[43]. Insofern P seine Chronologie von der Schöpfung her konstruiert, kann er
überhaupt erst und als erster Israelit »Weltgeschichte« schreiben. Die
Chronologie der Königsbücher gehört einer Episode an, die vergangen
ist und es nach P bleiben soll[44]. Die Regierungsjahre der persischen Könige seiner Gegenwart taugen nicht für die Vergangenheit.

Schon aufgrund der Mühe, die sich P mit der Chronologie gegeben
hat, verlangt, seinen Entwurf als wissenschaftliche Geschichtsschreibung mit den Mitteln der Zeit ernstzunehmen. Eine vergleichbare An-
strengung fehlt in den Geschichten der Deuteronomisten[45]. Dem steht
aber der Respekt gegenüber, den D seinen Quellen weitgehend bewahrt

mentarischen Quellen befragen lassen, cf. E.A. KNAUF, *Ismael. Untersuchungen zur Geschichte Palästinas und Nordarabiens im 1. Jahrtausend v. Chr.* (ADPV), Wiesbaden,
Harrassowitz, ²1989, pp. 96-99. In Gen bis Jos führt schon die Frage weithin ins Leere.

41. Vgl. Anm. 29.

42. H.P. MATHYS, *Philologia sacra: Das Beispiel der Chronikbücher*, in *TZ* 53
(1997), 64-73; p. 68.

43. Vgl. etwa die Šulgi-Chronik aus Uruk W.22289 (H. HUNGER, *Spätbabylonische
Texte aus Uruk I* [Ausgrabungen der Deutschen Forschungsgemeinschaft in Uruk-Warka,
9), Berlin, Mann, 1976], pp. 19f). Diese auf den 15. August 251 v. Chr. datierte Tafel
wird durch die einleitende Anrufung Z. 1 und das Kolophon Z. 5' – 10' als literarische
Einheit präsentiert und erzählt in den Z. 3-3' von Schuld und Strafe des Königs, dessen
»monographische Bearbeitung« durch die Angabe der Regierungsjahre seines Vorgän-
gers Z. 2 und seines Nachfolgers Z. 4' in mesopotamische Chronologie und Geschichte eingeordnet wird. Der Schreiber Anu-aḫa-ušabši konnte derart auf die kanonische
Historioghraphie verweisen und dem Leser das Nachschlagen erleichtern. P konnte letzteres offensichtlich noch nicht, sondern mußte seine Chronologie erst einmal selbst erstel-
len, natürlich unter Verwendung von Wissens-Stoff, der an der Jerusalemer Tempelschule
tradiert worden war.

44. Sie ist mit der »Sintflut« zuende und zugrunde gegangen (s.o. Abschnitt 1). P
schreibt die Geschichte von Bleibendem, was nicht mehr ist, ist so gut wie nie gewesen
(s. aber u. zu den »Königen«); cf. LOHFINK, *Geschichte*, pp. 247-252; ID., *Der Schöpfergott und der Bestand von Himmel und Erde* (1978); = ID., *Studien zum Pentateuch* (n. 4),
pp. 191-211.

45. Die Chronologie von D setzt P voraus, oder sie hängt in der Luft. Dabei kommt
als eigene chronographische Leistung von D nur die entsprechende Bearbeitung des
Richterbuches infrage – dessen Aufnahme in den »Kanon der Geschichten Israels« könnte aber nachpriesterschriftlich sein, s.u. Anm. 63.

hat, während man Vorlagen kaum radikaler umschreiben kann, als P es
getan hat. Als zweite historiographische Tugend der D-Schule erscheint
die relative Unabgeschlossenheit ihrer Sammlung – diese Geschichten,
als Geschichte gelesen, sind darauf angelegt, weiterzugehen, während P
es gegen Ende seiner Darstellung nicht an Signalen mangeln läßt, die
auf ein »Alles ist gesagt« hinauslaufen[46]. Sollte P bei einem Konflikt
der Quellen mit seiner Theorie gesagt zu haben »Umso schlimmer für
die Tatsachen«? Der Respekt für die theologische Leistung von P ver-
bietet es, von seinem historiographischen Können und seiner Berufs-
ethik so gering zu denken. P ist ein Wissenschaftler auf der Höhe seiner
Zeit, kosmologisch, geographisch, mathematisch[47]. Zur Haltung des
Wissenschaftlers damals wie heute gehört aber die Achtung vor den
Quellen – wenn es denn welche sind.

Ich glaube nun, daß P frei war, die Geschichten der Deuteronomisten
zum Gründungsmythos seiner Welt umzuschreiben, weil er die Überlieferungen von Abraham bis Josua – sachlich zutreffend! – für Geschichten von Gott und den Menschen, kurz, für Mythen hielt[48]. Die Ansicht
von P über die Historizität Abrahams unterschied sich vielleicht recht
wenig von der Kopenhagener Alttestamentler unserer Tage[49]. Mit den

---

46. S.u. Abschnitt 4 (d). Mit dem »Alles ist gesagt« gibt P offen zu, Ur-, Vor- und
Gründungsgeschichte zu schreiben, was die Deuteronomisten der Intention nach nicht anders taten. Geschichtsschreibung im Alten Orient ist allemal rückwärtsgewandte Prophetie, die der Vergangenheit sagt, wie sie gewesen sein soll, damit Gegenwart und Zukunft
so seien, wie sie der Prophet sich wünscht. Einmal mehr stellt P Israel eine von D ver-
schiedene Geschichte zur Wahl, die theologisch wie politisch zu einer Entscheidung
zwingt.

47. Die Kosmographie von Gen 1 ist alles andere als naiv, sondern auf mehr als einer
Ebene systematisch durchdacht. Geographisch dürfte P mit den Namen in Gen 10* (sowie
Gen 36*) mehr verbunden haben, als die Exegese nach 150 Jahren biblischer und vorder-
asiatischer Archäologie nachvollziehen kann. Uns fehlen immer noch einige Informationen, die P hatte. Zum mathematischen Wissen von P, das sich in seinen Zahlen und
Zahlensystemen verbirgt, nur soviel: nach der (hier ursprünglichen) Chronologie des sa-
maritanischen Pentateuch findet die Sintflut im A.M. 1307 statt; 1307 ist eine (ziemlich
große) Primzahl. Die Zahlen in Num 1 setzen sich aus Vielfachen und Brüchen von 2400
(= 12 x 200) zusammen, wobei gilt: Zahl der Israeliten = 11 x Gad + 2400 (Levi wird erst
in Num 4 behandelt), die Gesamtsumme beträgt (251 + 1/3 + 1/8 + 1/48) x 2400 = (251 +
23/48) x 251, wobei 251 und 23 wiederum Primzahlen sind.

48. Bei dem, was LOHFINK »Die Rückverwandlung der Geschichte in Mythus« (in
Geschichte, p. 227) nannte, handelt es sich m.E. weniger um eine Verwandlung als darum, die in der vermeintlichen »Geschichte« der Dtr enthaltenen mythischen Strukturen
kenntlich zu machen.

49. Insofern P schon vor dem Einsetzen der Offenbarung, d.h. vor Gen 17,1, Grundle-
gendes zum Verhältnis von Gott und Welt sagen kann, ist er ein Rationalist, für den die
Welt eine vernünftig nachvollziehbare Ordnung hat und diese Ordnung einen dem Ver-
stand erkennbaren Schöpfer. Insofern er die Geschichten der Deuteronomisten modifiziert
oder ablehnt, entmythologisiert er sie gründlich. Einst von einer »salomonischen Aufklärung« gesprochen zu haben, war ein grober Anachronismus – eine Art Farbfernseher im

Mitteln der Geschichtsschreibung, die er beherrscht, schreibt P die Vor- oder Gründungsgeschichte seiner Welt. Daß für P die Grenze zwischen Urgeschichte und Geschichte nicht zwischen der Völkertafel und Abraham, sondern nach Josua liegt, markiert er mit einem historiographischen Mittel, das ihm, seinen Kollegen und Vorgängern seit dem 3. Jahrtausend v. Chr. zur Verfügung stand: der Angabe unhistorisch langer Lebensalter[50]. Der letzte Protagonist, der ein solches Alter erreicht, ist Josua[51].

Mit dem Mittel seiner Chronographie hat P gegenüber D zweierlei dokumentiert: was D fehlt, um »Geschichte« zu sein, und daß man die Geschichten der Deuteronomisten nicht erst heute als Mythen rezipieren kann.

3. Warum P über Josua schreiben mußte, und warum der Schluß von P trotzdem nicht mehr im Pentateuch steht

Hinsichtlich der Abgrenzung der Priesterschrift besteht weitgehender Konsens. Schaut man aber aufs Detail, verflüchtigt sich die Harmonie. Zur Zeit konkurrieren drei Modelle: die »Normal«-»Priesterschrift« von Gen 1 – Dtn 34; die »Minimal«-»Priesterschrift« von Gen 1 – Ex 40/Lev 9[52]; und die »Maximal«-»Priesterschrift« von N. Lohfink, der mit einem freilich kleinen P-Bestand in Jos rechnet.

Gegen die Minimalisten spricht, daß die Mitte von P, die Einwohnung Gottes in Israel, schwerlich das Ende sein kann, denn solange Israel in der Wüste bleibt, ist auch Gott heimatlos. Damit er auf Erden real präsent werden kann, muß Israel in sein Land gelangen[53]. Die beste »Vor«-

---

Schlafzimmer Ludwigs XIV. P (Zeitgenosse des Xenophanes von Kolophon) kann, wer mag, einen Aufklärer nennen: P[g] teilt mit der Aufklärung die optimistische Anthropologie des *non peccare possumus*. Diesem Irrtum entgegenzutreten, ist das Verdienst nachpriesterlich-deuteronomistischer Schichten wie z. B. Gen 12,10-20, wo der Glaubensheld Abraham zum recht kleinmütigen Sünder wird.

50. Nach dem Vorgang der »*Sumerischen Königsliste*« (W.A.P. RÖMER, in *TUAT* I [1982] 328-327). – Freilich bilden die mythischen Lebensalter Klassen, die sich immer mehr vom gänzlich Unerhörten zum menschlich Vorstellbaren abstufen: Vor der Flut 930 bis 365 Jahre – nach der Flut 600 bis 148 Jahre – Väterzeit 180 bis 127 Jahre – Mosezeit 120 bis 110 Jahre.

51. S.u. Abschnitt 3 mit Anm. 65.

52. E. ZENGER et al., *Einleitung in das Alte Testament* (ST, 1,1), Stuttgart, Kohlhammer, ²1996, pp. 94-96. Entscheidend ist die Frage, ob P[g] in Dtn 34 vorliegt; m.E. in 34,1a*.b.c*.5*.7-9 durchaus. Den Sachverhalt וימת משה konnten weder P noch D mit wesentlich anderen Worten ausdrücken.

53. Es ist denkbar, daß mit dem Minimal-P eine »Studie und Vorarbeit« entdeckt worden ist (aus den Jahren 520-515?), die P benutzt und ausgebaut hat. Man sollte diese Quelle (P[Q]?) dann aber nicht P[g] nennen. Unter P[g] verstehe ich historisch den ältesten abgeschlossenen Entwurf der P-Gruppe in der Pentateuch-Redaktionsdebatte (ALBERTZ, *Religionsgeschichte* II, pp. 497-535; KNAUF, *Umwelt*, pp. 171-175; ID., »*Audiatur et altera*

»und Gründungsgeschichte« ist nutzlos, wenn sie nicht mit der zu be-
gründenden Gegenwart vermittelt wird.

Das gleiche Argument gilt auch gegenüber der Normal-Theorie, auch
wenn man ihr zugutehalten muß, daß sie immerhin bis unmittelbar an
die Grenze des Verheißenen Landes und damit zum Einsatzpunkt der
geschichtlichen Existenz Israels führt. Das Hauptargument für die Normal-Theorie ist zweifellos, daß mit dem Tod des Mose der priester-
schriftlich dominierte, geradezu konstituierte Pentateuch endet. Wenn P
so tonangebend war, wie es den Anschein hat, und einen Josua-Ab-
schnitt enthalten hätte, wieso hat P dann nicht dieses sein Schlußkapitel
auch für die Pentateuch-Erzählung durchsetzen können?

Damit ist das einzig schwerwiegende Argument gegen die Maximal-
Theorie genannt, das im folgenden beantwortet werden muß[54]. Für die
Maximal-Theorie sprechen zwei Argumente: (a) die Inklusion Gen
1,28f – Jos 18,1c durch das seltene[55] Verb כבשׁ, wobei dessen Nicht-
Vorkommen in Gen 9,1-2 genauso signifikant ist wie sein Vorkommen
in Jos 18,1[56]; und (b) der anhand von Gen 9 genugsam herausgestellte
Pazifismus von P[57], der nach einem Gegenentwurf zum extrem
bellizistischen Jos* aus josianischer Zeit[58] verlangte, denn wer schwieg,
schien auch damals zuzustimmen oder zumindest diese Möglichkeit of-
fenzulassen. Bei P zieht Israel unter Josua in ein leeres Land, das seine
hethitischen Bewohner zur Zeit Abrahams[59] offenbar gefressen hat[60];

pars« – zur Logik der Pentateuchredaktion, in BiKi 53 [1998] 118-126). Mir ist wahrscheinlicher, daß Pᵍ erst im Zuge der Debatte entstand, als daß die P-Gruppe schon den
ganzen Pᵍ-Bestand mitgebracht hätte. Erst dieses Modell löst Blums Versprechen »Weder
Quelle noch Redaktion« ein (BLUM, Studien zur Komposition, pp. 229-285), Blum selbst
bleibt bei einer Form der »Ergänzungshypothese«.

54. Kein Argument ist die »Gliederung« von P (gegen ZENGER, Einleitung, p. 96), da
es »die« Gliederung von P wohl nicht gibt, sondern eine Mehrzahl von sich über-
lagernden (und allesamt intentionellen) zweigliedriger wie mehrgliedriger Strukturen.
Auf einen dreigliedrigen Aufbau führen etwa die Gottesbezeichnungen Elohim – El
Schaddai – Jhwh, auf einen viergliedrigen die Lebensalter vor der Flut – nach der Flut –
Väterzeit – Mosezeit.

55. Im Pentateuch kommt das Verb nur noch Num 32,22.29 (Dˢ) vor, wo es von Jos
18,1 abhängig ist (cf. LOHFINK, Krieg, pp. 304-306; BLUM, Studien zur Komposition,
p. 378).

56. D. h. erst mit der »Landnahme« Israels und damit Gottes ist die in Gen 9 noch
unvollkommene restitutio in integrum der Gen 5* gefallenen Schöpfung abgeschlossen.

57. S. o. Abschnitt 1 mit Anm. 25.

58. LOHFINK, Krieg, pp. 269-279.

59. Falls Gen 23 zu Pᵍ gehört (gegen BLUM, Vätergeschichte, pp. 441-45; LEVIN,
Jahwist p. 193: Gen 23 ist über Gen 25,9; 35,29 mit 49,29-32 sehr wohl in der P-Theorie
von der Möglichkeit einer friedlich geordneten Welt verankert, und dem urbanen Hintergrund von P [Gen 11,31!] entstammt das Bemühen, die Tradition des Abraham-Grabes
womöglich vom flachen Land in in eine Bezirkshauptstadt zu verlegen); beim Familien-
gräberwerb Abrahams geht es aber nicht um den Beginn der »Landnahme«, sondern lediglich um die judäischen Rechte am schon damals bestehenden (Gen 25,9; 35,29)

hier ist ein Kompromiß mit der kriegerischen Landnahme-Theorie von D so wenig möglich, daß bis heute nicht alle Exegeten bereit sind die gänzlich unkriegerische Landnahmevorstellung von P überhaupt (an)zuerkennen. P konnte sich bei der Schlußredaktion in diesem Fall nicht anders durchsetzen als durch den Ausschluß von Jos aus der Grundurkunde der achämenidischen Jerusalemer Tempelgemeinde[61].

Schauen wir uns den P-Bestand in Jos genauer an, ist mit Lohfink Jos 4,19a; 5,10-12; 18,1 jedenfalls dazu zu rechnen[62].

Jos 4,19a	Das Kriegsvolk stieg vom Jordan auf am 10. des 1. Monats.
5,10a	Die Israeliten lagerten in Gilgal,
5,10b	und begingen das Passa am 14. Tag des Monats am Abend im Jordantalabschnitt von Jericho.
5,11	Sie assen vom Überfluss des Landes Mazzen und Gebratenes an ebendiesem Tag.
5,12a	Da hörte das Manna auf am Tag, nachdem sie vom Überfluss des Landes gegessen hatten.
5,12b	Inskünftig gab es für die Israeliten kein Manna mehr,
5,12c	sondern sie assen dieses Jahr vom Ertrag des Landes Kanaan.
18,1a	Die ganze Gemeinde der Israeliten versammelte sich in Schilo,
18,1b	dort errichteten sie das Begegnungs-Zelt,
18,1c	und das Land war vor ihnen unterworfen.

Mit 5,10-12 kommt die Wüstenwanderung (und damit die »vorhistorische« Existenz) Israels durch den Rückverweis auf Ex 16* zu ihrem Abschluß, mit 18,1 ist die Schöpfung ihrer ursprünglichen Intention gemäß (wieder-) hergestellt. Daß die Vorgeschichte Israels in Schilo endet, hat zwei Gründe: zum einen fand P diesen Ort in seinen Quellen zu den Anfängen der staatlichen Existenz Israels (1 Sam 4,3)[63], zum anderen hatte Schilo den Vorteil, weder mit Jerusalem und dem Zion noch

judäischen-idumäischen Simultanheiligtum von Mamre/Hebron (vgl. zum Weiterleben dieser Verhältnisse bis in die Spätantike O. KEEL – M. KÜCHLER, *Orte und Landschaften der Bibel 2*, Zürich, Benziger; Göttingen, Vandenhoeck & Ruprecht, 1982, pp. 702-705).

60. Num 13,32 (dazu LOHFINK, *Geschichte*, pp. 238-239); die »üble Nachrede« (14,36-37) der Kundschafter bestünde dann in der Erwartung, daß es auch seine zukünftigen israelitischen Bewohner fressen werde und, allgemeiner, in der Verkennung der mit Gen 9,13/Jos 18,1 angebrochenen Friedenszeit.

61. So entstand Jos in den gleichen Kreisen und in der gleichen Diskussion, die auch den Pentateuch redigiert hat, wurde aber bei der »Veröffentlichung« abgetrennt und der Tora als Appendix (oder erstes »deuterokanonische« Buch) nachgeordnet.

62. Gegen Lohfink ist vor 4,19 nicht unbedingt mit einer Lakune zu rechnen, da man zwischen den Arbot Moab und Gilgal, wie jeder weiß und auch damals wußte, nun einmal den Jordan überschreiten muß. 14,1f und 19,51 sind ohne Jos 13-19 einigermaßen sinn- und funktionslos und daher eher Pˢ.

63. Diese Beobachtung läßt fragen, ob zur Zeit von P das Richterbuch noch nicht zum »kanonischen« Geschichtsbild gehörte – unbeschadet der Existenz eines »Retterbuches« seit dem ausgehenden 8. oder 7. Jh. v. Chr. – Oder soll die Jer 7,14; 26,9 evozierte Geschichte annulliert werden?

mit Sichem und dem Garizim identisch und somit nach beiden Seiten hin offen zu sein[64]. Über Lohfink hinaus ist auch Jos 24,29b »Josua«, »Nun«'»s Sohn starb [«, »der Minister Jhwh«'»s«,] »im Alter von 110 Jahren« als chronologischer Schlußpunkt P zuzurechnen[65].

4. Das Problem der Könige

Nach der vorgetragenen Interpretation von Gen 9 (und 17) ist das ideale Israel mehr und etwas anderes als ein Staat. Wie verträgt sich damit Gen 17,6c, wonach aus Abraham nicht nur »Völkerschaften«, sondern auch »Könige« hervorgehen sollen? Mehrere Lösungsmöglichkeiten sind denkbar.

64. Vgl. zur Tora (und Jos!) als »Integrationsdokument« von Judäern und Samaritanern B.J. DIEBNER, »Auf einem der Berge des Landes Morija« (Gen 22,2) oder: »In Jerusalem auf dem Berge Morija« (2Chr 3,1)? in DBAT 23/24 (1987) 174-179; ID., Gottes Welt, Moses Zelt und das salomonische Heiligtum, in T. RÖMER (ed.), Lectio difficilior probabilior? L'exégèse comme expérience de décloisonnement. Mélanges offerts à Françoise Smyth-Florentin (DBAT, 12), Heidelberg, esprit Druckerei 1991, pp. 127-154 p. 131; KNAUF, Umwelt, p. 173.

65. S. zu seiner Funktion als Markierung der Grenze von »Vorgeschichte/Mythos« und »Geschichte« o. Abschnitt 2 mit Anm. 51; עבד יהוה ist schwerlich P, da die Wurzel עבד dort nur negativ besetzt ist (Ex 1,13-14; 2,23; 6,5; im Haushalt Abrahams werden die Sklaven in Gen 17 kunstvoll umschrieben); die Formulierung spricht sonst nicht dagegen, da der »reichen« Todesnotiz der Patriarchen (am vollständigsten im Falle Abrahams, Gen 25,8) schon in der Mose-Generation ein durchwegs ärmeres Formular entspricht. Der Übergang vom Mythos zur Geschichte ist bei P graduell und fein abgestuft (vgl. Anm. 54):

Lebensalter-Notiz

	w='lh/	w=yhyw	ymy	šny	ḥyy	PN	Zahl
Abraham 25,7	x		x	x	x	x	175
Ismael 25,17	x			x	x	x	137
Sara 23,1	x			x	x	x	127
Isaak 35,28	x		x			x	180
Jakob 47,28	x		x	x	x	x	147
Mose Dtn 34,7	w-MŠH bn Zahl šnh b-mtw						120
Josua Jos 24,29	w=ymt YHWŠᶜ bn NWN bn Zahl šnym						110

Todes-Notiz

	w=ygwᶜ	w=ymt	PN	b-śybh	ṭwbh	zqn	w-śbᶜ	ymym	w=y'sp	ᵓᶜ
Abraham 25,8	x	x	x	x	x	x				x
Ismael 25,17	x	x								x
Sara 23,2		x				x				
Isaak 35,29	x	x	x			x		x		x
Jakob 49,33	x									x
Miryam Num 20,1		x	x							
Aaron Num 20,28	x	x	x							x
Mose Dtn 34,5		x	x							x
Josua Jos 24,29		x	x							

(a) Es handelt sich nicht um P^g, sondern um einen Zusatz im deuteronomistischen Geist, also P^s (oder P^D)[66]. Diese nicht widerlegbare Möglichkeit hat den Nachteil, daß sie auch nicht recht beweisbar ist. Sie machte dem Exegeten das Leben leicht – m.E. zu leicht. Der Ergänzer wäre dann auch ausgesprochen konsequent gewesen und hätte die Könige auch 17,16e und 35,11f nachgetragen. Diese Gründlichkeit spricht eher gegen die Annahme einer Glosse[67].

(b) P dachte an die Könige der Ismaeliter (Kedrener, Nabatäer)[68] oder Edomiter/Idumäer[69]. Aber die Ismaeliter scheiden durch Gen 17,16e aus, die Edomiter durch 35,11f. Es muß sich schlechterdings um Könige Israels handeln.

(c) P hielt die Achämeniden für Nachfahren Abrahams und Jakobs – eine frühe Spekulation über den Verbleib der 10 »Stämme«. Mag man noch innen- oder außenpolitische Gründe finden, warum P deren Genealogie dann nirgends wenigstens angedeutet habe, scheitert diese Erwägung am völligen Fehlen eines entsprechenden Hinweises in der Tradition und vor allem an der in Gen 9,1-7 erfolgten radikalen Desakralisierung des Staates. Der Staat ist eine sinnvolle Auslegung – oder Applikation – der Schöpfungsordnung von Gen 9,4-6, eine göttliche explizite Setzung von Gottes Gnaden ist er, im Gegensatz zur Menschheit einerseits und Israel als Gottesvolk andererseits, nicht[70].

(d) P hatte doch, gegen allen Augenschein, eine Eschatologie: die Jerusalemer Tempel-Gemeinde ist eine vorläufige Institution, die vom messianischen Königreich letztendlich abgelöst werden wird[71]. Aber der

66. Vgl. für letzteres paradigmatisch Num 31 und dazu LOHFINK, *Krieg*, pp. 309-312.
67. Gegen die Annahme, diese Könige verdankten sich der makkabäischen Tora-Redaktion, die etwa auch die Zahlen in Gen 5 modifiziert hat (Sam → MT; LOHFINK, *Geschichte*, pp. 234-238) spricht das Vorkommen der »Könige« auch im Samaritanus.
68. Cf. KNAUF, *Ismael*, pp. 96-111.
69. Vgl. die »Edomitische Königsliste« Gen 36,31-39. Die literarische Stratigraphie von Gen 36 (P^Q, P^g, P^s) bereitet nach wie vor Kopfzerbrechen.
70. Überdies wäre dann dem jeremianischen Gottesknecht Nebukadnezar (Jer 27,6) und dem deuterojesajanischen Messias Kyros (Jes 45,1) die antinationalistische Spitze abgebrochen – zwei Texten, die wohl für das Staatsdenken von P prägend waren.
71. W. GROSS, *Israels Hoffnung auf die Erneuerung des Staates*, in J. SCHREINER, (ed.), *Unterwegs zur Kirche. Alttestamentliche Konzeptionen* (QD, 110), Freiburg, Herder, 1987, pp. 87-122, esp. 88-103. Gerade die Vergesellschaftung der »Königsverheißung« bei P mit der Verheißung von גוים oder עמים an Abraham (Gen 17,5c. 6b.c), Sara (Gen 17,16d.e) und Jakob (Gen 35,11e.f) zeigt, daß es hier nicht um eine Idealvorstellung für die Zukunft, sondern um einen Rückblick auf die reale Geschichte Israels vor dem Exil handelt. Während עם primär der »Heerbann« ist (so daß ein Plural von Milizarmeen innerhalb Israels immerhin denkbar wäre), bezeichnet גוי (Gen 17,5c.6c. 16d; 35,11e) eine territorial definierte Bevölkerung (vgl. besonders Gen 10,5.20.31). Solche mit eigenen Königen hat es in der Geschichte Israels nur von Eschbaal bis Hosea gege-

Augenschein ist doch übermächtig[72]: P schreibt die Geschichte von
Bleibendem, Vorläufiges, wie die Geschichte der Ammoniter und
Moabiter, kommt gar nicht erst vor. Wir haben P in Gen bis Jos als eine
einzige Kosmogonie verstanden. Mit Jos 18,1 ist die Welt von P fertig,
es steht nichts mehr aus.

(e) Dann sind die »Könige« am ehesten als eine Reverenz gegenüber
der Tradition von Sam und Kön zu verstehen wie Gen 6,13b vor der
Prophetie: das hat es gegeben[73] und diese Texte gehören weiterhin zum
Bildungs-Kanon. Aber Zukunftsbedeutung haben sie keine mehr. Gerade indem P königliche Prädikationen und Funktionen auf Josua überträgt[74], ihm den Titel aber nicht gibt, zeigt er, daß Könige in seiner
Idealverfassung nicht mehr vorgesehen sind, so wie die betreffenden
Funktionen Josuas an der Spitze des Heerbannes auch nur noch rituell,
parademäßig ausgeübt werden können, denn zu führende Kriege gibt es
jetzt nicht mehr[75]. Die Zukunft gehört der »Demokratisierung« der ehe-
dem königlichen Gottesebenbildlichkeit[76] und einer Welt-Chronologie,
die von den fundamentalen Lebenszusammenhängen von Geburt, Zeu-
gung und Tod ausgeht und nicht mehr von Regierungszeiten und Dyna-
stien. Und doch zeigt sich in diesen kleinen Sätzchen der Respekt, den P
als Historiker vor den Quellen der Geschichte Israels hatte – wo er eben
glaubte, Geschichtsquellen vor sich zu haben.

Universität Bern   Ernst Axel KNAUF

ben. Gerade diese Pluralität gehört in die Vergangenheit und nicht in »eine noch ferne«,
»ausstehende Zukunft« (gegen L. HOSSFELDT, *ibid.*, pp. 141f).
    72. L. SCHMIDT, *Studien zur Priesterschrift* (BZAW, 214), Berlin - New York, NY, de
Gruyter, 1993, p. 235 A. 95; LOHFINK, *Geschichte*, pp. 243-249.
    73. So schon SCHMIDT, *Studien*, p. 235: »Diese Ankündigung«(»sc. Gen 17«,6;
35,11) »soll aber lediglich die Mehrungsverheißung veranschaulichen. Sie ist im Rückblick auf die israelitische Königszeit formuliert.«. Die Diskussion ebd., 263-265, bleibt
ohne größeren Ertrag wegen der Koppelung mit der Mehrungsverheißung, die in Ägypten
erfüllt ist, ohne daß dort ein König Israels in den Blick kommt.
    74. Vgl. zu Num 27,15-23 L. SCHMIDT, *Studien*, pp. 232ff.
    75. LOHFINK, *Krieg*, pp. 282-284.
    76. Gen 1,26; 5,1-3; 9,6; und zum »königlichen Menschen« bei P GÖRG, *Menschen-
bild*, pp. 143-147. Doch kann man nicht sagen, daß der königliche Menschenentwurf ge-
scheitert und nach-sintflutlich gegenstandslos sei (so ebd. 147). Dagegen spricht schon
die Wiederholung der Gottesstandbildhaftigkeit in Gen 9,6, und auch der »Heilige
Krieg« gegen die Tiere 9,2-3 ist eine genuin königliche Rolle, dem Menschen an sich zu-
gesprochen. »Königliches« und »priesterliches« Menschenbild ersetzen sich nicht, sondern ergänzen sich: jeder Mensch ist ein König, aber nur jeder Israelit ist ein Priester.

IS THERE A FUTURE FOR
THE DEUTERONOMISTIC HISTORY?

One of the more remarkable developments in Old Testament study over the past half-century is the profound influence of Martin Noth's theories on the interpretation of the historical books[1]. His view of the composition of Deuteronomy through 2 Kings, contained in his *Über-lieferungsgeschichtliche Studien*, is especially impressive[2]. Noth argues that the books of Deuteronomy, Joshua, Judges, Samuel, and Kings constitute a continuous history characterized by a basic homogeneity in language, style, and content[3]. The Deuteronomist, according to Noth, incorporated the deuteronomic law into the beginning of his work, framing it with speeches by Moses[4]. The Deuteronomist then added other sources, such as tales of conquest and settlement, prophetic narratives and speeches, and official annals and records. The Deuteronomist ordered these sources, shaped them, introduced his own distinctive chronology, and inserted his own comments (often in the mouths of major characters) at critical junctures in his history.

Because the Deuteronomist's compositional technique included selection, edition, and composition, the resulting work was not merely a collection of sources, but a coherent work manifesting a deliberate design and a uniformity of purpose[5]. In advancing this point of view, Noth was reacting against both those scholars who focused their attention solely upon isolated historical books without recognizing their relationship to others and those who attempted to identify strands within the Deuteronomistic History continuous with or analogous to the sources of the Pentateuch. Noth's theory was so persuasive that most, albeit not all, schol-

---

1. An earlier version of this paper was read at the 1997 International SBL meeting in Lausanne. I wish to thank participants in the three Deuteronomistic History sessions for their helpful comments.

2. His work on the Chronicler's History, which also forms part of the same work (*Überlieferungsgeschichtliche Studien: Die sammelnden und bearbeitenden Geschichtswerke im Alten Testament*, 2nd ed., Tübingen, Max Niemeyer, 1957, pp. 110-180) was also important, but has been less influential on subsequent scholarship. See H.G.M. WILLIAMSON's introduction to his translation of this part of Noth's work, *The Chronicler's History* (JSOT SS, 50), Sheffield, JSOT Press, 1987, pp. 11-26.

3. M. NOTH, *Überlieferungsgeschichtliche Studien* (n. 2), pp. 3-12.

4. *Ibid.*, pp. 14-18, 27-40.

5. *Ibid.*, p. 10.

ars accepted it[6]. Hence, when I wrote the introduction to my two-volume work five years ago, I could presume that almost all scholars viewed the books of Deuteronomy through 2 Kings as one comprehensive corpus[7]. One could debate, of course, many difficult issues – sources, date, authorship, provenance, redaction, purpose, and theology – but one could assume the existence of the history itself. This is no longer the case. One can no longer assume a widespread scholarly consensus on the existence of a Deuteronomistic History. In the last five years an increasing number of commentators have expressed grave doubts about fundamental tenets of Noth's classic study.

The attacks against the very notion of a Deuteronomistic History have come from a variety of contexts and take a variety of forms. In this paper I propose to survey, discuss, and assess these recent challenges. I would like to argue that these recent challenges are important in at least two respects – they return to a number of pre-Noth propositions about the nature and limits of the Deuteronomistic History and they involve more than arcane debates about the composition of individual texts. They raise a series of larger questions about the range of techniques employed in ancient Mediterranean historiography, the import of literary diversity, the nature of ancient books, the character of ancient editing, and the definition of ancient authorship.

I. BOOKS, BLOCKS, AND ANCIENT HISTORIOGRAPHY

The objections to the Deuteronomistic History hypothesis can be grouped according to three broad categories. From the outset it should be acknowledged that these three categories are not mutually exclusive. Some writers hold to a combination of these views. First, there is what might be called the book model of composition advocated by Claus Westermann, Gordon McConville, and others[8]. These authors take issue with both the limits of the Deuteronomistic History and its unity.

6. Two notable exceptions were O. EISSFELDT, *The Old Testament: An Introduction*, New York, NY, Harper & Row, 1965, pp. 241-248, and G. FOHRER, *Introduction to the Old Testament*, Nashville, TN, Abingdon, 1968, who writes, "we have a series of books Deuteronomy–Kings, each composed or edited in a different way" (p. 195).

7. G.N. KNOPPERS, *Two Nations Under God: The Deuteronomistic History of Solomon and the Dual Monarchies*, vol. 1: *The Reign of Solomon and the Rise of Jeroboam* (HSM, 52), Atlanta, GA, Scholars Press, 1993, pp. 1-56.

8. C. WESTERMANN, *Die Geschichtsbücher des Alten Testament: gab es ein deuteronomistisches Geschichtswerk?* (TB AT, 87), Gütersloh, Kaiser, 1994, pp. 13-39; J.G. MCCONVILLE, *The Old Testament Historical Books in Modern Scholarship*, in *Themelios* 22/3 (1997) 3-13.

Westermann deems Noth's claim that Moses' speeches signal the beginning of an extensive history to be fundamentally mistaken. One cannot proceed from the situation in Deuteronomy, which prepares Israel for its entrance and life in the land, to the Babylonian exile, which ends that life in the land, and regard the sum as a complete unit[9]. According to Westermann, this vision of a Deuteronomistic History lacks a history of Israel's origins. Since various texts within Deuteronomy, Joshua, Judges, Samuel, and Kings point back toward the exodus, Westermann argues that the pre-Deuteronomistic narrative originally began here[10]. The exodus story purportedly supplies the tale of origins missing from Noth's Deuteronomistic History[11]. As for the rest of the so-called Deuteronomistic History, Westermann contends that the books within this work do not constitute a connected history[12]. To argue, as Noth did, that the Deuteronomist incorporated a variety of disparate sources into his history is rejected out of hand by Westermann, who thinks that no self-respecting historian would allow incongruous sources to stand alongside one another in a single work[13]. In Westermann's view, only loose connections exist between a series of books – Joshua, Judges, Samuel, and Kings – each of which was composed and edited in a distinctive way. Each of these books also exhibits its own distinctive subject matter and themes.

Westermann does not dispense with the notion of a Deuteronomist altogether. He thinks that a deuteronomistic editor supplied theological interpretations of certain events narrated within individual books[14]. Hence, in Westermann's presentation, one is left with a deuteronomistic editor, whose editing was fairly light. But proposals for either a deuteronomistic author or a deuteronomistic historian are rejected. On this point, however, McConville differs from Westermann[15]. McConville thinks that Deuteronomy through Kings is a history and one that manifests some continuity in themes, plot, and characterization[16]. Neverthe-

---

9. C. WESTERMANN, *Geschichtsbücher* (n. 8), pp. 39-40. So also MCCONVILLE, *Historical Books* (n. 8), p. 8.

10. For a list of relevant deuteronomic and deuteronomistic expressions, see M. WEINFELD, *Deuteronomy and the Deuteronomic School*, Oxford, Clarendon, 1972, pp. 326-330.

11. C. WESTERMANN, *Geschichtsbücher* (n. 8), pp. 40-49.

12. *Ibid.*, pp. 49-78.

13. *Ibid.*, pp. 55, 122.

14. *Ibid.*, pp. 16-18, 28-29, 97-124.

15. J.G. MCCONVILLE, *Narrative and Meaning in the Books of Kings*, in *Bib* 70 (1989) 31-49; ID, *Grace in the End: A Study in Deuteronomic Theology*, Grand Rapids, MI, Zondervan, 1993.

16. Hence, McConville retains the *siglum* of a Deuteronomic or Deuteronomistic History, *Historical Books*, pp. 9-11.

less, McConville, like Westermann, favors a focus upon individual books as discrete literary units within a larger, somewhat loosely edited corpus[17].

A second challenge to the consensus established by Noth comes from Ernst Axel Knauf, whose rebuttal to Noth is even more radical than that of Westermann[18]. Like Westermann and McConville, Knauf advocates a return to a concentration upon disparate, separately authored books, but unlike Westermann and McConville, Knauf regards these books as themselves resulting from a series of fundamentally unrelated exilic and postexilic redactions[19]. According to Knauf, the mode of composition found within most of these books does not qualify as historiography[20]. By labelling these books as something other than history, Knauf strikes against two central tenets of Noth's theory – that the Deuteronomist wrote an extensive national history of his people and that this history was written by a single author. Hence, for Knauf, the Deuteronomistic History is neither Deuteronomistic (at least, in the way that Noth thought) nor history.

A third challenge to Noth's case for the unity of the Deuteronomistic History comes from certain scholars, who advocate the block model of composition for Deuteronomy through Kings. This approach is not mutually exclusive with the first and second approaches, because books can be edited to form parts of larger blocks[21]. Moreover, by no means all commentators who adopt the block model of composition argue against the theory of a Deuteronomistic History[22]. Hence, it may be useful to

17. In this regard, McConville proposes a fusion between the block and redaction models of the Deuteronomistic History. See also E. CORTESE, *Theories Concerning DTR: A Possible Rapprochement*, in C. BREKELMANS – J. LUST (eds.), *Pentateuchal and Deuteronomistic Studies: Papers Read at the XIIIth IOSOT Congress* (BETL, 94), Leuven, Leuven University Press, 1990, pp. 179-190; H. WEIPPERT, *Das deuteronomistische Geschichtswerk. Sein Ziel und Ende in der neueren Forschung*, in *TR* 50 (1985) 213-249.

18. E.A. KNAUF, *L'"Historiographie Deutéronomiste' (DtrG) existe-t-elle?* in A. DE PURY – T. RÖMER – J.-D. MACCHI (eds.), *Israël construit son histoire: L'historiographie deutéronomiste à la lumière des recherches récentes* (Le Monde de la Bible, 34), Geneva, Labor et Fides, 1996, pp. 409-418.

19. *L'"Historiographie Deutéronomiste'* (n. 18), pp. 414-417.

20. See also T.L. THOMPSON, *Early History of the Israelite People: From the Written and Archaeological Sources* (SHANE, 4), Leiden, Brill, 1992, pp. 365-366, 383, who views the Deuteronomistic History as an "ethnographic aetiology".

21. In this context, the thesis of B. PECKHAM should be mentioned. He thinks that scholars should pay greater attention to the possibility that the "books" of the Deuteronomistic History are themselves deuteronomistic creations, *The Significance of the Book of Joshua*, in S.L. MCKENZIE – M.P. GRAHAM (eds.), *The History of Israel's Traditions: The Heritage of Martin Noth* (JSOT SS, 182), Sheffield, Sheffield Academic Press, 1994, pp. 231-232.

22. The examples are many, including: H. WEIPPERT, *Das deuteronomistische Geschichtswerk* (n. 17); N. LOHFINK, *Kerygmata des Deuteronomistischen Geschichtswerks*,

look at an example of a scholar who does. The recent book of Erik Eynikel on the Josianic reforms may serve as an illustration of this third challenge[23]. Eynikel prefers not to speak of a Deuteronomistic History, but of a variety of blocks that were written independently: Joshua through 1 Samuel 12, 1 Samuel 13 through 2 Samuel and 1 Kings 1-2, and 1 Kings 3 through 2 Kings 23[24]. Hence, whereas Westermann, McConville, and Knauf speak of separately authored, distinct books, Eynikel speaks of distinct blocks that incorporate separately authored books. The different blocks were not brought together until fairly late in the editorial process[25]. According to Eynikel, there were three editions of Kings that relate (or do not relate, as the case may be) to the union of the separate blocks: RI, who wrote sometime after Hezekiah, RII (= Cross's Dtr[1]), who wrote sometime after Josiah, and RIII (= Cross's Dtr[2]), who wrote during or after the exile[26]. RI and RII (Dtr[1]) did not extend beyond Kings. Later deuteronomistic redaction, perhaps by the

in J. JEREMIAS – L. PERLITT (eds.), *Die Botschaft und die Boten* Fs. H.W. Wolff, Neukirchen-Vluyn, Neukirchener Verlag, 1981, pp. 87-100; ID., *The Cult Reform of Josiah of Judah: 2 Kings 22-23 as a Source for the Story of Israelite Religion*, in P.D. MILLER – P.D. HANSON – S.D. MCBRIDE (eds.), *Ancient Israelite Religion. Essays in Honor of Frank Moore Cross*, Philadelphia, PA, Fortress, 1987, pp. 459-476; A.F. CAMPBELL, *Of Prophets and Kings: A Late Ninth-Century Document (1 Samuel 1-2 Kings 10)* (CBQ MS, 17), Washington, DC, The Catholic Biblical Association of America, 1986; I. PROVAN, *Hezekiah and the Book of Kings* (BZAW, 172), Berlin - New York, NY, de Gruyter, 1988; M.A. O'BRIEN, *The Deuteronomistic History Hypothesis: A Reassessment* (OBO, 92), Freiburg (CH), Universitätsverlag; Göttingen, Vandenhoeck & Ruprecht, 1989; A.G. AULD, *Salomo und die Deuteronomisten – eine Zukunftsvision?*, in *TZ* 48 (1992) 343-54; ID, *Kings Without Privilege: David and Moses in the Story of the Bible's Kings*, Edinburgh, T. & T. Clark, 1994; A. MOENIKES, *Zur Redaktionsgeschichte des sogenannten Deuteronomistischen Geschichtswerks*, in *ZAW* (1992) 333-348.

23. E. EYNIKEL, *The Reform of King Josiah and the Composition of the Deuteronomistic History* (OTS, 33), Leiden, Brill, 1996. See also C.H.W. BREKELMANS, *Joshua XXIV: Its Place and Function*, in J.A. EMERTON (ed.), *Congress Volume: Leuven, 1989*, Leiden, Brill, 1991, pp. 1-9.

24. An earlier, but different, example of this approach is E. WÜRTHWEIN, *Studien zum Deuteronomistischen Geschichtswerk* (BZAW, 227), Berlin, de Gruyter, 1994, pp. 1-11. In assessing the composition of Joshua through Kings, Würthwein speaks of both blocks and deuteronomistically edited (or created) layers. In this context, he posits substantially more deuteronomistic writing than some advocates of the block model do. Nevertheless, Würthwein does not believe that the Deuteronomistic History was ever a unified work.

25. In this, the approach of Eynikel differs quite remarkably from the "rolling corpus" compositional model advocated by A. LEMAIRE, which posits extensive editing at an early stage in the development of the Deuteronomistic History, *Les écoles et la formation de la Bible dans l'ancien Israël* (OBO, 39), Freiburg (CH), Universitätsverlag; Göttingen, Vandenhoeck & Ruprecht, 1981; ID., *Wisdom in Solomonic Historiography*, in J. DAY – R.P. GORDON – H.G.M. WILLIAMSON (eds.), *Wisdom in Ancient Israel*, Cambridge, Cambridge University Press, 1995, pp. 106-118.

26. F.M. CROSS, *Canaanite Myth and Hebrew Epic*, Cambridge, Harvard University Press, 1973, pp. 274-289.

same author (RIII/Dtr[2]) who wrote the end of Judah's history (2 Kings 24-25), fused the disparate blocks into a larger whole[27].

In addition to these three challenges, one might be tempted to add a fourth. In some recent scholarship on the Deuteronomistic History, so many narrative complexes and deuteronomistic editions are postulated that one wonders whether it makes sense to speak any longer of a unified work[28]. If seven or more editors contributed to the shape of the Deuteronomistic History, in what sense does this work manifest a deliberate plan? If such a long succession of redactors also incorporated, but did not overwrite, a variety of disparate sources, to what extent may one still claim that this corpus manifests a unified design?[29]

The aforementioned challenges assail central features of Noth's theory of a deuteronomistic historical work – its limits, unity, theme, and genre[30]. If earlier challenges to Noth's hypothesis accepted the unity of the Deuteronomistic History but debated its authorship and time of composition, these scholars reject the notion of deuteronomistic authorship itself. If signs of unity are manifest in the Deuteronomistic History, they reflect the work of editors, not authors.

II. CONTRIBUTIONS AND ASSESSMENT

Having provided a summary of these challenges, it may be useful to offer a brief assessment. I wish to begin with some contributions that these scholars have made to the current debate. First, they are right to take issue with Noth's simplistic understanding of the Deuteronomist's purpose. In Noth's presentation, the record of Israel's existence in the land is largely negative[31]. The history of Israel turns out to be a dismal failure, a record of "ever-intensifying decline". As many scholars have recognized, such a pessimistic understanding of the Deuteronomist's purpose does not do justice to the range of theological commentary found in the work[32].

---

27. Hence, Eynikel's RIII is more of an active, creative editor than CROSS' Dtr[2], *Canaanite Myth and Hebrew Epic* (n. 26), pp. 285-287.
    28. A point conceded by WÜRTHWEIN, who recognizes that positing a plurality of blocks and redactors augurs against the unity of the whole, *Deuteronomistischen Geschichtswerk* (n. 24), pp. 1-11.
    29. A point also stressed by T. RÖMER – A. DE PURY, *L'historiographie deutéronomiste (HD): Histoire de la recherche et enjeux du débat*, in *Israël construit son histoire* (n. 18), pp. 80, 84-86.
    30. These challenges recall, therefore, not only the book-centered approaches of some scholars who preceded Noth, but also the source-criticism of earlier scholars who sought to link certain texts in Joshua, Judges, Samuel and Kings with Tetrateuchal sources.
    31. M. NOTH, *Überlieferungsgeschichtliche Studien* (n. 2), pp. 100-110.

The diversity of themes extends, moreover, to deuteronomistic compositions[33]. In other words, one cannot attribute all of the diversity within the
Deuteronomistic History to heterogeneous sources that the Deuteronomist
incorporated, but did not rewrite, within his work. The thematic diversity
extends to deuteronomistic commentary itself[34].

Second, these challenges serve a useful purpose in reminding scholars
of the literary complexity inherent within the Deuteronomistic History.
In so doing, they complicate attempts by some new literary critics to
present the Deuteronomistic History as a completely integrated and carefully crafted work of art. By addressing issues of sources, genre, periodi-
zation, tensions, doublets, repetition, and stylistic variation, these scholars have called attention to the density and range of materials found in
Deuteronomy, Joshua, Judges, Samuel, and Kings. To this literary evidence can be added textual evidence. The differences between the
Masoretic Text, the Septuagint, the Old Latin, and the Dead Sea Scrolls
(where available) in Joshua, Judges, Samuel, and Kings are substantial
and should not be ignored[35]. I am thinking not only of the end of
Joshua[36], the beginning of Judges[37], the text of various passages in
Samuel[38], and the "miscellanies"[39] and "supplement"[40] of Kings, but

32. See most recently, W. DIETRICH, *Martin Noth and the Future of the
Deuteronomistic History*, in *The history of Israel's Traditions* (n. 21), pp. 153-175, and
the references cited there.

33. As a variety of scholars have observed (e.g., WEINFELD, *Deuteronomy and the
Deuteronomic School* [n. 10], pp. 320-365), deuteronomistic style is characterized by distinctive vocabulary and diction. Although this style can be imitated, this is no reason to
reject its importance altogether as one means to discern deuteronomistic authorship.

34. As stressed by T. VEIJOLA, *Martin Noth's Überlieferungsgeschichtliche Studien
and Old Testament Theology*, in *The History of Israel's Traditions* (n. 21), pp. 101-127.

35. KNOPPERS, *Two Nations Under God, 1* (n. 7), pp. 10-17.

36. A. ROFÉ, *The End of the Book of Joshua according to the Septuagint*, in *Henoch* 4
(1982) 17-36; E. TOV, *The Growth of the Book of Joshua in the Light of the Evidence of
the LXX*, in *ScrHie* 31 (1986) 321-339; A.G. AULD, *Reading Joshua after Kings*, in J.
DAVIES, *et al.* (eds.), *Words Remembered, Texts Renewed: Essays in Honour of J.F.A.
Sawyer* (JSOT SS, 195), Sheffield, JSOT Press, 1994, pp. 167-181.

37. J.C. TREBOLLE BARRERA, *Light from 4QJudg^a and 4QKgs on the Text of Judges
and Kings*, in D. DIMANT – U. RAPPAPORT (eds.), *The Dead Sea Scrolls: Forty Years of
Research*, Leiden, Brill, 1992, pp. 315-324; B. LINDARS, *Judges 1-5*, Edinburgh, T. & T.
Clark, 1995, pp. 3-109.

38. P.K. MCCARTER, *I Samuel* (AB, 8), New York, Doubleday, 1980, pp. 5-11; ID.,
Textual Criticism: Recovering the Text of the Hebrew Bible (Guides to Biblical Scholar-
ship), Philadelphia, PA, Fortress, 1986; E.C. ULRICH, *The Qumran Text of Samuel and
Josephus* (HSM, 19), Missoula, MT, Scholars Press, 1978; ID., *4QSam^c: A Fragmentary
Manuscript of 2 Samuel 14-15 from the Scribes of the Serek Hay-yahad (1QS)*, in *BASOR*
235 (1979) 1-25; ID., *The Canonical Process, Textual Criticism, and Latter Stages in the
Composition of the Bible*, in M. FISHBANE – E. TOV (eds.), *Sha'arei Talmon: Studies in
the Bible, Qumran, and the Ancient Near East Presented to Shemaryahu Talmon*,
Winona Lake, IN, Eisenbrauns, 1992, pp. 267-291.

also of the recently published 4QJosh[a] text, which has Joshua and the
Israelite leaders build the altar at a different location (Gilgal) than that
depicted in the MT (Mt. Ebal; Josh 8,30-35) and the LXX (Mt. Ebal;
Josh 9,3-8)[41]. The differences between these various textual witnesses
suggest a certain instability and history of development within the text
before the Common Era. In short, ignoring or defying evidence for dia-
chronic development in the Deuteronomistic History can lead to superfi-
cial or forced arguments for synchronic unity[42].

Third, the beginning of the Deuteronomistic History is a legitimate
issue. In dealing with this subject, Westermann and McConville are
not raising a new concern. Others have raised questions about the
composition and function of Deuteronomy 1-3[43]. To this, the issue
of so-called proto-deuteronomic, deuteronomic, or deuteronomistic
texts in the Tetrateuch may be added[44]. What does one make of these
texts?

39. E. Tov, *The LXX Additions (Miscellanies) in 1 Kings 2 (3 Reigns 2)*, in *Textus* 11
(1984) 89-111; R. Pennoyer, *Solomonic Apologetic: Text and Redaction in the Succession Narrative with Special Attention to the So-Called "Miscellanies" in 3 Reigns 2*, Dissertation, Johns Hopkins University, 1992.

40. J.C. Trebolle Barrera, *Salomòn y Jeroboán: Historia de la recensión y
redacción de 1 Reyes 2-12,14* (Institución San Jeronimo, 10), Valencia, Investigación
Biblica, 1980; Id., *Centena in Libros Samuelis et Regum. Variantes Textuales y
Composición literaria en los libros de Samuel y Reyes* (TECC, 47), Madrid, Consejo
Superior de Investigaciones Científicas Instituto de Filología, 1989; Knoppers, *Two
Nations Under God: The Deuteronomistic History of Solomon and the Dual Monar-
chies*, vol. 2: *The Reign of Jeroboam, the Fall of Israel, and the Reign of Josiah* (HSM,
53), Atlanta, GA, Scholars Press, 1994, pp. 79-91.

41. E.C. Ulrich, *4QJoshua[a] and Joshua's First Altar in the Promised Land*, in *New
Qumran Texts and Studies: Proceedings of the First Meeting of the International Organi-
zation for Qumran Studies*, Leiden, Brill, 1994, pp. 89-104; A. Rofé, *The Editing of the
Book of Joshua in the Light of 4QJosh[a]*, in *New Qumran Texts and Studies*, pp. 73-80; K.
Bieberstein, *Lukian und Theodotion im Josuabuch, Mit einem Beitrag zu den
Josuarollen von Hirbet Qumrān* (BN.B, 7), München, Görg, 1994, pp. 85-93.

42. J. Kugel, *On the Bible and Literary Criticism*, in *Prooftexts* 1 (1981) 217-336;
B.M. Levinson, *The human voice in divine revelation: The problem of authority in Biblical law*, in M.A. Williams – C. Cox – M.S. Jaffee (eds.), *Innovation in Religious Traditions* (RS, 31), Berlin, de Gruyter, 1992, pp. 46-61.

43. R. Rendtorff, for instance, views Deuteronomy as a hinge between the
Tetrateuch and the Deuteronomistic History that begins in Josh 1,1; *The Old Testament:
An Introduction*, Philadelphia, PA, Fortress, 1986, pp. 183-187.

44. See H.D. Preuss, *Deuteronomium* (EdF, 164), Darmstadt, Wissenschaftliche
Buchgesellschaft, 1982; Id., *Zum deuteronomistischen Geschichtswerk*, in *TR* 58 (1993)
230-245, 341-395; T. Römer, *The Book of Deuteronomy*, in *The History of Israel's Traditions* (n. 21), pp. 178-212; R. Albertz, *A History of Religion in the Old Testament Period, Volume I: From the Beginnings to the End of the Exile* (OTL), Louisville, KY,
Westminster/John Knox, 1994, pp. 195-236; M.A. O'Brien, *The Book of Deuteronomy*,
in *CR:BS* 3 (1995) 95-128; Römer – de Pury, *L'historiographie deutéronomiste* (n. 29),
pp. 65-71.

If the scholars opposing Noth have made a variety of contributions to the current debate, their work also raises a number of questions that extend beyond it. When modern scholars speak of an ancient author, what do they mean? When they use the term editor, what do they mean or what do they presuppose[45]? Similarly, what is a scribe? In debating these issues, it should be recognized that to a significant extent we are imposing modern constructs on ancient times. While Classical Hebrew has a word for a writer or scribe (*sōpēr*), it has no word for either an author or an editor.

Similar questions may be raised about the manner in which the terms blocks and books are used. Is a block a self-contained, coherent literary work or an edition that contains heterogeneous materials? Rofé's case for a pre-deuteronomistic Ephraimite History seems to assume the former definition, while Cross's Dtr[1] assumes the latter[46]. Moreover, what is a book? Is a book merely a collection of writings on a scroll? Is a book a long written composition? Or, is a book a major division of a longer literary work? My understanding of Westermann is that he has the second definition in view, but in the case of McConville the third definition is also operative. At this point in the dicussion, the contrast between the block approach and the book approach becomes instructive. Scholars such as Lohfink and Rofé argue that basic units within the narrative covered by Joshua through Kings are blocks, not canonical books. Scholarly definitions of these blocks differ. In the view of Lohfink, Deuteronomy 1 through Joshua 22* constitutes such a block[47]. But in the view of Noth, McCarthy, and others, the divisions between the primary units within the larger narrative are provided by speeches, prayers, and summarizing reflections[48]. Even David Jobling, who is primarily concerned with exploring literary issues, argues that the book divisions between Judges and Samuel are later developments that do not reflect the original creation of this literature[49]. Evidence supplied by the Septuagint

---

45. More attention has actually been paid to this question than to the question of authorship. See, for instance, M. FISHBANE, *Biblical Interpretation in Ancient Israel*, Oxford, Clarendon, 1985; B. PECKHAM, *Writing and Editing*, in A.H. BARTELT – A.B. BECK – C.A. FRANKE – P.R. RAABE (eds.), *Fortunate the Eyes That See: Essays in Honor of David Noel Freedman in Celebration of His Seventieth Birthday*, Grand Rapids, MI, Eerdmans, 1995, p. 383.

46. A. ROFÉ speaks of Joshua 24 through 1 Samuel 12* as constituting a coherent, (north) Israel oriented, pre-deuteronomistic unit, *Ephraimite versus Deuteronomistic History*, in D. GARRONE – F. ISRAEL (eds.), *Storia e Tradizioni di Israele: Scritti in Onore di J. Alberto Soggin*, Brescia, Paideia Editrice, 1991, pp. 221-235.

47. Attributed to Dtr[L], N. LOHFINK, *Kerygmata* (n. 22), pp. 87-100.

48. NOTH, *Überlieferungsgeschichtliche Studien* (n. 2), pp. 3-12; D.J. MCCARTHY, *II Samuel 7 and the Structure of the Deuteronomic History*, in *JBL* 84 (1965) 131-138.

49. D. JOBLING, *What, if Anything, is 1 Samuel?*, in *SJOT* 7 (1993) 17-31.

and the Dead Sea Scrolls adds credence to this assertion, *vis à vis* the
content and sequence of various books (e.g., Joshua in the MT, LXX,
and 4QJosh[b])[50], the books that are included in the historical books (e.g.,
the LXX includes Ruth), and the boundaries of these books (e.g., Joshua
and Judges, Samuel and Kings). Some twenty-five years before the publication of the first edition of Noth's *Überlieferungsgeschichtliche Studien*, Burney spoke of the original Book of Judges (note his terminology) as encompassing Joshua 24 through 1 Samuel 12[51]. The point is not
to decide between all these different points of view, but to acknowledge
them. In this context, one wonders whether Westermann, in speaking of
independent, discrete books has assumed too much and oversimplified
the issues.

A different set of questions may be raised about a pre-deuteronomistic
narrative that begins with the exodus. In this case, one wonders whether
Westermann is trying to have it both ways, proposing a book-centered
approach on the one hand, while arguing for a continuous pre-deuteronomistic narrative on the other hand. Assuming, for the sake of argument, the possibility of such a pre-deuteronomistic narrative, why would
such a work *ipso facto* require a story of national origins? Comparative
analysis of ancient Greek histories, such as those of Herodotus and
Thucydides, suggest that such stories were not an ineluctable component
of national histories[52]. Moreover, cannot the very question Westermann
poses about national origins be posed about his theory as well? Why
begin with the exodus? One could make the case that the exodus narratives themselves are not stories of national origin, but stories of national
liberation and lawgiving. The Book of Exodus begins with and presupposes the existence of a people that neither is Egyptian nor belongs in
Egypt. The people's origins lie elsewhere. Westermann speaks of allusions within the Deuteronomistic History to the exodus. But allusions to
"the fathers" also recur in Exodus[53]. Since various texts in Exodus refer

50. See E. Tov, *Textual Criticism of the Hebrew Bible*, Assen, Van Gorcum, 1992,
pp. 327-332, and the references cited there.

51. C.F. Burney, *The Book of Judges, with Introduction and Notes*, London,
Rivingtons, ²1920, pp. XLI-L.

52. As my colleague Paul Harvey points out (private communication), it was only
necessary to address such a question if a historian wished to take issue with a prevailing
misconception. See also the overview of J. Van Seters, *In Search of History*, New Haven, CT, London, Yale University Press, 1983, pp. 8-54.

53. The references to "the fathers" in Deuteronomy are more complicated, as T.
Römer has shown, *Israels Väter: Untersuchungen zur Väterthematik im Deuteronomium
und in der deuteronomistischen Tradition* (OBO, 99), Freiburg (CH), Universitätsverlag;
Göttingen, Vandenhoeck & Ruprecht, 1990. Do such citations refer to the ancestors or to
the exodus generation? N. Lohfink's booklength review of Römer's proposal contains a
response by Römer, *Die Väter Israels im Deuteronomium. Mit einer Stellungnahme von*

to the "God of the fathers" and allude to Israelite ancestors, most prominently Abraham, Isaac, and Jacob, could not one include material in the pre-deuteronomistic narrative from Genesis as well[54]?

III. A Moderate Defence of the Theory of a Deuteronomistic History

Having discussed books, blocks, and a putative pre-deuteronomistic exodus narrative, it remains to discuss the question of whether the deuteronomistic work constitutes a history. Actually, this complex issue involves three related questions. First, is the Deuteronomistic History historically reliable? Second, is it plausible or implausible that the Deuteronomist(s) incorporated disparate, pre-existing materials into his own narrative without completely reworking them? Third, do the components of the deuteronomistic work, whatever their origins, limits, and differences, form a continuous narrative?

First, with respect to the matter of historical reliability, one may take issue with the question. Historical reliability is an elusive and slippery issue. The positivistic way in which this matter is usually broached in biblical studies sidesteps more fundamental issues of historical epistemology, authorial commitments and contexts, the social construction of knowledge, and the fact that history is itself a form of literature, which exhibits its own rhetoric, forms, and tropes. The preoccupation with historical reliability in biblical studies reveals some *naïveté* about the complexities of history writing and, in any case, confuses a form-critical question with a historical one. The fundamental question should be, in the context of antiquity, what constitutes history writing? Does any writer, whether ancient or modern, have free, unmediated access to the past? Most modern historians would say no. One's apprehension of the past is limited by one's assumptions, intellectual tradition, interests, commitments, and geography. One's reconstruction of the past is limited by what evidence one admits and by what evidence one excludes, by what weight one places on certain kinds of evidence and by what means one assembles such evidence, by what line of interpretation one imposes on the evidence and by what role such an interpretation plays in forming a larger reconstruction.

Thomas Römer (OBO, 111), Freiburg (CH), Universitätsverlag; Göttingen, Vandenhoeck & Ruprecht, 1991.

54. In this context, the oft-repeated proposal of D.N. Freedman for further study of the *Primary History*, that is, Genesis through Kings, comes to mind. See D.N. FREEDMAN – J.C. GEOGHEGAN, *Martin Noth: Restrospect and Prospect*, in *The History of Israel's Traditions* (n. 21), pp. 128-152.

The issue, then, is not whether the deuteronomistic work is restricted in its scope, schematic, and tendentious – it clearly is all of these – but whether what the Deuteronomists believe about the past place some constraints upon what they say about the past[55]. Do the *bruta facta* of history, if one may still use such terminology, limit the extent to which deuteronomistic writers fabricate the past[56]? When the issue is examined in this light, can one make the case that the Deuteronomists wrote a history – a meaningful and sequential account of the past[57]? Like the historians of ancient Greece, the Deuteronomists exercised considerable latitude in researching, writing, and arranging their compositions, but their works can still be best classified as histories.

As to inclusion of source materials, one may again take issue with the way in which the question is framed. Does not any historian have to deal with disparate kinds of evidence, whether oral or written? Given the historian's task to comment meaningfully upon the past, what would preclude historians, especially ancient historians, from incorporating and employing different kinds of materials within their works? Far from being anathema to the pursuit of historical reconstruction, such engagement with sources would seem to be intrinsic to the task[58]. Historical writers inevitably have to confront, assess, and negotiate differences between a variety of perspectives on the past. To be sure, the acknowledgement of disparate perspectives, the inclusion of different kinds of sources, and the creation of new materials may create narrative tensions within a text, but the existence of those tensions does not disqualify the resulting work as a history. With respect to the Deuteronomist, I would argue that his recontextualization of tradition and his reinterpretation of

---

55. See further my *Two Nations Under God*, 2 (n. 40), pp. 181-187; ID., *The Vanishing Solomon: The Disappearance of the United Monarchy from Recent Histories of Ancient Israel*, in *JBL* 116 (1997) 19-44.

56. The important study of H. WHITE documents the literary tropes used in modern history writing and explores the extent to which the choice of a historical method affects the conclusions of one's historical study, *Tropics of Discourse: Essays in Cultural Criticism*, Baltimore, Johns Hopkins University Press, 1978. White is, therefore, concerned with interpretation in history and "the fictions of factual representation." Yet he also acknowledges that "Historians are concerned with events which can be assigned to specific time-space locations, events which are (or were) in principle observable or perceivable..." (p. 121).

57. So both VAN SETERS, *In Search of History* (n. 52) and B. HALPERN *The First Historians. The Hebrew Bible and History*, San Francisco, CA, Harper & Row, 1988, whatever their many differences.

58. This does not entail, however, that an ancient writer's sources were good sources or that a writer employed sources in such a way that their original shape and contexts were honored. One has only to look at the way in which the Chronicler used his biblical sources to see various counter-examples to such a proposition.

older materials, including the old deuteronomic law code, are intriguing and telling aspects of his craft[59].

Evidence for such a literary-critical model elsewhere in the Hebrew Bible is not long in coming. In the case of Chronicles one is not left completely in the dark about the matter of sources; we have some of these sources in the form of older biblical texts. The Chronicler quotes from his biblical sources, often at some length, often verbatim, often in succession. The Chronicler sometimes juxtaposes citations with little or no intervening material or with only slight editing[60]. Call the Chronicler what you will, and the Chronicler has been called many things, but the main outlines of his compositional technique are clear[61]. Such a model plays havoc, however, with the notion that a historical narrative has to be an internally consistent, flowing, seamless whole. Clearly, the Chronicler draws from unrelated sources and allows differences in vocabulary, style, and even theme to stand. In brief, the Chronicler's *Grundschrift*, however one reconstructs it, does not fit the literary model of history advocated by Westermann. The Chronicler and, I would argue, the Deuteronomists as well, tolerate heterogeneity within their texts[62].

To come to the third issue: does the narrative of Joshua through Kings constitute a continuous work? My concern in addressing this particular question is not with books or blocks *per se*, because a deuteronomistic writer may incorporate and supplement pre-existing materials within a larger narrative framework[63]. The question is whether the deuteronomistic historical work, whatever the origin of its constituent parts, is more than a lightly edited compilation of books or blocks. In

---

59. Close study of various passages in Kings supports the claim of Noth and many others that the authors of Kings used some form of Deuteronomy. The deuteronomistic use of *Urdeuteronomium* was, however, much more sophisticated and complex than Noth recognized, G.N. KNOPPERS, *The Deuteronomist and the Deuteronomic Law of the King: A Reexamination of a Relationship*, in ZAW 108 (1996) 329-346; ID., *Solomon's Fall and Deuteronomy*, in L.K. HANDY (ed.), *The Age of Solomon: Scholarship at the Turn of the Millennium* (SHANE, 11), Leiden, Brill, 1997, pp. 392-410. For a different view, see WESTERMANN, who thinks that Deuteronomy was a late insertion, *Geschichtsbücher*. (n. 8), pp. 140-142.

60. Within the Chronicler's history of the monarchy, the reign of Jehoshaphat serves as a good example. See my *Reform and Regression: The Chronicler's Presentation of Jehoshaphat*, in Bib 72 (1991) 500-524.

61. See most recently, I. KALIMI, *Zur Geschichtsschreibung des Chronisten* (BZAW, 226), Berlin – New York, NY, de Gruyter, 1995, and the references cited there.

62. *Two Nations Under God*, 2 (n. 40), pp. 73-112.

63. The question could be put even more strongly: even if one accepted the existence of books (Westermann, McConville) or large blocks (Rofé's *Ephraimite History*; Lohfink's *Dtr^L*) as the primary units incorporated into the deuteronomistic corpus, would the resulting corpus still qualify as a continuous work?

what follows, I would like to provide a moderate defense of the concept of a Deuteronomistic History.

To begin with, some of the alleged major discrepancies between various sections of the deuteronomistic presentation are more apparent than real. Westermann speaks of the sacral view of kingship in Samuel as opposed to that found in Kings[64]. But monarchs such as Solomon and Jeroboam are no less important to the fate of the people in Kings than Saul and David are in Samuel[65]. In both books, kings mediate the relationship between Yhwh and the people, whether for good or for ill[66]. Von Rad speaks of a cyclical view of time in the Judges stories as opposed to a linear view of time in the monarchy[67]. But the patterns of reform and regression that characterize the Deuteronomist's synchronistic history of Israel and Judah undermine a simply linear view of the monarchy[68]. In any case, the cycle of rebellion, divine wrath, punishment, and deliverance that von Rad claims is not found in Kings, is, in fact, pivotal to the deuteronomistic portrayal of disunion[69]. Briefer and more restricted versions of this cycle can also be found in the oracles against the northern dynasties[70]. This suggests that at least some of the differences between sections of the Deuteronomistic History have been exaggerated.

On a positive level, there are important indications of unity in the Deuteronomistic History[71]. Some of these are well-known – the prophecy-fulfillment schema[72], which operates on both short-range and long-

---

64. C. WESTERMANN, *Geschichtsbücher* (n. 8), pp. 57-74.

65. One should not conclude that a writer embraces a non-sacral view of kingship, because that writer depicts troubles befalling a king and his royal house. In the Kirta legend, for example, the dire effects of Kirta's illness on his family, land, and people only underscore how important the monarch is to the relationship between the people of Ḥubur and their gods, G.N. KNOPPERS, *Dissonance and Disaster in the Legend of Kirta*, in *JAOS* 114 (1994) 572-582.

66. G. KNOPPERS, *Two Nations Under God*, 2 (n. 40), pp. 229-254.

67. G. VON RAD, *Old Testament Theology*, vol. 1, New York, NY, Harper & Row, 1962, pp. 346-347; cf. WESTERMANN, *Geschichtsbücher* (n. 8), pp. 53-56; KNAUF, *L''Historiographie Deutéronomiste'* (n. 18), pp. 416-417.

68. H.-D. HOFFMANN, *Reform und Reformen. Untersuchungen zu einem Grundthema der deuteronomistischen Geschichtsschreibung* (ATANT, 66), Zürich, Theologischer Verlag, 1980, pp. 169-264.

69. G. KNOPPERS, *Two Nations Under God*, 1 (n. 7), pp. 135-168.

70. W. DIETRICH, *Prophetie und Geschichte* (FRLANT, 108), Göttingen, Vandenhoeck & Ruprecht, 1972; H.N. WALLACE, *The Oracles Against the Israelite Dynasties in 1 and 2 Kings*, in *Bib* 67 (1986) 21-40; S.L. MCKENZIE, *The Trouble with Kings: The Composition of the Book of Kings in the Deuteronomistic History* (SVT, 42), Leiden, Brill, 1991, pp. 81-100.

71. In this regard, see also the paper by T. Römer in this volume.

72. G. VON RAD, *The Problem of the Hexateuch and Other Essays*, New York, NY, McGraw-Hill, 1966, p. 219.

range levels[73], the division of Israelite history into sequential periods, the connections between individual sections and books[74], the links between Deuteronomy and later books[75], the deuteronomistically-worded speeches, prayers, and summarizing reflections that orchestrate the transitions between major epochs[76], and the reuse of themes from one part of the work in another, such as the citations of and allusions to the Davidic promises (from Samuel) in Kings. Other literary devices that unify the Deuteronomistic History are not so well-known. These include the use of divine wrath formulae, the collocation ב־ יהוה התאנף (or its alloform חרה אף יהוה ב־), to cap a stylized description of popular or royal regression[77], the use of intermarriage with the autochthonous Canaanite nations as a *topos* to explain Israel's decline both in the transition to the period of the Judges and in the transition to the dual monarchies (the second part of Solomon's reign)[78], and the creation of analogies between events that follow in sequence[79].

CONCLUSION

Given these indications of unity, a picture emerges of a work that is more than a catalogue of sources, books, or blocks, which has been unobtrusively spliced together. Addressing the record of Israel's life in the land, the Deuteronomistic History is shaped by concepts of causality and chronology and written with a view to certain standards. By speaking of a moderate defense of the theory of a Deuteronomistic History, I wish to avoid, however, the impression that the Deuteronomist was simply a grand inventor, someone who created his work out of whole cloth. To reduce the tremendous diversity of vocabulary, styles, forms, and idi-

73. H. WEIPPERT, *Geschichten und Geschichte: Verheißung und Erfüllung im deuteronomistischen Geschichtswerk*, in *Congress Volume: Leuven, 1989* (n. 23), pp. 116-131.

74. McCONVILLE, *Historical Books* (n. 8), pp. 9-10.

75. See, for instance, R.E. FRIEDMAN, *From Egypt to Egypt: Dtr¹ and Dtr²*, in B. HALPERN – J. LEVENSON (eds.), *Traditions in Transformation: Turning Points in Biblical Faith. Essays Presented to Frank Moore Cross, Jr.*, Winona Lake, IN, Eisenbrauns, 1981, pp. 167-192.

76. As many scholars have stressed, these are more numerous than Noth recognized, KNOPPERS, *Two Nations Under God*, 1 (n. 7), pp. 26-27.

77. D.J. McCARTHY, *The Wrath of Yahweh and the Structural Unity of the Deuteronomistic History*, in J.L. CRENSHAW – J.T. WILLIS (eds.), *Essays in Old Testament Ethics*, New York, NY, Ktav, 1974, pp. 97-110.

78. G.N. KNOPPERS, *Sex, Religion, and Politics: The Deuteronomist on Intermarriage*, in *HAR* 14 (1994) 121-141.

79. VAN SETERS, *In Search of History* (n. 52), pp. 31-40.

omatic expressions within this extensive corpus to a single creative author is reductive[80]. By the same token, the Deuteronomist was more than simply an editor, someone who simply gathered pre-assembled materials and slightly altered them, according to a particular purpose. In short, the Deuteronomist was both an editor and an author – someone who selected and reworked sources, but also someone who created his own material and arranged the whole into a broadly sequential and connected work. This brings us back to Noth, because my view of the Deuteronomist's compositional technique is indebted to his. It is unclear whether the current challenges to the very existence of a Deuteronomistic History are a temporary or a permanent feature of the scholarly landcsape. At any rate, perhaps the greatest credit to the impact of Noth's scholarship is that his work continues to set the contours, whether positively or negatively, for the present debate.

The Pennsylvania State University   Gary N. KNOPPERS
University Park, PA, USA

---

80. Nor is it necessary to deny that important differences exist between the various periods depicted in the larger work. Each of these eras may be characterized by its own tropes, characters, and themes, yet form part of a larger deuteronomistic historical corpus.

THE DIVIDED KINGDOM
IN THE DEUTERONOMISTIC HISTORY
AND IN SCHOLARSHIP ON IT

In the beginning was the Deuteronomistic History. It was not *tohu wabohu* but a well ordered creation by one author who had access to Israel's traditions. We knew not his name, though scoffers say it was Martin Noth. We called him simply "Dtr." And it was good. But as scholars multiplied on the Deuteronomistic History so did Dtrs. Soon, there arose a great division in the earth. Those in the North – of America – followed Cross while those across the Sea went after Smend. Each faction did what was right in its own eyes, and there was little interaction between them. Then in the 50th year an invitation went out from America saying, "Come, let us celebrate and let us reason together". And the Smendites came to Washington to gather with the Crossites at the SBL meeting. The Smendites did not fear and were not harmed, and some were very well housed. And now the scholars of the neutral land of Switzerland, the land of cheese and chocolate, have once again brought us together for fellowship and to reason together, and we thank them for their hospitality. It is indeed good that we assemble to speak about these matters, for the words of the former prophets have been heard and understood in different ways.

This paper follows up on the suggestion that the different theories about the composition of the Deuteronomistic History arose as a result of scholars concentrating on different sections of the work. The paper will assess some of the principal tenets of both the Cross and Smend hypotheses through the lens of 1 Samuel 8-12. It is rather unusual for a Cross student to look to Samuel for compositional analysis. It would be inaccurate to say that Cross ignored the book. But he limited the work of Dtr[2] in all of Samuel to just one verse, 1 Sam 12,25[1], without addressing the complex literary-critical issues in 1 Samuel 8-12 or any other section of the book. The adherents of the model have basically followed suit, so that Friedman[2] and Nelson[3], for example, also did not include any de-

---

1. F.M. CROSS, *Canaanite Myth and Hebrew Epic. Essays in the History and Religion of Israel*, Cambridge, MA – London, Harvard University Press, 1973, p. 287.

2. R.E. FRIEDMAN, *The Exile and Biblical Narrative* (HSM, 22), Chico, CA, Scholars Press, 1981.

3. R.D. NELSON, *The Double Redaction of the Deuteronomistic History* (JSOT SS, 18), Sheffield, JSOT Press, 1981.

tailed treatment of 1 Samuel 8-12. This is all the more surprising since
some of the literary-critical conclusions of Veijola and others for secondary additions in these chapters (see below) could have lent themselves quite well to Cross's theory. McCarter[4] and Halpern[5] are the only
adherents of the Cross model, so far as I know, to have dealt comprehen-
sively with these chapters, and McCarter was forced to do so by the nature of his work as a commentary. The proponents of Smend's theory
have been more comprehensive. While Smend's initial article dealt only
with a handful of texts in Joshua and Judges[6], the now classic studies of
Dietrich[7] and Veijola[8] essentially covered Samuel and Kings.

The treatments of 1 Samuel 8-12 in the Cross and Smend schools
have moved in opposite directions, though on somewhat similar grounds.
McCarter[9], influenced by Birch[10], found an earlier redaction that was
prophetic in nature, while Veijola found a later deuteronomistic reworking. But both built their cases on the grounds of the assumption that
there are *königsfreundliche* and *königsfeindliche* strands to be found in
those chapters. It is that assumption and the literary results that grow out
of it that I question. It is my view that 1 Samuel 8-12 is a unit.

At the 1994 annual meeting of the SBL in Chicago in a special reception honoring Frank Cross, I found myself eavesdropping on a conversa-
tion between Gary Knoppers and Robert Wilson. They were agreeing
that it was the books of Samuel they found problematic in trying to understand the Deuteronomistic History. Imagine my surprise to learn that
the trouble was not with Kings at all but with Samuel. As a student of
Cross's, my own work has also focused on Kings. I believed that it was
where the evidence relating to the date and authorship of the Deuteronomistic History surfaced most clearly. But now I would like to suggest

---

4. P.K. McCarter, Jr., *I Samuel* (AB, 8), Garden City, NY, Doubleday, 1980.
5. B. Halpern, *The Constitution of the Monarchy in Israel* (HSM, 25), Chico, CA,
Scholars Press, 1981.
6. R. Smend, *Das Gesetz und die Völker. Ein Beitrag zur deuteronomistischen Redaktionsgeschichte*, in H.W. Wolff (ed.), *Probleme biblischer Theologie. G. von Rad zum
70. Geburtstag*, München, Kaiser, 1971, pp. 494-509.
7. W. Dietrich, *Prophetie und Geschichte. Eine redaktionsgeschichtliche Untersuchung zum deuteronomistischen Geschichtswerk* (FRLANT, 108), Göttingen, Vandenhoeck & Ruprecht, 1972.
8. T. Veijola, *Die ewige Dynastie. David und die Entstehung seiner Dynastie nach
der deuteronomistischen Darstellung* (AASF B, 193), Helsinki, Suomalainen Tiedeakatemia, 1975; *Das Königtum in der Beurteilung der deuteronomistischen Historiographie. Eine redaktionsgeschichtliche Untersuchung* (AASF B, 198), Helsinki, Suomalainen Tiedeakatemia, 1977.
9. McCarter, *I Samuel* (n. 4), esp. pp. 18-21.
10. B.C. Birch, *The Rise of the Israelite Monarchy. The Growth and Development of
1 Samuel 7-15* (SBL DS, 27), Missoula, MT, Scholars Press, 1976.

that 1 Samuel 8-12 contains some keys to unlocking the mysteries relating to the composition of the Deuteronomistic History.

I initially developed the case for my view that 1 Samuel 8-12 is a unit (the *Wiederaufnahme* is intentional) three years ago in the essay now published in the volume compiled by our hosts, *Israël construit son histoire*[11]. Thanks to a fine critique of that essay by Mr. Christophe Nihan, a student here in Lausanne, I have now refined and enlarged some of my arguments. While I cannot repeat them, an overview is appropriate. In 1 Samuel 8-12 Dtr has expanded two older stories about Saul into a block describing the transition from judges to monarchy. The two older stories lie beneath 9,1-10,16 and chapter 11, and their original contours have been generally recognized since the 1970 work of Ludwig Schmidt[12]. The main change to both stories was the addition of Samuel's name in the role of the national prophet and leader who anointed Saul. Dtr tied the two stories together with his account of the lot ceremony directed by Samuel in 10,17-27a. The result was a core unit in chapters 9-11 that describes the accession of Israel's first king as a sequence of steps. Saul is first anointed by Samuel when he is in search of his father's asses. He is then publicly designated by lot and finally proves himself in battle against the Ammonites. Dtr further surrounded this core with the story of the people's request for a king in chapter 8 and Samuel's farewell address in chapter 12, which together lay out his theological response to kingship. Chapter 7 serves as a hinge from the unit about Samuel's life and the ark narrative in 1 Samuel 1-6 to the unit on the beginning of monarchy in 8-12. The figure of Samuel in chapter 7 in the roles of prophet, priest, and judge is especially artificial and a creation of Dtr.

This understanding of 1 Samuel 8-12 has important implications for the composition of the Deuteronomistic History. In the first place, it renders untenable the theory of a prophetic document underlying Dtr's account. There are two versions of this theory extant, one represented by the Australians Campbell[13] and O'Brien[14] and the other by Birch and

---

11. S.L. McKenzie, *Cette Royauté qui fait problème*, in A. de Pury – T. Römer – J.-D. Macchi (eds.), *Israël construit son histoire. L'historiographie deutéronomiste à la lumière des recherches récentes* (Le Monde de la Bible, 34), Geneva, Labor et Fides, 1996, pp. 267-295.

12. L. Schmidt, *Menschlicher Erfolg und Jahwes Initiative. Studien zu Tradition, Interpretation und Historie in Überlieferungen von Gideon, Saul und David* (WMANT, 38), Neukirchen-Vluyn, Neukirchener Verlag, 1970.

13. A.F. Campbell, *Of Prophets and Kings. A Late Ninth-Century Document (1 Samuel 1-2 Kings 10)* (CBQ MS, 17), Washington, DC, Catholic Biblical Association, 1986.

14. M.A. O'Brien, *The Deuteronomistic History Hypothesis. A Reassessment* (OBO, 92), Freiburg (CH), Universitätsverlag; Göttingen, Vandenhoeck & Ruprecht, 1989.

McCarter. A full-scale literary-critical response is not possible here. But Samuel's place in the story is Dtr's contribution. Also, Veijola has demonstrated the thoroughly deuteronomistic nature of these chapters, aside from the source materials[15]. In addition, one observation about form criticism is worth making. Birch's dates for the prophetic narratives that he isolated beneath Dtr's writing in 1 Samuel 8-12 were heavily dependent on Westermann's conclusions in his *Grundformen prophetischer Rede*[16]. But Westermann assumes that the oracles in the Deuteronomistic History come from the times in which they are set, so that his conclusions, and hence Birch's, are entirely unacceptable when it comes to dating the oracular forms.

A second important implication of 1 Samuel 8-12 is the exilic date that its references to Mizpah require for the Deuteronomistic History. Again, Veijola has explored this matter in detail[17]. It has also forced McCarter to adopt the literarily indefensible position that what he calls the "Mizpah material" in 1 Samuel 8-12 is secondary[18]. The situation may be summed up as follows. The depiction of Mizpah of Benjamin in these chapters, as in Judges 19-21, as the site of political and religious convocation reflects its status in the exile. The entire image of a national assembly is anachronistic and could not have occurred before the establishment of a centralized monarchic state. Mizpah was nothing more than a border fortress until 586 B.C.E., when it replaced Jerusalem as Judah's administrative and cultic center.

With this groundwork, let us turn our attention to the Cross and Smend theories. Cross's case was based on three themes dealing with references to Jeroboam, David, and Manasseh in the book of Kings. The first theme, that of the sin of Jeroboam, remains basically as Cross articulated it. It begins with the description of Jeroboam's establishment of the shrines and their cult at Dan and Bethel in 1 Kings 12,25-32 + 13,34 (the intervening material is secondary). Dtr then accuses each king of Israel in turn of perpetuating the "sin of Jeroboam". Each royal house rises and falls according to prophetic announcement until Israel's destruction by the Assyrians, which is explained in 2 Kings

---

15. VEIJOLA, *Das Königtum* (n. 8).

16. C. WESTERMANN, *Grundformen prophetischer Rede* (BEvT, 31), München, Chr. Kaiser, 1960; = ID., *Basic Forms of Prophetic Speech*, trans. H.C. WHITE, Louisville, KY, Westminster/John Knox, 1991.

17. T. VEIJOLA, *Verheissung in der Krise. Studien zur Literatur und Theologie der Exilszeit anhand des 89. Psalms* (AASF B, 220), Helsinki, Suomalainen Tiedeakatemia, 1982, pp. 178-210.

18. P.K. MCCARTER, *The Books of Samuel*, in S.L. MCKENZIE – M.P. GRAHAM (eds.), *The History of Israel's Traditions. The Heritage of Martin Noth* (JSOT SS, 182), Sheffield, Sheffield Academic Press, 1994, pp. 260-280, esp. 278-280.

17,20-23 as the consequence of Jeroboam's sin. Hence, through this theme Dtr offered a theological explanation for both the succession of coups and royal houses in Israel and the nation's ultimate demise in 721 B.C.E.

The second and primary theme isolated by Cross provided a contrast to Jeroboam in the form of David. Cross found the beginning of this theme with the promise to David through Nathan in 2 Samuel 7. He also pointed out that David is the standard of comparison for kings of Judah and that in the cases of Abijah (1 Kings 15,4-5a) and Jehoram (2 Kings 8,19), Judah's survival despite wicked kings is explained as the benefit of Yahweh's loyalty to his promise to David. Arguing that the ideology of an eternal dynasty was that of the royal house itself, Cross concluded that it reflected a pre-exilic setting and that its climax was to be found in the account of Josiah's reign.

There is no doubt that David and Yahweh's promise to him form one of Dtr's major themes. But looking at it through the lens of 1 Samuel 8-12 results in a very different image from the one Cross described based solely on 2 Samuel 7 and the book of Kings. In the first place, we must assume that the setting of the theme is exilic, not only because that is where it ends but also because the Mizpah references in the key Dtr unit in 1 Samuel 8-12 point to that period. As van Keulen has recently observed, the assumption of a pre-exilic date by dual redactionists colors the reading of the material in the Deuteronomistic History and is unwarranted to the extent that it neglects the burden of proof they bear in light of the work's ending[19].

Secondly, and no less important, 1 Samuel 8-12 sets the stage ideologically for the Davidic promise in a way that has generally been overlooked. There is an ambivalence about kingship in these chapters that deserves fuller explication than can be given here. The bottom line is that both monarchy and the monarch are subordinate to Yahweh. Kingship comes about in Israel only because Yahweh permits it, and he does so with certain conditions. One of those is that he choose the king. This is ironic in view of the fact that permanence in the form of dynastic rule appears to be one of the reasons why the people reject the system of rule under judges in preference to monarchy in the first place. The process of charismatic designation is clear in the series of royal houses in the north, each of which is appointed and then rejected by a prophet. Thus, both the royal houses in Israel and the Davidic dynasty in Judah are subject to

19. P.S.F. VAN KEULEN, *Manasseh through the Eyes of the Deuteronomists. The Manasseh Account (2 Kings 21:1-18) & the Final Chapters of the Deuteronomistic History* (OTS, 38), Leiden, Brill, 1996, pp. 49, 191-192.

Yahweh, which means that their existence is ultimately contingent on obedience to the law.

Of course, the primary issue with regard to the Davidic covenant is how it should be understood in light of the exile. How could Dtr write of an eternal promise to David when he knows that the kingdom has ended? The simplest answer to this question, and one that has frequently been suggested, is that "forever" does not really mean forever. Long expresses this idea eloquently when he refers to the eternal covenant as hyperbolic language of royal legitimation "rooted in the literary styles of ancient Near Eastern monarchies" and argues that it should not be taken literally[20]. This view may be correct; it assumes, with Cross, that Dtr borrowed the idea of the Davidic covenant from the royal ideology of the Judahite court. If so, however, Dtr has invested the ideology with a theological content that it did not originally intend. I would suggest that Dtr sees the promise to David as both fulfilled and yet never abrogated by Yahweh and therefore open to the future. In the first place, the David theme begins not with 2 Samuel 7 but with 1 Samuel 8-12 or at least shortly thereafter. First Samuel 13,13-14, which is part of a Dtr insertion (13,7b-15a), says that Saul had the opportunity for an eternal kingdom: "Yahweh would have established your kingdom over Israel forever." This is the same eternal house promised to David and then offered to Jeroboam. Saul and Jeroboam are both disobedient and so do not receive the promise. Neither of their houses is established eternally; each has just one heir who sits on the throne before their entire line is exterminated. Hence, the contrast in the establishment of David's house is with theirs. In part, Dtr is explaining why the Davidic dynasty far outlasted Saul's and all of those in the North – because Yahweh established David's house in accordance with his promise. The contrast with Saul is explicit in 2 Sam 7,15 where Yahweh promises not to remove (*hēsîr*) his *hesed* from David's son as he removed it from Saul, whom he removed from the throne. It is striking that the same verb is found in reference to Jeroboam and Israel in 2 Kings 17,18.23. What is meant by this verb, as the history makes clear, is annihilation of the royal line.

Other texts also show that Yahweh fulfilled his word to David. When Solomon dedicates the temple in 1 Kings 8, he acknowledges as much (vv. 20, 24):

> Yahweh established his word that he spoke since I have arisen in the place of David my father and have sat on the throne of Israel just as Yahweh promised; and I have built the temple to the name of Yahweh God of Israel.

20. B.O. LONG, *I Kings, with an Introduction to Historical Literature* (FOTL, 9), Grand Rapids, MI, Eerdmans, 1984, pp. 16-17.

You have kept what you promised to David my father; you have fulfilled with your hands what you spoke with your mouth as this day.

Solomon's accession and his completion of the temple fulfill Yahweh's promise to David (vv. 20, 24). Solomon goes on to ask that Yahweh keep another promise to David:

Now oh Yahweh God of Israel, keep for your servant David my father what you promised to him saying, "Your male heirs will never be cut off before me from sitting on the throne of Israel if only your sons will keep their way to walk before me as you walked before me".

The intention of this verse is debated. The references to Israel and the conditionality of the promise have led some scholars to propose that the verse alludes to the division of the kingdom as punishment for Solomon's sin. It would be the "rod of mortals" to which 2 Sam 7,14 refers, with which David's son will be disciplined without the removal of Yahweh's *ḥesed*. What is clear is that this speech describes Yahweh as having faithfully kept his word to David.

It is in this light that the references to David in 1 Kings 15,4 and 2 Kings 8,19 should be read. Both verses indicate that the kingdom of Judah continues despite wicked kings because of (*lĕmă'an*) David. But this should not be construed (*pace* Cross) as the benefit of an eternal decree by which Yahweh himself is bound nor as a license for Judah or its kings to behave as they will without consequences. Dtr does not intend to subordinate Yahweh to the Davidic covenant. Rather, for Dtr Yahweh has kept his word, and Yahweh is supreme. Judah was not destroyed, according to 2 Kings 8,19, because Yahweh did not will it (*wĕlō' 'ābāh yhwh lĕhašḥît 'et-yĕhûdāh*), and this was for David's sake.

What is more, Dtr seems to regard the Davidic promise as still open. It is never explicitly cancelled or abrogated in the book of Kings or the Deuteronomistic History. The description of it as *lĕ'ôlām* and for *kol-hayyāmîm* implies that it is ongoing. The case of Athaliah is instructive here (2 Kings 11). She was not a Davidid. Dtr's account of her seven year reign lacks the usual regnal formulas, showing that he does not consider her a legitimate ruler. Yet there is no indication that she represents a breach of the Davidic promise. Indeed, the story's outcome attests the preservation of the Davidic line. The ending of the Deuteronomistic History also supports this point, as von Rad noted. Jehoiachin is released from Babylonian prison. The Davidic line is alive and well. It has not been destroyed like those of Saul, Jeroboam, and the rest of the northern kings. The exile may be another "rod of mortals," but Yahweh has not removed his *ḥesed* from the house of David. Yahweh is supreme. He will decide if and when and how to restore the kingdom. He has kept his promise, but it also remains open to the future.

Cross's third theme, or subtheme as he calls it, concerns the wicked-
ness of Manasseh as the cause for the exile. Cross took this as an indication of exilic editing, arguing that it was unexpectedly tacked on to what
was otherwise an optimistic account that culminated with Josiah. Our
review of this theme is significantly aided by van Keulen's recent study
of the Manasseh pericope in 2 Kings 21,1-18, which concludes that it is
essentially a Dtr(G) composition[21]. Indeed, I am skeptical of van Keulen's
own contention that vv. 4, 8-9aα, and 15 are later additions. Where his
work is particularly valuable, though, is in dealing with the contrast between Manasseh and Josiah. Van Keulen points out that Manasseh is
described in terms that recall Jeroboam and especially Ahab, the two
worst kings of the North. It may not be stretching the point too far to say
that Manasseh is depicted as worse than all the kings of Israel put together. Second Kings 21,11 states that he was worse than the Amorites
whom Yahweh dispossessed before Israel. Van Keulen then argues that
we should take the statements about Manasseh in 2 Kings 21,11-12 and
especially 23,26-27 at face value when they say Manasseh was so bad
that even Josiah could not prevent the disastrous consequences of his
reign. The fact that Josiah corrects Manasseh's cultic aberrations only
highlights this claim.

I would add two small observations to those of van Keulen. First,
Manasseh's fifty-five year reign, the longest of all the kings of Israel and
Judah, gave him unprecedented opportunity to do evil in Dtr's scheme.
Secondly, due to the final outcome of the history and the overall impres-
sion of the book of Kings, it is often overlooked that up to the time of
Josiah there are actually more good kings in Judah than bad according to
Dtr's evaluations: Asa, Jehoshaphat, Joash, Amaziah, Azariah, Jotham,
Hezekiah, and Josiah "did what was right," while Rehoboam, Abijam,
Jehoram, Ahaziah, Ahaz, Manasseh, and Amon "did evil." (The list
does not include David or Solomon, who ruled the united kingdom.
David, of course, is judged righteous, while the evaluation for Solomon
is mixed. Nor does it include Athaliah, whose reign is considered illegitimate.) Following Josiah, the final four kings of Judah (Jehoahaz,
Jehoiakim, Jehoiachin, and Zedekiah) are all judged evil. At first, this
appears to support Cross's contention that an optimistic history has been
radically and unexpectedly altered at the end. But a closer look suggests
another viewpoint; it is not really after Josiah that Judah's fortunes
change, as Cross suggests, but after Hezekiah. Up to and including
Hezekiah, the kings of Judah are basically righteous. The reigns of
wicked kings are qualified in some way or seen as less significant. Un-

---

21. VAN KEULEN, *Manasseh through the Eyes of the Deuteronomists* (n. 19).

der Rehoboam it is Judah rather than the king who does evil (1 Kings 14,22). For Abijam and Jehoram, Dtr explains that Judah was preserved because of Yahweh's loyalty to David. Ahaziah only reigns one year. Evil Ahaz is balanced by righteous Hezekiah, whose trust in Yahweh saves Jerusalem from the Assyrians, with whom Ahaz had linked Judah in the first place. But from Manasseh on the only good king was Josiah. For Dtr, laboring to explain the past theologically, Judah's duration beyond that of Israel was explained in part by its history of better kings. But Manasseh's unequaled tenure immediately following Hezekiah suggested the occasion for unparalleled sin leading to a plunge that even Josiah could not halt. Thus, Manasseh, rather than being an afterthought to Dtr's historical structure, is actually the crux at which Judah's fortunes change.

Turning now to the Smend hypothesis, like Cross's Dtr[1], Smend's DtrN was also to be recognized by two themes: *das Gesetz und die Völker*, specifically foreign peoples remaining in the land. Cross used his themes to isolate an earlier *Grundschrift*, while Smend used his to separate a later *Schicht*. But Cross's theory also had a *schichtliches* element to it, since he attributed a series of secondary texts throughout the Deuteronomistic History to Dtr[2] (even though they sometimes had little in common – in this regard Smend was more consistent). Of course, Smend did work in a completely different portion of the Deuteronomistic History than Cross.

This last difference adumbrates one of the problems of the Smend theory when viewed through the lens of 1 Samuel 8-12. While Smend's followers have been more comprehensive than Cross's in their application of his theory to the Deuteronomistic History, they have not always been so consistent in using Smend's two themes to find DtrN texts. Mommer exaggerates only slightly when he says that the law and the people left in the land play absolutely no role in 1 Samuel 8-12[22]. Becker has observed as much for chapter 8[23], and so really does Veijola[24] when he makes a feable attempt to connect the people's demand for a king in order to be like the nations with Smend's theme of the people left in the land. Thus, as Mommer goes on to point out, the most important criteria, according to Smend, for distinguishing DtrN

22. P. MOMMER, *Samuel. Geschichte und Überlieferung* (WMANT, 65), Neukirchen-Vluyn, Neukirchener Verlag, 1991, p. 53.

23. U. BECKER, *Der innere Widerspruch der deuteronomistischen Beurteilung des Königtums (am Beispiel von 1 Sam 8)*, in M. OEMING – A. GRAUPNER (eds.), *Altes Testament und christliche Verkündigung. Festschrift für A. H. J. Gunneweg zum 65. Geburtstag*, Stuttgart, Kohlhammer, 1987, pp. 246-270.

24. VEIJOLA, *Das Königtum* (n. 8), p. 67.

are lacking in 1 Samuel 8-12. Mommer[25] and Becker[26] have also shown the weakness of the linguistic and ideological criteria. As recognized by adherents of the Smend theory, DtrG and DtrN stand in the same tradition and belong to the same theological circle, so that the evidential basis for distinguishing between them is very thin. (Indeed, I doubt that it exists.) In 1 Samuel 8-12 the distinction between DtrP and DtrN levels is really based on the perception of *königsfeindliche* and *königsfreundliche* Tendenzen.

First Samuel 8-12 thus raises serious doubts about the Smend hypothesis in two respects. First, the ease with which the transition is made away from the themes identified by Smend to completely different features as criteria for isolating DtrN does not inspire confidence in the results. The reliance on perceived ideology about kingship, especially, raises a question about how good the literary criteria for more than one editor really are. But even assuming that the followers of Smend have isolated secondary material in 1 Samuel 8-12 and that Smend was correct in his isolation of secondary material in Joshua and Judges (and I am not ready now to concede either assumption) there is no real reason for ascribing both sets of additions to the same editor. Secondly, the extremely narrow base in linguistic evidence for separating editorial levels easily gives way to more extreme solutions that have appeared more than once in the Smend sphere. Instead of two or three redactors, as many as a dozen are posited. The end result is that any meaningful text disintegrates and scholarship itself becomes little more than an exercise of self-gratification. Is there any example of a piece of literature elsewhere in the world with such a complicated development?

In conclusion, 1 Samuel 8-12 indicates that Dtr was capable of sublety and ambivalence of which redactional theories have robbed him. At the same time, it also represents the beginning of themes in Dtr's work that he has skillfully carried throughout his history all the way to the end of 2 Kings. It therefore tends to confirm Noth's hypothesis of a single deliberate historical work encompassing the Former Prophets with Deuteronomy at its head. It is ironic that just as dialogue between the Cross and Smend schools begins in earnest, the consensus about the existence of the Deuteronomistic History has begun to dissolve. By way of an *inclusio,* though the Smendites and Crossites have dominated the land, scholars and theories have continued to multiply. Of late, some have arisen from among the faithful who no longer believe in the one

25. MOMMER, *Samuel* (n. 22), pp. 53-54.
26. BECKER, *Der innere Widerspruch* (n. 23), pp. 257-262.

History. These are men of renown – Auld[27], Knauf[28], Westermann[29], and now Kaiser[30]. There are indeed many facets to the Deuteronomistic History and of writing books about it there is no end. Who is able to comprehend it all? But as for me and my house we will follow Noth, at least for the time being.

Rhodes College   Steven L. McKENZIE
2000 North Parkway
Memphis, TN 38112
USA

27. See esp. A.G. AULD, *The Deuteronomists and the Former Prophets or What Makes the Former Prophets Deuteronomistic?*, in L.S. SCHEARING –S.L. McKENZIE (eds.), *Those Elusive Deuteronomists: The Phenomenon of Pan-Deuteronomism* (JSOT SS, 268), Sheffield, Sheffield Academic Press, 1999, pp. 116-126, as well as *The Former Prophets* in S.L. McKENZIE – M.P. GRAHAM (eds.), *The Hebrew Bible Today: An Introduction to Critical Issues*, Louisville, KY, Westminster/John Knox, 1998, pp. 53-68.

28. E.A. KNAUF, *L'"Historiographie Deutéronomiste" (DtrG) existe-t-elle?* in DE PURY – RÖMER – MACCHI (eds.), *Israël construit son histoire* (n. 11), pp. 409-418.

29. C. WESTERMANN, *Die Geschichtsbücher des Alten Testaments. Gab es ein deuteronomistisches Geschichtswerk?* (TB, 87), Gütersloh, Kaiser, 1994.

30. O. KAISER, *Das Verhältnis der Erzählung vom König David zum sogenannten Deuteronomistischen Geschichtswerk*, in A. DE PURY – T. RÖMER (eds.), *Die sogenannte Thronfolgegeschichte Davids. Neue Einsichten und Anfragen* OBO, 176), Freiburg (CH), Universitätsverlag; Göttingen, Vandenbroeck & Ruprec ht, 2000, pp. 94-122.

LE(S) RÉCIT(S) DTR DE L'INSTAURATION
DE LA MONARCHIE EN 1 SAMUEL[1]

Dans leur forme «finale», les textes qui mettent en scène l'émergence de l'institution monarchique en Israël (soit, classiquement, 1 S 8–12[2]) présentent une complexité littéraire évidente: en attestent les différentes tensions dont l'intrigue qui s'y développe a conservé la trace, jusque dans l'image – controversée – qu'elle donne de la royauté. C'est pourquoi, depuis les travaux de M. Noth[3], la discussion de ces ch. a surtout porté sur la reconstruction d'éditions pré-[4] ou post-[5] dtr. De

1. Cet article n'aurait jamais vu le jour sans les encouragements et le soutien des professeurs S.L. McKenzie (Rhodes College, Memphis, TN) et T. Römer (Lausanne). La relecture par T. Römer des versions successives de ce texte m'a également permis d'en perfectionner l'argumentation. Tous deux voudront bien trouver ici l'expression de ma reconnaissance, même si (selon la formule consacrée) les considérations qui suivent n'engagent que ma responsabilité.
2. Ces ch. sont délimités comme suit depuis J. WELLHAUSEN (*Die Composition des Hexateuchs und der historischen Bücher des Alten Testaments,* Berlin, W. de Gruyter, 1963⁴, pp. 239-246): 8; 9,1-10,16; 10,17-27; 11; 12.
3. *Überlieferungsgeschichtliche Studien. Erster Teil. Die sammelnden und bearbeitenden Geschichtswerke im Alten Testament,* trad. anglaise *The Deuteronomistic History* (JSOTS SS, 15), Sheffield, JSOT Press, 1981², chap. 7, pp. 47-53.
4. Dans la recherche récente, voir particulièrement H.-J. STOEBE, *Das erste Buch Samuelis* (KAT, 8/1), Gütersloh, G. Mohr, 1973; B.C. BIRCH, *The Rise of the Israelite Monarchy: The Growth and Development of 1 Samuel 7-15* (SBL DS, 27), Missoula, MT, Scholars Press, 1976; T.N.D. METTINGER, *King and Messiah. The Civil and Sacral Legitimation of the Israelite Kings* (CB OT, 8), Lund, C.W.K. Gleerup, 1976; F. CRÜSE-MANN, *Der Widerstand gegen das Königtum. Die antiköniglichen Texte des Alten Testaments und der Kampf um den frühen israelitischen Staat* (WMANT, 49), Neukirchen-Vluyn, Neukirchener Verlag, 1978; P.K. McCARTER, *1 Samuel. A New Translation with Introduction, Notes and Commentary* (AB, 8), Garden City, NY, Doubleday, 1980; H. SEEBASS, *David, Saul und das Wesen des biblischen Glaubens,* Neukirchen-Vluyn, Neukirchener Verlag, 1980; A.D.H. MAYES, *The Story of Israel between Settlement and Exile. A Redactional Study of the Deuteronomistic History,* London, SCM Press, 1983; A. F. CAMPBELL, *Of Prophets and Kings. A Late Ninth-Century Document (1 Samuel 1-2 Kings 10)* (CBQ MS, 17), Washington, DC, The Catholic Biblical Association of America, 1986; W. DIETRICH, *David, Saul und die Propheten* (BWANT, 122), Stuttgart, W. Kohlhammer, 1987; ID., *Histoire et Loi. Historiographie deutéronomiste et Loi deutéronomique à l'exemple du passage de l'époque des Juges à l'époque royale,* in A. DE PURY – T. RÖMER – J.-D. MACCHI (eds.), *Israël construit son histoire. L'historiographie deutéronomiste à la lumière des recherches récentes* (Le Monde de la Bible, 34), Genève, Labor et Fides, 1996, pp. 297-323; M. O'BRIEN, *The Deuteronomistic History Hypothesis: A Reassessment* (OBO, 92), Freiburg (CH), Universitätsverlag; Göttingen, Vandenhoeck & Ruprecht, 1989; P. MOMMER, *Samuel. Geschichte und Ueberlieferung* (WMANT, 65), Neukirchen-Vluyn, Neukirchener Verlag, 1991; A. MOENIKES, *Die grundsätzliche Ablehnung des Königtums in der Hebraïschen Bibel* (BBB, 99), Weinheim, Beltz, 1995. Dans la mesure où ces travaux ont souvent attribué l'édition pré-dtr des récits sur les débuts de la royauté à des

ce fait, la question de l'étendue et de la cohérence de l'édition dtr de 1 S
8–12 a été reléguée au second plan, alors qu'elle mérite vraisemblablement un traitement plus approfondi. Ainsi, S. McKenzie[6] a récemment
établi le caractère dtr de la majorité des liens rédactionnels unissant ces
ch. Pour ma part, je chercherai à montrer, en partant de l'analyse du vo-
cabulaire des ch. attribués par Noth à l'édition dtr de Samuel, que Noth
avait raison de considérer ces ch. comme une création originale de Dtr
sur les débuts de la monarchie en Israël. Cependant, l'intention de Dtr[7]
en composant ce récit n'est pas d'encadrer des traditions favorables à la
royauté israélite par une perspective «antimonarchique»[8], mais de situer, au commencement de la succession des rois dans HD, un débat sur
la royauté comme institution en rapport avec le problème de la souveraineté de Yhwh[9]. Cette approche permet de faire droit à la cohérence et à

cercles prophétiques (notamment en raison de la présence de la figure du prophète Samuel),
l'ouvrage de A. WEISER (*Samuel. Seine geschichtliche Aufgabe und religiöse Bedeutung.
Traditionsgeschichtliche Untersuchungen zu 1 Samuel 7-12* [FRLANT, 81], Göttingen,
Vandenhoeck & Ruprecht, 1962) occupe également une place importante. Pour un état de
la recherche sur l'hypothèse d'une édition prophétique des livres de Samuel, cf. P.K.
MCCARTER, *The Books of Samuel*, in S.L. MCKENZIE – M.P. GRAHAM (eds.), *The History of
Israel's Traditions: The Heritage of Martin Noth* (JSOT SS, 182), Sheffield, JSOT Press,
1994, pp. 260-280; pour une critique de cette hypothèse (dans le cas des livres de Samuel-
Rois), voir S.L. MCKENZIE, *The Trouble with Kings. The Composition of the Book of Kings
in the Deuteronomistic History* (SVT, 42), Leiden, Brill, 1991, part. pp. 10-14.
    5. Surtout dans la perspective d'une rédaction de type «nomiste»: ainsi, T. VEIJOLA,
*Das Königtum in der Beurteilung der deuteronomistischen Historiographie. Eine
redaktionsgeschichtliche Untersuchung* (AASF B, 198); Helsinki, Tiedeakatemia, 1977;
R. BICKERT, *Die Geschichte und das Handeln Jahwes. Zum Eigenart eines deutero-
nomistischen Offenbarungsauffassung in den Samuelbüchern*, in A.H.J. GUNNEWEG –
O. KAISER (eds.), *Textgemäss. Aufsätze und Beiträge zur Hermeneutik des Alten Testa-
ments. FS E. Würthwein*, Göttingen, Vandenhoeck & Ruprecht, 1979, pp. 9-27; MAYES,
Story of Israel; R.W. KLEIN, *1 Samuel* (WBC, 10), Waco, TX, Word Books, 1983;
F. FORESTI, *The Rejection of Saul in the Perspective of the Deuteronomistic School. A
Study of 1 Samuel 15 and Related Texts* (Studia Theologica, 5), Rome, Ed. del Teresia-
num, 1984; DIETRICH, *David*; ID., *Histoire et Loi*; O'BRIEN, *Reassessment*.
    6. S.L. MCKENZIE, *Cette royauté qui fait problème*, in DE PURY – RÖMER – MACCHI,
Israël construit son histoire, pp. 267-295.
    7. Dans ma terminologie, ce sigle désigne une «école», vraisemblablement composée
d'exilés à Babylone, non un auteur-rédacteur unique; sur ce point, voir T. RÖMER, A. DE
PURY, *L'historiographie deutéronomiste. Histoire de la recherche et enjeux du débat*, in
Israël construit son histoire, pp. 9-120, ici pp. 86-88.
    8. *Contra* NOTH, *Deuteronomistic History*, pp. 47s.
    9. Ma propre recherche a bénéficié des nombreuses études «littéraires» qui sont pa-
rues ces dernières années sur les livres de Samuel. À ce titre, je mentionnerai particulièrement J.P. FOKKELMAN, *Narrative Art and Poetry in the Books of Samuel. A Full Interpretation Based on Stylistic and Structural Analyses* (SSN, 23), Assen, Van Gorcum,
1986 (Vol. II, *The Crossing Fates*), 1993 (Vol. IV, *Vow and Desire*); M. GARSIEL, *The
First Book of Samuel. A Literary Study of Comparative Structures, Analogies and
Parallels*, Ramat-Gan, Revivim Publishing House, 1985; A. WÉNIN, *Samuel et l'instauration de la monarchie. Une recherche littéraire sur le personnage (1 S 1–12)*, Frankfurt
am Main, P. Lang, 1988; D. JOBLING, *Deuteronomic Political Theory in Judges and 1*

la complexité de la représentation dtr de la royauté dans ces récits. Elle me conduira également à revenir, au terme de cette analyse, sur la possibilité d'une édition pré-exilique des livres de Samuel.

I. LIMINAIRE: LE RÉSEAU SÉMANTIQUE DE LA COMPOSITION DTR

Un examen attentif des ch. que Wellhausen attribuait à sa source «tardive» (soit 1 S 7; 8; 10,17-27; 12; auxquels il faut rajouter 1 S 15; 16,1-13[10]) permet de faire, au niveau formel, deux constatations. D'une part, ces ch. sont particulièrement imprégnés du style et de la terminologie dtr; d'autre part, ils ont en commun tout un réseau de termes récurrents, qui esquissent un champ sémantique distinctif. Il s'agit essentiellement des racines suivantes.

שמע   («écouter, obéir»): 7,7; 8,7.9.19.21.22; 12,1.14.15; 15,1.4.14. 19.20.22 (2x).24; 16,2.

שמע בקול («écouter, obéir à la voix de»)[11]: 8,7.9.19.22; 12,1.14.15; 15,19.22.24.

מאס   («rejeter»): 8,7 (2x); 10,19; 15,23 (2x).26 (2x); 16,1.7.

שאל   («demander»): 8,10; 10,22; 12,13.17.19.

עשה   («faire»): 8,8 (2x).12.16; 12,6.7.16.17.20.22; 15,2.6.19; 16,3.4.

Samuel 1–12, in *The Sense of Biblical Narrative. Structural Analyses in the Hebrew Bible*, II (JSOT SS, 39), Sheffield, JSOT Press, 1986, pp. 44-87; U. BERGES, *Die Verwerfung Sauls. Eine thematische Untersuchung* (FzB, 61), Würzburg, Echter Verlag, 1989. On peut également se référer à D.M. GUNN, *The Fate of King Saul. An Interpretation of a Biblical Story* (JSOT SS, 14), Sheffield, JSOT Press, 1981; L. ESLINGER, *Viewpoints and Points of View in 1 Samuel 8-12*, in *JSOT* 26 (1983) 61-76; ID., *Kingship of God in Crisis. A Close Reading of 1 Samuel 1-12* (BiLiSe, 10), Decatur, Almond, 1985; P.D. MISCALL, *1 Samuel. A Literary Reading*, Bloomington, IN, Indiana University Press, 1986; R. POLZIN, *Moses and the Deuteronomist. A Literary Study of the Deuteronomic History. Part 2: 1 Samuel*, San Francisco, CA, Harper & Row, 1989; V.P. LONG, *The Reign and Rejection of King Saul. A Case for Literary and Theological Coherence* (SBL DS, 118), Atlanta, GA, Scholars Press, 1989; D. EDELMAN, *King Saul in the Historiography of Judah* (JSOT SS, 121), Sheffield, JSOT Press, 1991.

10. WELLHAUSEN, *Composition*, pp. 240-241. Wellhausen attribue le ch. 15 à une étape intermédiaire («ein Zwischenstück») du développement des récits de 1 Samuel (*Composition*, p. 246). Pour l'attribution de ce ch., avec 16,1-13, à la rédaction dtr, voir mon analyse ci-dessous.

11. Les occurrences de cette tournure dans ces ch. représentent la moitié de ses occurrences totales dans les deux livres de Samuel (soit 10 sur 19). Sur l'importance de cette tournure dans ces ch., voir J. ARAMBARRI, *Der Wortstamm «Hören» im Alten Testament. Semantik und Syntax eines hebräischen Verbs* (SBB, 20), Stuttgart, Verlag Katholisches Bibelwerk, 1990, pp. 76s.: «Die Häufigkeit der Belege von שמע בקול in 1 Sam 8; 12; 15 (und 28) ist deutlich; das geschieht nur in diesen Kapiteln und innerhalb des Themas Königtum. Die Wendung verbindet die einzelnen Abschnitte dieser Kapitel» (p. 78). A noter que les occurrences de cette tournure en 1 S 8; 12; 15 se répartissent en deux catégories: «écouter la voix du peuple» (8,7.9.22; 12,1; 15,24) et «écouter la voix de Yhwh» (8,19; 12,14.15; 15,19.20.22 [2x]). Sur l'importance et la signification de cette distinction, voir mon analyse ci-dessous.

שפט   («juger» ou «juges»)[12]: 7,6.15.16.17; 8,1.2.5.6.20; 12,7.

משפט   («justice»): 8,3.9; 10,25.

מלך   («roi, régner»): 8,5.6.7.9 (2x).10.11 (2x).18.19.20.22; 10,19. 24; 12,1.2.9.12 (4x).13 (2x).14 (2x).17.19.25; 15,1.8.11.17.20. 23.26.32; 16,1 (2x)[13].

בחר   («choisir, élire»): 8,18; 10,24; 12,13; 16,8.9.10.

נצל מיד   («délivrer de la main de»): 7,3.14; 10,18 (2x); 12,10.11. Avec ישׁע: 7,8.

ירא   («craindre»): 7,7; 12,14.18.20.24; 15,24.

זעק   («crier»): 7,8.9; 8,18; 12,8.10; 15,11.

שׂים   («instituer»)[14]: 7,12; 8,1.5.11.12; 10,19; 15,2.

פלל   («intercéder»): 7,9; 8,6; 12,19.22.

Dans le cadre de cet article, je me contenterai de faire quelques remarques sur cette liste. D'abord, les racines שפט, משפט, ירא, זעק, פלל, מאס[15], שׁאל, שׂים, בחר, et les tournures שׁמע בקול, ainsi que נצל מיד, sont attestées uniquement dans les ch. 7; 8; 10,17-27; 12; 15,1 – 16,13, et constituent donc un ensemble de motifs qui leur est propre. Pour le reste, שׁמע est peu attesté en dehors des ch. mentionnés ci-dessus – et jamais au sens théologique de l'«obéissance» – (cf. 9,27; 11,6Q; 13,3 [2x].4; 14,23.27), tout comme מלך (11,12.14.15; 13,1 [2x]; 14,47; cf. aussi 10,16; 11,14 avec la mention de la «royauté», מלוכה) et נצל (14,48). Enfin, on relèvera que la plupart des termes en jeu ici sont caractéristiques de la littérature dtr (cf. notamment «écouter/suivre la voix de», «élire», «délivrer de la main de», «craindre [Yhwh]»), ou du moins, sont fréquents dans HD.

En résumé, ces remarques, qui demanderaient à être complétées par une analyse plus approfondie, suggèrent cependant que dans le cas des récits sur les origines de la monarchie en Israël, l'activité rédactionnelle et éditoriale de Dtr se concentre plus spécifiquement sur quelques chapitres, à savoir 1 S 7; 8; 10,17-27; 12; 15,1–16,13, ce qui correspond globalement (à l'exception de 15,1–16,13) à l'hypothèse de Noth. Non seulement ces ch. sont étroitement associés par un réseau sémantique complexe, mais on verra par la suite que les différents motifs qu'ils dévelop-

---

12. On relèvera qu'on ne rencontre, dans l'ensemble du livre des Juges, que 14 occurrences de cette racine.

13. Cf. encore la mention de la «royauté», מלוכה, en 10,25.

14. Ce verbe est associé à trois reprises avec מלך: cf. 8,5; 10,19; 15,2.

15. Le cas de מאס est particulièrement intéressant, dans la mesure où ce terme totalise 9 occurrences en 1 S 7,2–16,13*, pour un total de 13 occurrences dans l'ensemble de HD (Jg 9,38; 2 R 17,15.20; 23,27). De manière générale, j'aurais voulu vérifier statistiquement mon intuition selon laquelle la fréquence d'une partie des termes de cette liste est significativement plus élevée dans ces ch. que dans le reste de HD. Je n'avais malheureusement pas à ma disposition les données quantitatives nécessaires (nombre total de mots dans l'ensemble de HD et dans chaque livre en particulier, etc.).

pent sont au centre du débat mis en scène ici par Dtr entre Yhwh et le peuple au sujet de la royauté. Ainsi, le «rejet» de Yhwh, l'«obéissance» (au peuple et à Yhwh), la «délivrance» du peuple par Yhwh, la «demande» d'un roi par le peuple et son «élection» par Yhwh, sont des éléments essentiels à la structuration de l'intrigue par laquelle HD rapporte la transition de l'époque des juges à celle de la monarchie en Israël. Selon toute vraisemblance, on a donc affaire, dans les ch. que relie le réseau sémantique exposé ci-dessus, à une composition d'ensemble, de facture dtr, dont il s'agit maintenant d'examiner en détail la cohérence rédactionnelle et thématique.

1 S 8 ET 12: INTRODUCTION À LA MONARCHIE COMME PROBLÈME *THÉOLOGIQUE*

Il paraît légitime de limiter, dans un premier temps, la problématique de l'instauration de la monarchie en Israël aux ch. 8–12, qui sont encadrés par la notice finale sur la judicature de Samuel (7,15-17) et par la première notice royale de l'historiographie dtr (13,1)[16]. On a donc essentiellement affaire, dans ces ch., à la transition d'une époque à l'autre de HD. En ce sens, il est significatif que les récits sur l'accession de Saül au trône (1 S 9–11) soient disposés, dans l'édition dtr, autour des ch. 8 et 12, qui débattent des conséquences du passage à la monarchie en Israël. Ainsi, 1 S 8 et 12 constituent ensemble le *cadre de référence* des récits sur les origines de la royauté comme le signale la correspondance structurelle de ces deux ch., puisque le discours de Samuel en 12,1s., reprenant les termes de 8,22b, prétendra résoudre l'intrigue ouverte en 8,4s. par la demande du peuple[17]. L'analyse de ces deux ch. dégagera cependant quelques motifs centraux qui demanderont à être prolongés par l'examen de l'ensemble de la composition dtr en 1 S 7,2–16,13.

---

16. D.J. McCarthy, *The Inauguration of Monarchy in Israel. A Form Critical Study of 1 Samuel 8–12*, in *Int* 27 (1973) 401-412, ici p. 402; Wénin, *Instauration*, pp. 117-118; A.D.H. Mayes, *The Rise of the Israelite Monarchy*, in *ZAW* 90 (1978) 1-19, ici p. 1.

17. Cf. ‏ויאמר יהוה אל־שמואל שמע בקולם והמלכת להם מלך‎ (8,22)

‏ויאמר שמואל אל־כל־ישראל הנה שמעתי בקלכם לכל אשר־אמרתם לי ואמליך עליכם מלך‎ (12,1)

À ce sujet, voir Fokkelman, *Vow and Desire* (p. 323): «The request for a king in chapter 8 opens a macroplot which needs the whole Act [i.e., les ch. 8-12] as a radius of action».

Les autres principaux parallèles entre les ch. 8 et 12 sont les suivants. L'emploi du verbe ‏לקח‎, en 12,3, rappelle les agissements du roi décrits dans le ‏משפח המלך‎ du ch. 8; de manière générale, l'ensemble du dialogue entre Samuel et le peuple en 12,3-5 doit être compris sur le fond de 8,11-17, puisque ces vv. visent clairement à disculper la judicature de Samuel des reproches faits à la royauté. Enfin, l'intégration de la demande par le peuple d'un roi dans l'histoire du péché d'Israël en 12,12 reprend explicitement les termes de 8,7-8.

1 Samuel 8. McKenzie a récemment défendu l'hypothèse de l'unité rédactionnelle (dtr) de ce ch[18]. Sa démonstration trouve un soutien important dans un article récent de S. Kammerer, qui analyse 8,1-5 comme une création dtr[19]. Il n'y a donc plus lieu de chercher les éléments d'une édition pré-dtr dans ce ch.[20]. Quant aux tentatives pour y retrouver une seconde rédaction dtr (DtrN), elles surévaluent les tensions présentes dans le récit[21]. De manière générale, l'hypothèse d'une divergence dans

La présence d'une tension entre les ch. 8 et 12 (selon 12,12, l'origine de la demande d'un roi par le peuple n'est plus la faute des fils de Samuel – qui n'est d'ailleurs pas rappelée en 12,1-5 –, mais l'agression de Nahash l'Ammonite) a conduit certains exégètes à postuler l'existence de deux traditions divergentes sur l'émergence de la monarchie en Israël derrière ces ch. (ainsi, STOEBE, *Buch Samuelis*, pp. 237-238; et, non sans hésitations, H.W. HERTZBERG, *I and II Samuel. A Commentary* [OTL], Londres, SCM Press, 1964, p. 99). Mais cette hypothèse est intenable; comme je le montrerai par la suite dans mon analyse, ces deux ch. ne contiennent aucune tradition sur les origines de la monarchie, mais doivent être compris – à l'exception possible de 8,11-17 – comme une création dtr. En ce sens, la tension entre 8,1-5 et 12,12 dépend de la place et de la fonction respectives des ch. 8 et 12 dans l'élaboration de l'intrigue qu'ils encadrent (sur ce point, cf. FOKKELMAN, *Vow and Desire*, p. 323: «The two chapters do what their location leads us to expect: open and close»). En 1 S 8, le motif de l'injustice des fils de Samuel permet d'illustrer, avec une ambiguïté délibérée, la transition d'une époque à l'autre dans HD, par quoi le ch. 8 ouvre, en s'appuyant sur le récit de 1 S 7, l'intrigue au terme de laquelle la judicature charismatique sera remplacée par la monarchie. Par contre, le ch. 12 recourt à un tableau idyllique de l'époque des juges pour les besoins de sa démonstration (cf. mon analyse de ce ch. ci-dessous). C'est pourquoi, ici, ce n'est plus la conduite des fils de Samuel qui est invoquée, mais l'épisode de Nahash (établissant ainsi un lien rédactionnel avec le ch. 11; cf. NOTH, *Deuteronomistic History*, p. 51).

18. McKENZIE, *Cette royauté*, pp. 282-285. Cf. déjà R.E. CLEMENTS, *The Deuteronomistic Interpretation of the Founding of Monarchy in 1 Sam VIII*, in *VT* 24 (1974) 398-410; A.D.H. MAYES, *The Rise of the Israelite Monarchy*; U. BECKER, *Der innere Widerspruch der deuteronomistischen Beurteilung des Königtums (am Beispiel von 1 Sam 8)*, in M. OEMING – A. GRAUPNER (eds.), *Altes Testament und christliche Verkündigung. FS A.H.J. Gunneweg*, Stuttgart, W. Kohlammer, 1987, pp. 246-270.

19. S. KAMMERER, *Die mißratenen Söhne Samuels*, in *BN* 88 (1997) 75-88. Selon l'analyse de Kammerer, le v. 2 serait un ajout tardif, apparenté à la littérature chroniste.

20. Je laisse ici ouverte la question de savoir si 8,11-17 constitue ou non un document pré-dtr; mais les vv. qui l'encadrent sont, quant à eux, clairement dtr (cf. 8,9 et 8,18).

21. *Contra* VEIJOLA, *Königtum*, p. 55 (qui a été suivi depuis par MOMMER, *Samuel*, p. 56; DIETRICH, *David*, p. 134), la distinction entre les «Anciens» (8,4) et le «peuple» (8,7s.) ne constitue pas un indice suffisant pour un découpage rédactionnel. La mention du peuple se retrouve en 8,21, qui est nécessaire au récit (O'BRIEN, *Reassessment*, p. 110, n. 97; il relève également que les termes «peuple», «anciens» et «hommes d'Israël» paraissent parfaitement interchangeables en 1 S 11). À mon sens, la mention des Anciens en 8,5 s'explique par le fait qu'ils sont associés, dans HD, à chaque changement d'époque. De même, je ne crois pas que la divergence dans l'emploi des formules «un roi *pour* [ל] le peuple» (8,5.6.22) et «un roi *sur* [על] le peuple» (8,9.11.19) provienne de rédactions différentes (*contra* DIETRICH, *David*, p. 133; ID., *Histoire et Loi*, pp. 305, 308; MOMMER, *Samuel*, p. 56). D'une part, on retrouve successivement ces deux formulations dans le ch. 12 (cf. 12,1.12.13.14., pour la seconde formulation, et 12,17.19, pour la première). D'autre part, la loi dt(r) de Dt 17,14-20, à laquelle 8,5 se réfère explicitement (comp. 1 S 8,4-5 et Dt 17,14s.), se sert de la préposition על; il faut donc reconnaître que la rédaction dtr est susceptible d'employer les deux formules alternativement. Enfin, si l'usage de על

l'appréciation de la monarchie entre les vv. 1-5 et le v. 6 est trop simpliste[22]. Car, contrairement au schéma habituel de l'époque des juges[23],

signalait une perspective spécifiquement *négative* à l'égard de la royauté, on comprend mal que la rédaction nomiste se serve également de ce terme pour qualifier la suzeraineté de Yhwh (cf 8,7; 12,12).

Dans l'ensemble, la «césure» (postulée par plusieurs auteurs à la suite de Veijola) entre les vv. 5 et 6 se justifie mal, dans la mesure où la réponse de Yhwh en 8,22 présuppose que Samuel lui ait rapporté les paroles du peuple (avec MOMMER, *Samuel*, p. 63). Or, le v. 6 appartient à la rédaction responsable des ch. 7 et 12, puisque la «plainte» (פלל) de Samuel constitue la contrepartie de son «intercession» en faveur d'Israël en 7,9 (avec KLEIN, *1 Samuel*, p. 75) et en 12,19.23; la présence de ce motif en 8,6 doit donc être attribuée à la composition d'ensemble dtr en 7,2–16,13. DIETRICH (*Histoire et Loi*, p. 308) voudrait remplacer le rapport de Samuel à Yhwh du v. 6 par celui du v. 21, mais la mention וישמע שמואל את כל־דברי העם au v. 22 suppose visiblement l'ordre de Yhwh en 8,7. Il faut donc tenir le v. 6 pour la suite logique des vv. 1-5 dans la rédaction dtr du ch. 8.

Je pense similairement que l'attribution de tout ou partie des vv. 7-8 à une couche rédactionnelle secondaire ne se justifie pas (*contra* O'BRIEN, *Reassessment*, pp. 111-112; MOENIKES, *Ablehnung*, pp. 24-26; DIETRICH, *Histoire et Loi*, p. 306). Outre les arguments de MCKENZIE (*Cette royauté*, pp. 283-84, n. 58), j'aimerais mentionner, d'une part, que la plainte de Samuel au v. 6 (qui appartient à la rédaction dtr originale, cf. *supra*) demande nécessairement l'arbitrage et les explications supplémentaires de Yhwh au vv. 7-8. De plus, comme je l'ai déjà relevé, la formulation du v. 21 suppose l'ordre de Yhwh au v. 7. D'autre part, il est exagéré de dire que les vv. 7 et 8 se contredisent (*contra* O'BRIEN, *Reassessment*, p. 112; MOENIKES, *Ablehnung*, p. 25); ils apparaissent bien plutôt complémentaires l'un de l'autre. En 8,7, Yhwh ne conteste pas que la demande populaire suppose le rejet de Samuel, mais il en explicite la portée véritable (avec F. STOLZ, *Das erste und zweite Buch Samuel* [ZBK AT, 9], Zürich, Theologischer Verlag, 1991, pp. 59-60): en réalité, le rejet de Samuel équivaut au rejet de l'origine divine de l'inspiration des sauveurs charismatiques.

Par contre, le v. 8 cherche à intégrer la demande du peuple dans le cycle traditionnel d'apostasie d'Israël: en ce sens, il présente le rejet de la judicature de Samuel comme une étape supplémentaire de l'histoire du rejet continuel de Yhwh par le peuple. L'une et l'autre affirmation ne sont donc pas en tension: derrière l'autorité du juge se tient celle de Yhwh (v. 7); par conséquent, le rejet de Samuel peut être égalé au rejet «traditionnel» de Yhwh (v. 8). En ce sens, la recommandation faite par Yhwh à Samuel au v. 7 d'écouter «toutes les paroles du peuple» signale que Samuel, qui ne relève dans la demande du peuple que la volonté d'avoir un roi pour le juger (v. 6), ne voit pas la véritable portée de cette demande, qui est d'avoir un roi «comme toutes les nations» (cf. la mention du v. 5, qui n'est pas reprise au v. 6), en quoi consiste véritablement le rejet de la souveraineté de Yhwh sur le peuple. C'est donc le discours de Yhwh aux vv. 7-8 qui va établir la nature exacte de la demande du peuple. Enfin, les vv. 7-8, pris ensemble, se retrouvent ailleurs en 1 S 8-12: cf. 10,18-19 (qui est très proche quant à sa formulation), mais aussi 12,7-12, qui évoque les mêmes motifs: *rejet de Yhwh* (bien que le terme technique de «rejet», מאס, n'apparaisse pas en 12,7-12, ce qui est probablement dû au contexte: le ch. 12 intègre la monarchie dans l'alliance entre Yhwh et Israël) et *insertion de la demande populaire dans le cadre plus large du cycle d'apostasie en Israël*. On notera également que ces deux vv. ne sont pas antimonarchiques *stricto sensu*, puisque Yhwh y ordonne à Samuel d'instituer un roi.

22. *Contra* VEIJOLA, *Königtum*, pp. 54-55, dont les critères «idéologiques» ont été adoptés depuis par plusieurs auteurs. Selon Veijola, Dtr porte un regard favorable sur la monarchie en 8,1-5.22b, et négatif en 8,6-22a. Son argument se fonde notamment sur la distinction dans les deux rédactions entre motifs de politique «intérieure» et «extérieure» dans l'instauration de la monarchie en Israël. Dans la mesure où le contexte immédiat du

la conduite des fils de Samuel (8,1-3) amène ici le peuple à chercher sa délivrance dans le recours à une nouvelle forme de gouvernement en Israël (8,4-5), et non plus auprès de Yhwh[24]. De la sorte, Dtr présente l'introduction du gouvernement monarchique comme une rupture radicale dans l'histoire d'Israël.

Cette rupture est illustrée par l'association dans la demande populaire entre «justice» et «roi»[25], qui est, à ce stade de HD, tout à fait originale[26]. Cet artifice terminologique évoque immédiatement la transition au-delà de l'époque des juges, et il en désigne exemplairement l'enjeu de fond – savoir *à qui* il appartient de *juger* (שפט, avec toute la gamme des registres théologico-politiques que ce terme couvre) Israël, soit en définitive qui détient le pouvoir et l'autorité. Avec le passage à l'*institution* monarchique, qui remplace désormais la judicature charismatique[27],

ch. 7 suggère que le שפט de 8,5 doit être compris dans son sens large (puisque Samuel y apparaît à la fois comme juge-sauveur et comme juge-administrateur), cette distinction n'est vraisemblablement pas fondée ici.

23. Soit la séquence suivante: péché d'Israël – oppression étrangère – cris du peuple vers Yhwh – délivrance du peuple par Yhwh, qui envoie un juge-sauveur. La présence de ce schéma à l'arrière-fond du ch. 8 est clairement suggérée par le récit de la délivrance du peuple au ch. 7, avec lequel se clôt l'époque des juges, et qui est rappelé en 12,11.

24. On trouve un exposé identique en 12,7-12, qui évoque le cycle de l'époque des juges de manière explicite. Or, au v. 12, l'agression de Nahash provoque la demande d'un roi, alors que jusque là, le peuple avait crié vers Yhwh sous l'oppression étrangère (12,8.10). KLEIN (*1 Samuel*, p. 113) relève finement que, pour le ch. 12, l'artifice de Dtr consiste à inverser la séquence habituelle péché – oppression (puisqu'en 1 S 8 et 12, l'oppression n'est précédée d'aucun péché du peuple), de façon à ce que la demande par le peuple d'un roi apparaisse à la place du péché d'Israël. En 1 S 8, cependant, la demande du peuple n'est précédée d'aucune oppression étrangère; mais elle est encadrée par deux formes d'exploitation d'Israël par lui-même: celle des juges corrompus (les propres fils de Samuel) en 8,1-3, et celle (plus grave encore) des rois israélites qui régneront successivement (cf. 8,11-18), ce qui s'explique vraisemblablement par la volonté dtr de dénoncer les dangers de toute forme dynastique de gouvernement en Israël.

25. Cf. FOKKELMAN, *Vow and Desire*, p. 328.

26. Alors que 8,5 reprend explicitement les termes de Dt 17,14-20, le שפט n'est précisément pas mentionné dans la loi dt(r) comme un attribut du roi. DIETRICH (*Histoire et Loi*, p. 305) soutient que l'absence de ce terme en Dt 17,14s. est due à la délimitation opérée dans ce ch. entre les offices de «juge«et de «roi» (la loi sur les juges précède de peu celle sur les rois, cf. Dt 16,18-20). Mais cette hypothèse n'explique pas pour quelle raison le שפט est attribué au roi en 8,5s., ce qu'il faut comprendre à mon avis comme une variation dtr sur la loi dt(r) pour les besoins de la composition du ch. 8.

27. La problématique de la transition d'une forme de gouvernement à l'autre est explicitement introduite par le motif de la *succession dynastique* dès le début du livre de Samuel (mais déjà en Juges, cf. les récits sur Gédéon et Abimélek, Jg 6-9), avec la faute des fils d'Elie en 1 S 2,12s., dont le parallèle avec les fils de Samuel est évident (sur ce point, cf. en dernier lieu KAMMERER, *Söhne*, pp. 83-84). Sur ce motif, trop peu étudié, cf. JOBLING, *Deuteronomic Political Theory*; BERGES, *Verwerfung Sauls*, p. 60. On relèvera la subtilité de la composition dtr, qui attribue l'origine de l'institution monarchique à l'échec du programmme dynastique de Samuel en 8,1-3, le lien étant d'autant plus explicite que Dtr se sert pour condamner la conduite des fils de Samuel de la formule en usage

la problématique centrale de Dtr est de préserver la toute-puissance de Yhwh, que ce changement d'époque et de régime remet en cause (cf., explicitement, 8,20[28]). Pour cette raison, Dtr compose dans ce ch. un récit qui esquisse, à travers le «débat» entre Yhwh et le peuple sur la monarchie, deux options politiques: une royauté «comme les autres nations» (vv. 5.20) – où le roi, par conséquent, détient les attributs qui étaient ceux de Yhwh jusque là[29] – et le gouvernement théocratique et charismatique de l'époque des juges, qui garantissait *per se* la suprématie de Yhwh[30]. C'est *précisément* parce que l'enjeu de Dtr est ici de réaffirmer la souveraineté *sans partage* de Yhwh, que ces deux formes de gouvernement sont représentées en opposition radicale[31]: en ce sens, il ne peut y avoir qu'un seul règne, celui de Yhwh (8,7), et la demande par le peuple d'un roi humain se présente comme le point culminant du cycle d'apostasie en Israël (8,8).

On voit alors comment cette problématique (qui ne trouve sa résolution, partielle, qu'au ch. 12) structure l'ensemble de la composition dtr en 1 S 8. Le «droit» (ou «coutume») du roi en 8,11-17 met en question l'association faite au v. 5 entre «roi» et «justice»[32]. Il sert en même temps à «avertir» (הֵעֵד, v. 9) le peuple des implications de sa demande: puisque l'instauration de la monarchie signifie le rejet de Yhwh, le peuple ne pourra plus compter sur l'assistance divine (v. 18). Ici, l'abandon par le peuple du gouvernement théocratique est vu comme un péché à ce point ultime, qu'il rompt le cycle «apostasie – délivrance» en usage jusque là dans HD. Le refus du peuple d'écouter cet avertissement est l'oc-

---

dans le livre des Rois pour évaluer le règne d'un souverain: «X marcha/ne marcha pas sur les traces de son père» (O'BRIEN, *Reassessment*, p. 109). À cet égard, le tableau dressé par Dtr de la «judicature dynastique» des fils de Samuel est typiquement un motif de transition, qui sert à articuler les deux époques de l'histoire d'Israël dans HD. Pour un traitement plus détaillé de cette question, voir mes *Remarques sur la fonction de 1 S 8,1-5 dans son contexte littéraire*, in BN 92 (1998) 26-32.

28. 8,20 détourne les formules traditionnelles de la guerre sainte, appliquées cette fois au roi et non à Yhwh (comparer avec Jos 23,3.10).

29. Dans les termes de 8,20, il rend la justice et il mène au combat. A noter que ce sont exactement les attributions de Samuel (sous l'inspiration de Yhwh) au ch. 7.

30. D'accord avec MOMMER, *Samuel*: «Hinter den Richtern steht aber Jahwe selbst [...] Er *selbst* rettete *durch* sie Israel, nachdem Israel im Hilfeschrei sein ganzes Vertrauen auf Jahwe gesetzt hatte» (p. 130; l'auteur souligne).

31. En ce sens, la thèse selon laquelle l'institution monarchique ne serait pas mauvaise en soi, seule la demande populaire qui témoigne d'un «manque de foi» à l'égard de Yhwh étant condamnée (cf. KLEIN, *1 Samuel*, p. 79; MCKENZIE, *Cette royauté*, pp. 284-85), passe à côté de la problématique de ce ch., et ne fait pas droit au regard porté par Dtr sur la monarchie comme institution. En 8,20, le peuple ne témoigne pas seulement d'un «manque de foi», il se décide (en toute conscience) pour une alternative politique et théologique qui implique de fait le rejet (v. 7) définitif (v. 18) de la souveraineté de Yhwh.

32. Mais une lecture attentive des vv. précédents montre que c'est déjà le cas dans le discours de Yhwh en 8,7-9; cf. FOKKELMAN, *Vow and Desire*, pp. 339s.

casion pour la rédaction dtr d'introduire un motif classique de HD, où le peuple ratifie sa propre condamnation[33]. C'est ce qui explique que la formulation de 8,20 soit plus clairement idolâtre que celle du v. 5[34]. Le récit peut ainsi ouvertement établir la responsabilité du peuple dans l'avènement du régime monarchique en Israël, ce qui me paraît être une des fonctions centrale du *redoublement dialogal* sur lequel est construit le ch. 8[35].

Il demeure alors deux problèmes au terme de l'analyse du ch. 8, qui sont essentiels pour comprendre l'intention de la rédaction dtr en 1 S 8-12, et au-delà. D'une part, comment expliquer que l'instauration de la monarchie en Israël soit rapportée (bien qu'indirectement) à Yhwh, malgré la condamnation par Dtr de la royauté dans ce ch. (8,7.9.22)? D'autre part, que va devenir l'offense faite à Yhwh par le peuple? Quel traitement reçoit-elle dans la suite du récit? Il faut par conséquent examiner la manière dont le ch. 12 répond à ces questions, et clôt, provisoirement, l'intrigue ouverte par le ch. 8.

1 Samuel 12. La terminologie du ch. 12 est clairement dtr[36], y compris pour les vv. 1-5[37], qui supposent de toute manière la rédaction dtr du ch.

---

33. VEIJOLA, *Königtum*, pp. 58-59; KLEIN, *1 Samuel*, p. 78.

34. D'accord en cela avec VEIJOLA, *Königtum*, p. 55; DIETRICH, *Histoire et Loi*, pp. 307-308.

35. WÉNIN, *Instauration*, pp. 131-134; ainsi que FOKKELMAN, *Vow and Desire*, p. 324, ont tous deux bien vu que ce ch. était construit sur le *redoublement* systématique de chaque scène dialogale entre les différents acteurs du débat engagé sur la monarchie – soit du peuple à Samuel (vv. 4-5), de Samuel à Yhwh (v. 6), de Yhwh à Samuel (vv. 7-9) et de Samuel au peuple (vv. 10-18), répété dans le même ordre aux vv. 19-22. A mon sens, ce phénomène n'est pas fortuit, mais vise un effet littéraire déterminé, qui apparaît mieux lorsqu'on réalise qu'il est provoqué par l'ordre de Yhwh à Samuel d'avertir le peuple des dangers de la monarchie (au lieu que Yhwh donne *directement* l'ordre à Samuel d'instituer un roi, comme en 8,22). La construction «en double» de ce ch. sert ainsi à Dtr simultanément à expliciter la demande des Anciens dans ses dernières conséquences théologiques et politiques (v. 18), et à condamner l'endurcissement du peuple (vv. 19-20). C'est en ce sens qu'il faut comprendre également la répétition du commandement divin d'«écouter la voix du peuple». Outre l'effet de redondance recherché ici, 8,22 répond, dans le second discours de Yhwh, à 8,9 dans le premier. Quant au «doublet» des vv. 7 et 9, il encadre le discours extrêmement critique à l'égard de la royauté par le commandement divin d'instaurer la royauté en Israël (sur les enjeux de cette construction littéraire pour la compréhension de ces vv., cf. FOKKELMAN, *Vow and Desire*, p. 337), ce qui est typique de la composition dtr en 1 S 8-12, où les deux aspects sont indissolublement liés: cf. 10,18-19 et 10,20-25; 12,12b-13.

36. Cf. les analyses du langage de ce ch. chez VEIJOLA, *Königtum*, pp. 84-91; KLEIN, *1 Samuel*, p. 114; MOMMER, *Samuel*, pp. 124-125.

37. *Contra* BIRCH, *Rise*, pp. 64-65; D.J. MCCARTHY, *Treaty and Covenant. A Study in Form in the Ancient Oriental Documents and in the Old Testament* (AnBib, 21A), Rome, Biblical Institute Press, 1978, p. 207; MCCARTER, *1 Samuel*, pp. 217-218; MOENIKES, *Ablehnung*, p. 37, ces vv. ne constituent donc pas un document pré-dtr.

8[38]. Il faut donc traiter ce ch. comme une unité littéraire[39]. Cependant, plusieurs difficultés demeurent, qui rendent l'interprétation de ce ch. difficile. Parmi celles-ci, je mentionnerai principalement la question du rapport des vv. 1-5 aux vv. (6)7-25, qui demeure obscure, ainsi que la présence de différents éléments de la terminologie postexilique[40]. Faut-il alors postuler l'existence de deux rédactions dtr différentes dans ce ch.[41]? Mais les vv. 1-5 pris isolément ne signifient pas grand chose[42], et ne représentent pas une résolution satisfaisante des caractéristiques dtr de 1 S 8-11[43]. De plus, on ne trouve dans le reste du ch. aucune des problématiques de la rédaction nomiste, telle que R. Smend l'a définie[44]. En d'autres termes, la signification du ch. 12 considéré comme une unité littéraire demeure peu claire.

À mon sens, deux éléments de réponse peuvent être apportés. D'abord, plusieurs auteurs ont déjà identifié différentes gloses tardives dans le texte[45], dont la suppression élimine une partie des tensions, et rend

38. VEIJOLA, *Königtum*, p. 83, établit la liste des références aux ch. précédents présentes en 1 S 12.

39. VEIJOLA (*Königtum*, pp. 92-93) a montré que ce ch. était principalement structuré par la répétition de ועתה (respectivement גם־עתה au v. 16), qui permet de distinguer trois séquences principales: 12,1-5(6).7-15.16-25. Voir également T. RÖMER, *Israels Väter. Untersuchungen zur Väterthematik im Deuteronomium und in der deuteronomistischen Tradition* (OBO, 99), Freiburg (CH), Universitätsverlag; Göttingen, Vandenhoeck & Ruprecht, 1990, p. 330.

40. Cf. MAYES, *Story of Israel*, p. 101; RÖMER, *Israels Väter*, p. 334.

41. Ainsi DIETRICH (*Histoire et Loi*, pp. 312 [n. 51] et 313), avec beaucoup de prudence. Mais le découpage rédactionnel qu'il propose, et qui attribue à DtrH les vv. 1-6a.13b, est particulièrement peu convaincant.

42. O'BRIEN (*Reassessment*, p. 122) relève que les «discours d'adieux» parallèles de Moïse et de Josué sont toujours accompagnés de dispositions pour l'avenir, telles qu'elles apparaissent dans la suite de 1 S 12. 12,1-5 s'explique donc mieux dans le contexte de l'ensemble du ch.

43. *Contra* O'BRIEN, *Reassessment*, pp. 120-128, qui considère le ch. 12 comme une insertion tardive dans HD. Cf. sur ce point les critiques de McKENZIE, *Cette royauté*, pp. 286-287. Comme le rappelle justement McKenzie, en 1 S 12, «[…] l'idéologie du discours de Samuel ressemble à celle des textes dtr du ch. 8 et de 10,17-27a» (p. 286).

44. Cf. R. SMEND, *Das Gesetz und die Völker: Ein Beitrag zur deuteronomistischen Redaktionsgeschichte*, in H.W. WOLFF (ed.), *Probleme biblischer Theologie. Gerhard von Rad zum 70. Geburtstag*, Münich, C. Kaiser, 1971, pp. 494-509. Avec MOMMER, *Samuel*, pp. 127-128; RÖMER, *Israels Väter*, p. 334 («Von einer typisch "nomistischen" Terminologie und Ideologie ist hier jedoch nichts zu merken»); *contra* VEIJOLA, *Königtum*, pp. 83-92; DIETRICH, *Histoire et Loi*, pp. 311-312.

45. Cf. notamment 12,6b (avec STOEBE, *Buch Samuelis*, pp. 233, 237; VEIJOLA, *Königtum*, p. 85, n. 10; MOMMER, *Samuel*, p. 126), 12,21 (STOEBE, *Buch Samuelis*, pp. 234, 239; VEIJOLA, *Königtum*, p. 90, n. 46; MOMMER, *Samuel*, p. 126), ainsi que la mention d'Aaron à côté de celle de Moïse en 12,8 (MOMMER, *Samuel*, p. 126) et celle de l'«oint» de Yhwh en 12,3.5 (VEIJOLA, *Königtum*, p. 94; McCARTER, *1 Samuel*, p. 213; O'BRIEN, *Reassessment*, p. 123, n. 137).

compte de la présence d'une terminologie postexilique dans ce ch. Ensuite, la recherche exégétique s'est souvent efforcée de caractériser le
genre littéraire du ch. 12, sans envisager la possibilité qu'il soit *délibérément* composite. C'est pourquoi les modèles habituellement proposés demeurent trop simples pour envisager la complexité de ce ch. Ainsi,
P. Mommer, contestant le caractère juridique du discours de Samuel en
12,7-25, a récemment proposé d'interpréter ces vv. comme étant uniquement une parénèse prophétique[46]. Par ailleurs, différents exégètes ont
voulu rendre compte de la fonction du ch. 12 à partir des traités de vassalité (hittites ou assyriens) du Proche Orient ancien, que la rédaction dtr
aurait employés comme modèles[47]. Aucune de ces solutions n'est pleinement satisfaisante. La distinction de Mommer, aussi habile qu'elle soit,
est trop simpliste[48]; et si Samuel ne fonctionne plus comme juge *après* 1
S 12[49], il est présenté par la rédaction dtr comme prophète bien avant le
ch. 12, et parfois simultanément à sa représentation comme *juge* (cf 1 S
7). La comparaison avec les traités d'alliance assyriens est pertinente jusqu'à un certain point, et elle a permis de rendre compte de certains aspects
de 1 S 12, ainsi que des similitudes de ce ch. avec Jos 24. Mais 1 S 12
présente également de nombreuses divergences avec le modèle conven-
tionnel des traités. Ainsi, les vv. 1-5 n'ont pas de parallèle strict ailleurs (y
compris dans les discours d'adieux des autres grandes figures de l'histoire
d'Israël)[50]. De plus, le ch. se clôt singulièrement sur une formule de malé-

---

46. MOMMER, *Samuel*, pp. 130-133. Dans le schéma de Mommer, seul 12,1-5 serait à
interpréter comme discours *juridique* (puisque Samuel s'y décharge de sa fonction de
juge), alors que 12,7-25 correspondrait à la fonction de *prophète* que Samuel va endosser
dans les ch. ultérieurs.

47. Cf. principalement J. MUILENBURG, *The Form and Structure of the Covenantal
Formulations*, in *VT* 9 (1959) 347-365, part. pp. 361-365; WEISER, *Samuel*, pp. 83s.; K.
BALTZER, *The Covenant Formulary*, Philadelphia, PA, Mack, 1971; BIRCH, *Rise*, pp. 68-
70; R.J. VANNOY, *Covenant Renewal at Gilgal. A Study of 1 Samuel 11,14–12,25*, New
Jersey, NJ, Mack, 1978; McCARTHY, *Treaty and Covenant*, pp. 213-221; McCARTER, *1
Samuel*, pp. 220-221; WÉNIN, *Instauration*, pp. 228-230. Pour une évaluation des apports
et des limitations de la «treaty euphoria» qui s'est développée dans la recherche
vétérotestamentaire, cf. T. RÖMER, *The Book of Deuteronomy*, in McKENZIE – GRAHAM,
The History of Israel's Traditions, pp. 178-212, ici 196-199.

48. Il me paraît difficile de contester la dimension juridique de 12,7-15 (avec H.J.
BOECKER, *Die Beurteilung der Anfänge des Königtums in der deuteronomistischen
Abschnitten des 1. Samuelsbuches* [WMANT, 31], Neukirchen-Vluyn, Neukirchener
Verlag, 1969, pp. 72s.; VEIJOLA, *Königtum*, pp. 95-96; BERGES, *Verwerfung*, pp. 92-93;
RÖMER, *Israels Väter*, p. 332). Par contre, Mommer pourrait bien avoir raison en ce qui
concerne 12,16-25, qui correspond effectivement mieux au genre du discours prophétique.

49. Encore qu'il soit associé à des problématiques liées au respect de la loi dtr, cf. 1 S
13,7-15 et 15. Sur ce point, cf. BERGES, *Verwerfung*, pp. 163-211.

50. La tentative de McCARTHY, *Treaty*, p. 217, visant à interpréter les vv. 1-5 comme
une «liturgie de pénitence» illustre exemplairement les difficultés qu'il y a à faire rentrer
1 S 12 dans le cadre strict des traités d'alliance.

diction sans contrepartie positive (cf. 12,25)[51]. Enfin, le prologue historique (vv. 7-12) sert habituellement à légitimer l'établissement du roi, alors
que c'est l'inverse qui se produit ici[52]. On évitera par conséquent d'interpréter ce ch. comme un «calque» formel des traités d'alliance, même si la
composition dtr a pu leur emprunter certains éléments[53].

À mon sens, il faut donc prendre acte du caractère «hybride» de 1 S
12, lequel s'explique par les différentes fonctions de ce ch. dans le contexte de la composition d'ensemble dtr, et de la problématique inaugurée
au ch. 8.

D'une part, 1 S 12 établit clairement que ce ne sont ni Samuel (vv. 1-
5), ni Yhwh (vv. 7-11) qui sont responsables de l'avènement de la monarchie, et que *seul le peuple* (v. 12) porte par conséquent le poids de la
faute d'une institution injuste (8,11-18) et ennemie du gouvernement
théocratique en Israël (8,7.20)[54]. C'est pourquoi le texte contient une dimension «prophétique» aussi bien que «juridique»: une fois établie, la
faute doit être reconnue et confessée par le peuple (vv. 16-19), suite à
quoi des prescriptions pourront être énoncées (par l'intermédiaire du
prophète de Yhwh) pour l'avenir de l'Israël monarchique (vv. 20-25).
C'est sans doute également pour cette raison que le ch. 12 masque délibérément la faillite du gouvernement des juges évoquée en 1 S 8,1-3,
afin qu'aucune circonstance atténuante ne puisse être invoquée en faveur
du peuple. Enfin, la rédaction dtr met en pleine lumière la faute du peuple en contrastant de manière récurrente l'«agir» (עשה) du peuple et celui de Yhwh (cf. 12,7-11.19.23).

D'autre part, le ch. 12 vise à permettre l'intégration de la monarchie
dans l'alliance d'Israël avec Yhwh, comme il ressort clairement des vv.
14-15. C'est ici que le rapprochement avec les traités de vassalité prend
toute sa signification; car les tensions (relevées ci-dessus) qui se déga-
gent entre le ch. 12 et son «modèle» littéraire éclairent de manière sin-

---

51. Avec BERGES (*Verwerfung*, p. 96), qui relève également l'absence d'une affirmation finale de la part du peuple de sa volonté de demeurer obéissant à Yhwh; comparer
sur ce point avec Jos 24,24. Même si l'on considère avec BOECKER (*Beurteilung*, pp. 77-
82) que l'*apodosis* ne manque pas au v. 14b (où il faudrait lire par conséquent: «Aussi
longtemps que vous et votre roi reconnaîtrez Yhwh par roi»), la formule de bénédiction
de 12,14 surprend par son absence de promesse concrète.

52. Comme le relève BIRCH (*Rise*, p. 69).

53. Pour une conclusion similaire, cf. KLEIN, *1 Samuel*, p. 113; O'BRIEN, *Deuteronomistic History*, p. 128 n. 156.

54. L'originalité de 12,1-5 est due, pour une part, à ce que Dtr intègre une déclaration
d'innocence (construite sur l'arrière-fond du «droit du roi» de 8,11-17) dans le discours
d'adieu de Samuel. Ainsi, l'établissement au ch. 12 de la part de responsabilité de Samuel, de Yhwh et du peuple dans l'avènement de l'époque monarchique en Israël relie les
vv. 1-5 aux vv. 6s. La démonstration de Dtr rejoint ici celle du ch. 8, avec la mise en
garde de Yhwh et le refus de la part du peuple d'écouter (8,20).

gulière l'accord donné par Yhwh à la royauté. En particulier, le fait que le rappel des actes de délivrance continuels de Yhwh (12,7-11), qui sert à établir la culpabilité du peuple, constitue *simultanément* le préalable à l'intégration de la monarchie dans l'alliance (selon le schéma habituel des traités de vassalité) laisse entendre que la problématique du «rejet» de Yhwh impliqué, depuis le ch. 8, par l'institution monarchique, est encore présent à l'arrière-plan.

En réalité, si le ch. 12 décrit l'intégration de la monarchie dans l'alliance, c'est au sens de la *soumission* de cette institution à la seigneurie de Yhwh. L'acceptation de la monarchie est conditionnée à l'obéissance inconditionnelle du peuple *et du roi*, qui sont pareillement soumis aux obligations de l'alliance mosaïque (cf. vv. 14.24)[55] et aux enseignements (ירה) du prophète de Yhwh (v. 23). Comme l'expose clairement l'«*Alternativpredigt*» de 12,14-15, la monarchie n'est pas en soi garantie de salut, et l'Israël monarchique dépend toujours autant de Yhwh, contrairement aux attentes du peuple en 8,20[56]. À cet égard, on est en droit de considérer que le ch. 12 résoud la problématique «théologique» ouverte au ch. 8 par le passage du gouvernement charismatique des juges à l'institution monarchique en réaffirmant l'autorité absolue de Yhwh sur la royauté.

Ainsi, au terme du procès complexe mis en scène par le ch. 12, *un certain type* de monarchie est instauré, conformément à l'ordre de Yhwh en 8,22. La tension présente dès le ch. 8 entre la condamnation sans appel de la royauté par Yhwh et sa décision de se conformer au souhait du peuple (cf. 8,7.9.22) est ici résolue dans le sens de l'établissement d'une royauté «idéale», entièrement soumise aux préceptes de la Tora et à la souveraineté de Yhwh – et qui n'est donc plus la royauté «comme les autres nations» souhaitée par le peuple en 8,5.20.

Toutefois, l'intrigue rebondit désormais, car deux questions au moins restent en suspens. La royauté *effectivement* établie dans l'intervalle (1 S 9-11), celle de Saül, correspond-elle aux critères de la royauté telle qu'elle a été acceptée *en principe* par Yhwh? Le récit du règne de Saül en 1 S 13-15 suggère explicitement le contraire[57]. Mais comment expli-

---

55. Cf. ESLINGER (*Kingship of God*, pp. 405, 424); WÉNIN (*Instauration*, pp. 224-227): «En confirmant les stipulations du pacte qui lie le peuple à Yhwh, Samuel détermine également le statut du roi. Le nouveau monarque est soumis à Yhwh comme le peuple [...] Aux yeux de Yhwh, le peuple et le roi, c'est tout un» (p. 226).

56. Cf. déjà NOTH (*Deuteronomistic History*, p. 51): «Despite the institution of monarchy, things can remain as they were before». BOECKER (*Beurteilung*, pp. 87-88) remarque finement que les vv. 20-24 se concentrent sur le peuple, et que c'est par conséquent uniquement de son obéissance que dépend l'avenir d'Israël.

57. Tout comme, par ailleurs, l'évocation de la pente «exilique» de la monarchie sur laquelle se clôt le ch. 12.

quer alors que Yhwh soit lui-même à l'origine de l'élection (בחר) de Saül (10,24)? Par ailleurs, on relèvera que l'offense liée au rejet de Yhwh (1 S 8), et rappelée entre temps (10,18-19; 12,8-12), n'est toujours pas punie au terme du ch. 12, bien que le peuple ait depuis confessé son crime (12,19), et qu'il sache désormais que le terme de la royauté en Israël est l'exil (12,25). Cette offense demeure donc, au terme du ch. 12, comme une interrogation suspendue à l'avenir de la royauté. Ces questions excèdent le cadre strict des ch. 8-12, et demandent à être traitées dans le contexte de l'ensemble de la rédaction dtr en 1 S 7,2-16,13[58].

DEUX FIGURES DE LA ROYAUTÉ ISRAÉLITE: SAÜL ET DAVID DANS LE RÉCIT DTR DE 1 S 7,2–16,13

Les ch. 15 et 16,1-13 complètent la représentation dtr de la monarchie en figurant, à travers le rejet du règne de Saül et l'élection de David, deux aspects de la monarchie israélite. En ce sens, le regard que porte Dtr sur cette monarchie est *double*, selon que le modèle politique qu'elle désigne apparaît, à l'origine, divinement institué (ch. 12), ou, à l'inverse, inspiré par les nations alentours d'Israël (8,5.20). On verra alors comment cette interprétation permet de rendre compte de l'ambivalence du récit complexe de 1 S 10,17-27 (l'élection de Saül), qui souligne exemplairement les préoccupations de la composition dtr en 7,2–16,13.

1 Samuel 15,1–16,13. Dans l'état actuel de la recherche, le ch. 15 présente plusieurs difficultés: l'attitude de Samuel à l'égard de Saül est ambiguë (comparer 15,11.35 et 15,13-31), et la fonction du long dialogue qui les oppose est peu claire et demanderait une analyse détaillée[59]. Par contre, le langage de ces ch. contient de nombreux éléments dtr[60].

---

58. *Contra* plusieurs études des récits de l'instauration de la royauté en 1 S 8-12, qui voient dans le ch. 12 l'aboutissement de l'intrigue ouverte par la demande du peuple au ch. 8; ainsi, ESLINGER, *Kingship of God*; JOBLING, *Deuteronomic Political Theory*; WÉNIN, *Instauration*, et, dans une moindre mesure, FOKKELMAN, *Vow and Desire*.

59. Aucun des traitements synchroniques qui en a été proposé ne me satisfait pleinement; cf. GUNN, *Fate*, pp. 44-55; FOKKELMAN, *Crossing Fates*, pp. 95-110; LONG, *Reign*, pp. 141-155; EDELMAN, *King Saul*, pp. 104-108. La question de savoir si Saül ment ou s'il est tout à fait honnête quant à ses intentions en préservant le meilleur du bétail (vv. 9.15) demeure peu claire. Quoi qu'il en soit, l'essentiel pour mon propos est que le discours de Samuel à Saül au ch. 15 débouche sur la condamnation sans appel de ce dernier, et le rejet de sa royauté (cf. STOLZ, *Das erste und zweite Buch Samuel*, p. 99: «Alles ist auf die Verwerfung Sauls hin ausgerichtet»).

60. Cf. les analyses de FORESTI (*Rejection*, pp. 67-90), et de J. VAN SETERS (*In Search of History. Historiography in the Ancient World and the Origins of Biblical Historiography*, New Haven, CT – London, Yale University Press, 1983, pp. 259-260).

Il n'y a donc aucune raison de les assigner à une édition pré-dtr[61]; et à l'exception de 15,26-30 qui est clairement un ajout secondaire[62], il n'est pas nécessaire d'y voir l'intervention de plusieurs rédactions dtr[63]. J. Van Seters considère à juste titre l'ensemble formé par 15,1–16,13 comme une insertion secondaire dans le récit dtr du règne de Saül[64]. Mais je ne crois pas, contrairement à lui, qu'il faille pour autant attribuer ces ch. à une rédaction post-dtr: à l'exception des vv. 26-30, le langage et le style de 15 et 16 ne justifient pas cette décision, et les motifs de ces ch. correspondent à ceux qui ont déjà été rencontrés auparavant dans la rédaction dtr. À mon avis, le caractère secondaire de 15,1–16,13 s'explique mieux par l'hypothèse d'une double édition dtr des récits sur le début de la monarchie en 1 Samuel, comme je le montrerai plus loin.

Pour l'essentiel, les ch. 15 et 16,1-13 servent à mener à son terme le débat engagé par Dtr sur le statut et la légitimité de la monarchie en 1 S 8 et 12. Considérés ensemble[65], ils indiquent d'abord que le destin de

---

61. *Contra* BIRCH, *Rise,* pp. 103-104; SEEBASS, *Wesen*, pp. 96-99; CAMPBELL, *Prophets and Kings*, pp. 42-45; DIETRICH, *David*, pp. 10-25; O'BRIEN, *Reassessment*, p. 130; MOMMER, *Samuel*, pp. 145-162.

62. Le v. 25 forme un doublet avec le v. 30 (cf. aussi les vv. 23 et 26). NOTH (*Deuteronomistic History*, p. 55) propose de considérer les vv. 24-31 comme une insertion secondaire, mais dans ce cas, le doublet est reporté dans l'insertion. Il vaut donc mieux considérer soit le v. 25, soit le v. 30 comme faisant partie de la rédaction originale du ch. 15. MOMMER (*Samuel*, pp. 147-150) tient les vv. 24-29 pour secondaires. CAMPBELL (*Prophets and Kings*, pp. 63-90) considère que ce sont les vv. 26-30 qui ont été ajoutés. Dans la mesure où 15,26 vise explicitement à contredire 15,24-25, il me paraît effectivement préférable de suivre cette dernière proposition. L'aveu de Saül en 15,24 («Car j'ai craint le peuple et j'ai écouté sa voix»), absent en 15,30, sert à clore la confrontation entre Samuel et Saül et à indiquer la nature du péché de Saül; il est donc nécessaire à la bonne compréhension du récit. Puisque le principal «plus» de 15,30 par rapport à 15,24-25 consiste dans le remplacement d'une partie du motif de la demande de Saül (en 15,30, Saül demande à Samuel de l'«honorer» [כבד] devant les Anciens du peuple et devant tout Israël, alors qu'en 15,25, il lui demande d'«enlever son péché» [שׂא נא את־ חטאתי]), l'insertion de 15,26-30 vise à infléchir la rédaction initiale afin de souligner le fait que Saül n'obtiendra pas le pardon de Samuel, puisque désormais Samuel n'accepte de revenir avec Saül qu'après que celui-ci ait renoncé à demander son pardon. Quant à 15,29, il s'agit clairement d'une glose tardive visant à corriger 15,11.35.

63. *Contra* FORESTI, *Rejection* (pp. 25-62); DIETRICH, *David* (pp. 10-25).

64. VAN SETERS, *Search*, pp. 261-264, suivi en cela par McKENZIE (*Cette royauté*, p. 290). Les ch. 15,1-16,13 interrompent le récit du règne de Saül, et sont insérés juste après la notice de 14,47-52 sur la fin de son règne, qui est dtr. Il en va d'ailleurs de même pour le ch. 28, qui est vraisemblablement de la même main que le ch. 15, et qui se présente également comme une insertion secondaire. Enfin, il n'est plus fait mention par la suite du rejet de Saül par Yhwh, sinon en 1 S 28. Toutefois, je pense que Van Seters et McKenzie ont tort de voir dans le ch. 15 un doublet de 13,7b-15a, dans la mesure où ce dernier passage n'est pas concerné par le rejet personnel de Saül comme roi (le terme מאס n'y apparaît d'ailleurs pas), mais par le refus divin de toute hérédité dynastique pour Saül (avec McCARTER, *1 Samuel*, p. 270; O'BRIEN, *Reassessment*, p. 131, n. 4).

65. Les deux ch. sont étroitement reliés, comme l'indiquent 15,35 et 16,1 (VAN SETERS, *Search*, p. 263).

l'institution royale ne dépend pas de celui du roi Saül, puisqu'alors même que Saül est destitué, Samuel reçoit l'ordre de désigner un nou-veau roi[66]. Ensuite, et surtout, le contraste établi dans ces ch. entre deux figures royales antithétiques (Saül et David) vise clairement à signaler deux types incompatibles de royauté. Saül (שָׁאוּל), qui est devenu roi suite à la demande (שׁאל) du peuple[67], et parce que Yhwh a «écouté la voix du peuple» (8,7.9.22), est finalement rejeté pour avoir «écouté la voix du peuple» au lieu d'écouter les ordres et les paroles de Yhwh (cf. 12,14-15), comme il le reconnaît lui-même en 15,24[68]:

ויאמר שאול אל־שמואל חטאתי כי־עברתי את־פי־יהוה ואת־דבריך כי יראתי את־העם ואשמע בקולם[69].

Saül personnifie donc vraisemblablement l'origine *populaire*, non di-vine, de la royauté en Israël dans la conception dtr exilique. C'est pour-quoi le «rejet» (מאס) de sa royauté répond, en définitive, au rejet de la souveraineté de Yhwh par le peuple; la réciprocité impliquée par la sen-tence de 15,23 est à cet égard saisissante[70]:

ויּמאסך ממלך את־דבר יהוה יען מאסת (v. 23b)

Si l'offense faite à Yhwh par la demande populaire (8,5), constam-ment rappelée depuis[71] mais non résolue, peut être finalement reportée sur Saül, c'est uniquement parce que dans le récit dtr celui-ci incarne, au-delà de sa propre faute, le péché du peuple[72].

---

66. À cet égard, WEISER, *1 Samuel 15*, in *ZAW* 54 (1936) 1-28, avait également avancé une remarque intéressante, qui est malheureusement passée inaperçue. Il relève le fait que Samuel exécute le roi Agag à la place de Saül (15,32-34), qui avait pourtant été choisi par Yhwh comme roi pour accomplir cette mission selon 15,1. Ainsi, Samuel com-pense la défaillance de Saül, et remplit le mandat de la royauté à sa place. On peut prolon-ger ici la réflexion de Weiser: le fait que ce soit précisément Samuel, c-à-d le «porte-parole» de la loi de Yhwh depuis le ch. 12, qui se substitue momentanément à la royauté défaillante de Saül me paraît tout à fait révélateur de l'intention de la rédaction dtr.

67. Cf. 8,10; 10,22; 12,13.17.19.

68. Cf. GUNN, *Fate*, p. 74.

69. Le fait que Saül reconnaisse avoir «craint le peuple» (כי יראתי את־העם) contredit explicitement l'encouragement de Samuel à craindre Yhwh en 12,24.

70. «Puisque tu as rejeté ma parole, je te rejette comme roi». BIRCH (*Rise*, p. 100) re-lève en ce sens que cette sentence exprime une relation de causalité inhabituelle dans les jugements prophétiques. Cf. également FOKKELMAN, *Vow and Desire*, pp. 337s., qui a bien vu que le motif du rejet de Yhwh parcourait l'ensemble des ch. 8-15, avant d'être finalement reporté sur Saül en 15,23: «The judgement runs there: "Because you have rejected the word of the Lord, he has rejected you as king". This "measure for measure" logic did not appear out of thin air and has been prepared for after 8,7-9» (p. 342).

71. Cf. 8,7; 10,19; 12,12.

72. En ce sens, si la condamnation de Saül peut paraître disproportionnée par rapport à sa faute (GUNN, *Fate*, p. 44), elle est par contre à la hauteur de l'offense faite à Dieu par l'instauration en Israël de la monarchie, cette autorité rivale de la sienne. À mon avis, c'est dans le contexte du rejet de Saül que le jeu de mots entre la racine de son nom et celle de la demande populaire prend tout son sens.

À l'opposé, David, qui est désigné en 16,7 comme le roi «selon le cœur» de Yhwh, apparaît comme le paradigme de la royauté idéale, d'origine divine. Ainsi, en rejetant Saül, la rédaction dtr condamne définitivement la royauté «exogène» souhaitée par le peuple en 8,5.20; en consacrant David, elle réaffirme, à la suite du ch. 12, que seule une royauté entièrement soumise aux prescriptions de Yhwh est politiquement et théologiquement viable pour Israël. Au-delà de cette séquence inaugurale, c'est donc – sauf exception – l'ensemble de la succession des rois israélites qui se trouve condamné pour n'avoir pas imité l'obéissance de David.

En ce sens, Saül et David figurent dans la perspective dtr les termes d'une alternative indépassable dont dépend le sort de la royauté, et sur laquelle le «récit d'origine» de la monarchie israélite élaboré par Dtr se conclut. Une question reste cependant à élucider, celle de la mention par la composition dtr de l'élection *divine* de Saül à la royauté.

1 Samuel 10,17-27. Bien que, dans l'état actuel, cette péricope présente certaines difficultés textuelles et littéraires, je pense toutefois qu'elle s'explique mieux comme une composition dtr (ainsi que McKenzie l'a récemment rendu vraisemblable) que comme un «collage» de traditions sur l'accession de Saül à la royauté. Malgré ses tensions apparentes, les différentes séquences du récit paraissent bien intégrées; en ce sens, les vv. 20-21bα et 22-25[73] sont trop fragmentaires pour représenter des sources autonomes, comme le relevait déjà Noth[74]. McKenzie remarque, en ce qui concerne 10,20-21, que la pratique du tirage au sort est attestée ailleurs dans HD (cf. Jos 7 et 1 S 14), et que la mention de «toutes les tribus d'Israël» est dtr[75]. 10,20-21 présuppose les données sur l'ascendance de Saül transmises par 9,1–10,16; de plus, le récit de la désignation de Saül reprend, dans l'ordre inverse, les termes

---

73. Cf. O. EISSFELDT, *Die Komposition der Samuelisbücher*, Leipzig, Hinrichs, 1931, p. 7, qui attribuait le premier récit à E, et le second à sa source «L».

74. *Deuteronomistic History*, p. 50: «The passage 10:21bβ-27a would lack the necessary introduction and 10:17-21abα the necessary conclusion if they were seen as belonging to separate narratives». De même, O'BRIEN (*Reassessment*, p. 117): «It seems unlikely therefore that one can recover the complete text of the two versions. The lot-drawing ceremony conducted by Samuel really requires v. 24a as its climax, but this verse incorporates a feature of the second account, namely Saul's incomparable stature (1 Sam 10:24aβ). The second account (vv. 21bβ-23) appears to have lost its beginning by being thoroughly incorporated into the lot-drawing ceremony [...]». Parmi les tentatives récentes pour reconstruire un récit pré-dtr de l'élection de Saül, cf. principalement BIRCH, *Rise*, pp. 42-54; CRÜSEMANN, *Widerstand*, pp. 54-60; McCARTER, *1 Samuel*, p. 195; SEEBASS, *Wesen*, pp. 77-81; MAYES, *Story of Israel*, pp. 100; DIETRICH, *David*, pp. 136-145; MOMMER, *Samuel*, pp. 69-80.

75. *Cette royauté*, p. 270.

par lesquels Saül met en question son titre à la royauté en 9,21[76], selon un schéma typique des récits de vocation dtr[77], et qui doit faire partie de la première édition dtr de 9,1-10,16 (cf. mon analyse de l'édition dtr de ces ch. ci-dessous). La mention de la «loi du roi» en 10,25, qui entérine un changement d'époque dans HD, et qui fait allusion à Dt 17,14-20 et 1 S 8,11-17, est clairement un motif dtr[78]. De même, la mention de l'«élection» (בחר) de Saül par Yhwh au v. 24 suit le programme de Dt 17,15[79]; ce point est essentiel, et j'y reviendrai par la suite. La mention de la taille de Saül au v. 23 reprend l'indication de 9,2[80]; elle joue d'ailleurs un rôle important dans la composition de ce récit par Dtr, comme je le montrerai plus loin. Enfin, McKenzie a démontré que les vv. 18-19 ne doivent pas être tenus pour secondaires, mais sont nécessaires à la compréhension du récit[81]. Or leur style les identifie à la rédaction dtr des ch. 8 et 12. Quant à 10,26-27, il s'agit d'une notice rédactionnelle dtr reliant le récit du ch. 11 avec la désignation de Saül en 10,17-27[82].

Toutefois, deux difficultés demeurent dans l'analyse du récit de 10,17-27, soit la formulation peu claire de 10,22, ainsi que la raison de l'absence de Saül en 10,21bβ. La raison pour laquelle le récit représente le peuple consultant Yhwh une *seconde* fois (עוד, 10,22a) tient à ce que le tirage au sort constitue déjà une première forme de consultation, comme le signalent explicitement Jos 7,14 et 1 S 14,40-41. Il n'y a donc aucun besoin de postuler, derrière la seconde consultation du peuple, un oracle divin (désormais égaré) recommandant d'élire comme roi un homme de stature exceptionnelle[83].

---

76. Comparer particulièrement:

(9,21a) ויען שאול ויאמר הלוא בן־ימיני אנכי מקטני שבטי ישראל

(10,20) ויקרב שמואל את כל־שבטי ישראל וילכד שבט בנימן

La mention du *clan* de Saül, absente de 9,21, peut s'expliquer par le contexte du tirage au sort, cf. Jos 7,14. La mention des «Matrites», qui n'est attestée nulle part ailleurs dans HD, pourrait être traditionnelle.

77. Cf. à ce sujet J. VAN SETERS, *The Life of Moses: The Yahwist as Historian in Exodus-Numbers*, Louisville, KY, Westminster / John Knox Press, 1994, pp. 42-44.

78. Cf. BOECKER, *Beurteilung*, pp. 51-56; MCKENZIE, *Cette royauté*, p. 271 n. 1.

79. Cf. VEIJOLA, *Königtum*, pp. 49-50.

80. *Contra* MOMMER (*Samuel*, p. 76), qui défend l'antériorité de 10,23 sur 9,2. Si Mommer avait raison en ce qui concerne le caractère secondaire de 9,2bβ, il devrait s'agir d'une intervention rédactionnelle destinée à préparer 10,23, et provenant de la même main.

81. *Cette royauté*, p. 271: «Il y a de bonnes raisons d'inclure les v. 18b-19 dans l'ensemble, car en leur absence on ne comprendrait pas pourquoi Samuel rassemble le peuple ni à quelle fonction Saül est destiné».

82. MCKENZIE, *Cette royauté*, pp. 273-274.

83. *Contra* EISSFELDT, *Komposition*, pp. 7s.; il a été suivi depuis notamment par NOTH, *Deuteronomistic History*, p. 50; BOECKER, *Beurteilung*, pp. 45-46; CRÜSEMANN,

En ce qui concerne le motif de l'absence de Saül lors du tirage au sort, on a généralement considéré qu'il servait à relier les deux traditions sur l'élection de Saül, en introduisant le fragment sur la requête du peuple auprès de Yhwh. Pour T. Veijola[84], le récit de 10,17-27 suggérerait que Saül s'est caché parce qu'il savait (cf. 9,20; 10,1) qu'il allait être désigné par le sort, ce qui n'est guère convaincant. Van Seters et McKenzie[85] supposent, pour leur part, que l'absence de Saül correspondrait à la pratique antique du tirage au sort[86]: mais cette explication est douteuse dans le cas présent (elle est contredite par les épisodes parallèles de Jos 7 et 1 S 14), et elle ne rend pas compte de la signification de ce motif en 10,17-27. À mon avis, il vaut mieux s'interroger sur la *fonction* de l'absence de Saül dans le récit. La dissimulation de Saül est un artifice qui sert essentiellement à introduire en 10,17-27 l'association entre שאל, «demander» (v. 22a) et שאול[87], afin de rappeler ici que c'est la demande du peuple (selon le récit de 1 S 8) qui est à l'origine de l'élection de Saül. De plus, l'absence du premier roi d'Israël démontre la dépendance du peuple à l'égard de Yhwh, puisque celui-ci est obligé de recourir à l'assistance divine pour élire son roi, alors que la monarchie devait être, selon les termes du ch. 8, une institution garantissant l'autonomie du peuple. Enfin, la dissimulation de Saül «parmi les bagages» (v. 23) sert aussi l'ambivalence de la représentation dtr de la royauté dans ce récit, sur laquelle je vais maintenant me pencher.

De manière générale, la discussion de 10,17-27 a plus porté sur la reconstruction d'un hypothétique matériau traditionnel à l'arrière-fond de ce passage que sur la signification de ces versets. Quelques exégètes ont cependant remarqué que le récit de 10,17-27 semblait entretenir l'équivoque sur la désignation de Saül[88]; et McKenzie s'est récemment efforcé de faire un relevé systématique des ambiguïtés rencontrées[89]. Il

---

Widerstand, p. 56; DIETRICH, *David*, pp. 139s.; O'BRIEN, *Reassessment*, p. 117; MOMMER, *Samuel*, pp. 75-76. Rien ne garantit qu'un tel oracle ait jamais existé en Israël; et de toute manière, le motif de la taille de Saül est rédactionnel (voir ci-dessus). En ce qui concerne le second עוד, la correction proposée par McCARTER (*1 Samuel*, p. 190) à la suite de la LXX est suggestive (voir aussi McKENZIE, *Cette royauté*, p. 270 n. 16); mais la leçon de la LXX n'est pas *lectio difficilior* (avec MOMMER, *Samuel*, p. 76). Plus vraisemblablement, la version du TM, si elle n'est pas fautive, vise à souligner l'absence de Saül lors du tirage au sort de 10,20-21.

84. *Königtum*, p. 39.
85. VAN SETERS, *Search*, p. 252; McKENZIE, *Cette royauté*, p. 270.
86. Cf. principalement J. LINDBLOM, *Lot-Casting in the Old Testament*, in VT 12 (1962) 164-178.
87. Avec McCARTER (*1 Samuel*, pp. 193, 196), et FOKKELMAN (*Vow and Desire*, p. 446).
88. Voir p. ex. McCARTER, *1 Samuel*, p. 196.
89. *Cette royauté*, pp. 271-272.

mentionne ainsi 1) la présence d'une formule de jugement en 10,18-19a, qui sert d'introduction à la désignation de Saül, laquelle s'insère ainsi à la place de la sentence[90]; 2) le fait que l'élection par tirage au sort serve à désigner un criminel dans les récits de Jos 7 et 1 S 14; 3) la figure de Saül se cachant, assez ridiculement, dans les bagages; 4) le caractère trompeur de sa taille, dénoncé en 16,1-13; 5) la description d'une opposition à Saül qui succède immédiatement au récit de son élection, laquelle est donc décrite, dès le départ, comme ne faisant pas l'unanimité[91]. Pour ma part, je rajouterai à cette liste deux éléments, qui ont précisément à voir avec la problématique de l'origine populaire (et non divine) de la royauté de Saül: l'allusion faite aux circonstances qui ont conduit à la consécration du premier roi d'Israël selon le ch. 8, aux vv. 18-19, d'abord, puis à travers le rappel au v. 22a du lien entre la demande par le peuple d'un roi et le nom de celui-ci; et le fait que l'établissement de Saül comme roi n'est rapporté à Yhwh que de manière indirecte, puisque c'est le peuple qui consacre Saül en l'acclamant par les paroles de «Vive le roi!», alors que le texte se contente de mentionner (encore qu'indirectement, par la bouche de Samuel) que Yhwh a «choisi/élu» Saül (בהר). La royauté de Saül semble ainsi (au moins)

90. À la suite de BIRCH (*Rise*, pp. 48-51). L'interprétation avancée par Birch pour expliquer ce phénomène est intenable, et elle ne rend pas compte des motifs qu'a Dtr de faire précéder le récit de la désignation royale de Saül par une formule de jugement (à ce sujet, cf. les critiques de BERGES, *Verwerfung*, pp. 83-84). Certains auteurs ont suggéré que la sentence était constituée par l'établissement de la royauté en Israël. Mais cette position est excessive (selon le récit de 1 S 12, la royauté est intégrée, moyennant certaines conditions, dans l'alliance du peuple avec Yhwh), et elle ne tient pas suffisamment compte de ce qu'en 10,17-27, c'est Yhwh qui élit Saül à la royauté conformément au schéma de Dt 17,15. La désignation royale de Saül ne saurait donc s'expliquer uniquement comme la punition d'Israël par Yhwh. Il paraît préférable de considérer la présence de la formule de jugement en 10,17-27 comme une allusion faite par Dtr à la condamnation qui attend la royauté de Saül au ch. 15, dans la mesure où ce dernier personnifie la royauté «populaire», désobéissante à Yhwh. Significativement, Dtr fait d'ailleurs figurer dans la formule de jugement des vv. 18-19 le rappel du rejet de Yhwh impliqué par la demande populaire d'un roi, qui trouve sa conclusion dans le récit du ch. 15. La véritable sentence du jugement porté par Yhwh sur la royauté populaire tombe par conséquent avec le récit du rejet de la royauté de Saül; elle débute cependant dès le récit de la désignation de Saül en 10,17-27 dans la mesure où ce dernier n'est pas destiné à être le roi «selon le cœur de Yhwh», mais à figurer la royauté issue du péché du peuple.

91. Cet argument gagne encore en poids si l'on relève, avec STOEBE (*Buch Samuelis*, p. 174) que la figure de Samuel est toujours associée, dans ces ch., à la mention de «tout Israël»: cf. 7,3.5; 10,20.24; 12,1 (en 8,4, on a la mention de «tous les anciens d'Israël»). 10,26-27 suggère ainsi, par contraste, que Saül ne parviendra jamais à garantir l'unité d'Israël, comme Samuel l'avait fait jusque là. Le fait que les adversaires de Saül en 10,27 soient qualifiés de בני בליעל ne traduit pas une perspective favorable à Saül, mais s'explique dès lors que Yhwh a accepté le principe de la monarchie, et qu'il a participé à la désignation de Saül. En s'opposant à Saül, ses adversaires s'opposent donc à la décision divine elle-même (avec HERTZBERG, *1 & 2 Samuel*, p. 90; KLEIN, *1 Samuel*, p. 100; ESLINGER, *Kingship of God*, pp. 356-358).

autant le fait du peuple que celui de Yhwh. C'est pourquoi la composition dtr ajoute au récit de la désignation de Saül par tirage au sort le récit de sa quête par le peuple (vv. 22s.), afin de souligner la responsabilité de ce dernier dans le couronnement du premier roi d'Israël[92].

Les observations de McKenzie sont judicieuses, mais la réponse qu'il avance quant à l'intention de Dtr en plaçant le récit de la désignation royale de Saül sous le signe de l'équivoque est trop simple, et demande quelques développements[93]. Il me semble que cette intention apparaît mieux si l'on compare ce récit à celui de la désignation de David en 16,1-13, qui en est comme l'antitype. Le parallèle entre les scènes est explicite: dans chaque cas, c'est Samuel qui dirige l'élection au nom de Yhwh; les candidats défilent devant Samuel; l'élu est absent au moment du choix. Les différences sont dues au contexte: l'onction de Saül a déjà eu lieu en 9,1-10,16; et l'absence de tirage au sort s'explique précisément par la connotation négative dont ce motif bénéficie dans le cas de la désignation de Saül.

Or les critères qui ont servi à désigner Saül en 10,17-27 sont explicitement démasqués comme étant d'origine humaine, non divine, lors de l'élection de David, qui se fera précisément selon les critères inverses. C'est pourquoi, comme le relève R. Polzin[94], Eliav (16,7) est le seul parmi les fils de Jessé à être *rejeté* (מאס, cf. 15,23), parce qu'il est lui aussi de grande taille (cf. 10,24), alors que les autres fils ne sont simplement pas choisis (לא־בחר, 16,8.9.10). De façon générale, tout le récit de 16,1-13 est composé autour de l'opposition entre *apparence* et *réalité*[95], afin d'établir que la royauté de Saül était née d'une erreur de jugement du peuple, et n'avait jamais reçu l'aval de Yhwh. En 10,17-27, c'est le peuple qui a proclamé Saül roi parce qu'il était frappé par sa grande taille (v. 24): Yhwh n'a fait que le désigner de loin au peuple (v. 22). En 16,1-13, Samuel, qui allait répéter l'erreur du peuple (16,6-7), se voit déjugé par Yhwh, qui a «vu» (רהע, 16,1), autrement que Samuel et le peuple ne l'ont fait, le roi «selon son cœur» (13,14; 16,7) – c.-à-d., le roi qui remplira les conditions de l'alliance mosaïque du ch. 12. On notera encore, à cet égard, que le peuple est absent lors de la désignation royale de David, dans laquelle il ne joue aucun rôle[96].

92. C'est la *particula veri* des travaux qui ont présupposé une tradition distincte sur l'élection royale de Saül en 10,22s. sur la base du constat que c'est le peuple, et non plus Samuel, qui prend l'initiative ici (ainsi CRÜSEMANN, *Widerstand*, p. 56; DIETRICH, *David*, p. 140; MOMMER, *Samuel*, p. 75).

93. Pour McKenzie, l'ambiguïté du récit dtr de 10,17-27 exprimerait la méfiance de Dtr à l'égard de la demande populaire, et du manque de foi que traduit le passage à la monarchie en Israël (*Cette royauté*, p. 272).

94. POLZIN, *Samuel*, p. 155; EDELMAN, *King Saul*, p. 115.

95. Comme l'a montré POLZIN, *Samuel*, pp. 152-155; cf. 16,1.7.

96. L'absence du peuple en 16,1-13 s'explique peut-être par le fait que le récit de

Ainsi, en 10,17-27, Yhwh, qui élit (בחר) Saül, non sans l'avoir désigné auparavant par le procédé infamant du tirage au sort, remplit le programme de Dt 17,15 et accède à la demande du peuple (conformément à
8,7.9.22; 12,13). En somme, Dtr joue ici sur deux aspects de la figure de
Saül en 10,17-27. Dans la mesure où Saül est le représentant de l'institution royale à ce stade du récit, Yhwh agit en conformité avec les prescriptions de Dt 17,14-20, et élit Saül. Mais dans la mesure où Saül est
bientôt destiné à personnifier une royauté désobéissante à Yhwh, le récit
remet explicitement en cause la légitimité de Saül et rapporte son établissement comme roi au peuple. C'est pourquoi, dans les ch. qui encadrent 10,17-27, le discours de Samuel peut inverser les rôles respectifs
de Yhwh et du peuple selon Dt 17,15 pour attribuer l'élection (בחר) de
Saül au peuple, et non à Yhwh (8,18; 12,13), qui s'est contenté de le
donner pour roi (נתן) au peuple selon 12,13. De la sorte, Dtr fait valoir
que Yhwh, s'il a respecté les engagements définis par la loi dtr sur la
royauté, ne se porte pas pour autant garant du succès de la royauté de
Saül. En résumé, l'ambivalence du récit de la désignation royale de Saül
tient à la nécessité pour Dtr de suivre le modèle de la loi sur la royauté,
afin de placer dès le départ la succession des rois sous le signe de l'élection divine, tout en dégageant la responsabilité de Yhwh dans la faillite
programmée de la royauté de Saül.

Il reste à conclure le parcours de la composition dtr en 1 S 7,2–16,13
par un rapide survol de 1 S 7,2-17. Le caractère dtr de ce ch. ne fait
aucun doute[97], et il ne présente pas de tension particulière, à l'exception
du doublet des vv. 3 et 5[98]. La présence de traditions sur Samuel dans ce
ch. est à mon avis douteuse[99]; la représentation simultanée de Samuel
comme «juge-sauveur» et comme juge administrant la justice en Israël
(7,15-17) est une création dtr[100], qui prépare les ch. 8 et 12, de même
que le motif de l'intercession (פלל) de Samuel en faveur du peuple anticipe sur 8,6 et 12,23. Tant la mention de la faute du peuple que celle de
l'oppression philistine présupposent les ch. précédents. Le récit de la dé-

---

l'onction de David suit le modèle de l'onction de Saül par Samuel, qui se déroule en secret (cf. 9,27-10,1). Mais la comparaison est limitée (l'onction de David ne se déroule pas
véritablement en secret, puisque la famille de Jessé y assiste), et il n'en reste pas moins
que la désignation de David à la royauté israélite ne doit rien au peuple, contrairement à
celle de Saül.

97. Voir les analyses de VEIJOLA, *Königtum*, pp. 30-34.

98. Ainsi VEIJOLA, *Königtum*, p. 31; DIETRICH, *David*, pp. 126-127; O'BRIEN,
Reassessment, p. 106.

99. Voir notamment les analyses de BIRCH, *Rise*, pp. 11-21; P. WEIMAR, *Die Jahwekriegserzählungen in Exodus 14, Josua 10, Richter 4 und 1 Samuel 7*, in *Bib* 57 (1976)
38-73; DIETRICH, *David*, pp. 124-130; CAMPBELL, *Prophets and Kings*, pp. 67-68;
SEEBASS, *Wesen*, pp. 64-66; MOMMER, *Samuel*, pp. 32-51; O'BRIEN, *Reassessment*,
pp. 105-108.

100. VEIJOLA, *Königtum*, p. 33.

livrance d'Israël par Yhwh en 7,7-12 présente différents traits dtr[101], et sert à mettre en perspective l'ensemble des récits sur la royauté en 8-12 (voir ci-dessous). Enfin, les lieux mentionnés dans le circuit juridique de Samuel en 7,16 ont une fonction rédactionnelle importante: Béthel renvoie au début du livre de Samuel, alors que Gilgal et Mizpa sont (avec Rama, v. 17) les lieux où prendront place les ch. suivants de la composition dtr[102].

Il vaut donc mieux considérer le récit de 1 S 7,2s. comme une création dtr[103] qui vise à articuler les ch. précédents (notamment le récit de l'arche, 4,1–7,1, mais aussi les traditions sur le jeune Samuel aux ch. 1-3) avec le début des récits sur la royauté israélite. À cet égard, le ch. 7 constitue un arrière-fond indispensable pour apprécier les événements des ch. 8-12. Dire (à la suite de Boecker[104]) que le récit de la délivrance d'Israël au ch. 7 rend inutile la demande d'un roi est abusif: c'est oublier que ce récit débouche sur la crise de la justice en Israël (8,1-3), puisqu'il présente Samuel comme dernier représentant de l'époque des juges. Plus précisément, la narration des actes de salut de Yhwh en 1 S 7 clôt le gouvernement de l'époque des juges sur un bilan positif[105], dont le rappel servira par la suite à évaluer les dangers et les limitations de cette autre forme de gouvernement qu'est la royauté «comme les autres nations» (8,7-8; 10,18-19; 12,7-12). Dans ce contexte, on relèvera qu'Israël se trouve à son tour menacé par le «tonnerre» de Yhwh suite à l'intercession de Samuel au ch. 12, tout comme les Philistins au ch. 7 (comparer 12,17-18 à 7,9-10, dont la formulation est proche). De la sorte, la rédaction dtr encadre significativement le changement d'époque et le passage à la royauté en Israël par la démonstration de la toute-puissance de Yhwh.

101. Ainsi, la mention de la «crainte» d'Israël en 7,7, d'Israël «sauvé de la main des Philistins» en 7,8 (comp. avec 10,18), du «cri» de Samuel vers Yhwh en 7,8.9b (cf. VEIJOLA, *Königtum*, p. 32); *contra* p. ex. WEIMAR (*Jahwekriegserzählungen*, p. 66) qui voit dans les vv. 7.8.9b.10b.11 le récit original (pré-dtr) à l'arrière-plan du ch. 7.
102. Dans un ordre strictement inverse à celui de l'énumération de 7,16-17, comme le relève FOKKELMAN (*Vow and Desire*, p. 312): Rama en 8,4; Mizpa en 10,17; Gilgal en 11,14-12,25.
103. Avec STOEBE, *Buch Samuelis*, pp. 160s.
104. *Beurteilung*, pp. 93s.
105. La clôture idyllique de l'époque des juges en 1 S 7 inverse artificiellement la tendance de la succession des juges en Israël, qui allait jusque là dans le sens d'une dégradation croissante de l'office charismatique; cf. à ce sujet DIETRICH, *Histoire et Loi*, p. 298 n. 4.

LA «DOUBLE ORIGINE» DE LA ROYAUTÉ ISRAÉLITE
SELON LE RÉCIT DTR À L'ÉPOQUE DE L'EXIL

En faisant de Saül le repoussoir d'un David idéalisé, la rédaction dtr établit la «double origine» de la royauté en Israël. D'un côté, l'institution monarchique, réinterprétée dans les termes théocratiques du ch. 12 et exemplifiée par la figure de David en 16,1-13, apparaît divinement instituée. De l'autre, la royauté saülide, qui personnifie la rebellion contre la souveraineté de Yhwh (cf. 15,22-23) d'une institution «séculière», et donc *a priori* contraire au principe théocratique, est rapportée au seul peuple d'Israël. En ce sens, la perspective dtr dans ces ch. n'est pas «anti-monarchique» au sens strict: son principal souci est de réaffirmer la souveraineté inconditionnelle de Yhwh, qui accepte *en principe* la monarchie aussi longtemps que celle-ci lui reste soumise. De même, le regard porté par Dtr sur la monarchie n'est pas simplement «ambigü» (McKenzie), mais délibérément *double*. De la sorte, Dtr place Yhwh au principe de l'époque qui s'ouvre désormais dans l'histoire d'Israël, puisque c'est lui qui rend possible en définitive la fondation de la royauté (1 S 12). Simultanément, Dtr laisse clairement entendre que l'instauration de ce nouveau régime politique n'oblige que le peuple et son roi, et non Yhwh.

L'enjeu de cette distinction est évident. Dans le contexte de l'exil, Dtr peut faire remonter à Yhwh le principe d'une institution dont il fallait sans doute justifier la permanence dans l'histoire du peuple juif. En même temps, les égarements de la royauté, ainsi que son échec final, conduisent Dtr à attribuer l'origine de la royauté effective, représentée par Saül, au peuple lui-même, dont la demande d'un roi est présentée significativement comme le point culminant de l'histoire de l'apostasie d'Israël. Du point de vue de son origine *divine*, la royauté est une forme de gouvernement comme les autres, et son succès est conditionné à l'obéissance de tous (du roi comme du peuple, cf. 12,14-15). Mais du point de vue de son origine *populaire*, «saülide», c'est une institution condamnée (12,25).

Un dernier mot, qui concerne la datation de la composition dtr. Les ch. que je lui attribue présentent dans l'ensemble certaines caractéristiques (de style et de terminologie) dtr tardives. Le ch. 12 constitue le terrain de débat le plus favorable pour la datation de l'ensemble de la composition dtr, en raison du rôle central qu'il occupe dans celle-ci. O'Brien a récemment défendu l'hypothèse d'une attribution post-dtr de ce ch[106]. Alors que O'Brien pourrait bien avoir raison de considérer 1 S 12

---

106. *Reassessment*, pp. 120-128; 281; similairement, VEIJOLA, *Königtum*, pp. 83-99; MAYES, *Story of Israel*, p. 101; DIETRICH, *Histoire et Loi*, pp. 311-312.

comme une insertion secondaire dans les ch. qui l'entourent (voir ci-des-sous), plusieurs éléments invitent cependant à ne pas en situer trop tardi-vement la rédaction. D'une part, T. Römer a comparé les formules se référant aux «pères» d'Israël dans ce ch. à celles utilisées en Dt et dans le reste de HD. Sur ce point précis, il conclut que la terminologie em-ployée en 1 S 12, si elle n'est pas originale, est néanmoins antérieure à certaines formulations tardives comme celle de Jos 24[107]. D'autre part, E. Blum[108] relève que la version dtr du récit d'Ex 14, qu'il attribue à sa composition «D» («KD»), a pour *Vorlage* le texte de 1 S 12, puisque Ex 14,13.31 reprend, en les disjoignant, les termes de 1 S 12,16.18. Pour ces raisons, il paraît préférable d'attribuer le ch. 12 (et avec lui, l'ensem-ble de la composition dtr en 7,2-16,13) à l'édition exilique de HD, sans doute à un stade déjà avancé de son développement. Enfin, je réserve à un traitement ultérieur la question des parallèles langagiers et thémati-ques de 1 S 7,3-4; 8,7-8; 10,18-19 et 12,6-25 avec certains passages dtr de Jg (voir notamment Jg 2; 6,7-10; 10,6-16).

UNE OU DEUX ÉDITIONS DTR?

Je voudrais, pour terminer, revenir sur le rapport de la composition dtr au reste des ch. qui forment l'ensemble de 7,2–16,13. Dans la mesure où ces ch. présentent une version cohérente et clairement divergente des origines de la royauté en Israël, il faut reconsidérer la possibilité d'une édition antérieure à HD des livres de Samuel.

Je partirai pour cela du cas de 1 S 9,1–10,16. Ces ch. présentent plu-sieurs difficultés, aussi bien sur le plan de l'analyse textuelle que litté-raire, qui sont loin d'être résolues[109]. Il existe cependant un consensus assez général dans la recherche récente pour distinguer la tradition de la quête des ânesses de Qish du récit de l'onction de Saül par Samuel (9,15-17; 10,1), qui serait rédactionnel[110]. Certains auteurs ont correcte-

---

107. T. RÖMER, *Israels Väter*, pp. 334, 336. En Jos 24, la généalogie d'Israël remonte jusqu'à Abraham (comp. avec Moïse en 1 S 12), ce qui signale la volonté d'établir un lien entre HD et les livres du Pentateuque.

108. E. BLUM, *Studien zur Komposition des Pentateuch* (BZAW, 189), Berlin - New York, NY, W. de Gruyter, 1990, pp. 30-31.

109. Même si MCKENZIE (*Cette royauté*, p. 275) a raison de considérer l'étude de L. SCHMIDT (*Menschlicher Erfolg und Jahwes Initiative. Studien zu Tradition, Interpretation und Historie in Überlieferung von Gideon, Saul und David* [WMANT, 38], Neukirchen-Vluyn, Neukirchener Verlag, 1970) comme étant toujours inégalée, elle n'en pose pas moins de nombreux problèmes, notamment en ce qui concerne l'analyse de 10,1-16.

110. Cf. particulièrement K.D. SCHUNCK, *Benjamin. Untersuchungen zur Entstehung und Geschichte eines israelitischen Stammes* (BZAW, 86), Berlin, Töpelmann, 1963, pp. 85-89; W. RICHTER, *Die sogenannten vorprophetischen Berufungsgeschichte. Eine li-

ment identifié ces vv. rédactionnels comme étant dtr[111], ce qui signifie qu'il faut vraisemblablement attribuer la rédaction de 9,1–10,16 à Dtr, étant donné le caractère central de l'épisode de l'onction dans le récit sous sa forme finale[112]. Or 9,16 est en tension avec 1 S 7,8. Ces deux passages sont en effet formulés de manière similaire, comme le relève M. Buber[113]: dans l'un et l'autre, le peuple «crie» vers Yhwh, qui a le pouvoir de «sauver» (ישׁע) son peuple «de la main des Philistins» (מיד פלשׁתים)[114]. Mais alors que selon 9,16 Saül apparaît comme l'instrument de Yhwh dans la délivrance du peuple, le ch. 7 attribue celle-ci (suite à l'intercession de Samuel) à l'action de Yhwh seul.

Il faut donc vraisemblablement postuler deux rédactions dtr en 1 S 7-15[115]. La tension observée entre 7,8 et 9,16 est en effet significative des préoccupations de la composition dtr exilique. Au ch. 7, le prophète Samuel apparaît comme l'unique médiateur entre Israël et Yhwh (cf. part. 1 S 12), alors qu'en 9,16, Yhwh entend le cri de son peuple sans recourir à la médiation de Samuel. Surtout, le passage de 7,8s. insiste sur le fait que Yhwh intervient en personne pour délivrer son peuple; le récit culmine ainsi avec la démonstration de la toute-puissance de Yhwh en 7,10. Cette représentation vise clairement à corriger la mention du mandat divin en 9,16 par lequel Yhwh délègue au roi la libération d'Israël, ce qui contredit explicitement le constat par Dtr de l'asservissement du peuple par le roi en 8,11-18. En faisant précéder les récits sur l'accession de Saül au trône par le récit de la délivrance du peuple d'Israël par *Yhwh seul*, la royauté de Saül perd sa motivation originale, puisque la menace

teraturwissenschaftliche Studie zu 1 Sam 9,1-10,16; Ex 3f. und Ri 6,11b-17 (FRLANT, 101), Göttingen, Vandenhoeck & Ruprecht, 1970; SCHMIDT, *Menschlicher Erfolg*, pp. 58-119; VEIJOLA, *Königtum*, pp. 73-82; METTINGER, *King and Messiah*, pp. 64-79; MOMMER, *Samuel*, pp. 92-110; H.-C. SCHMITT, *Das sogenannte vorprophetische Berufungsschema. Zur «geistigen Heimat» des Berufungsformulars von Ex 3,9-12; Jdc 6,11-24 und 1 Samuel 9,1-10,16*, in ZAW 104 (1992) 202-216, même si l'étendue de la tradition originale qui est reconstruite varie d'une étude à l'autre.

111. VEIJOLA, *Königtum*, pp. 76-82; MCKENZIE, *Cette royauté*, pp. 278-280.

112. McKenzie repère d'ailleurs des éléments de la terminologie dtr en d'autres endroits de 9,1-10,16.

113. Cf. les analyses de M. BUBER, *Die Erzählung von Sauls Königswahl*, in VT 6 (1956) 113-173, ici pp. 114-115.

114. On notera que les termes communs à 7,8 et 9,16 sont caractéristiques de la littérature dtr.

115. Un argument supplémentaire pour la présence de deux rédactions dtr en 9,1–10,16 se trouve dans la tension rédactionnelle entre 10,7 et 10,8. SCHMIDT (*Menschlicher Erfolg*, p. 66) a bien montré que le v. 8 contredisait le v. 7. Or le v. 7 contient des éléments de la terminologie dtr (cf. la formule «Car Yhwh est avec toi»; avec F.M. CROSS, *Canaanite Myth and Hebrew Epic. Essays in the History and the Religion of Israel*, Cambridge, MA – London, Harvard University Press, 1973, pp. 252-253), et il est donc (au moins pour 7bβ) rédactionnel. Le v. 8 est clairement un ajout secondaire, qui prépare l'insertion (dtr) de 13,7b-15a.

philistine est désormais déjà écartée. C'est pourquoi, conformément aux préoccupations de la rédaction exilique, la royauté est présentée en 8,1-5 comme étant issue de la demande du peuple, et non plus de la stratégie de Yhwh pour faire face à la crise philistine comme c'est le cas en 9,16. Par conséquent, 9,16, et avec lui l'ensemble de la rédaction de 9,1–10,16 (sans certains ajouts secondaires comme 10,8) doivent être attribués à une première édition dtr (dtr[1]) des livres de Samuel.

En ce qui concerne la datation de cette rédaction dtr[1], puisqu'elle est antérieure à l'édition exilique de HD et cependant clairement dtr, elle doit être située dans le contexte d'une édition préexilique des livres des Rois. À ce sujet, I. Provan a montré que l'édition préexilique de Rois devait sans doute inclure une partie des livres de Samuel[116]. À mon sens, il ne s'agit pas encore d'une première édition de HD, laquelle n'interviendra qu'à l'époque de l'exil, mais d'une collection de documents (avec une première version des récits de conquête de Jos, ainsi que de Dt*[117]) constituant une «littérature de propagande» en faveur de la politique expansionniste de Josias[118]. C'est dans ce contexte que le récit de l'onction de Saül s'explique le mieux puisque la désignation de Saül représente ici la stratégie choisie par Yhwh afin de faire face à la crise philistine en Israël (ce qui serait impensable dans le cadre de la composition dtr exilique), sans qu'intervienne autrement une quelconque considération sur les dangers de la monarchie.

L'édition préexilique des récits du règne de Saül en Israël devrait inclure 1 S 11,1-11.15* (sans la mention de Samuel en 11,7). En effet, les vv. 12-14 interrompent clairement le récit du couronnement de Saül[119]. De plus, ils en altèrent doublement la signification. Dans la première version dtr du récit de la victoire de Saül sur les Ammonites, le noeud de l'intrigue réside dans la question désespérée des habitants de Jabesh-Gilead: «Qui pourra nous sauver?» (cf. v. 3), et la résolution intervient lorsque Saül révèle, sous la conduite de l'esprit de Yhwh, qu'il est ce sauveur (vv. 6-11), ce qui conduit logiquement au dénouement, à savoir

116. I.W. PROVAN, *Hezekiah and the Books of Kings. A Contribution to the Debate about the Composition of the Deuteronomistic History* (BZAW, 172), Berlin – New York, NY, W. de Gruyter, 1988, pp. 158-159.

117. Sur ce point, cf. N. LOHFINK, *Kerygmata des Deuteronomistischen Geschichtwerkes*, in J. JEREMIAS – L. PERLITT (eds.), *Die Botschaft und die Boten*. FS H.W. Wolff, Neukirchen-Vluyn, Neukirchener Verlag, 1981, pp. 87-100.

118. Voir RÖMER – DE PURY, *Histoire de la recherche*, pp. 76-80, part. 78-79; T. RÖMER, *Transformations in Deuteronomistic and Biblical Historiography. On «Book-Finding» and other Literary Strategies*, in ZAW 109 (1997) 1-11, part. pp. 2-4.

119. *Contra* MCKENZIE (*Cette royauté*, pp. 273-274), 11,15 est sans doute déjà rédactionnel, puisqu'en 11,1-11 on a affaire à un récit classique de juge-sauveur, transformé en récit d'élection à la royauté par le v. 15.

l'intronisation de Saül comme roi. Par contre, les ajouts de 10,26-27 et de 11,12-13 introduisent une micro-intrigue supplémentaire, qui se résoud par l'attribution de la victoire non plus à Saül, mais à Yhwh. Ceci correspond bien à la perspective de la rédaction dtr², qui met constamment l'accent sur l'exclusivité de Yhwh comme sauveur d'Israël[120]. Quant au v. 14, il est en tension avec le v. 15, notamment quant à la mention de la nécessité d'un «renouvellement» (חדשׁ) de la monarchie israélite, qui signale la remise en question de la royauté telle qu'elle est déjà établie[121]. En ce sens, le v. 14 sert sans doute à préparer la transition vers le ch. 12 et la redéfinition de l'institution monarchique dans le contexte de l'alliance.

De même, l'édition dtr¹ doit comprendre 1 S 13-14*, avec notamment les notices traditionnelles de début et de fin de règne en 13,1 et 14,47-52, qui sont rédactionnelles. La distinction de deux éditions dtr dans les récits du règne de Saül permet ainsi de rétablir la continuité des formules de 11,15 et 13,1[122]. De même, 16,14 constitue selon toute vraisemblance le prolongement original de 14,47-52[123], ce qui confirme l'attribution de 15,1–16,13 à la rédaction exilique. Enfin, avec 13,7b-15a, il s'agit clairement d'une insertion secondaire, préparée par 10,8 (dont j'ai montré plus haut qu'il était en tension rédactionnelle avec la première édition dtr en 9,1–10,16), et qui traduit les préoccupations des Dtr exiliques dans la mesure où elle met l'accent sur la nécessité de l'obéissance à Yhwh, dans le prolongement des prescriptions du ch. 12[124]. Ainsi, la notice finale sur le règne de Saül en 14,47-52 clôt l'ensemble narratif constitué par l'accession de Saül au trône d'Israël (9,1–10,16; 11) et par les récits sur son règne contenus dans les ch. 13-14, alors que la mention de l'envoi par Yhwh d'un «esprit mauvais» sur Saül en 16,14 inaugure un autre ensemble narratif, celui du «récit de l'ascension de David», qui rapporte de quelle manière David en vient à succéder à Saül. Par conséquent, à partir de 16,14 la perspective du récit se modifie, et n'a plus en vue les réalisations du règne de Saül (cf. ch. 13–14)[125],

---

120. Outre le récit de délivrance du ch. 7 (en tension délibérée, comme je l'ai indiqué plus haut, avec la mission confiée à Saül en 9,16), on relèvera notamment le rappel récurrent des «hauts faits» de Yhwh en 8,8; 10,18; 12,7-11.

121. À mon sens, il est difficile de concevoir que la rédaction dtr se serve de ce terme simplement pour unifier les différents récits sur la royauté en 1 Samuel 9-11, comme on le prétend généralement.

122. Cf. VEIJOLA, *Königtum*, pp. 91-92; MAYES, *Story of Israel*, p. 101.

123. Cf. FORESTI, *Rejection*, p. 165; VAN SETERS, *Search*, pp. 263-264.

124. *Contra* VEIJOLA (*Ewige Dynastie*, pp. 55-56), les vv. 13-14 sont nécessaires à la compréhension de 13,7-15, et il n'y a donc aucune raison de les tenir pour secondaires.

125. Mais la fonction des récits des ch. 13–14 est peu claire, et demanderait à être examinée plus étroitement. Certains éléments sont vraisemblablement destinés à préparer

mais le conflit qui oppose le premier roi d'Israël à son successeur[126]. La transition d'un ensemble narratif à l'autre est préparée en 14,52 par la mention (rédactionnelle) de la politique de recrutement de Saül dans le contexte de la guerre contre les Philistins, laquelle dura tout au long de son règne selon le récit de HD[127].

En résumé, l'édition dtr pré-exilique de Samuel-Rois comprendrait ici 1 S 9,1–10,16*; 11*; 13–14*. Saül y est présenté comme l'instrument pressenti par Yhwh en vue de la délivrance d'Israël; c'est pourquoi la légitimité de son règne est entièrement suspendue à la présence de l'esprit de Yhwh à ses côtés. Mais la notice finale du règne de Saül en 14,52 signale l'incapacité de Saül à accomplir la mission que lui avait confiée Yhwh selon les termes de 9,16, puisqu'il n'a pas su mettre fin à la domination philistine. En ce sens, le remplacement de Saül par David (introduit par l'abandon de Saül par Yhwh au commencement du «récit de l'ascension de David») s'explique bien dans le contexte de l'élaboration d'une littérature de propagande en faveur de la politique expansionniste de Josias, présenté comme le «David *redivivus*». Pour les Dtr josianiques, ce n'est pas Saül, originaire du Nord, qui était destiné à libérer *tout Israël* de l'oppression étrangère, mais bien David, dont le règne est sanctionné par la promesse d'une dynastie éternelle en 2 S 7.

CONCLUSION (D'UN RÉCIT À L'AUTRE)

J'ai voulu montrer dans cet article que la rédaction dtr s'efforçait, dans le contexte de l'édition exilique de HD, d'insérer au commencement de la royauté un débat politico-théologique sur le statut et la légitimité de l'institution monarchique au regard de la souveraineté inconditionnelle de Yhwh. Pour ce faire, Dtr compose une version cohérente de l'émergence de la monarchie en Israël, dans laquelle il attribue à celle-ci une double origine, l'une populaire, l'autre divine. Selon la première, la monarchie (conçue sur le modèle des autres nations) est une institution

---

la transition depuis le récit de l'accession de Saül au trône vers le «récit de l'ascension de David»: cf. p. ex. l'émergence de Jonathan comme protagoniste essentiel du récit; voir à ce sujet D. JOBLING, *Saul's Fall and Jonathan's Rise: Tradition and Redaction in 1 Sam 14,1-46*, in *JBL* 95 (1976) 367-376.

126. En réalité, la présence de la notice finale sur le règne de Saül dès 14,47-52 suffit à indiquer que les préoccupations de l'édition dtr pré-exilique de Samuel ne concernent plus, à ce point du récit, le règne de Saül mais l'avènement de la royauté davidique.

127. Cf. FORESTI, *Rejection*, p. 165: «Evidently, 14,52 could not be the introduction of the war against the Amalekites, that now follows in MT, 1 Sm 15. The verse intends, rather, to announce the dominant theme of the literary complex which follows on the *Saul-Überlieferung*, that is, to introduce the *Aufstiegsgeschichte*, which begins in 16,14. There, in fact, Saul is repeatedly presented as confronting the Philistine peril».

illégitime et contraire au principe théocratique dont dépend l'identité de l'Israël exilique. Selon la seconde, une royauté entièrement soumise à Yhwh (d'après le paradigme davidique) aurait pu subsister en Israël, ce qui signale essentiellement que Yhwh, malgré sa désapprobation du principe du gouvernement monarchique (et moyennant une redéfinition de ce gouvernement, telle qu'elle est opérée par 1 S 12) a entériné le changement d'époque en Israël. Dans la perspective divine, les conditions de la survie du peuple sont donc demeurées inchangées dans la transition d'une forme de gouvernement à l'autre dans HD: et ce dernier répond seul par conséquent (du fait de sa désobéissance) de ce que l'époque monarchique se conclut par l'exil.

Par là, la composition dtr exilique infléchit en profondeur l'intention de la première édition dtr, josianique, des récits sur les origines de la royauté, dont était absente toute remise en cause de l'institution monarchique. Ensemble, les deux récits témoignent de l'évolution, liée à l'expérience de l'exil, du regard porté par le mouvement dtr sur l'histoire de l'Israël monarchique.

Université de Lausanne   Christophe NIHAN

L'ÉCOLE DEUTÉRONOMISTE
ET LA FORMATION DE LA BIBLE HÉBRAÏQUE

I. INTRODUCTION

La «déconstruction» qui a frappé la science vétérotestamentaire ces dernières années a atteint son point culminant avec la contestation récente de l'existence d'une «historiographie dtr»[1]. Si ce pilier qui a fourni aux exégètes une si solide attache dans la tempête des bouleversements divers (qui secouèrent surtout le Pentateuque) semble lui aussi s'écrouler, alors que reste-t-il encore de «sûr»? La réponse que l'on voudrait donner à cette question peut paraître paradoxale: ce qui reste, après tout, ce sont les «Deutéronomistes». En effet, personne ne conteste le rôle qu'a joué ce groupe dans la formation de la première partie des *Nebiim*, et d'autre part le terme «dtr» apparaît de plus en plus dans la discussion sur l'élaboration d'un nouveau modèle rédactionnel du Pentateuque. En même temps certains livres des *Ketubim* reçoivent parfois eux-mêmes le prédicat «dtr». Le profil de ces «Dtrs» reste cependant assez flou, on a souvent l'impression que le Dtr de l'un n'est pas forcément celui de l'autre. Un même flou surgit lorsque tel ou tel texte biblique ou simple verset porte le sigle «dtr», sans que les critères de définition aient été explicités.

Avant de commencer notre bref tour d'horizon sur le rôle des Dtrs dans la formation de la Bible hébraïque, il paraît donc nécessaire d'aborder les questions touchant la définition du terme «dtr».

1. *Qu'est-ce qu'un texte «dtr»?*

Le premier critère qui puisse permettre de définir un texte «dtr» devrait être d'ordre stylistique – ce qui est communément admis. La meilleure présentation de la phraséologie dtr, telle qu'elle se décèle dans le Dt et les livres historiques, se trouve toujours dans les annexes de

---

1. Cf. C. WESTERMANN, *Die Geschichtsbücher des Alten Testaments. Gab es ein deuteronomistisches Geschichtswerk?* (TB AT, 87), Gütersloh, Kaiser, 1994; E. WÜRTHWEIN, *Erwägungen zum sog. deuteronomistischen Geschichtswerk. Eine Skizze*, in *Studien zum deuteronomistischen Geschichtswerk* (BZAW, 227), Berlin – New York, NY, W. de Gruyter, 1994, pp. 1-11; E.A. KNAUF, *L'"historiographie deutéronomiste" (DtrG) existe-t-elle?*, in A. DE PURY – T. RÖMER – J.-D. MACCHI (eds.), *Israël construit son histoire. L'historiographie deutéronomiste à la lumière des recherches récentes* (Le Monde de la Bible, 34), Genève, Labor & Fides, 1996, pp. 409-418.

l'ouvrage fondamental de M. Weinfeld[2]. Comme l'a montré cet auteur ainsi que d'autres après lui[3], le style dtr est baroque et se caractérise par des formules stéréotypées. Il est directement influencé par celui des annales et des traités assyriens, et fait son apparition dans le royaume de Judah grosso modo aux VIII-VIIe siècles avant notre ère[4].

On pourrait ajouter aux observations de Weinfeld certaines préférences syntaxiques propres aux Dtrs, comme l'utilisation redondante de propositions infinitives, à la différence des auteurs sacerdotaux qui n'apprécient guère ce type de subordonnées[5].

Pourtant, l'application du seul critère stylistique dans ce travail de repérage n'est pas suffisante. En effet, la phraséologie dtr est très facile à imiter – on la retrouve jusqu'à l'époque néo-testamentaire (cf. Za 1; Dn 9; Act 7; etc[6].). Si l'on voulait qualifier tous ces textes de «dtr», le terme lui-même deviendrait alors inutilisable pour désigner le milieu producteur d'une époque (plus ou moins) précise.

Il faut donc recourir, à côté du critère stylistique, au critère théologique, c'est-à-dire déterminer les notions fondamentales qui semblent typiques de la pensée dtr. Mais ce critère est plus difficile à manier que le précédant, car la description d'une idéologie est toujours conditionnée par la propre subjectivité de l'exégète. On peut certainement énumérer quelques thèmes théologiques chers à HD, tels que la *berît*, l'élection, l'importance de la loi mosaïque, le pays promis et conquis, la vénération exclusive de Yhwh, etc. Mais est-il si évident, comme le pensent actuellement plusieurs chercheurs[7], que l'idéologie dtr soit principalement royaliste, voire même nationaliste? L'élaboration de ce qu'on pourrait appeler une théologie dtr se complique encore du fait que certains thè-

2. M. WEINFELD, *Deuteronomy and Deuteronomic School*, Oxford, Clarendon, 1972.

3. Cf. en dernier lieu H.U. STEYMANS, *Deuteronomium 28 und die adê zur Thronfolgeregelung Asarhaddons. Segen und Fluch im Alten Orient und in Israel* (OBO, 145), Fribourg (CH), Universitätsverlag; Göttingen, Vandenhoeck & Ruprecht, 1995.

4. Dans cet article, je renonce à la distinction chère à l'exégèse germanique entre «deutéronomique» (dt, se rapportant au Dt avant son insertion dans HD) et «deutéronomiste» (dtr, désignant les différentes rédactions de HD à l'époque exilique). Cette distinction pose de toute façon problème, si l'on s'imagine les origines de HD à l'époque de Josias.

5. N. LOHFINK, *Gab es eine deuteronomische Bewegung?*, in W. GROSS (ed.), *Jeremia und die »deuteronomistische Bewegung«* (BBB, 98), Weinheim, Beltz Athenäum Verlag, 1995, pp. 313-382, esp. 323.

6. T. RÖMER – J.-D. MACCHI, *Luke, Disciple of the Deuteronomistic School*, in C.M. TUCKETT (ed.), *Luke's Literary Achievement. Collected Essays* (JSNT SS, 116), Sheffield, Sheffield Academic Press, 1995, pp. 178-187.

7. Ainsi notamment R. ALBERTZ, *Die Intentionen und Träger des Deuteronomistischen Geschichtswerks*, in R. ALBERTZ et al., *Schöpfung und Befreiung, FS C. Westermann*, Stuttgart, Calwer, 1989, pp. 37-53 et E.A. KNAUF, *L'"historiographie deutéronomiste" (DtrG) existe-t-elle?*

mes, comme l'alliance ou le recours à l'Exode comme mythe fondateur, ne se restreignent nullement au milieu dtr.

Quoi qu'il en soit, il est impossible de privilégier le critère idéologique au détriment du critère stylistique, sous peine de mener à une sorte de pan-deutéronomisme incontrôlé et incontrôlable. Un exemple de cette dérive: l'attribution d'Es 1-39 à des rédacteurs dtrs[8]. Le premier Esaïe n'est pas écrit dans le style dtr et les catégories théologiques de la désobéissance du peuple ou de l'annonce du jugement n'appartiennent pas au seul milieu dtr[9]. Cette remarque devrait nous mettre en garde contre toute «inflation dtr», inflation qui, en fin de compte, ne saurait guère nous permettre d'avancer dans l'histoire rédactionnelle de la Bible hébraïque.

Pour pouvoir identifier un texte dtr, il faut combiner les critères stylistique et idéologique. Ces critères devraient ensuite être limités, dans leur application, par des arguments de datation. Il me semble utile de restreindre le sigle «dtr» à des textes rédigés entre le VIIe et IVe siècle avant notre ère, ce qui constitue déjà un laps de temps considérable[10].

2. Qui étaient les «Deutéronomistes»?

La question de l'identité des Dtrs et celle de leur nombre reçoit actuellement plusieurs réponses. Le spectre va d'un seul individu-écrivain (Van Seters) à tout un mouvement dtr (Steck). En partant de l'idée que des textes dtrs existent au moins depuis l'époque de Josias et que la rédaction principale de Dt – Rois présuppose les événements de 597/87, il convient d'imaginer un groupe de scribes voire de hauts fonctionnaires[11]. N. Lohfink s'est opposé récemment dans un long article à l'idée

8. Cf. notamment O. KAISER, *Das Buch des Propheten Jesaja: Kapitel 1-12* (ATD, 17), Göttingen, Vandenhoeck & Ruprecht, 1981, 5e éd.; *Der Prophet Jesaja: Kapitel 13-39* (ATD, 18), Göttingen, Vandenhoeck & Ruprecht, 1983, 3e éd.; et J. VERMEYLEN, *Du prophète Isaïe à l'apocalyptique. Isaïe I-XXXV, miroir d'un demi-millénaire d'expérience religieuse en Israël* (Etudes bibliques), Paris, Gabalda, 1977-1978.

9. C. BREKELMANS, *Deuteronomistic Influence in Isaiah 1-12*, in J. VERMEYLEN (ed.), *The Book of Isaiah. Le livre d'Isaïe. Les oracles et leur relectures. Unité et complexité de l'ouvrage* (BETL, 81), Leuven, University Press - Peeters, 1989, pp. 167-176. Cf. également L. PERLITT, *Jesaja und die Deuteronomisten*, in V. FRITZ – K.-F. POHLMANN – H.-C. SCHMITT (eds.), *Prophet und Prophetenbuch. Festschrift für Otto Kaiser zum 65. Geburtstag* (BZAW, 185), Berlin - New York, NY, W. de Gruyter, 1989, pp. 133-149.

10. Pour une proposition comparable concernant l'étendue des rédactions dtr, cf. A. ROFÉ, *Joshua 20 Historico-Literary Criticism Illustrated*, in J.H. TIGAY (ed.), *Empirical Models for Biblical Criticism*, Philadelphia, PA, University of Pennsylvania Press, 1985, pp. 131-147. On pourrait éventuellement distinguer trois phases: a. *dtrJ* (les origines de la production littéraire dtr, à l'époque de Josias, voire même avant); b. *dtr* (l'édition de HD et d'autres textes à l'époque de l'exil); c. *dtrT* (= dtr tardif; édition, voire rédaction de textes pendant l'époque perse).

11. Peut-être devrait-on parler, à la suite d'Albertz, d'une coalition qui aurait regroupé

d'un «mouvement dtr»[12], parce que ce terme implique un large courant porté par une grande partie de la population. Il est plus adéquat de parler d'une «école» ou d'un «parti» dtr, si l'on se base sur les définitions suivantes données par «Le Petit Robert»: «école»: «groupe ou suite de personnes... qui se réclament d'un même maître ou professent les mêmes doctrines»; «parti»: «groupe de personnes défendant la même opinion».

On pourrait éventuellement préciser le «profil» des Dtrs en recourant à une analyse sociologique inspirée des travaux de Max Weber. Dans une enquête sur les réactions intellectuelles face à la crise moderniste, symbolisée par la Révolution française, le politologue Steil distingue trois attitudes: celle du «prophète» (eschatologique), celle du «prêtre» (mythico-cyclique) et celle du «mandarin» (distante-explicative)[13]. Ce modèle s'applique fort à propos aux courants idéologiques majeurs du judaïsme confrontés à la crise de la destruction de Jérusalem et de l'exil babylonien[14]. L'attitude prophétique se manifeste dans les courants eschatologiques qui surgissent vers la fin de la domination babylonienne et au début de l'époque perse (cf. notamment le Deutéro-Esaïe). La position dite du «prêtre», celle qui est consignée dans le document «P», transfère toute la réflexion théologique sur Dieu, le monde et Israël, dans un temps mythique, pré-étatique. Selon «P», l'exil ne peut pas perturber la stabilité du monde prévue par le Dieu créateur[15].

C'est l'attitude du «mandarin» qui a son équivalent vétérotestamentaire dans l'œuvre du parti dtr. Les Dtrs étaient en effet des «mandarins»: hauts fonctionnaires et anciens enseignants de l'école du palais. Fins connaisseurs de l'idéologie assyro-babylonienne, ce sont eux qui, au moment de l'exil, élaborent pour la première fois un projet d'historiographie judéenne[16]. Avec cette grille d'analyse empruntée à la sociologie

---

des haut fonctionnaires, des prêtres jérusalémites et des prophètes, cf. *Intentionen*, pp. 48-49.

12. N. LOHFINK, *Bewegung*.

13. A. STEIL, *Krisensemantik. Wissenssoziologische Untersuchungen zu einem Topos moderner Zeiterfahrung*, Opladen, Leske & Budrich, 1993.

14. Pour plus de détails, cf. T. RÖMER, *L'Ancien Testament. Une littérature de crise*, in *RTP* 127/4 (1995) 321-338.

15. Cf. N. LOHFINK, *L'écrit sacerdotal et l'histoire*, in *Les traditions du Pentateuque autour de l'exil* (CE, 97), Paris, Cerf, 1996, pp. 9-25. Original allemand: *Die Priesterschrift und die Geschichte*, in *Congress Volume. Göttingen 1977* (SVT, 29), Leiden, Brill, 1978, pp. 189-225; = ID, *Studien zum Pentateuch* (SBAAT, 4), Stuttgart, Katholisches Bibelwerk, 1988, pp. 213-253.

16. Cette remarque n'exclut pas une activité littéraire dtr à l'époque de Josias. À mon avis, la production dtr à cette époque se comprend comme littérature de propagande. Il ne s'agit pas encore d'une conception du style «HD» (cf. T. RÖMER, *Transformations et influences dans «l'historiographie» juive de la fin du VIIe s. av. notre ère jusqu'à l'époque*

moderne, la théorie de Martin Noth selon laquelle HD se comprendrait, dans son édition exilique, comme un constat d'échec[17], paraît tout à fait défendable malgré toutes les critiques qu'elle a suscitées. Face à la crise de 597/87, les Dtrs n'adoptent ni une attitude utopique ni une conception cyclique et restauratrice. Leur démarche est plutôt «analytique». La présentation dtr de l'histoire d'Israël permet d'élaborer une théodicée sans pourtant envisager immédiatement une finalité ultérieure à la crise. La crise en tant que telle est agréée; il ne s'agit pas de la surmonter, ni en amont ni en aval. Il s'agit plutôt de s'installer dans la crise, de «valoriser» celle-ci. En acceptant la disparition des institutions de la monarchie, en leur substituant une histoire écrite, le parti dtr se trouve à l'origine du canon[18] vétérotestamentaire.

II. L'HISTORIOGRAPHIE DTR ET LES DÉBUTS DU CANON BIBLIQUE

1. 2 R 22-23 et la prétention à la canonicité

2 R 22-23 constitue en quelque sorte le mythe d'origine du parti dtr. Selon ce texte, la politique de centralisation et de yahwisation de Josias aurait été provoquée par la découverte d'un livre. Les versets qui appartiennent au *Auffindungsbericht* (22,8.10.11.13*.16-18.19*.20a*; 23,1-3) ne peuvent guère être datés avant l'édition exilique du livre des Rois[19]. Les parallèles entre le récit de la découverte du livre et le motif assyro-babylonien de l'invention de la pierre de fondation lors de la (re-)construction d'un sanctuaire sont flagrants[20]. Or, ce qu'il faut remarquer ici, c'est le remplacement de la pierre de fondation (contenant le plan du temple) par le Livre qui devient dans ce récit l'unique référence à la-

perse, in *Trans* 13 [1997] 47-63]. Je n'entre pas dans la discussion de savoir si le terme «historiographie» est adapté pour l'ensemble (Dt)Jos-Rois. Il ne s'agit pas d'une entreprise historiographique au sens grec, on y décèle néanmoins une volonté évidente d'établir une suite chronologique des «origines» jusqu'au «présent». Cf. J. VAN SETERS, *In Search of History. History in the Ancient World and the Origin of Biblical History*, New Haven, CT, London, Yale University Press, 1983.

17. M. NOTH, *Überlieferungsgeschichtliche Studien. Die sammelnden und bearbeitenden Geschichtswerke im Alten Testament* (*1943*), Darmstadt, Wissenschaftliche Buchgesellschaft, 1967³.

18. Le terme «canon» est utilisé ici dans un sens très large pour désigner un ensemble de textes qui ont une prétention constitutive, cf. C. DOHMEN, *Vom Umgang mit dem Alten Testament* (NSK AT, 27), Stuttgart, Verlag Katholisches Bibelwerk, 1995, pp. 55-57.

19. Selon C. LEVIN, *Joschija im deuteronomistischen Geschichtswerk*, in *ZAW* 96 (1984) 351-371, il s'agirait d'une addition postexilique.

20. Cf. L.K. HANDY, *Historical Probability and the Narrative of Josiah's Reform in 2Kings*, in S.W. HOLLOWAG – L.K. HANDY (eds.), *The Pitcher is Broken. Memorial Essays for Gösta W. Ahlström* (JSOT SS, 190), Sheffield, Academic Press, 1995, pp. 252-275.

quelle doivent se soumettre roi, prêtres et prophétesse. 2 R 22-23 met ainsi en œuvre la substitution par l'espace du «livre» de l'espace sacral et politique. Dans la suite du livre des Rois, le temple va bientôt être détruit et la royauté disparaître. Reste alors le livre, tel un nouveau sanctuaire où la Loi se fait performante, proposant au lecteur (ou plutôt: à l'auditeur) une nouvelle «alliance» et une nouvelle identité «scripturaire». Cette prétention à une «historiographie canonique», comme le dit Françoise Smyth[21], rend plausible l'hypothèse selon laquelle HD formerait le premier écrit «canonique» de l'AT[22].

2. La cohérence rédactionnelle de HD

Je reste donc (au moins pour le moment) convaincu qu'il a bel et bien existé une «historiographie dtr» rédigée à Babylone. Ceux qui contestent une telle HD devraient pouvoir expliquer les faits suivants:

– les différents «chapitres de réflexion»[23] (Jos 1; 23; Jug 2,6ss; 1 Sam 12; 1 R 8; 2 R 17). Ces chapitres constituent en quelque sorte des «Deutéronomes en miniature» et délimitent les différentes époques de la construction dtr de l'histoire – lesquelles ne coïncident pas avec les délimitations actuelles des livres historiques. Ils contiennent de nombreux liens stylistiques et thématiques qui s'expliquent le mieux par l'idée d'une activité rédactionnelle voulant donner une cohérence à l'ensemble Dt – 2 R.

– les nombreux renvois que fait le Dt aux livres suivants. En voici quelques exemples[24]. Jos 1,6 reprend presque mot à mot Dt 31,7, et l'ordre que Josué donne aux tribus transjordaniennes en Jos 1,12 correspond à celui de Dt 3,18ss (cf. le renvoi en Jos 1,13). Dt 11,29 trouve son accomplissement en Jos 8,30. Les mises en garde de Dt 6,12 préparent très clairement les remarques au sujet de la désobéissance du peuple en Jg 2,12ss.

– le fait que certains passages du Dt préparent les «dénouements» de la fin du livre des Rois. L'appel à aimer Yhwh en Dt 6,5 se retrouve mot à mot dans l'appréciation dtr du règne de Josias en 2 R 23,25. Ce sont

---

21. F. SMYTH, *Quand Josias fait son œuvre ou le roi bien enterré. Une lecture synchronique de 2 R 22,1-23,28*, in A. DE PURY – T. RÖMER – J.-D. MACCHI (eds.), *Israël construit son histoire* (n. 1), pp. 325-339, esp. 339.

22. A. DE PURY, *Le canon de l'Ancien Testament. Ecritures juives, littérature grecque et identité européenne*, in *Protestantisme et construction européenne. Actes du Colloque des Facultés de théologie protestante des pays latins d'Europe (8-12 septembre 1991)*, Bruxelles, Ad Veritatem, 1991, pp. 25-46, esp. 32.

23. L'expression est de M. Noth.

24. Cf. encore L. SCHMIDT, *Deuteronomistisches Geschichtswerk*, in H.J. BOECKER *et al.* (eds.), *Altes Testament* (Neukirchener Arbeitsbücher), Neukirchen-Vluyn, Neukirchener Verlag, 1983, pp. 101-114, esp. 104.

les deux seuls textes de tout l'AT qui utilisent *m^e'od* comme substantif. Les malédictions de Dt 28,36ss font clairement allusion à l'exil du peuple tel qu'il sera relaté en 2 R 17 et 2R 24-25. Plus précisément encore, le retour en Égypte annoncé dans la dernière malédiction de Dt 28,68 s'accomplit en 2 R 25,26, ce qui a inspiré Friedman lorsqu'il a caractérisé HD exilique par le slogan «From Egypt to Egypt»[25].

Il s'ensuit que le Dt a davantage de liens avec Jos – Rois qu'avec les livres du Tétrateuque[26].

Jusqu'à nouvel avis, nous devons donc partir de l'idée d'une rédaction cohérente de Dt – Rois aux alentours de 570/60 av. notre ère. Cette édition se fait, comme nous l'avons vu, dans une volonté de proposer une interprétation «canonique» de l'histoire et de remplacer les anciennes institutions et autres médiations. Le nouveau médiateur est désormais le scribe dtr[27]. Cette focalisation sur le livre va s'accompagner de l'idée de la «fin de la prophétie» (cf. Dn 9,24; Bb 12b), qui est sans doute une invention dtr et qui constitue, selon Assmann, une «Vorbedingung des Kanons»[28].

3. Les Dtrs et le début de la formation du corpus des «prophètes postérieurs»

Il est en effet plausible que l'école dtr soit à l'origine du recueil des livres prophétiques. Les mandarins dtrs ne pouvaient que s'opposer au prophétisme eschatologique qui se développait au début de l'époque perse. En revanche, les oracles de jugement des prophètes du VIIIe/VIIe siècle sonnaient bien avec la finale de HD. Dès lors, on comprend facilement que ces mêmes Dtrs ou plutôt leurs collègues se soient mis à éditer pendant – ou peu après – l'exil un certain nombre de livres prophétiques. Les prophètes sont placés sous l'autorité de Moïse (cf. Dt 18,18-20) et la mention de «prophètes, serviteurs de Yhwh» dans le livre des Rois (2 R 9,7; 17,13.23; 21,10; 24,2), fait peut-être allusion à la collection d'oracles prophétiques destinée à accompagner HD. Quels livres faisaient partie de cette collection? Ce point restera encore longtemps en discus-

---

25. R.E. FRIEDMAN, *From Egypt to Egypt: Dtr¹ and Dtr²*, in B. HALPERN – J.D. LEVENSON (eds.), *Traditions in Transformation. Turning Points in Biblical Faith*, Winona Lake, IN, Eisenbrauns, 1981, pp. 167-192.

26. Les liens avec le Tétrateuque concernent surtout les «traditions parallèles» qu'on trouve en Dt 1-3; 9-10; Ex et en Nb 10-36. Les textes d'Ex et Nb semblent présupposer les récits parallèles en Dt, cf. J. VAN SETERS, *The Life of Moses. The Yahwist as Historian in Exodus-Numbers*, Louisville, KY, Westminster / John Knox Press, 1994.

27. Cf. à ce sujet F. SMYTH, *Quand Josias fait son œuvre*.

28. J. ASSMANN, *Das kulturelle Gedächtnis. Schrift, Erinnerung und politische Identität in frühen Hochkulturen*, München, C.H. Beck, 1992, p. 208.

sion, bien que les candidats les plus probables soient sans doute Os, Am, Mi et Jr[29] (et dans un deuxième temps peut-être aussi Za[30]).

Il existe néanmoins une différence considérable entre Am, Os, Mi d'un côté, et le livre de Jr de l'autre. Dans les trois premiers livres, la rédaction dtr semble plutôt discrète, du moins difficile à circonscrire[31], au lieu qu'elle est omniprésente dans Jr. Cette différence s'explique par le fait qu'Os, Am et Mi avaient été publiés[32] avant l'activité littéraire des Dtrs, si bien que ces derniers se sont contentés de retoucher des livres déjà existants. Tel ne semble pas être le cas de Jr, dont la première édition est à attribuer à un groupe dtr[33]. En effet, il y a une quantité impressionnante de *Querverweise* entre le livre de Jr et HD. Le discours sur le temple, en Jr 7,1-15, est conçu comme le pendant du texte-clé sur le temple dans HD, à savoir le discours de Salomon en 1 R 8 et sa suite en 9,1-9[34]. Ces textes ont beaucoup d'expressions et de thèmes communs. On pourrait même dire que Jr 7 est construit comme une suite de 1 R 8

---

29. O. KAISER, *Grundriß der Einleitung in die kanonischen und deuterokanonischen Schriften des Alten Testaments. Band 2: Die prophetischen Werke*, Gütersloh, Gütersloher Verlagshaus, 1994, p. 22

30. Cf. R.F. PERSON, *Second Zechariah and the Deuteronomic School* (JSOT SS, 167), Sheffield, Academic Press, 1993.

31. Ce que N. LOHFINK, *Bewegung*, a récemment contesté, pp. 325-333; cf. par contre D.U. ROTTZOLL, *Studien zur Redaktion und Komposition des Amosbuchs* (BZAW, 243), Berlin – New York, NY, W. de Gruyter, 1996, notamment pp. 56-59, 188-192, 287. Pour Os, cf. les approches divergentes de T. NAUMANN, *Hoseas Erben. Strukturen der Nachinterpretation im Buch Hosea* (BWANT, 131), Stuttgart – Berlin – Köln, Kohlhammer, 1991, pp. 178-179 (seul 8,1b serait dtr) et G.A. YEE, *Composition and Tradition in the Book of Hosea. A Redaction Critical Investigation* (SBL DS, 102), Atlanta, GA, Scholars Press, 1987 (deux rédactions dtrs substantielles).

32. Pour Am et Os, cf. J. JEREMIAS, *Die Anfänge des Dodekapropheton: Hosea und Amos*, in J.A. EMERTON (ed.), *Congress Volume: Paris 1992* (SVT, 61), Leiden, Brill, 1995, pp. 87-106; pour Am également D.U. ROTTZOLL, *Studien*. Pour Mi, cf. B. RENAUD, *La formation du livre de Michée. Tradition et actualisation* (Études bibliques), Paris, Gabalda, 1977, notamment pp. 383-393.

33. Pour plus de détails et aussi pour la suite, cf. T. RÖMER, *La conversion du prophète Jérémie à la théologie deutéronomiste*, in A.H.W. CURTIS – T. RÖMER (eds.), *The Book of Jeremiah and Its Reception – Le livre de Jérémie et sa réception* (BETL, 128), Leuven, University Press - Peeters, 1997, pp. 27-50. L'existence d'une rédaction dtr en Jr a été récemment contestée par K. SCHMID, *Buchgestalten des Jeremiabuches. Untersuchungen zur Redaktions- und Rezeptionsgeschichte von Jer 30-33 im Kontext des Buches* (WMANT, 72), Neukirchen-Vluyn, Neukirchener Verlag, 1996, *passim*. Malgré son refus de parler d'une rédaction dtr qui serait à l'origine du livre de Jr, il admet néanmoins que «bei aller notwendigen inneren Differenzierung der vor allem in Dtn-2Kön und in Jer gefundenen 'deuteronomistischen' Texte bildet deren schulsprachliche Verfaßtheit und doch einigermaßen geschlossene Sprachwelt eine Auffälligkeit, die einer kollektiven Erklärung bedarf» (pp. 348-349). Pour Schmid cette explication devrait se situer au niveau des traditions et non des rédactions. Reste le fait qu'il faut aussi expliquer les liens (rédactionnels) qui existent entre Jr et HD.

34. Je remercie John Van Seters d'avoir attiré mon attention sur cette suite du discours de Salomon.

et 9,1-9. La possibilité de la destruction du sanctuaire annoncée en 1 R 8,46ss et 9,7 est entérinée par le prophète en Jr 7,8ss. Il existe également des liens très clairs entre Jr 25,1-13 et la récapitulation de l'histoire en 2 R 17. Le cas le plus flagrant de cette volonté dtr d'établir des corrélations entre Jr et HD se trouve dans les deux versions du «rouleau»: le récit du rouleau trouvé en 2 R 22-23 et celui du rouleau brûlé puis réédité, en Jr 36. Il n'est pas nécessaire de faire l'inventaire de tous les parallèles qui mettent en rapport ces deux textes[35] et qui indiquent qu'ils doivent être lus et entendus ensemble[36]. Dans ces deux passages, l'intervention prophétique s'effectue par rapport au livre. Hulda ne fait qu'expliciter ce qui se trouve déjà dans le *sepher*, et le prophète Jérémie, à cause d'un «empêchement» (36,5) qui le prive d'aller parler au peuple, se fait remplacer par le livre et le scribe.

On pourrait encore se demander, suivant J. Blenkinsopp[37], si les Dtrs considéraient Jr comme le dernier des «vrais» prophètes. En effet, ce livre commence par un récit de vocation qui s'inspire de Dt 18,18 (Jr 1,7b.9b) et se termine (selon TM et LXX) comme 2 R 24-25[38].

Il ne fait donc aucun doute que la formation du corpus des *Nebiim* est intimement liée à l'activité intellectuelle (et politique?) du parti dtr.

Qu'en est-il du Pentateuque?

III. LES DTRS ET LE PENTATEUQUE

1. La thèse de la «composition D»

Aucun des différents modèles qui dominent aujourd'hui le débat sur le Pentateuque ne peut ignorer la question dtr. D'ailleurs, la tendance actuelle va plutôt vers une accentuation de l'apport dtr à la formation du Pentateuque. Cela est particulièrement vrai pour le Yahwiste deutéro-

---

35. Cf. R.P. CARROLL, *Jeremiah* (OTL), London, 1986, pp. 663-664 et récemment C. MINETTE DE TILLESSE, *Joiaqim, repoussoir du >Pieux< Josias: Parallélismes entre II Reg 22 et Jer 36*, in *ZAW* 105 (1993) 352-376.

36. On pourrait faire remarquer qu'un tel *Querverweis* existe aussi entre 2 R 18-20 et Es 36-38. A la suite de Ruprecht ce parallèle doit être interprété différemment. 2 R 20 (+18-19*) était un récit indépendant (écrit vers 588) que Dtr aurait intégré dans l'historiographie. L'ajout d'Es 36ss ne se situe pas avant 400 (cf. E. RUPRECHT, *Die ursprüngliche Komposition der Hiskia-Jesaja-Erzählung und ihre Umstrukturierung durch den Verfasser des deuteronomistischen Geschichtswerkes*, in *ZTK* 87 [1990] 33-66).

37. J. BLENKINSOPP, *The Pentateuch. An Introduction to the First Five Books of the Bible* (The Anchor Bible Reference Library), New York, NY, *et al.*, Doubleday, 1992, p. 235.

38. Pour l'histoire rédactionnelle de ces chapîtres, cf. R.F. PERSON, JR., *II Kings 24,18-25,30 and Jeremiah 52: A Text-Critical Case Study in the Redaction History of the Deuteronomistic History*, in *ZAW* 105/2 (1993) 174-205.

nomisé de M. Rose et pour le modèle élaboré par E. Blum[39]. Selon ce dernier, la grande majorité des textes non-sacerdotaux du Pentateuque proviendraient d'une activité rédactionnelle et littéraire d'un groupe dtr, et seraient à dater à la fin de l'exil, voire à l'époque postexilique. Selon ce modèle, le Pentateuque apparaît comme un compromis entre le courant sacerdotal et le courant dtr à l'époque perse. Cette thèse est séduisante par sa (relative) simplicité.

Pourtant, on peut se demander s'il est légitime de classer mécaniquement tous les textes non-sacerdotaux du Pentateuque dans la catégorie «dtr». Le seul ensemble où nous soyons manifestement en présence du style et de l'idéologie dtr est Ex 1-32* (vocation prophétique de Moïse, promesse d'une conquête militaire impliquant l'extermination de la population autochtone, explicitation des signes et prodiges en Égypte, la sortie d'Égypte comme guerre de Yhwh, conclusion, rupture et renouvellement de l'alliance). Dans le livre de la Genèse, l'écriture et la théologie dtrs sont beaucoup plus discrètes, comme l'a de nouveau fait remarquer C. Levin[40] (Abraham cohabite avec ses voisins; Joseph s'intègre avec succès dans un pays étranger). Le livre du Lévitique est quant à lui un produit principalement sacerdotal. Reste le livre des Nombres. Y retrouve-t-on vraiment la composition D dans tous les textes non-sacerdotaux? Regardons brièvement les deux premiers récits des Nb considérés souvent comme dtr.

2. *L'exemple de Nb 11-12*

Nb 11 réunit (au moins) deux thèmes: celui du mécontentement du peuple à l'égard de la nourriture – sanctionné finalement par l'envoi des cailles; et celui du mécontentement de Moïse face à sa responsabilité – sanctionné par le don de l'esprit.

À qui faut-il attribuer la conflation de ces deux thèmes? S'agit-il d'une «œuvre deutéronomiste», comme le pensent notamment Blum, Crüsemann et Albertz [41]?

---

39. M. ROSE, *Deuteronomist und Jahwist* (ATANT, 67), Zürich, Theologischer Verlag, 1981; E. BLUM, *Studien zur Komposition des Pentateuch* (BZAW, 189), Berlin - New York, NY, de Gruyter, 1990.

40. C. LEVIN, *Der Jahwist* (FRLANT, 157), Göttingen, Vandenhoeck & Ruprecht, 1993, p. 436

41. E. BLUM, *Studien*, pp. 76-84; F. CRÜSEMANN, *Die Tora. Theologie und Sozialgeschichte des alttestamentlichen Gesetzes*, München, Kaiser, 1992, pp. 111-113; cf. également R. ALBERTZ, *Religionsgeschichte Israels in alttestamentlicher Zeit* (GAT, 8), Göttingen, Vandenhoeck & Ruprecht, 1992, pp. 515-516, et F. AHUIS, *Der klagende Gerichtsprophet. Studien zur Klage in der Überlieferung von den alttestamentlichen Gerichtspropheten* (CTM), Stuttgart, Calwer, 1982, p. 57, qui postule cependant une couche yahwiste de base (contenant notamment l'ébauche de la complainte de Moïse).

Dans sa forme actuelle, Nb 11 oppose d'une manière quasi pauli-
nienne la chair (בשׂר) et l'esprit (רוח)[42]. Une telle opposition n'est pas
typique de la pensée dtr, de toute manière peu charismatique. La concordance montre que le terme רוח est rarement attesté à l'intérieur de HD[43].
De plus, Nb 11 se singularise par le fait qu'il y est question de l'esprit de
Moïse répandu sur les anciens. En dehors d'Es 66,13, il n'existe pas de
parallèle où Dieu aurait mis son esprit en Moïse[44].

On pourrait observer, en faveur du caractère dtr de Nb 11, que le
thème de la décharge de Moïse est attesté en Dt 1,9-18 (et en Ex 18,13-
26). Et en effet, il est très probable que Nb 11 présuppose Dt 1,9ss[45].
Cependant, il n'y a pas d'affinités stylistiques entre ces textes, la racine
נשׂא mise à part (cf. Nb 11,14 // Dt 1,9); et le problème de Moïse en Nb
11 ne relève pas de la sphère juridique: il ressortit à la question plus générale de la médiation entre Dieu et le peuple.

Cette question est résolue en Nb 11, toutefois non pas de manière dtr
(la torah mosaïque), mais selon une conception caractéristique de la prophétie postexilique[46]. Au reste, les connections entre Nb 11 et le
Deutéro-Esaïe sont nombreuses[47]. Les protestations que Moïse adresse à
Yhwh sous-entendent que Dieu devrait assumer ses responsabilités
comme mère du peuple. Cette métaphore se trouve en Es 42,14; 46,3;
49,15[48]. De telles analogies avec Es 40ss se poursuivent dans la suite du
texte. Ainsi la question de 11,23: הֲיַד יְהוָה תִּקְצָר trouve un écho dans Es
50,2: הֲקָצוֹר קָצְרָה יָדִי (cf. לֹא־קָצְרָה יַד־יְהוָה, Es 59,1). Enfin, le vœu final
de Moïse: «Que tout le peuple de Yhwh devienne des prophètes. Que
Yhwh donne son esprit sur eux» (11,29), correspond aux attentes formu-

---

42. Cf. H. SEEBASS, *Numeri* (CBK, IV/2), Neukirchen, Neukirchener Verlag, 1993, p.
32.

43. Il est fréquemment question de l'esprit divin dans le cyle de Samson, mais là il
s'agit justement d'une œuvre non-dtr, voire post-dtr.

44. Nb 27,18 et Dt 34,9 parlent de l'esprit de Josué. Ces deux textes sont généralement considérés comme sacerdotaux, voire post-dtr.

45. Cette thèse semble s'imposer de plus en plus, cf. M. ROSE, *Deuteronomist*,
pp. 224-263; E. AURELIUS, *Der Fürbitter Israels. Eine Studie zum Mosebild im Alten Testament* (CBOT, 27), Stockholm, Almqvist & Wiksell, pp. 180-181; J. VAN SETERS, *Life
of Moses*, pp. 212-219.

46. Déjà la complainte du peuple au v. 4: וְעַתָּה נַפְשֵׁנוּ יְבֵשָׁה rappelle l'expression du
désespoir du peuple telle qu'elle se trouve en Ez 37,11: הִנֵּה אֹמְרִים יָבְשׁוּ עַצְמוֹתֵינוּ. Face à
cette complainte d'un peuple qui se considère comme mourant, Dieu répond dans les
deux cas par le don de l'esprit (Ez 37,5 et 14: «Je mets mon esprit sur vous»; cf. Nb
11,17). De plus, ces deux textes établissent un lien entre l'esprit et la capacité de prophé-
tiser (Ez 37,1-5; Nb 11,25-26).

47. Cf. notamment J. VAN SETERS, *Life of Moses*, pp. 231-232.

48. Pour d'autres textes du 2e Es, cf. J. BRIEND, *Dieu dans l'Écriture* (LD, 150), Paris,
Cerf, 1992, pp. 78-83. Cf. encore Es 66,13. L'image maternelle de Dieu n'est attestée à
l'intérieur de HD qu'en Dt 32,18; ce chapitre est à considérer comme une insertion tardive; cf. en dernier lieu M. ROSE, *5. Mose, Vol. 2. 5. Mose 1-11 und 26-34: Rahmenstücke
zum Gesetzeskorpus* (ZBK AT, 5), Zürich, Theologischer Verlag, 1994, pp. 566-567.

lées en Es 44,3; Ez 36,27; 39,29; Jl 3,1[49]. L'auteur de Nb 11 appartient donc au milieu de la prophétie eschatologique postexilique. Il connaît la production littéraire de l'école dtr mais il veut la corriger, voire la critiquer[50].

Dans ce sens, on pourrait voir dans le personnage de Josué (présenté en Nb 11,28 comme en Jos 1,1) le représentant du milieu des Deutéronomistes qui s'auto-percevaient comme les successeurs de Moïse. Dans sa réponse à Josué, Moïse justifie en fait la légitimité d'une prophétie non-institutionnelle, indépendante même de la tradition mosaïque[51]. C'est notamment ce que suggère l'épisode d'Eldad et de Médad (11,26). Car l'esprit qui tombe sur eux n'est apparemment pas «prélevé» de Moïse, il vient directement de Yhwh (ce qui est d'ailleurs contraire à la conception de la prophétie selon Dt 18,15ss). Le texte opère donc un élargissement du don de l'esprit: depuis les 70 anciens qui représentent en quelque sorte tout le peuple jusqu'à ceux qui se trouvent en marge[52]. Derrière les noms énigmatiques d'Eldad et de Médad se cache sans doute un mouvement charismatico-eschatologique[53], au sein duquel on pourrait chercher l'auteur de Nb 11.

Nb 12 est un texte aussi complexe que le précédent. Le noyau, vv. 2-9*, peut être caractérisé comme «dtr», mais «dtr tardif». En insistant sur l'incomparabilité de Moïse par rapport aux prophètes «communs», Nb 12,6-8 se rapproche de Dt 34,10, un ajout lui aussi tardif relevant sans doute d'une des dernières rédactions du Pentateuque[54]. Ces deux

---

49. Pour d'autres textes, cf. R. ALBERTZ – C. WESTERMANN, *art.* «רוח», *THAT* 2, München, C. Kaiser; Zürich, Theologischer Verlag, 1976, cc. 726-753; 751-752.

50. Il accepte bien sûr l'autorité mosaïque. On notera néanmoins que Moïse en Nb 11 formule un projet de mort (!) auquel Dieu va opposer le don de l'esprit.

51. Cf. également C. SCHÄFER-LICHTENBERGER, *Josua und Salomo. Eine Studie zu Autorität und Legitimität des Nachfolgers im Alten Testament* (SVT, 58), Leiden - New York, NY - Köln, Brill, 1995, p. 135: «Das Machtwort Moses beläßt der Prophetie einen Freiraum jenseits der mosaischen Gebote». Il semble alors plus logique de lire en Nb 11,25 la racine סוף au lieu de יסף, cf. E. BLUM, *Studien*, p. 80; A.H.J. GUNNEWEG, *Das Gesetz und die Propheten. Eine Auslegung von Ex 33,7-11; Num 11,4-12,8; Dtn 31,14f.; 34,10*, in *ZAW* 102 (1990) 169-180, esp. p. 176.

52. Le thème des 70 anciens «privilégiés» (cf. la racine אצל en Ex 24,11 et Nb 11,17.25) renvoie à Ex 24,9-11, un texte postexilique qui n'est ni dtr ni sacerdotal.

53. Cf. M. NOTH, *Das 4. Buch Mose. Numeri* (ATD, 7), Göttingen, Vandenhoeck & Ruprecht, 1977, pp. 80-81. La thèse de R. ALBERTZ, *Religionsgeschichte Israels*, pp. 515-516, qui y voit une allusion à une commission laïque d'inspiration dtr, chargée de défendre les intérêts de D lors de la publication du Pentateuque, ne me convainc guère.

54. G. BRAULIK, *Deuteronomium II, 16,18-34,12* (NEB, 28), Würzburg, Echter Verlag, 1992, p. 246, l'attribue à la rédaction finale du Pentateuque.

passages modifient la conception dtr traditionnelle de Dt 18,18ss[55]. Par son insistance sur la séparation entre Moïse et les prophètes, Nb 12,2-8 peut, en effet, être lu comme une réponse (dtrT) à Nb 11[56]. Cela montre que les textes dits «dtr» du Pentateuque ne se situent pas tous au même niveau rédactionnel. On peut déceler des voix et des idéologies deutéro-nomisantes jusqu'aux dernières retouches du Pentateuque.

Les versets 12,1 et 10ss, par contre, ne pourraient guère être interprétés comme «dtr». Ils défendent le mariage mixte de Moïse (interdit selon Dt 7) par le récit de Miryam, qui sera punie pour avoir critiqué cette union[57]. L'auteur de ces versets est apparemment issu d'un courant libéral du judaïsme. Il a greffé son récit autour de la présentation lumineuse de Moïse (Nb 12,2ss) afin de légitimer les mariages suspects aux yeux de l'orthodoxie jérusalémite (cf. Esd 9; Ne 10).

Cette brève analyse rend compte de la grande complexité littéraire de Nb 11-12, et nous invite à rester prudents vis-à-vis de certaines théories trop globalisantes, en tout cas en ce qui concerne le livre des Nombres.

3. Les Dtrs entre Pentateuque et Hexateuque

Cela ne signifie pas que la thèse du Pentateuque comme document de compromis doive être abandonnée. Notre analyse demande seulement si les deux courants théologiques «P» et «D» sont les seuls qui aient eu «voix au chapitre». Même si l'existence de la fameuse «autorisation impériale» n'est pas aussi établie que certains veulent le faire croire, le parti dtr a sans doute joué un rôle important dans la «publication» du Pentateuque. Comme conséquence de la séparation (canonique) du Dt de sa suite, la Torah (l'enseignement) dtr encadre la Torah sacerdotale (Ex 25*-Lv) par Ex 1-32* et le Dt. Il semble d'ailleurs que le *Penta*teuque n'ait pas été la seule option possible. Certains membres de la commission de publication (surtout du côté «dtr», mais non pas exclusivement) ont dû militer en faveur d'un ensemble Gn – Jos, comme le montre Jos 24 qui, en récapitulant toute l'histoire depuis les Patriarches jusqu'à la conquête, a voulu promouvoir un Hexateuque[58] (et se trouve pour ainsi

---

55. Ce texte qui fait de Moïse le premier d'une série de prophètes appartient sans doute à la rédaction dtr du Dt; cf. p. ex. M. ROSE, *5. Mose, Vol. 1. 5. Mose 12-25: Ein-führung und Gesetze* (ZBK AT, 5), Zürich, Theologischer Verlag, 1994, pp. 99-106.

56. Cf. M. NOTH, *Das 4. Buch Mose Numeri* (ATD, 7), Götingen, Vandenhoeck & Ruprecht, ³1977, pp. 83-86.

57. Pour cette interprétation, cf. notamment B.J. DIEBNER, *»... for he had married a Cushite woman«(Num 12,1)*, in *Nubica* I/II (1990) 499-504.

58. Cf. notamment E. BLUM, *Studien*, pp. 363-365, et le motif de la promenade des ossements de Joseph (Gn 50,25; Ex 13,19) qui aboutit en Jos 24,32. L'hypothèse énoncée

dire en concurrence avec Dt 34). Quoi qu'il en soit, l'option retenue, celle d'un Pentateuque, reflète finalement le souci commun à P et à D de circonscrire les fondements par rapport à Moïse.

IV. LES DTRS ET LES KETUBIM

Contrairement aux *Nebiim* et à la Tora, la troisième partie du canon vétérotestamentaire ne témoigne pas d'une influence dtr prononcée. Le livre des Chroniques certes reprend le style dtr, ce qui n'a rien d'étonnant. Mais leur idéologie n'est nullement dtr: comme l'a montré notamment Sara Japhet, les Chroniques semblent promouvoir l'image d'un Israël quasi autochtone. Les références à l'exode sont réduites au stricte minimum et la conquête de Josué est passée sous silence. Quant à l'exil babylonien, il n'est, contrairement à son traitement dans les livres des Rois, qu'un «accident mineur»[59].

Le livre d'Esd-Ne est le seul parmi les livres des *Ketubim* à présenter des caractéristiques «dtr».

Tous les chapitres ne font pas apparaître un style dtr «pur», mais cela peut s'expliquer par l'utilisation de sources et par la transformation de la langue hébraïque vers la fin de l'époque perse. La présentation du retour de la Golah à la manière de l'Exode et de la conquête sous Josué, et la large place donnée aux préoccupations identitaires (cf. la dissolution des mariages mixtes, Esd 9; Ne 10) permettent de considérer ce livre comme le produit d'une frange du parti dtr[60].

Mais à part cela, la main dtr est quasiment absente des Écrits. On trouve certes quelques Psaumes qu'on pourrait qualifier de dtr (Ps 78; 89, etc.), mais quel est le courant théologique qui n'aurait pas réussi à insérer dans le Psautier quelques compositions de son cru? La plupart de la production littéraire qu'on trouve dans les *Ketubim* fait plutôt apparaître une théologie non-dtr, voire anti-dtr, comme notamment Job et Qoh, mais aussi d'autres livres (p. ex. le livre de Ruth, qui constitue un plaidoyer pour un «Israël multi-ethnique»). Cela signifie sans doute que le parti dtr en tant que force sociale était, à l'époque hellénistique, en voie de dissolution, ou en éclatement. L'époque hellénistique produira de

---

ci-dessus explique aussi l'observation que Jos est le seul parmi les livres historiques contenant des textes qu'on peut qualifier de «sacerdotaux».

59. Cf. S. JAPHET, *L'historiographie post-exilique: comment et pourquoi?*, in A. DE PURY – T. RÖMER – J.D. MACCHI (eds.), *Israël construit son histoire*, pp. 123-152; P. ABADIE, *Une «Histoire corrective»: le modèle du Chroniste*, in *Theophilyon* 2/1 (1997) 65-90.

60. Selon A.H.J. GUNNEWEG, *Esra. Mit einer Zeittafel von Alfred Jepsen* (KAT, XIX,1), Gütersloh, Gütersloher Verlagshaus, 1985, Esd-Ne aurait été écrit comme suite de HD.

nouvelles constellations de groupes sociaux, dont certains intégreront telle ou telle préoccupation dtr. Le langage dtr continue à être utilisé, voire à être imité, comme le montrent par ex. les derniers ajouts du livre de Jr, mais aussi des textes deutéro-canoniques comme Tobie, Judith ou 1Macc[61]. Mais dans ces cas-là, il convient de parler d'«héritage dtr» plutôt que de dtr tout court.

V. CONCLUSION

Le parti dtr est à l'origine des *Nebiim*; les prophètes antérieurs se constituent sur la base de HD et la première collection des livres prophétiques se comprend fort bien à partir du souci dtr de consigner la catastrophe de l'exil dans la littérature prophétique. Quant au Pentateuque, les Dtrs ont joué un rôle non négligeable au moment de sa publication mais, comme nous l'avons vu, ils n'étaient de loin pas le seul groupe ayant marqué le Pt de son empreinte. La «discrétion dtr» dans les *Ketubim*, montre que le parti dtr se désintègre à cette époque. Ainsi, la troisième partie de la BH nous fait entendre des voix non-dtr et souligne cette grande diversité théologique, à partir de laquelle le judaïsme va finalement trouver son identité[62].

Université de Lausanne   Thomas C. RÖMER

---

61. H. ENGEL, «*Das Buch Tobit*», «*Das Buch Judit*», «*Die Bücher der Makkabäer*», in *Einleitung in das Alte Testament* (Studienbücher Theologie), Stuttgart – Berlin – Köln, Kohlhammer, 1995, pp. 183-191, 192-201, 210-223.
62. On pourrait également se demander pourquoi des livres évoquant le style et la théologie dtr (Tob, Jud et 1Macc) n'ont pas été acceptés dans les *Ketubim*.

DOES A COMPREHENSIVE "LEITMOTIV" EXIST
IN THE DEUTERONOMISTIC HISTORY?

I

If scholarly opinion is correct in believing that the Deuteronomistic History (=Dtr) was written by *one* author, one would expect that this author would have introduced a basic explanation or principle, an overarching "Leitmotiv", in order to highlight the homogeneity of his work. This is the opinion of Julius Wellhausen[1], who writes concerning the Book of Kings: "Vom Ende aus wird hier auf die Königsperiode zurückgeschaut wie auf eine abgeschlossene Vergangenheit, über welche das Urteil gesprochen ist.... [es] steht überall die Vernichtung der Nation und ihrer beiden Reiche im Hintergrunde. Das gibt dem Ganzen die Beleuchtung: es wird gezeigt, warum es so kommen mußte. Wegen der Untreue gegen Jahve, wegen der grundverkehrten Richtung, an der man trotz der Thora Jahves und seiner Propheten beharrlich festgehalten habe. Die Darstellung wird gewissermaßen zu einem großen Sündenbekenntnis der exilirten Nation über ihre Vergangenheit". Wellhausen is certainly right: an overarching principle in the Dtr has to be connected with the political catastrophes which terminated the two kingdoms respectively.

If Wellhausen's impression could be verified, we would have to accept the unity of Dtr as a reality and attribute this unity to a single author, as Noth did. But if Wellhausen's impression turns out to be incorrect, then we have to abandon the theory of a uniform Dtr.

We shall approach this problem in a more general manner, which also enables us to find a basic principle, even if it differs somewhat from Wellhausen's definition[2]. We shall examine the following motifs, asking

---

1. J. WELLHAUSEN, *Prolegomena zur Geschichte Israels*, Berlin – Leipzig, de Gruyter, ⁶1927, pp. 275f. Wellhausen formulated his principle in relation to the Book of Kings only, but in the same connection he states that the redaction of Kings is basically the same as the redaction of the two preceding historical books. Therefore it is justified to examine the whole Dtr according to this principle.

2. M. NOTH, *Überlieferungsgeschichtliche Studien* I, Halle a.d. Saale, 1943 = Darmstadt, Wissenschaftliche Buchgesellschaft, ³1973, p. 100, defines the "theologische Leitgedanken" of Dtr as "Erkenntnis, daß Gott in dieser Geschichte erkennbar gehandelt hat, indem er auf den ständig wachsenden Abfall mit Warnung und Strafen und schließlich, als diese sich als fruchtlos erwiesen hatten, mit der völligen Vernichtung geantwortet hat". This explanation contains two phases of punishment. It surpasses a one-dimensional explanation, but according to our examination it is also unacceptable.

especially whether they constitute a comprehensive historical concept:
I. The sin of Israel (and its leaders); II. The (emotional) reaction of God;
III. The punishment of God; IV. Future salvation.

The most important texts for examination are the programmatic texts
of the historical books, which contain the farewell speeches and the
theological reflections at important points of the history, specifically:

1. The Book of Deuteronomy, mainly texts at the beginning and end;
2. The frame of the Book of Joshua, ch. 1 and ch. 23-24;
3. The frame of the Book of Judges, ch. 2 and related texts in ch. 6; 8
and 10;
4. The speech of Samuel, 1 Sam 7,3.4, the speech of God in 1 Sam 8,
the farewell speech of Samuel, 1 Sam 12, the story of Saul's rejection, 1
Sam 15, and 2 Sam 7, the promise to David;
5. The texts related to Solomon's building of the temple, 1 Kings 8-9,
and to his wives, 1 Kings 3; 11, the prophecies of Ahija, 1 Kings 11; 14.
Additional shorter texts include 1 Kings 13,34; 21,26; 2 Kings 13,2-
6.23, the reflections on the occasion of the destruction of the northern
kingdom, 1 Kings 17, the reflections related to kings Manasseh and
Josiah, and finally the short explanation of the destruction of Judah, 2
Kings 24,2.20.

TABLE: SIN AND PUNISHMENT IN THE DEUTERONOMISTIC HISTORY[3]

sin	divine reaction	punishment	salvation
Dt 4,25 ועשׂיתם פסל תמונת כל הרע בעיני יהוה אלהיך להכעיסו		Dt 4,26 אבד תאבדון מהר מעל הארץ לא תאריכן ימים עליה כי השמד תשמדון v. 27 והפיץ יהוה אתכם בעמים ונשׁארתם מתי מספר	Dt 4,30 ושׁבת עד יהוה אלהיך ושׁמעת בקלו v. 31 כי אל רחום יהוה אלהיך לא ירפך ולא ישׁחיתך ולא ישׁכח את ברית אבתיך
Dt 7,2 לא תכרת להם ברית v. 3 ולא תתחתן בם			

3. To keep the tables brief we use the abbreviations: Dt = Deuteronomy, 1-2 S = 1-2
Samuel, 1-2 K = 1-2 Kings. For the same reason verses are not quoted completely. – The
notes in the last column explain why a certain text is of little relevance for our examination.

sin	divine reaction	punishment	salvation
Dt 7,4 כי יסיר את בנך v. 4 מאחרי ועבדו אלהים אחרים	Dt 7,4 וחרה אף יהוה בכם (similar Dt 6,15)	Dt 7,4 והשמידך מהר (similar Dt 6,15)	
Dt 8,19 והיה אם שכח תשכח את יהוה אלהיך והלכת אחרי אלהים אחרים ועבדתם והשתחוית להם		Dt 8,19 כי אבד תאבדון	
Dt 11,16 וסרתם ועבדתם אלהים אחרים והשתחויתם להם	Dt 11,17 וחרה אף יהוה בכם	Dt 11,17 ועצר את השמים ואבדתם מהרה מעל הארץ	
		Dt 28,36 יולך יהוה אתך ואת מלכך אל גוי אשר לא ידעת ועבדת שם אלהים אחרים	note: Dt 28 mostly speaks of punishments (curses), which will strike the people being *in* its country.
Dt 29,24 על אשר עזבו את ברית יהוה v. 25 וילכו ויעבדו אלהים אחרים וישתחו להם	Dt 29,26 ויחר אף יהוה בארץ ההוא	Dt 29,27 ויתשם יהוה מעל אדמתם באף וישלכם אל ארץ אחרת	
			Dt 30,1-10: future salvation, but not in direct connection with punishment v. 3 ושב יהוה אלהיך את שבותך וקבצך מכל העמים v. 5 והביאך אל הארץ v. 6 ומל את לבבך
Dt 30,17 והשתחוית לאלהים אחרים ועבדתם		Dt 30,18 כי אבד תאבדון לא תאריכו ימים על האדמה	
Dt 31,16 וקם העם הזה וזנה אחרי אלהי נכר הארץ ועזבני והפר את בריתי	Dt 31,17 וחרה אפי בו ביום ההוא	Dt 31,17 ועזבתים והסתרתי פני מהם ומצאהו רעות רבות וצרות	note: "God's remoteness as punishment": Dt 31,16ss is very unusual in Dt.

sin	divine reaction	punishment	salvation
Josh 23,7 לבלתי בוא בגוים האלה ובשם אלהיהם לא תשביעו ולא תעבדום ולא תשתחוו להם v. 12 ודבקתם ביתר הגוים האלה והתחתנתם בהם v. 16 בעברכם את ברית יהוה אלהיכם ועבדתם אלהים אחרים והשתחויתם להם	Josh 23,16 וחרה אף יהוה בכם	Josh 23,15 כל הדבר הרע עד השמידו אותכם מעל האדמה הטובה הזאת v. 16 ואבדתם מהרה מעל הארץ הטובה	
Josh 24,20 כי תעזבו את יהוה ועבדתם אלהי נכר		Josh 24,20 ושב והרע לכם וכלה אתכם	
Judg 2,11 ויעשו בני ישראל את הרע בעיני יהוה ויעבדו את הבעלים v. 12 ויעזבו את יהוה וילכו אחרי אלהים אחרים וישתחוו להם ויכעסו את יהוה			
v. 13 ויעזבו את יהוה ויעבדו לבעל ולעשתרות v. 19 ללכת אחרי אלהים אחרים לעבדם ולהשתחות להם	Judg 2,14 ויחר אף יהוה	Judg 2,14 ויתנם ביד שסים וימכרם ביד אויביהם מסביב	
v. 20 יען אשר עברו את בריתי ולא שמעו לקולי	Judg 2,20 ויחר אף יהוה	Judg 2,21 גם אני לא אוסיף להוריש איש מפניהם מן הגוים	
Judg 4 as example for the frame of the stories of the Judges: v. 1 ויספו בני ישראל לעשות הרע בעיני יהוה		Judg 4,2 וימכרם יהוה ביד יבין	Judg 4,23 ויכנע אלהים ביום ההוא את יבין
Judg 6,10 לא תיראו את אלהי האמרי			
Judg 8,33 ויזנו אחרי הבעלים וישימו להם בעל ברית לאלהים v. 34 ולא זכרו בני ישראל יהוה אלהיהם			
Judg 10,6 לעשות הרע בעיני יהוה ויעבדו את הבעלים ואת העשתרות ואת אלהי ארם ויעזבו את יהוה ולא עבדוהו	Judg 10,7 ויחר אף יהוה	Judg 10,7 וימכרם ביד פלשתים	

sin	divine reaction	punishment	salvation
v. 13 ואתם עזבתם אותי ותעבדו אלהים אחרים		Judg 10,13 לכן לא אוסיף להושיע אתכם	
(1 S 7,3 הסירו את אלהי הנכר מתוככם והעשתרות v. 4 ויסירו בני ישראל את הבעלים ואת העשתרת) (similar Judg 10,16)			
1 S 8,7 כי אתי מאסו v. 8 ככל המעשים אשר עשו מיום העלתי אתם ממצרים ועד היום הזה ויעזבני ויעבדו אלהים אחרים			
1 S 12,9 וישכחו את יהוה אלהיהם v. 10 חטאנו כי עזבנו את יהוה ונעבד את הבעלים ואת העשתרות		1 S 12,9 וימכר אתם ביד סיסרא	
		1 S 12,25 ואם הרע תרעו גם אתם גם מלככם תספו	

In 1 S 15 these motifs do not appear

In 2 S 7 these motifs do not appear

sin	divine reaction	punishment	salvation
1 K 3,2 רק העם מזבחים בבמות v. 3 רק בבמות הוא מזבח ומקטיר			
			1 K 6,13: conditional salvation without previous judgment or punishment
1 K 8,46 כי יחטאו לך כי אין אדם אשר לא יחטא	1 K 8,46 ואנפת בם	1 K 8,46 ונתתם לפני אויב ושבום שביהם אל ארץ האויב	1 K 8,49 ושמעת השמים את תפלתם ואת תחנתם ועשית משפטם v. 50 וסלחת לעמך ונתתם לרחמים לפני שביהם ורחמום
			note: 1 K 8,46ss is very unusual in Dtr.

sin	divine reaction	punishment	salvation
1 K 9,6 אם שוב תשבון מאחרי ולא תשמרו מצותי ועבדתם אלהים אחרים והשתחויתם להם		1 K 9,7 והכרתי את ישראל מעל פני האדמה ואת הבית אשלח מעל פני והיה ישראל למשל ולשנינה	
1 K 11,4 נשיו הטו את לבבו אחרי אלהים אחרים v. 5 וילך שלמה אחרי עשתרת ואחרי מלכם v. 6 ויעש שלמה הרע בעיני יהוה ולא כדוד v. 7 אז יבנה שלמה במה לכמוש v. 9 כי נטה לבבו מעם יהוה v. 10 לבלתי לכת אחרי אלהים אחרים v. 11 ולא שמרת בריתי וחקתי	1 K 11,9 ויתאנף יהוה בשלמה	1 K 11,11 קרע אקרע את הממלכה מעליך	
1 K 11,33 יען אשר עזבוני וישתחוו לעשתרת לכמוש ולמלכם ולא הלכו בדרכי לעשות הישר בעיני וחקתי ומשפטי כדוד אביו		1 K 11,31 הנני קרע את הממלכה מיד שלמה	
		1 K 13,34 ויהי בדבר הזה לחטאת בית ירבעם ולהכחיד ולהשמיד מעל פני האדמה	
1 K 14,8 ולא היית כעבדי דוד אשר שמר מצותי v. 9 ותרע לעשות ותעשה לך אלהים אחרים ומסכות להכעיסני ואתי השלכת אחרי גוך		1 K 14,10 הנני מביא רעה אל בית ירבעם והכרתי לירבעם משתין בקיר v. 11 יאכלו הכלבים עוף השמים	
1 K 14,15 יען אשר עשו את אשריהם מכעיסים את יהוה		1 K 14,15 והכה יהוה את ישראל ונתש את ישראל מעל האדמה הטובה וזרם מעבר לנהר	

After usual prophecy against king and his house (here against Ahab):

1 K 21,26 ויתעב מאד ללכת אחרי הגללים ככל אשר עשו האמרי

.

sin	divine reaction	punishment	salvation
2 K 13,2 ויעש הרע בעיני יהוה וילך אחר חטאת ירבעם אשר החטיא את ישראל לא סר ממנה (Usually such evaluations of kings appear without the motifs of punishment, etc.)	2 K 13,3 ויחר אף יהוה בישראל	2 K 13,3 ויתנם ביד חזאל וביד בן הדד	2 K 13,5 ויתן יהוה לישראל מושיע v. 23 ויחן יהוה אתם וירחמם ויפן אליהם למען בריתו את אברהם ולא אבה השחיתם ולא השליכם מעל פניו עד עתה 2 K 14,27 ולא דבר יהוה למחות את שם ישראל מתחת השמים ויושיעם ביד ירבעם
		(2 K 15,37 החל יהוה להשליח ביהודה רצין ואת פקח)	
2 K 17,7 כי חטאו בני ישראל ליהוה וייראו אלהים אחרים v. 8 וילכו בחקות הגוים v. 9 ויבנו להם במות בכל עריהם v. 10 ויצבו להם מצבות ואשרים על כל גבעה v. 11 ויקטרו שם בכל במות כגוים ויעשו דברים רעים להכעיס v. 12 ויעבדו הגללים v. 14 ולא שמעו ויקשו את ערפם v. 15 וימאסו את חקיו ואת בריתו וילכו אחרי ההבל ואחרי הגוים אשר סביבתם v. 16 ויעזבו את כל מצות יהוה אלהיהם ויעשו להם מסכה ויעשו אשרה וישתחוו לכל צבא השמים ויעבדו את הבעל	(2 K 17,13 ויעד יהוה בישראל וביהודה ביד כל נביאו לאמר שבו מדרכיכם)		

sin	divine reaction	punishment	salvation
ויעבירו את בניהם v. 17 באש ויתמכרו לעשות הרע בעיני יהוה להכעיסו	ויתאנף 2 K 17,18 יהוה מאד בישראל	ויסרם מעל 2 K 17,18 פניו	
גם יהודה לא שמר v. 19 את מצות יהוה והחטיאם חטאה v. 21 גדולה	וימאס יהוה v. 20 בכל זרע ישראל	ויענם ויתנם ביד v. 20 שסים עד אשר השליכם מפניו	
וילכו בני ישראל v. 22 בכל חטאות ירבעם		עד אשר הסיר v. 23 יהוה את ישראל מעל פניו כאשר דבר ביד כל עבדיו הנביאים ויגל ישראל מעל אדמתו אשורה	
על אשר לא 2 K 18,12 שמעו בקול יהוה אלהיהם ויעברו את בריתו את כל אשר צוה משה		ויגל מלך 2 K 18,11) אשור את ישראל אשורה)	
ויעש הרע בעיני 2 K 21,2 יהוה כתועבת הגוים ויבן את הבמות v. 3 ויקם מזבחת לבעל ויעש אשרה וישתחו לכל צבא השמים והעביר את בנו v. 6 באש ועונן הרבה לעשות הרע בעיני יהוה להכעיס ולא שמעו ויתעם v. 9 מנשה לעשות את הרע מן הגוים			
	וידבר 2 K 21,10) יהוה ביד עבדיו הנביאים לאמר)		
יען אשר עשה מנשה v. 11 התעבות האלה הרע ויחטא גם את יהודה בגלוליו יען אשר עשו את v. 15 הרע בעיני ויהיו מכעסים אתי מן היום אשר יצאו אבותם ממצרים		הנני מביא 2 K 21,12 רעה על ירושלם ויהודה ונטיתי על v. 13 ירושלם את קו שמרוך ונטשתי את v. 14 שארית נחלתי ונתתים ביד איביהם	
תחת אשר עזבוני 2 K 22,17 ויקטרו לאלהים אחרים למען הכעיסני	חמתי 2 K 22,17	הנני מביא 2 K 22,16 רעה אל המקום הזה	

sin	divine reaction	punishment	salvation
	2 K 23,26 אך לא שב יהוה מחרון אפו הגדול אשר חרה אפו ביהודה		
2 K 23,26 על כל הכעסים אשר הכעיסו מנשה		2 K 23,27 גם את יהודה אסיר מעל פני ומאסתי את העיר הזאת ואת הבית	
		2 K 24,2 וישלח יהוה בו את גדודי כשדים ביהודה להאבידו כדבר יהוה ביד עבדיו הנביאים v. 3 ביהודה להסיר	
2 K 24,3 בחטאת מנשה		מעל פניו	
	2 K 24,20 כי על אף יהוה היתה בירושלם וביהודה	2 K 24,20 עד השלכו אתם מעל פניו	

After examining the foregoing texts, it is interesting to note that several basic texts do not mention the motifs we are looking for: Josh 1 is set on the eve of conquest and settlement, but it is surprisingly silent on the possible fate of the people in the country and the related alternative of serving the Lord or apostasy. Similarly in 1 Sam 15 and 2 Sam 7 where a "Leitmotiv" of sin and punishment would have been very appropriate, it nevertheless was not developed[4]. 1 Kings 8 deals with the motif of "sin" in a completely different manner than does the rest of Dtr. All this does not support the supposed unity of Dtr.

Let us now turn to the positive findings from our examination of the motifs:

1. If one compares the motifs of sin and punishment, one realizes that the motif of *sin* is the more important; its treatment simply takes up more space[5]. The punishments that are mentioned differ from one another. Usually the motif of the end of the two kingdoms is not prominent. This changes, not surprisingly, only at the end of the Book of Kings.

4. This is correct, although the motif appears in 2 Sam 7,14.
5. The explanation that, unlike the punishment, the existence of sin had to be proven and was therefore emphasized is insufficient. It does not explain why there is a divergence in the conceptions of punishment and why the end of the two kingdoms is mentioned so rarely in this context.

If we explore the motif of אלהים אחרים, which is one of the most important motifs describing sin, we discover that this motif is not connected to a specific punishment. It can appear without any punishment or with different punishments, for example, with the motif of a fast destruction of the people[6], which usually does not relate to the historical end of either of the two kingdoms. Alternatively it can be connected – in the Book of Judges – with the motif of periodic oppression by enemies[7] or with a prophecy against a dynasty: 1 Kings 14,9f.

The next motif for "sin" we will examine takes a verbal form: כעס (Hif.). Some of the relevant biblical passages are to be found in the Book of Deuteronomy[8]; more (17) are found in the Book of Kings, to which Judg 2,12 may be added[9].

According to their contents, these passages can be divided into two groups. In the first group, individual kings, usually of the northern kingdom, are the subject; in the second group, Israel is the subject. The first group, which is restricted to the Book of Kings, mostly speaks about the end of a dynasty. A wider historical and theological perspective characterizes only the second group, which includes some passages in Kings and all passages outside the Book of Kings.

This leads us to the conclusion that, at an early stage, there existed only a deuteronomistic Book of Kings[10] which contained the appropriate motif of the kings as a cause of God's anger. In the course of development of the deuteronomistic historical books, the application of this motif was widened; it was used in connection to Israel. The only transfer of this motif to a king of Judah, Manasseh, in 2 Kings 21,6, was not part of the earliest stage, as was the case for some passages of the theologically developed chapters, 2 Kings 17 (vv. 11.17) and 2 Kings 23 (v. 19). It is relevant that the summary expression "the kings of Israel" appears as a subject only in the last passage.

2. The most characteristic expression of the emotional reaction of God is ויחר אף יי / וחרה. It is interesting that this sentence appears almost exclusively in the books of Deuteronomy and Judges[11]. This is not by chance: the motif of God's anger is more suited to the conception of

6. Compare Deut 4,26; 7,4; 11,17; Josh 23,16.
7. Judg 2, compare 10,13.
8. Deut 4,25; 9,18; 31,29. H.-D. HOFFMANN, *Reform und Reformen. Untersuchungen zu einem Grundthema der deuteronomistischen Geschichtsschreibung* (ATANT, 66), Zürich, Theologischer Verlag, 1980, p. 332, adds Deut 32,16.21 in brackets.
9. The motif is often connected to prophets, see Jeremiah and, in the Book of Kings, especially 2 Kings 22,17.
10. This book was, of course, smaller than the present one.
11. And see 2 Kings 13,3.

immediate punishment, which is basic in Judges and Deuteronomy. In other words, the distribution of this expression for God's anger hints at different conceptions of the punishment in Dtr. Therefore, the unity of Dtr becomes doubtful.

3. Concerning the motif of salvation (after punishment) in Dtr, we may add that this motif is not only quite rare, it also is not uniform.

We arrive at the conclusion that the political catastrophe at the end of the period of the Kings was not used as a "Leitmotiv" by the supposed author of Dtr. Therefore the unity of Dtr and even its very existence become questionable. The impact of this catastrophe cannot be felt in important parts of Dtr[12]; consequently it cannot be regarded as a literary unity.

II

Let us examine, now, whether a different "Leitmotiv" could save the unity of Dtr. Using the formulation of Hans-Detlef Hoffmann[13], it is the cultic theme of "reform and reforms". Is this the basic theme of deuteronomistic historiography, that unifies Dtr and makes it attributable to one single author?

Hoffmann developed the thesis that texts in the Books of Kings that deal with cultic changes are connected to the chapter, 2 Kings 23, dealing with the reform of Josiah, and he summarized it in a table[14] that can serve as a basis for our examination. The following texts are relevant for Hoffmann:

1	1 K 11,1-13 **Solomon**	theme: high places	target: 2 K 23,13
2	1 K 12,26-33 **Jeroboam**	high places, northern kingdom	target: 2 K 23,19
		Intermediate texts: Evaluation of all kings of Judah, texts No 15a,b	
3	1 K 14,21-24 **Rehoboam**	a. high places, southern kingdom	target: 2 K 23,8
		Intermediate texts: Evaluation of all kings of Judah,	
		text No 16 (Hezekiah), text No 17 (Manasseh)	
		b. (male) hierodules	target: 2 K 23,7
		Intermediate texts: text No 4 (Asa), text No 6 (Jehoshaphat)	
4	1 K 15,9-15 **Asa**	*see text No 3b*	
5	1 K 16,29-33 **Ahab**	cult of Baal, Asherah	target: 2 K 23,4.6.14
		Intermediate texts: texts No 7 (Ahazia), No 8 (Jehoram),	
		No 9 (Jehu), No 10 (Jehoiada), No 12 (Jehoahaz), No 17 (Manasseh)	

---

12. It is interesting to note that the main motif that explains the destruction of Jerusalem and Judah is the motif of the sin of (the late king) Manasseh, which by its very (chronological) nature cannot serve as an overarching "Leitmotiv".

13. H.-D. HOFFMANN, *Reform und Reformen* (n. 8).

14. *Ibid.*, p. 253.

6	1 K 22,41-47	**Jehoshaphat**	*see text No 3b*	
7	1 K 22,52-54	**Ahazia**	*see text No 5*	
8	2 K 3,1-3	**Jehoram**	*see text No 5*	
9	2 K 9-10	**Jehu**	*see text No 5*	
10	2 K 11,1-20	**Jehoiada**	a. *see text No 5*	
			b. commitment	target: 2 K 23,1-3
11	2 K 12,1-17	**Jehoash**	renovation of the temple	target: 2 K 22,3-7.9
			Intermediate Text: text No 13 (Jotham)	
12	2 K 13,1-9	**Jehoahaz**	*see text No 5*	
13	2 K 15,32-38	**Jotham**	*see text No 11*	
14	2 K 16,1-4	**Ahaz**	child-sacrifice	target: 2 K 23,10
			Intermediate text: text No 17 (Manasseh)	
15a	2 K 17,7-23	**(balance)**	*see texts No 2.5.14.17*	
15b	2 K 17,24-33	**the northern**		
		kingdom after its		
		fall	*see text No 2*	
16	2 K 18,1-6	**Hezekiah**	*see text No 3a*	
17	2 K 21,1-16	**Manasseh**	a. 'host of heaven'	target: 2 K 23,11
			b. familiar spirits and wizards	target: 2 K 23,24
			see also texts No 3a.5.14	
(18	2 K 22-23	**Josiah**	appears as target-text in the right column)	

Although this table looks very impressive, a caveat must be heeded: the table lists 18 separate texts, but it turns out, that the "intermediate texts" appear a second time with running numbers. If one takes the intermediate texts only as such and does not list them again seperately, the number of texts is reduced by half.

Let us now reexamine the different motifs which, according to Hoffmann, culminate in 2 Kings 22-23. First, we must clarify the aim of our examination: we can easily dismiss the possibility that the texts always reflect historical events; rather they must be seen to reflect a high degree of creativity by the author or authors. Therefore, we are left with two alternative models to explain the texts and their possible relations:

1. *One* author wrote all the texts mentioned in the table. This author composed the texts, which describe cultic changes of the (earlier) kings in view of his target-composition on the reform of Josiah 2 Kings 23. In this case, the "target-composition" should be a well composed, organic structure.

2. If this characterization of 2 Kings 23 proved incorrect or, more importantly, if substantial differences emerged between the texts and the "target-composition", we would have to conclude that *different* authors were involved.

In view of these alternatives, we shall examine the texts: *theme No 1* deals with the motif of high places, which were erected by Solomon (1 Kings 11,1-13) and abolished by Josiah (2 Kings 23,13). In 1 Kings 11 this motif appears directly only in v. 5 and v. 7. Therefore, we can confine our comparison to these two verses with 2 Kings 23,13.

ואחרי מלכם שקץ עמנים	וילך שלמה אחרי עשתרת אלהי צדנים	1 Kings 11,5
אז יבנה שלמה במה לכמוש שקץ מואב בהר אשר על פני ירושלם		1 Kings 11,7
ולמלך שקץ בני עמון		
אשר על פני ירושלם	ואת הבמות	2 Kings 23,13
אשר מימין להר המשחית		
אשר בנה שלמה לעשתרת שקץ צידנים		
ולמלכם תועבת בני עמון	ולכמוש שקץ מואב	

After comparing these texts, we conclude that 2 Kings 23,13 is a compilation of 1 Kings 11,5 and 1 Kings 11,7. Or as expressed by Hoffmann[15]: "2 K 23,13 ist also ein 'Zitat' von 1 K 11,5+7, das zugleich die Vorlage zusammenfaßt und vereinfacht". But the mere fact that 2 Kings 23,13 is a compilation does not exclude the possibility that this verse is of later origin than the verses in 1 Kings 11. This is even probable, because of several differences between the verses: only in 2 Kings 23 is a high place attributed to Ashtoreth. A second difference exists in the doubling of the location in 2 Kings 23,13.

It seems that they do not belong to the same author. The motif of the high places in 1 Kings 11 and 2 Kings 23 cannot then be explained as a unifying theme introduced by one and the same deuteronomistic author, as Hoffmann proposes.

According to Hoffmann, *theme No 2*, "the high places of the northern kingdom", leads from 1 Kings 12,26-33, which is the basic text concerning the "sin of Jeroboam", *via* the evaluations of the kings of northern Israel and the balance of 2 Kings 17 to the target-text 2 Kings 23,19.

It becomes obvious that all these texts contain different conceptions and can hardly be attributed to the same author: 2 Kings 23,19 speaks about "all the houses of the high places (כל בתי הבמות) that were in the cities of Samaria[16], which the kings of Israel had made". On the other hand 1 Kings 12,31 (textus receptus) mentions the one house of high places, which Jeroboam made. In 2 Kings 17 the conception is different again. V. 9 speaks of high places (במות, not בתי במות), which the children of Israel (not Jeroboam or the kings) built. Only later, in the general accusation of v. 22, are the sin(s) of Jeroboam mentioned, but now in

---

15. H.-D. HOFFMANN, *Reform und Reformen* (n. 8), p. 52.
16. This is the same formulation as in 1 Kings 13,32, which is not surprising, as the chapters are related directly to one another.

relation to the children of Israel. And בית הבמות appears in this chapter only in vv. 29.32, i.e. in the final part of this chapter, which does not deal with the northern kingdom at all, but, after its fall, with the Samaritans. Again it is obvious that one cannot speak of an overarching set of motifs which was conceived in advance.

Theme No 3a, "high places of the southern kingdom", also is not attributable to one single author. This becomes clear when we compare the relevant part of the text at the beginning, 1 Kings 14,23, with the "target" 2 Kings 23,8:

ויבנו גם המה להם במות ומצבות ואשרים	1 Kings 14,23
ויטמא את הבמות אשר קטרו שמה הכהנים ונתץ את במות השערים	2 Kings 23,8

In 1 Kings 14,23 the high places (במות) appear merely as *one* element by the side of *masseboth* and *asherim*, whereas 2 Kings 23,8 deals with the high places *only*. Yet 2 Kings 23 also mentions the related priests, who are missing in 1 Kings 14. Finally, special high places in Jerusalem only appear in 2 Kings 23,8 without preparation in one of the earlier texts.

Theme No 3b. The verses, which mention the (male) hierodules are:

וגם קדש היה בארץ	1 Kings 14,24
ויעבר הקדשים מן הארץ	1 Kings 15,12
ויתר הקדש אשר נשאר בימי אסא אביו בער מן הארץ	1 Kings 22,47
ויתץ את בתי הקדשים אשר בבית יהוה אשר הנשים ארגות	2 Kings 23,7
שם לאשרה	

It is striking, that – disregarding the "target" 2 Kings 23,7 – this theme is restricted to the *First* Book of Kings. This is appropriate for matters of content, as the problem is finally eliminated in 1 Kings 15,12; 22,47[17].

Although the *qadesh* does not exist any longer, it nevertheless appears after a long interval in 2 Kings 23,7. Yet the details are new: Only now *houses* of the *qedeshim* are mentioned. Likewise the location in the temple (of Jerusalem) is unique; normally it appears with the general statement "in the land" or "out of the land". Finally, we read about women who weave for Asherah only in 2 Kings 23,7.

Reasons of form and content lead us to the conclusion that more than one author[18] contributed to the development of this motif as well.

---

17. For our argument it is irrelevant, whether 1 Kings 22,47 is a later addition or not, see H.-D. HOFFMANN, *Reform und Reformen* (n. 8), p. 94 and n. 74.

18. This also is the opinion of H. SPIECKERMANN, *Juda unter Assur in der Sargonidenzeit* (FRLANT, 129), Göttingen, Vandenhoeck & Ruprecht, 1982, pp. 184-191. He thinks, however, that the verses in 1 Kings are very late, even later than DtrN. –

Theme No 5, "cult of Baal, Asherah", has its beginning, according to Hoffmann, in the tradition of Ahab and its "target-text" in 2 Kings 23,4.6.14.

In connection with Ahab, the relevant verses are 1 Kings 16,31-33. The motif of Baal is briefly mentioned during the rule of Ahab's successors, but Jehu (2 Kings 10,26-28) eliminated the problem once and for all, as stated in v. 28:

וישמד יהוא את הבעל מישראל.

Therefore it is surprising, that we read in connection with the revolution of the priest Jehoiada (2 Kings 11,18)[19] about a בית בעל in *Jerusalem*, which was destroyed. The reader did not gain any information about the installation of such a cult in Judah. Later, altars for Baal are attributed to the Judean king Manasseh, this in a verse (2 Kings 21,3), which mentions Ahab explicitly.

There can be no doubt that an overarching connection exists, but this connection probably cannot be attributed to an early author. It is unlikely that the same author who accused Ahab of serving Baal introduced this motif into the tradition of Manasseh, because as we have shown this motif originally belonged to the northern kingdom, and the revolution of Jehu marked its end, which also explains the difficulties of 2 Kings 11,18.

The foregoing discussion has implications for our understanding of 2 Kings 23,4.6.14. One could say, of course, that this theme ("cult of Baal, Asherah") was brought to a conclusion here in the representation of Josiah's reform. But this could not have been done by the same author who introduced the theme into the tradition of the northern kingdom.

As there is no need to examine Hoffmann's "intermediate texts" seperately, we can proceed to theme No 10b.

We should notice that here, and even more obviously in the following themes, the texts that introduce the motifs appear in the middle of 2

N. NA'AMAN, *The Dedicated Treasures Buildings within the House of YHWH where Women Weave Coverings for Asherah (2 Kings 23,7)*, in *BN* 83 (1996) 17ff., proposes a different solution viz., that 2 Kings 23,7 originally spoke of "treasure buildings" and not of "buildings for the *kedeshim*".

19. H.-D. HOFFMANN, *Reform und Reformen* (n. 8), pp. 42-43, relates 2 Kings 11,17f. to 2 Kings 10,26f. (Jehu and the Baal); he sees in the "Gegenüber dieser beiden Texte... das 'Scharnier'..., das den Baalskult – bislang ausschließliches Spezifikum des Nordreiches – auf das Südreich überträgt". Still it is strange that the *installation* of this cult in Judah is not reported. Likewise Hoffmann's "Scharnier"(hinge) is much weaker than he leads his readers to believe (*ibid.*, p. 42): 2 Kings 11,18 mentions a priest of Baal, not so 2 Kings 10,26f. (*Pace* HOFFMANN).

Kings or even later. This implies that even if we documented literary connections belonging to one author, these "short" connections would not demonstrate single authorship for the Books of Kings, much less for the whole Dtr.

Concerning *theme No 10b*, "commitment (to covenant)", the fact that this theme is mentioned in two texts relating to the priest Jehoiada (2 Kings 11,17) and the king Josiah (2 Kings 23,3), has no relevance at all to the question of authorship of Dtr.

In connection with *theme No 11*, "renovation of the temple", Hoffmann quotes three texts: 2 Kings 12,1-17; 2 Kings 15,32-38, and the "target-text" 2 Kings 22,3-7.9. It is obvious that 2 Kings 12, explaining the regulations concerning donations to the temple, serves as preparation for 2 Kings 22, where this motif appears again. But one cannot say that this connection is an important one, especially because the "intermediate text" 2 Kings 15,32-38 does not belong to this line at all; v. 35 only mentions the building of a new gate in the temple.

Theme No 14a, "child-sacrifice", relates to Ahaz, Manasseh and Josiah:

וגם את בנו העביר באש	2 Kings 16,3
והעביר את בנו באש	2 Kings 21,6
וטמא את התפת אשר בגי בני הנם לבלתי להעביר איש את בנו	2 Kings 23,10
ואת בתו באש למלך	

The last verse (2 Kings 23,10) differs from the preceding verses: only here are concrete details mentioned, one of them being the Molech. Likewise, only in 2 Kings 23 is "the daughter" added to the son. Finally, the "democratization of sin" in 2 Kings 23 is absent from the two other verses. Therefore, it is unlikely that all these verses were written by the same author.

The last theme "host of heaven" and "familiar spirits and wizards" (*theme No 17a,b*) leads only from Manasseh (2 Kings 21,1-16) to Josiah (2 Kings 23,11.24). Note that 2 Kings 23,11 does not mention the "host of heaven" of 2 Kings 21,3.5. Hoffmann should have quoted 2 Kings 23,5. Also note, regarding "familiar spirits and wizards", that according to the location "in the land of Judah and in Jerusalem", 2 Kings 23,24 speaks about general offences of the people. 2 Kings 21,6, however, deals with a personal sin[20] of king Manasseh.

---

20. We are convinced that it is of importance whether a sin is attributed to a king or to the people. It is remarkable that in large parts of the Book of Kings only the kings and their families are punished for their sins. Therefore, we cannot agree with H.-D. HOFFMANN, *Reform und Reformen* (n. 8), p. 75, who explains: "Das Verhältnis von

Having concluded our examination of all the texts and themes that are vital for Hoffmann's thesis, our conclusion is diametrically opposed to that of Hoffmann: Almost everywhere we found indications of several deuteronomistic authors. Even the Books of Kings are not uniform with regard to the subject of "Reform und Reformen". And concerning the *Reformbericht* of Josiah in 2 Kings 23, we reached the conclusion that this chapter does not constitute an integral climax of Dtr, because it was not composed by the original author but rather by a relatively late deuteronomistic author[21].

In answer to the question addressed in the title of this paper: there is no comprehensive "Leitmotiv" in the deuteronomistic historical books. On the contrary, central motifs appear in different and sometimes even contradictory formulations. This is one reason for concluding that one should abandon the theory of a single and uniform deuteronomistic history.

University of Haifa   Hartmut N. RÖSEL
Israel

König und Volk ist im Verständnis des DtrG nie alternativ zu sehen. Die Könige handeln stellvertretend für das Volk, ihre Verschuldung ist die des Volkes und ihre kultischen Sünden führen den Untergang des Volkes herbei". We think that this characterization is incorrect for DtrG and prefer a more differentiating reading of Dtr.

21. This may have far-reaching conclusions for the historicity of the reform-measures and also for the "deuteronomic question". See now B. GIESELMANN, *Die sogenannte josianische Reform in der gegenwärtigen Forschung*, in *ZAW* 106 (1994) 223-242 and the contributions of H. NIEHR and C. UEHLINGER in W. GROSS (ed.), *Jeremia und die 'deuteronomistische Bewegung'* (BBB, 98), Weinheim, Beltz, 1995.

THE DEUTERONOMISTIC HISTORY:
CAN IT AVOID DEATH BY REDACTION?

Within two or three decades after Martin Noth made the compelling case for a single comprehensive history extending from Deuteronomy to 2 Kings, a number of scholars set about to modify his thesis by introducing the notion that the history has undergone significant editorial alteration and transformation by one or more redactors. Two schools quite independent of each other at the outset, and with little agreement, set out to identify these redactions. The one group, initiated by Frank M. Cross and developed by his students and followers[1], focuses on the theme of God's unconditional promise of an eternal dynasty to David in 2 Samuel 7 which came to final flower in Josiah's reign, at which time the first edition was written. Only with the failure of the successors of Josiah and the demise of the state and monarchy did an editor feel compelled to modify the Davidic promise as conditional and explain the failure as the result of disobedience to the law. The second group, begun by Rudolf Smend with an initial focus on some texts in Joshua and Judges[2], considered the special emphasis upon obedience to the law (DtrN) as a later revision of an earlier history (though both in the exilic period). This was followed up by monographs of his students Timo Veijola and Walter Dietrich[3], the latter supporting yet another redactional layer with special prophetic interests (DtrP). These two schools between them now claim the largest number of adherents among those advocating a DtrH. Yet, at

---

1. F.M. CROSS, *The Themes of the Book of Kings and the Structure of the Deuteronomistic History,* in *Canaanite Myth and Hebrew Epic*, Cambridge, MA, Harvard University, 1973, pp. 274-289. Also R.N. NELSON, *The Double Redaction of the Deuteronomistic History* (JSOT SS, 18), Sheffield, JSOT Press, 1981. For a review of the scholarship on Dtr see S.L. MCKENZIE, *The Trouble with Kings: The Composition of the Book of Kings in the Deuteronomistic History* (SVT, 42), Leiden, Brill, 1991, pp. 1-19.

2. R. SMEND, *Das Gesetz und die Völker. Ein Beitrag zur deuteronomistischen Redaktionsgeschichte,* in H.W. WOLFF (ed.), *Probleme biblischer Theologie. FS G. von Rad*, München, Kaiser, 1971, pp. 494-509.

3. T. VEIJOLA, *Die ewige Dynastie. David und die Entstehung seiner Dynastie nach der deuteronomistischen Darstellung* (AASF B, 193), Helsinki, Suomalainen Tiedeakatemia, 1975; ID., *Das Königtum in der Beurteilung der deuteronomistischen Historiographie* (AASF B, 198), Helsinki, Suomalainen Tiedeakatemia, 1977; W. DIETRICH, *Prophetie und Geschichte* (FRLANT, 108), Göttingen, Vandenhoeck & Ruprecht, 1972. See also E. WÜRTHWEIN, *Die Bücher der Könige. 1. Könige 1-16* (ATD, 11,1), Göttingen, Vandenhoeck & Ruprecht, [2]1985; ID., *1. Kön. 17-2. Kön. 25* (ATD, 11,2), Göttingen, Vandenhoeck & Ruprecht, 1984.

the same time they have spawned a proliferation of further redactions and the gradual dissolution of a single comprehensive history.

It is not my purpose in this short paper, to outline and critique these positions in greater detail. Instead, I want to focus on the position of Cross and his followers and on a particular text, the story of the man of God from Judah in 1 Kings 13, and the way in which it has come to function in support of this particular school. It will also be important for a discussion about what it means to identify redactional activity within the historical work as a whole and whether redaction criticism can, in fact, salvage Noth's original contribution of a single unified history by Dtr instead of ruin it. In this respect it will have some important implications for the Göttingen school as well.

In his initial study of DtrH, Cross identified the prediction of the man of God in 1 Kings 13,2-5 that Josiah would destroy the altar at Bethel and its fulfillment in 2 Kings 22,1–23,25 as basic to understand the character and dimensions of the Dtr literary work, but he gave little detailed examination of the relevant texts[4]. Special examination of 1 Kings 13, however, was taken up by his student Werner Lemke[5] and more recently in a comprehensive defense of Cross's position by Gary Knoppers[6].

The first task is to set the limits of the account about the man of God from Judah and its relationship to its context. In my view we have Dtr's presentation of the reform of the northern cult in 1 Kings 12,26-32. Since it presupposes Deuteronomy's view of cult reform I regard it as a complete Dtr invention[7]. Nevertheless, the unit is not without some difficulties[8]. The account seems fairly clear within vv. 26-30 (restoring v. 30 with LXX) and recounts the setting up of two calves, one at Bethel and the other at Dan and that this act became the primary offense of the peo-

---

4. *Canaanite Myth*, pp. 279-280.

5. W.E. LEMKE, *The Way of Obedience: 1 Kings 13 and the Structure of the Deuteronomistic History*, in F.M. CROSS *et al.* (eds.), *Magnalia Dei, The Mighty Acts of God. In Memoriam G. Ernest Wright*, Garden City, NY, Doubleday, 1976, pp. 301-326. Based on this study NELSON (*Double Redaction*, p. 82) makes the statement: "Today it is generally recognized that 1 Kings 12:32-13:32 is an integral part of the Deuteronomistic history", and therefore needs no further debate. The same viewpoint is reflected most recently in D.W. VAN WINKLE, *1 Kings XII 25-XIII 34: Jeroboam's cultic innovations and the man of God from Judah*, in *VT* 46 (1996) 101-114.

6. G.N. KNOPPERS, *Two Nations under God: The Deuteronomistic History of Solomon and the Dual Monarchies*, 2 vols. (HSM, 52-53), Atlanta, GA, Scholars Press, 1993-1994.

7. See H.-D. HOFFMANN, *Reform und Reformen* (ATANT, 66), Zürich, Theologischer Verlag, 1980, pp. 59-73, esp. 73; J. VAN SETERS, *In Search of History*, New Haven, CT, Yale University Press, 1983, pp. 313-314; McKENZIE, *The Trouble with Kings*, p. 57.

8. Knoppers radical surgery, however, hardly seems warranted. See his remarks on the text in *Two Nations*, vol. 2, pp. 25-29.

ple and king. In what follows in vv. 31-32 the king's subsequent actions are not so clear. His first action seems to be the establishing of *bāmôt*, "high places", and staffing these with non-Levitical priests[9]. Nevertheless, v. 31 introduces a new subject not related to the golden calves and is therefore suspect. Jeroboam's next act is to establish a festival on the fifteenth day of the eighth month "like the festival in Judah". On the one hand this clearly has in mind a rival pilgrimage festival and Dtn's centralization of such festivals in the one chosen place. But Deuteronomy does not date the festivals in this way[10]. It is in P that we have a festival of booths on the fifteenth day of the **seventh** month (Lev 23,33-36). So the detail about this festival is suspect as a late addition, although it may only be the dating that is late, in which case the identity of the festival would be uncertain. The next item in v. 32aß is rather garbled. As it stands it reads: "He went up upon the altar; thus he did in Bethel to sacrifice to the calves that he had made". The shift to a particular action, "he went up on the altar", does not fit the series of reforms both before and after it and must be a modification or corruption influenced by the following verse, v. 33. The phrase, "in Bethel", is also awkward with the reference to both calves. Perhaps one could reconstruct the verse to say originally in the Dtr version: "Jeroboam set up a festival; thus [the people] went up in order to sacrifice to the calves which he had made"[11]. This would make the whole unit coherent with the one theme of the golden calves apostasy. All of this would presuppose the D code and be consistent with Dtr's view that Jeroboam had violated it. The immediate sequel to 12,32a* is in 13,34–14,20 in which the act of apostasy is followed by divine condemnation through the prophet Ahijah, the one who anointed him in the first place.

---

9. Verse 31 actually speaks of a *bēt bāmôt*, "house of the high places". One might be inclined to correct *bet* to the plural (versions), but the same phrase occurs in 2 Kings 17,29.32. S. TALMON, *Polemics and Apology in Biblical Historiography – 2 Kings 17:24-41*, in R.E. FRIEDMAN (ed.), *The Creation of Sacred Literature*, (University of California Publications, Near Eastern Studies, 22), Berkeley, CA, University of California Press, 1981, p. 63, wants to understand the singular as a reference to Bethel but the context certainly suggests a plurality of sanctuaries in the various cities.

10. KNOPPERS (*Two Nations*, p. 25) retains in his original Dtr text the reference to this late dating system, which is hardly likely.

11. The association of a festival and the offering of sacrifices to the golden calf/calves is also found in Exod 32,5-6, a text that is directly dependent upon DtrH.

The following statement about installing in Bethel the priests of the high places that he had made, however, is suspect and secondary, along with v. 31. The usage of *'md* in the hiph. in the sense of "to install", esp. of priests, is late and common to Chronicles (see 2 Chron 8,14; 31,2). The import of this addition is to vilify the cult of Bethel by suggesting that its priesthood is derived from the non-Levitical priests mentioned in v. 31 even though this action hardly makes sense in the present context.

This means that the whole of 12,33–13,33 is a *post*-Dtr addition. The technique of resumptive repetition to incorporate the new story is obvious both at the beginning in 12,33 and at the end in 13,33. Yet this is not just an editorial seam since the whole of what precedes, and 12,33 specifically, are entirely necessary to what follows. The unit 12,33–13,33 was not a part of the DtrH[12]. Furthermore, the redactional transition in 12,33 not only repeats the reference to the festival but also the addition of the post-P date change of the festival and then uses this calendar change as the specific date for the beginning of the story, shifting the focus from a series of general cult changes to a single occasion[13]. He also introduces the notion of "the altar which he [Jeroboam] had made" which is not in Dtr's list of cult changes. But this altar becomes the focus of the story that now follows. The redactional seams are not part of Dtr's effort to integrate into his work an older prophetic story but rather the work of the later writer of 1 Kings 13 to tie his story into the DtrH.

This means that I would oppose all of those attempts by both schools of Deuteronomistic redactors to see in the story of the man of God in 1 Kings 13 two older prophetic legends that have come together in an extended traditio-historical and redactional process until it was taken up by Dtr or a subsequent dtr redactor and fitted into the history. On the contrary, I want to affirm with A. Jepsen the view that the story as it stands is a unity and that it must be taken together with 2 Kings 23,16-18 as a part of the same story, not as a redactional addition[13a]. The two parts, 13,1-10 and 11-32, cannot be considered as two separate stories that have been skillfully combined by a later writer. The first part is incom-

---

12. This position is similar to that of MCKENZIE (see *The Trouble*, pp. 51-52) except that he distinguishes between the prophetic legend in 13,1-32a and the redactional seam in 12,33 and 13,23b-33 which he attributes to a **post**-Dtr redactor who inserted the piece into the DtrH.

13. KNOPPERS (*Two Nations*, 2, pp. 25-29) gets around the problem of construing 12,33 as a redactional seam by eliminating everything in the verse except the last phrase, "And he ascended the altar to burn incense" thereby retaining v. 33 in this form as part of the previous Dtr account. However, this drastic solution will not do. In his reconstruction "the altar" has not been mentioned and the shift from a series of "reforms" to a specific action is too abrupt. Since the following story makes much of this altar and since 2 Kings 23,15 specifically mentions an altar that Jeroboam made and the location "in Bethel" this strongly points to retaining the opening sentence and the explanation of the particular occasion for Jeroboam's mounting the altar.

The reason for the date of the festival in the eighth month is given in v. 33 as "in the month he devised himself", but this would be more appropriate with the date in v. 32. It would suggest that the addition of the date in v. 32 is actually the work of the "redactor" of v. 33.

13a. A. JEPSEN, *Gottesmann und Prophet. Anmerkungen zum Kapitel 1 Könige 13*, in H.W. WOLFF (ed.), *Probleme biblischer Theologie. FS G. von Rad*, München, Kaiser, 1971, pp. 171-82.

plete and meaningless without its completion in the second while the second demands the background of the first, and both halves are incomplete without the fulfillment of the predictions, both of the man of God and of the old prophet, in the actions of Josiah in 2 Kings 23,15-20. Thus, to give but one example from Jepsen's treatment, the instruction of the old prophet to be buried in the same grave in Bethel as the man of God because he believes in his prophecy against the altar in the first part of the story, relates specifically to the mention in v. 2 of the burning of human bones on the altar. This only becomes clear in 2 Kings 23,16-18 when Josiah uses the bones of the graves in Bethel to desecrate the altar but is prevented from doing so with the bones of the man of God by the report of the local population about this earlier prediction of Josiah's actions. So out of respect for the man of God he does not disturb that tomb *and this allows the old prophet's remains which have been buried with him to lie in peace as well.* Only at this point is the story actually complete and the old prophet's instructions intelligible! Furthermore, one cannot remove the story of 1 Kings 13 or 2 Kings 23,16-18 from their present context, put them together and then view them as an independent tale. The first makes sense only in the context of the Jeroboam apostasy which it assumes without mention, the second is attached directly to the Josiah reform as an episode within it. They are narratives that were specifically written for the contexts in which they are found. The redactional fit, as additions to DtrH, was the work of the narrator himself.

The secondary character of the man of God story is also obvious from the content. As Alexander Rofé pointed out[14], the vocabulary is late and not characteristic of DtrH, even when it deals with a common theme of the prophetic judgment speech. It repeatedly uses the phrase, "by the word of Yahweh" (*bdbr yhwh*), which is quite rare elsewhere and not Dtr usage[15]. It refers to the prophetic announcement by the phrase "to cry/proclaim against" (*qr' 'l*), vv. 2.4.32, which is otherwise used in prophetic narratives only in Jonah 1,2. Rofé has pointed to many other features that the story shares with Jonah[16]. Furthermore, the idea of a

---

14. A. ROFÉ, *Classes in the Prophetical Stories: Didactic Legenda and Parable*, in *Studies in Prophecy* (SVT, 26), Leiden, Brill, 1974, pp. 158-163; = ID., *The Prophetical Stories*, Jerusalem, Magnes Press, 1988, pp. 170-182.

15. Vv. 1.2.5.9.17.18.32. It is found also in 1 Kings 20,35, a story that is a late addition to DtrH, and 1 Sam 3,21 where the reading is very doubtful. It is clearly not Dtr usage.

16. *Prophetical Stories*, pp. 171-172. There are also similarities with the Balaam story, with its insistence upon absolute obedience to the word of God, as well as the wondrous aspects of the talking ass.

prophet giving a sign in the sense of producing a wonder (*ntn mwpt*) for a foreign king (v. 3) has its closest parallel in P in the story of Moses and Aaron before Pharaoh (Exod 7,9). These features consistently point to a very late date for this addition.

It should also be observed that the man of God says nothing about the golden calves that Jeroboam has made, which is everywhere else regarded by Dtr as **the great sin** of Jeroboam and the Northern Kingdom. Instead he 'cries against' the altar of Bethel as the king's primary evil deed. But Dtr never says anything about Jeroboam building an altar in 12,26-32 and it is never mentioned again until we come to 2 Kings 23,15-20. (To this we will return.) After the altar is split as a "sign" and the king is temporarily disabled, the prophet gives no word of judgment on Jeroboam and his house, as one would expect from the subsequent prophetic judgment narratives of Ahijah (14,1-20, cf. 11,29-33), Jehu, son of Hanani (16,1-4), and Elijah (21,17-24). In no case in Dtr does a prophet intercede with God for an evil king. And at the end of the interview the king and the man of God are almost on friendly terms. The nature of the prophecy uttered by the man of God (vv. 2-3) is also unparalleled in Dtr. It concerns the destruction of a holy site, but says nothing about the king's dynasty or even the destiny of the Northern state as is consistently done by Dtr. As McKenzie has argued[17], this is Dtr's constant refrain in the prophetic speeches from Jeroboam to Jehu and makes 1 Kings 13 a remarkable exception.

Let us turn again to the final prediction in 13,32 which recalls the man of God's proclamation against the altar in Bethel "and against the houses of the high places which are in the cities of Samaria". Some view this as a phrase added by Dtr because it was not mentioned by the man of God in the earlier part of the narrative[18]. But this cannot be, because the reference to the "cities of Samaria" is a blatant anachronism that is nowhere else used by Dtr for the Northern Kingdom during the monarchy period. Verse 33 is also part of the narrative that suggests that in spite of the dramatic events of 13,1-10 Jeroboam was unrepentant and it highlights the details of the additions in 12,31 and 32b about the illegitimate priests, while saying nothing about the golden calves[19]. It is also the fate of these priests, not any images of worship, that is specifically picked up in the later fulfillment.

---

17. *The Trouble with Kings*, pp. 61-80, esp. 79-80.
18. See G.H. JONES, *I and 2 Kings* (NCBC), Grand Rapids, MI, Eerdmans, 1984, vol. 1, p. 268. MCKENZIE *(The Trouble*, p. 52) attributes 13,32b to a **post**-Dtr redactor, but on pp. 124-125 its parallel in 2 Kings 23,19-20 becomes part of Dtr.
19. The phrase "to fill the hand" as it relates to the priesthood is also late, frequently in P and Chronicles, also in Judg 17,5.12.

This story with its precise prediction of Josiah's reform is then given its corresponding fulfillment in 2 Kings 23,15-20. There has been a lot of discussion about the limits of this unit and its redactional history. Certainly, if 1 Kings 12,33–13,33 is a later addition to DtrH then all of 2 Kings 23,16-20 must also be secondary. But what of v. 15? This verse is likewise suspect for a number of reasons:

1) The action against Bethel in v. 15 interrupts the royal activity in Jerusalem that continues in vv. 21ff[20].

2) Bethel does not fit the limits of the realm given in v. 8, "from Geba to Beersheba" and one cannot create out of v. 15 a "northern campaign" as a counterpart to the reform in Judah. The initial "and moreover" ($w^e gam$) is a pretty obvious indication of this addition.

3) The focus of Josiah's activity in v. 15 is "the altar in Bethel that Jeroboam... had made", but this information is given to us only in the story of the man of God (1 Kings 12,33). In both cases it is specifically the building of that altar that is identified as Jeroboam's great sin, not the golden calves about which nothing is said, even though the preceding reform narrative lists the destruction of many such cult objects. The description of how the altar was demolished is simply borrowed from the previous texts.

The remark in v. 19 that "all the temples of the high places that were in the cities of Samaria, which the kings of Israel had made... Josiah removed" recalls the anachronistic prediction of 1 Kings 13,32 and clearly belongs to the same source. Yet it also has some interesting connections with 2 Kings 17,24-34. This tells about how foreigners were placed by the Assyrians in the cities of Samaria (understood as an Assyrian province)[21] and since there were no priests of Yahweh left in the land one had to be returned by the Assyrians to teach the new population the religion of the land. But this foreign population still put their own gods in the "temples of the high places which the Samarians (foreigners) had made, each nation in their own cities where they were living". The terminology which refers to "the cities of Samaria" and "the temples of

---

20. At the end of the addition (vv. 15-20) the redactor adds the remark about Josiah's return to Jerusalem. This would suggest that the addition begins at a point where Josiah was still in Jerusalem in v. 14.

21. For a discussion of the historical background of Assyrian policy see M. COGAN and H. TADMOR, *II Kings* (AB, 11), New York, Doubleday, 1988, pp. 209-214. See also I. EPH'AL, *"The Samarian(s)" in the Assyrian Sources*, in M. COGAN, I. EPH'AL (eds.), *Ah, Assyria...: Studies in Assyrian History and Ancient Near Eastern Historiography Presented to Hayim Tadmor* (ScrHie, 33), Jerusalem, Magnes Press, 1991, pp. 36-45.

the high places" is shared by the story of the man of God but nowhere else in the book of Kings.

It is common for those of the Cross school to ascribe most of the text in 2 Kings 17,24-34 to Dtr[22] and therefore associate it with the same source as the references in 1 Kings 13,32 and 2 Kings 23,19-20. The reason for this is obvious, since the whole of Cross's thesis rests on Josiah's northern campaign against the high places of Samaria. However, the idea expressed in 2 Kings 17,24-34 that there were no priests of Yahweh and no Israelites left in the northern province of Samaria after the fall of Samaria is obviously unhistorical. And it is scarcely conceivable that anyone in the preexilic or early exilic period would have suggested any such thing. It seems to me that Würthwein is entirely correct when he argues that this is merely anti-Samaritan propaganda to discredit any association with the northern worshipers of Yahweh[23]. It cannot be earlier in date than late Persian or early Hellenistic.

The story of the man of God in 1 Kings 12,33–13,33 is directly dependent upon this text and has exactly this same purpose. It has shifted attention away from the golden calves, which have long since ceased to be a problem in Samaria, to that of the altar and temple of Bethel and all the other religious places of worship in the north. Since 2 Kings 17,29-34 suggests that all of the priests of these high places were foreign priests of foreign deities, the author of 2 Kings 23,19-20 has Josiah not only destroy the temples of the high places but also "sacrifice" (i.e. put to death) all of these priests upon their altars. This is fundamentally different from the treatment of the priests of the high places in Judah who were permitted to "eat unleavened bread among their brethren" in their local communities in conformity with Deuteronomic law.

Concerning the meaning or moral of the story about the man of God and the old prophet of Bethel, Jepsen has argued quite persuasively that the whole story is directed towards a vilification of Bethel as a cult place. The author is no longer concerned about the fate of the Northern Kingdom as in Dtr but about the continuing existence of cult places in Samaria and especially the important temple in Bethel. The message of the unit is twofold. First, the altar was completely desecrated by divine decree so that it is no longer an appropriate place of worship and the priesthood is entirely illegitimate from the beginning. Secondly, one is

---

22. KNOPPERS, *Two Nations*, pp. 8-9, 39, 67-70; McKENZIE, *The Trouble*, p. 141. See also JONES, *1 and 2 Kings*, 2, pp. 543-544, with a survey of views.

23. WÜRTHWEIN, *Die Bücher der Könige*, 2, pp. 397-403. See also TALMON, *Polemics and Apology*, pp. 57-68. I would dispute Talmon's suggestions that an old Ephraimite chronicle lies behind vv. 24.29-31, but his reasons (pp. 66-68) for seeing the rest as contemporary with Ezra-Nehemia are quite convincing.

to have no further communal association (to eat and drink) with anyone in Bethel, even those who worship Yahweh, as represented by the old prophet. This reflects the same kind of anti-Samaritan vilification that is represented by 2 Kings 17,24-34, and since it shares so much of the same terminology it could actually stem from the same hand.

The implications of this analysis are clear. There was no northern campaign against Bethel or any other of the northern cult centers by Josiah. Any reform activity and cult centralization was entirely restricted to Judah "from Geba to Beersheba", and this is confirmed by the corresponding archaeological evidence. Josiah is not presented in Dtr as someone who would revive the Davidic empire. Nor does he bring to fulfillment the divine judgment against Jeroboam. For Dtr that is realized in the destruction of the Northern Kingdom (2 Kings 17,16-18.21-23). This means that the primary reason for dating DtrH to the time of Josiah is invalid.

Furthermore, the approach of the Göttingen school as it relates to these texts is no more helpful since scholars of this school have been inclined to see in the redactions a series of dtr editors reworking previous editions or incorporating new material into older work. Thus Dietrich suggests that the story of the man of God in 1 Kings 13 is an addition by DtrP to the base DtrG, while 2 Kings 23,15-20 is distributed among several redactors. This methodology I believe is in error. What we have in both parts of this story is a late post-dtr addition that makes use of some dtr terminology in its resumptive repetition in the seams but is otherwise not in the least Deuteronomistic in its content and concerns. Once such blocks of material are bracketed, then we are left with much greater clarity about the limits and nature of DtrH.

In a similar fashion I have argued that the Court History of David is a later addition to the DtrH that goes directly counter to the basic theme of the idealization of David throughout the DtrH. Again, if this work is bracketed as secondary, then it becomes clear that in the original DtrH 2 Samuel 7 almost immediately preceded the scene in 1 Kings 2,1-4.10-12 in which David, after he has been given the divine promise by God at the end of his life, exhorts Solomon to obedience to God's laws as his final swan song. He dies and is succeeded by Solomon. This is followed in turn by 1 Kings 3ff. which leads quickly to the fulfillment of the promise of David's son building a house for God's name.

This brings us to the second pillar of Cross's position, viz, the distinction between the conditional and unconditional promise to David. Why is there no conditionality to the promise to David as there is in the case of Jeroboam? Because the promise comes to David at the end of his career as a reward for his obedience whereas it is given to Jeroboam at the beginning of his career as a future possibility. This difference has been completely obscured by the addition of the Court History which suggests that it was offered to David at the beginning of his reign in Jerusalem and that it was totally unaffected by his sin against Uriah and adultery with Bathsheba.

The first task of redaction criticism of the DtrH is not to continue to split it up into small fragments on the basis of rather dubious principles, but to identify the large amount of later additions and to retrieve the core work. It is only in this way that its unity and consistency of perspective will become apparent. Redaction criticism need not be the death of the DtrH as Noth understood it. On the contrary, it can be the means by which to revive this important thesis to new life and vitality.

University of North Carolina   John VAN SETERS
Chapel Hill, NC

L'ÉCOLE DEUTÉRONOMISTE AURAIT-ELLE
IMAGINÉ UN PREMIER CANON DES ÉCRITURES?

À moins d'être incompréhensible, aucun texte n'est entièrement isolé d'autres textes ou d'un corps de paroles: il fait appel à des notions connues de quelques lecteurs au moins, il utilise des mots usités. Bref, il s'inscrit dans une culture, dans l'entrelac infini des paroles échangées et des textes écrits. Il en va de même, bien sûr, pour les textes de la Bible. Ceux-ci forment un réseau ouvert sur l'extérieur, car chaque parole fait écho à d'autres paroles, dans la Bible elle-même et dans les cultures qui l'entourent.

Si l'on s'interroge sur la nature des liens qui relient les textes bibliques entre eux, trois types au moins peuvent être distingués. Il y a tout d'abord l'utilisation – consciente ou inconsciente – d'un texte plus ancien par l'auteur d'un nouveau texte; cette utilisation peut prendre diverses formes: citation explicite, citation implicite, commentaire, allusion, réminiscence...[1]. Pour qualifier le deuxième type de lien, je parlerai de «parallélisme». En effet, un même auteur ou une même école (au sens large) répétera spontanément – et souvent sans s'en rendre compte – les mêmes expressions, les mêmes images, les mêmes messages. Ici, les textes ne dépendent pas les uns des autres mais portent en quelque sorte la même marque de fabrique; ce phénomène peut s'observer en l'absence de tout projet d'ensemble. Le troisième type de lien concerne des textes qui forment système, et qui doivent donc être lus ensemble. Toute unité littéraire implique la présence d'un tel système: qu'elle soit longue ou courte, cette unité a sa structure propre, plus ou moins complexe, dont les éléments sont interconnectés, et donc inséparables. Certaines structures sont de type linéaire (dans une logique narrative, par exemple), d'autres de type concentrique, et différentes combinaisons sont possibles. Une telle structure s'explique bien par le projet d'un auteur qui compose son œuvre, même s'il utilise un certain nombre de matériaux qui le précèdent: il les choisit, les agence et les enrichit en fonction de son but éditorial propre.

Dans certains cas, plusieurs péricopes qui forment système proviennent manifestement du même auteur. Prenons un exemple bien connu dans le livre de Jérémie:

---

1. Ainsi, par exemple, la reprise de concepts théologiques des prophètes de malheur par le Deutéronome, étudiée par K. ZOBEL, *Prophetie und Deuteronomium* (BZAW, 199), Berlin - New York, NY, de Gruyter, 1992.

1. En 19,1–20,6, Jérémie pose un geste spectaculaire devant le peuple: il brise une cruche, signifiant ainsi la fin prochaine de Jérusalem; le prophète explique que le malheur de la ville est lié au refus d'écouter la parole divine (19,15). Le prophète est alors mis au carcan par Pashehur, chef de la police du Temple; cet événement n'est pas daté.
2. Au chap. 26, au début du règne de Yoyaqim fils de Josias, Jérémie prononce un discours dans la cour du Temple; il est alors menacé de mort par «les prêtres, les prophètes et le peuple entier» (v. 8). Au v. 3, YHWH commente les instructions qu'il donne au prophète: «peut-être écouteront-ils et se détourneront-ils chacun de sa voie perverse: alors, je me repentirai du malheur que je suis en train de méditer contre eux pour la perversité de leurs actes». L'accueil de la parole prophétique apparaît ainsi comme la dernière chance de salut pour Jérusalem.
3. Le chap. 36, enfin, est situé la quatrième et la cinquième année de Yoyaqim, et la correspondance avec le chap. 26 est soulignée par la similitude des introductions des deux péricopes (26,1; 36,1). À nouveau, la mission confiée à Jérémie est présentée comme une dernière chance de salut pour le peuple: «peut-être qu'en entendant tout le mal que j'ai le dessein de leur faire, ceux de la maison de Juda reviendront chacun de sa voie mauvaise; alors, je pourrai pardonner leur iniquité et leur péché» (v. 3). Cette fois, Jérémie fait mettre par écrit toutes ses paroles antérieures; le roi détruit le document et veut faire saisir prophète, ainsi que Baruch. Cette réaction violente de Yoyaqim apparaît donc comme un refus global et définitif du message prophétique.

Jérémie a exprimé son message par un geste prophétique, puis par un discours et enfin par un écrit. Pashehur, puis les prêtres, les prophètes et le peuple, puis enfin le roi lui-même ayant refusé de l'écouter, il ne reste plus qu'à raconter comment Jérusalem fut prise par Nabuchodonosor et quel fut le sort du prophète lui-même (chap. 37–43)[2].

Cet ensemble littéraire, qui appartient aux récits biographiques en prose du livre de Jérémie («source B», selon la terminologie de S. Mowinckel), forme un tout indissociable[3], lui-même enrichi par une ou

---

2. Certains matériaux des chap. 27–29 semblent avoir été rédigés en même temps que l'essentiel des chap. 19–20, 26 et 36, mais ils n'interviennent pas de la même manière dans la progression logique de l'ensemble. Cette dernière est malheureusement ignorée par H.-J. STIPP, *Jeremia im Parteienstreit. Studien zur Textentwicklung von Jer 26,36-43 und 45 als Beitrag zur Geschichte Jeremias, seines Buches und judäischer Parteien im 6. Jahrhundert* (BBB, 82), Frankfurt/M., Hain, 1992.

3. G. WANKE, *Untersuchungen zur sogenannten Baruchschrift* (BZAW, 122), Berlin, de Gruyter, 1971, distingue dans les récits en prose du livre de Jérémie trois ensembles

plusieurs rédactions ultérieures. Depuis les travaux de G. Wanke[4], l'attribution de ces récits à Baruch a perdu de sa vraisemblance; d'ailleurs Jr 26 (texte de type «B») dépend de Jr 7 (discours en prose de type «C»)[5]. Sans doute les textes de type «B» et «C» proviennent-ils les uns comme les autres de l'école deutéronomiste[6], à répartir en deux ou – plus vraisemblablement – trois strates successives[7]. Le fond ancien des

---

traditionnels: 1° 19,1–20,6, 26–29 et 36 proposent une série de récits complets, qui présentent toujours le même schéma: longue introduction (orale, gestuelle, écrite) de Jérémie, exposé du conflit (message contesté par les autorités), puis réaffirmation de la proclamation initiale et condamnation des opposants. 2° Les chap. 37–43 forment un seul long récit, avec divers épisodes qui s'enchaînent. 3° Les sections 45,1-5 et 51,59-64 forment deux courts récits constitués autour de paroles authentiques de Jérémie. Les chap. 37–43 présentent des caractéristiques propres, mais cela ne signifie pas qu'il faille attribuer a priori cette section à un rédacteur différent: c'est en quelque sorte le point d'orgue nécessaire de l'ensemble; il est possible cependant que ces chapitres soient plus anciens.

4. Voir la note 3. Le livre de Wanke a été suivi par de nombreux autres travaux, qui montrent toute la complexité de la question.

5. Voir H.G. REVENTLOW, *Gattung und Überlieferung in der 'Tempelrede Jeremias' Jer 7 und 26*, in *ZAW* 81 (1969) 315-352; H. WEIPPERT, *Die Prosareden des Jeremiabuches* (BZAW, 132), Berlin - New York, NY, de Gruyter, 1973, pp. 26-48, s'appuie sur cette relation de dépendance pour affirmer – d'une manière imprudente, me semble-t-il – l'authenticité jérémienne des discours en prose. La provenance deutéronomiste des chap. 7 et 26, mais aussi la probabilité de plusieurs rédactions dtr dans le livre, sont d'ailleurs confirmées par T. SEIDL, *Jeremias Tempelrede: Polemik gegen die joschijanische Reform? Die Paralleltraditionen Jer 7 und 26 auf ihre Effizienz für das Deuteronomismusproblem in Jeremia befragt*, in W. GROSS (ed.), *Jeremia und die «deuteronomistische Bewegung»* (BBB, 98), Weinheim, Beltz Athenäum, 1995, pp. 141-179; voir aussi, la confirmation, avec quelques correctifs, de J.P. FLOSS, *Methodologische Aspekte exegetischer Hypothesen am Beispiel von Theo Seidls Beitrag zur 'Tempelrede'*, in *Jeremia und die «deuteronomistische Bewegung»*, pp. 181-185.

6. Cette position a été défendue en particulier par E.W. NICHOLSON, *Preaching to the Exiles. A Study of the Prose Tradition in the Book of Jeremiah*, Oxford, Blackwell, 1970. La présence d'éléments deutéronomistes dans le livre de Jérémie a été contestée par plusieurs auteurs (R. Albertz et H.-J. Stipp, notamment), qui croient pouvoir relever des contractions entre l'Histoire deutéronomiste (Josué-Rois) et les passages deutéronomisants du livre de Jérémie; cette position critique a été réfutée par T. RÖMER, *Y a-t-il une rédaction deutéronomiste dans le livre de Jérémie?*, in A. DE PURY et al. (eds.), *Israël construit son histoire. L'historiographie deutéronomiste à la lumière des recherches récentes* (Le Monde de la Bible, 34), Genève, Labor et Fides, 1996, pp. 419-441; ID., *La conversion du prophète Jérémie à la théologie deutéronomiste*, in A.H.W. CURTIS – T. RÖMER (eds.), *The Book of Jeremiah and Its Reception – Le livre de Jérémie et sa réception* (BETL, 128), Leuven, Leuven University Press-Peeters, 1997, pp. 27-50. L'auteur parle d'une «rédaction dtr cohérente de Jr» (*La conversion*, p. 39), qui s'étendrait du chap. 7 au chap. 35, le chap. 36 appartenant à une rédaction postérieure (Dtr2); il me semble cependant que ce dernier chapitre est indissociable des épisodes racontés aux chap. 19–20 et 26.

7. Les récits de type «B», qui s'appuient sur les discours de type «C», sont eux-mêmes retravaillés par un rédacteur dont la phraséologie et la théologie fondamentale restent proches des écrits Dtr. Prenons par exemple Jr 26. Depuis longtemps déjà, on a relevé la double présentation de l'attitude du peuple à l'égard de Jérémie: aux vv. 8-9 et 24, le peuple est hostile au prophète et veut le condamner à mort; au v. 16, en revanche, «les princes et le peuple entier» s'opposent à une telle mesure et protègent Jérémie contre les prê-

discours en prose remonte à la rédaction du début de l'époque exilique
(que j'appelle Dtr575)[8], tandis que les récits en prose, qui en dépendent,
sont pour l'essentiel une composition du milieu de l'époque exilique
(Dtr560), avec des additions encore plus récentes (Dtr525).

Qu'un livre biblique ou un ensemble articulé comme le Pentateuque
forme système n'étonnera personne. Dans trois cas au moins, cependant,
on rencontre des systèmes qui affectent des blocs de textes bibliques appartenant à des grands ensembles littéraires en principe bien distincts: le
livre de Jérémie et l'histoire deutéronomiste[9], le livre d'Isaïe et la même

---

tres et les prophètes. Le v. 16 fait double emploi avec les vv. 17-19, où les Anciens prennent la défense de Jérémie; en outre, il trouve sa contrepartie exacte au v. 11, formulé en
des termes presque identiques. Autrement dit, il semble que les vv. 11 et 16, formulés
d'une manière semblable, constituent deux additions complémentaires destinées à opposer en Juda deux groupes antagonistes: d'un côté les prêtres et les prophètes, hostiles à
Jérémie, et de l'autre les princes et le peuple, qui prennent sa défense. Le récit ancien
parlait d'une prédication visant toute la population (vv. 2-6), et c'était encore toute la population qui condamnait le prophète aux vv. 8-9; celui-ci était sauvé grâce à l'intervention de «quelques anciens» (v. 17), dont en particulier Ahiqam fils de Shaphan (v. 24);
en d'autres termes, seuls quelques amis se sont montrés solidaires de lui. Le texte actuel,
au contraire, restreint la condamnation de Jérémie au groupe des prêtres et des prophètes
(vv. 11 et 16). Rien n'empêche les versets ajoutés de provenir d'un nouveau rédacteur
deutéronomiste; en tout cas, le fait de situer les prêtres et les prophètes officiels dans le
mauvais camp correspond à Dt 18, où YHWH semble instituer un nouveau clergé
(lévitique et non aaronide) et un nouveau prophétisme (à la manière de Moïse, non sur le
mode des prophètes cultuels); sur Dt 17–18 comme programme d'une restauration nationale sans les élites déportées à Babylone, voir J. VERMEYLEN, *Un programme pour la restauration d'Israël. Quelques aspects de la Loi dans le Deutéronome*, in C. FOCANT (ed.),
La Loi dans l'un et l'autre Testament (LD, 168), Paris, Cerf, 1997, pp. 45-80 (en particulier 60-63).

8. La date suggérée n'est qu'approximative, évidemment. J'ai utilisé jusqu'ici le
même sigle pour parler du rédacteur principal de l'Histoire deutéronomiste et de la première rédaction deutéronomiste du livre de Jérémie. Aujourd'hui, je n'exclus pas une première rédaction de l'Histoire deutéronomiste entre 597 et 587, comme le propose C.R.
SEITZ, *Theology in Conflict. Reactions to the Exile in the Book of Jeremiah* (BZAW, 176),
Berlin - New York, NY, de Gruyter, 1989, pp. 201-202. M. ROSE, *Idéologie deutéronomiste et théologie de l'Ancien Testament*, in A. DE PURY, *et al.* (eds.), *Israël construit son
histoire*, pp. 445-476 (spéc. 460 n. 34), refuse cette hypothèse; cependant son analyse littéraire de la finale de 2 R (pp. 453-457) va dans la même direction: la conclusion originelle de l'ouvrage se trouve en 24,20 («Cela arriva à Jérusalem et à Juda à cause de la
colère de YHWH, tant qu'enfin il les rejeta loin de sa face»), immédiatement suivi par
25,21b («Ainsi, Juda fut déporté loin de sa terre»); l'essentiel du chap. 25 paraît constituer une addition résumant Jr 39–41. Il faut ajouter que cette notice finale se rattache dif-
ficilement à 24,17-19 (règne de Sédécias); selon la meilleure vraisemblance, elle se rapporte plutôt au récit de la première déportation aux vv. 10-16. Cela n'implique pas que
l'auteur ait fait partie des déportés.

9. Déjà N. LOHFINK, *Gab es eine deuteronomistische Bewegung?*, in GROSS, *Jeremia
und die «deuteronomistische Bewegung»*, pp. 313-382 (360), signale ce qu'il appelle des
«Querverweisen» entre 2 R 24–25 et Jr 39–41 et 52. Je ne suis pas certain, cependant,
que les références croisées soient l'œuvre de rédacteurs deutéronomistes, comme Lohfink
le suggère. Ainsi, 2 R 25,22-26 paraît résumer Jr 40,5–41,18, texte auquel il emprunte
presque toute son information; l'addition pourrait provenir non de Dtr, mais d'un rédac-

histoire deutéronomiste[10], le livre de l'Exode et celui du Deutéronome. Et, dans les trois cas, le système, qu'on peut aussi qualifier de «réseau», me paraît marqué par la même rédaction deutéronomiste du milieu de l'époque exilique, comme l'exemple proposé ci-dessus. Si cette observation est pertinente, les implications pour le projet éditorial de l'école deutéronomiste pourraient s'avérer considérables.

I. Jr 36 et 2 R 22–23

Au chap. 36 du livre de Jérémie (chap. 43 dans la LXX), le prophète dicte à Baruch un rouleau contenant tous ses oracles antérieurs. Ce rouleau est lu successivement devant le peuple, devant les princes et devant le roi, qui réagit avec violence: il détruit le rouleau et veut s'emparer du prophète.

Dès 1978, C.D. Isbell[11] a rapproché Jr 36, qui forme le sommet de la série déjà évoquée ci-dessus, et le récit de la découverte du rouleau de la Tôrah par Josias en 2 R 22–23. L'auteur note une série de similitudes: dans les deux cas, le lecteur apprend l'apparition d'un livre revêtu de l'autorité prophétique et présenté comme parole de YHWH (2 R 22,19; Jr 36,2.4.6); cet écrit, dont le contenu chargé de menaces[12] est inconnu jusque là, fait l'objet de trois lectures successives – au cours de la même journée – devant des auditoires différents: Shaphan, le roi Josias et le peuple dans 2 R 22–23; le peuple, les princes fils de Shaphan et le roi Yoyaqim fils de Josias en Jr 36. En même temps, les deux épisodes s'opposent: Josias brûle (*sārap*[ʰ]) les objets de culte païen (23,4), le «chariot du soleil» (23,11), le pieu sacré de Béthel (23,15), les ossements des idolâtres (23,16), les os des prêtres des hauts-lieux (23,20), tandis que Yoyaqim brûle le rouleau (Jr 36,27.28.32; cf. vv. 25.29)[13].

---

teur de l'époque perse, soucieux de montrer que le pays a été vidé de toute population judéenne (v. 26; voir déjà le v. 21b, qui peut avoir été écrit en même temps); c'est le point de vue des Sionistes (voir 2 Ch 36,20; Esd 4,1-5). De même, la reprise de 2 R 24,18–25,30 en Jr 52 n'est pas forcément l'œuvre d'un rédacteur deutéronomiste. De toute manière, le phénomène qui m'intéresse ici dépasse de loin le cas de références croisées.

10. Comme on le sait, 2 R 18–20 et Is 36–39 apparaissent comme deux variantes d'un même texte. Sur les relations entre ces deux ensembles, je me permets de renvoyer à mon article *Hypothèses sur l'origine d'Isaïe 36–39*, in J. van Ruiten – M. Vervenne (eds.), *Studies in the Book of Isaiah* (BETL, 132), Leuven, Leuven University Press-Peeters, 1997, pp. 95-118. Ce n'est pas ce genre de doublet que j'envisage ici.

11. C.D. Isbell, *2 Kings 22:3–23:24 and Jeremiah 36: A Stylistic Comparison*, in *JSOT* 8 (1978) 33-45.

12. Il est chaque fois question de la «grande colère» de YHWH (2 R 22,13; Jr 36,7).

13. Jr 36,24 ajoute que Yoyaqim ne déchire pas ses vêtements comme Josias en 2 R 22,11; cependant ce verset est sans doute secondaire.

2 R 22,11.18.19 insiste sur le fait que Josias «écoute», mais on ne fait que lire le rouleau en présence de Yoyaqim, sans parler d'«écoute».

Comment faut-il imaginer le rapport entre les deux textes? Pour Isbell, Jr 36 dépend de 2 R 22–23, car on reconnaît généralement dans ce dernier texte au moins une «base» antérieure à l'école deutéronomiste. Pour C. Minette de Tillesse[14], au contraire, 2 R 22–23 serait une composition deutéronomiste inspirée par le récit de la réforme de Joas (2 R 12)[15] et par Jr 36, composition qui aurait pour but de donner son explication ultime au drame de l'année 587. Les deux auteurs raisonnent en termes de dépendance littéraire, la priorité étant déterminée par l'ancienneté supposée plus grande de l'un ou de l'autre texte. Pour ma part, je remarque surtout qu'ils forment système, comme le souligne en d'autres termes Th. Römer: «Ces deux textes opposent deux archétypes de comportement face à la parole divine et... ils peuvent être lus comme des récits de réforme et d'anti-réforme»[16]. Plus précisément, il y a opposition entre la génération des pères qui font bon accueil au livre de YHWH et celle des fils (les fils de Shaphan, le fils de Josias) qui veulent, au contraire, le détruire. En raison de son attitude exemplaire, Josias est «entendu» par YHWH (2 R 22,19), mais la génération des fils ne veut pas entendre la parole divine et perd ainsi sa chance d'éviter le grand malheur (cf. Jr 36,3). Il me semble donc que les deux textes sont inséparables et renvoient l'un à l'autre: c'est de leurs ressemblances comme de leurs oppositions que ressort leur message essentiel, qui correspond en tous points aux préoccupations de Dtr560[17]: la parole prophétique comme dernier appel à la fidélité et donc comme ultime chance de salut de Juda, la rétribution de chaque génération en fonction de sa propre conduite.

En effet, et même si le texte comporte un fond antérieur[18], 2 R 22–23 porte la marque de la rédaction deutéronomiste du milieu de l'époque

---

14. C. Minette de Tillesse, *Joiaqim, repoussoir du 'pieux' Josias: parallélismes entre II Reg 22 et Jer 36*, in *ZAW* 105 (1993) 352-376.

15. Voir déjà H.-D. Hoffmann, *Reform und Reformen. Untersuchungen zu einem Grundthema der deuteronomistischen Geschichtsschreibung* (ATANT, 66), Zürich, Zwingli Verlag, 1980, pp. 169-170.

16. T. Römer, *Y a-t-il une rédaction deutéronomiste dans le livre de Jérémie?*, p. 440. Le même auteur écrit dans *La conversion du prophète Jérémie*, p. 47: «Peu nous importe ici de connaître la dépendance littéraire des deux récits; ce qui est important, c'est le fait que ces deux textes veulent être lus et entendus l'un en relation avec l'autre». Je ne pourrais mieux dire!

17. Sur ce point, voir J. Vermeylen, *L'affaire du veau d'or (Ex 32–34). Une clé pour la «question deutéronomiste»?*, in *ZAW* 97 (1985) 1-23; Id., *Le Dieu de la promesse et le Dieu de l'Alliance* (LD, 126), Paris, Cerf, 1986, pp. 113-131.

18. Le récit joue déjà un rôle structurel dans l'Histoire deutéronomiste sous sa forme initiale (Dtr575), comme l'a montré notamment T. Römer, *Transformations in Deutero-*

exilique (Dtr560). Cela vaut en particulier pour l'intervention de la prophétesse Hulda (2 R 22,11-20), généralement considérée comme un élément secondaire du récit. Outre l'intérêt pour la parole prophétique, rele-
vons en particulier l'affirmation de Josias au v. 13, selon laquelle la colère de YHWH «s'est enflammée contre *nous* parce que *nos pères* n'ont
pas obéi». La punition injuste de la génération des fils des coupables se
trouve au cœur de la problématique de Dtr560 (voir Dt 1,35.39; 2,14-
25), selon le principe énoncé en Jr 31,29-30: «En ces jours-là, on ne
dira plus: 'Les pères ont mangé des raisins verts, et les dents des fils
sont agacées', mais chacun mourra pour sa propre faute». Ici, les vv. 19-
20 supposent également que la génération fidèle est épargnée, mais
qu'une autre génération verra de grands malheurs frapper Jérusalem. Jr
36 raconte précisément comment la génération des fils (Yoyaqim et ses
princes) a refusé le livre du prophète, alors que la génération des pères
avait au contraire mis en pratique le livre de la Tôrah, authentifié par la
parole de la prophétesse. En 2 R 22, ce sont les éléments introduits par
Dtr560 (vêtements déchirés, colère de YHWH, noms des princes, consultation de la prophétesse) qui permettent d'établir le lien avec Jr 36.

Jr 36 a également connu une histoire littéraire en deux étapes. G.
Wanke[19] a relevé dans le récit trois parenthèses (vv. 17-19; 24-25; 29-
31), qui font figure d'additions:

– Le v. 20 (ambassade auprès du roi) suit logiquement le v. 16 (nécessité d'informer le roi); les vv. 17-19, qui interrompent le fil du récit,
  insistent sur l'origine prophétique du rouleau et interprètent la frayeur
  des princes (*pāḥ^adû*, v. 16), comme s'ils craignaient pour la vie de Jérémie. Les princes prennent ainsi le parti du prophète, contre le roi.
– Les vv. 24-25 disent curieusement ce que le roi ne fait pas. Encore
  une fois, les princes sont du côté du prophète, alors que le roi et ses
  serviteurs détruisent le livre des paroles de Jérémie.
– Au v. 28, YHWH ordonne à Jérémie de réécrire ses paroles sur un
  autre rouleau; au-delà des vv. 29-31, qui parlent du sort personnel de
  Yoyaqim et de la fin de la monarchie judéenne, ces ordres sont exécu-
  tés point par point au v. 32. Comme au v. 24, le roi est associé à ses
  «serviteurs» (*^{ca}bādāyw*, v. 31).

nomistic and Biblical Historiography. On «Book Finding» and Other Literary Strategies,
in *ZAW* 109 (1997) 1-11. L'auteur rappelle (p. 6) que le v. 8 (découverte du livre de la
Tôrah) interrompt l'exposé de la réparation du Temple (vv. 3-7 et 9), et qu'il différencie
le récit de la réforme de Josias des autres récits comparables. On peut donc penser que cet
élément est secondaire; dans ce cas, il a pu avoir été introduit soit par Dtr575, soit par
Dtr560.
    19. G. WANKE, *Untersuchungen zur sogenannten Baruchschrift*, pp. 65-70.

Les additions des vv. 17-19, 24-25 et 29-31 ont pour point commun de distinguer à l'intérieur de la nation les partisans de Jérémie (les princes) et ses opposants (le roi et ses serviteurs)[20]. Cela a pour effet de brouiller la progression logique qui sous-tend les récits en prose depuis le chap. 19 (refus de la parole prophétique par le chef de la police du Temple, puis par les prêtres, les prophètes et le peuple, et enfin par le roi). Sans les parenthèses, le récit du chap. 36 présente un ordre régulier très élaboré[21], et il apparaît comme la suite logique des sections 19,1–20,6 et 26,1-10.12-15.17-24, où nous avons reconnu la marque de Dtr560. C'est également dans ce récit primitif qu'on rencontre les analogies avec 2 R 22–23.

J'en conclus que la même école deutéronomiste du milieu de l'époque exilique a conçu un ensemble de textes opposant Josias et Yoyaqim, reliant ainsi de manière organique l'Histoire deutéronomiste et le livre de Jérémie. Pour atteindre cet objectif, elle a remanié l'histoire de Josias (2 R 22–23) et a écrit la série des récits sur le refus de la parole du prophète. En d'autres termes, nous ne sommes pas en présence d'un simple cas d'emprunt ou d'imitation d'un texte plus ancien par un nouveau rédacteur: l'opposition entre l'attitude exemplaire de Josias et celle, désastreuse, de son fils est une création délibérée, qui suppose un seul système réunissant des écrits jusque-là bien distincts.

II. Is 36–37 (2 R 18–19), Is 7, 2 R 22–23 et Jr 36

Un deuxième système, relié au premier, a pour pièce centrale le récit de l'ambassade de l'échanson envoyé par Sennachérib à Ézéchias en l'an 701, récit qui figure sous deux formes presque identiques en Is 36,2–37,9a.37-38 et 2 R 18,17–19,9a.36-37 et que plusieurs exégètes désignent par le sigle «B1»[22]. Selon l'hypothèse classique, nous serions en présence d'un texte ancien, qui a d'abord fait partie du livre des Rois avant d'être transféré dans celui d'Isaïe[23]. K.A.D. Smelik[24] a mis cepen-

---

20. Le phénomène est en tous points semblable à l'addition des vv. 11 et 16 au chap. 26; voir ci-dessus, la note 7. On attribuera logiquement cette rédaction à Dtr525.

21. Voir le plan proposé par G. WANKE, *Untersuchungen zur sogenannten Baruchschrift*, p. 71.

22. Notamment F. GONÇALVES, *L'expédition de Sennachérib en Palestine dans la littérature hébraïque ancienne* (Publications de l'Institut Orientaliste de Louvain, 34), Louvain-la-Neuve, Institut Orientaliste, 1986, pp. 373-444.

23. Voir encore R.F. PERSON, Jr., *The Kings–Isaiah and Kings–Jeremiah Recensions* (BZAW, 252), Berlin - New York, NY, de Gruyter, 1997, p. 5.

24. K.A.D. SMELIK, *Distortion of Old Testament Prophecy. The Purpose of Isaiah xxxvi and xxxvii*, in COLL., *Crises and Perspectives. Studies in Ancient Near Eastern Polytheism, Biblical Theology, Palestinian Archaeology and Intertestamental Literature*

dant en évidence plusieurs indices permettant de penser qu'au contraire, le récit a été conçu dès son origine en fonction du livre d'Isaïe, et je crois qu'il faut lui donner raison[25]. Plus précisément, le rédacteur du récit B1 utilise la brève notice A (36,1) et s'inspire de B2 (37,9b-20.33-35), tout en reprenant d'autres éléments du livre, comme les noms des hauts fonctionnaires (22,15-23; 36,3). D'autre part, j'ai cru pouvoir montrer que ce texte porte, comme les passages évoqués ci-dessus, la marque de l'école deutéronomiste[26]. Le récit B1 d'Is 36–37 (ou son parallèle dans le livre des Rois) forme système à la fois avec l'histoire d'Achaz rapportée en Is 7 et avec celles de Josias (2 R 22–23) et de Yoyaqim (Jr 36).

Considérons tout d'abord le parallélisme entre Is 7 («histoire d'Achaz») et Is 36–39 («histoire d'Ézéchias»):

– Les deux récits sont rédigés à la troisième personne et s'inscrivent dans le cadre de l'invasion par une armée étrangère (les armées syro-éphraïmites, 7,1-2; l'armée assyrienne commandée par l'échanson de Sennachérib, 36,2);
– Un discours à ce sujet est tenu au même endroit précis, «près du canal de la piscine supérieure, sur le chemin du champ du foulon» (discours d'Isaïe, 7,3; discours de l'échanson, 36,2);
– Isaïe délivre chaque fois un «oracle de guerre», qui s'ouvre par l'appel à ne pas craindre (*'al-tîrā'*) et annonce la défaite ennemie (7,4-9; 37,6-7)[27].

(OTS, 24), Leiden, Brill, 1986, pp. 70-93; ID., *King Hezekiah Advocates True Prophecy: Remarks on Isaiah XXXVI and XXXVII // II Kings XVIII and XIX*, in ID., *Converting the Past. Studies in Ancient Israelite and Moabite Historiography* (OTS, 28), Leiden, Brill, 1992, pp. 93-128.

25. Ainsi, toute une série d'éléments du texte sont empruntés ou tout au moins apparentés à la tradition isaïenne. Par exemple, on retrouve associés en Is 36,3.11 les noms des maîtres du palais Élyaqim fils de Hilqiyyahu (Is 22,20) et Shebna (Is 22,15), alors qu'en Is 22 le second est destitué au profit du premier. Pour une évaluation des indices pour et contre la priorité d'Is 36–39, voir J. VERMEYLEN, *Hypothèses*, pp. 96-108.

26. J. VERMEYLEN, *Hypothèses*, pp. 113-115. Tel est aussi l'avis de S. DE JONG, *Het verhaal van Hizkia en Sanherib. 2 Koningen 18,17–19,37 / Jesaja 36–37 als narratieve reflectie op de Ballingschap*, in *ACEBT* 10 (1989) 57-91, p. 68; l'auteur ne distingue cependant pas entre B1 et B2. Is 36,17 fait allusion à la déportation. E. BEN ZVI, *Who Wrote the Speech of Rabshakeh and When?*, in *JBL* 109 (1990) 79-92, pp. 85-88, relève un certain nombre d'expressions du discours de l'échanson qui trouvent leur meilleur parallèle dans des textes réputés deutéronomistes ou apparentés (comme les discours en prose de Jérémie); il pense cependant que ces deutéronomismes sont le fait d'additions (voir surtout p. 92). D'autre part, Isaïe déclare, au nom de YHWH: «Voici que je vais mettre en lui (Ézéchias) un esprit et, sur une nouvelle qu'il entendra, il retournera dans son pays»; le don de cet esprit peut être rapproché de 1 R 22 Dtr, où l'Esprit va tromper Achab, de telle sorte qu'il meure à Ramot de Galaad.

27. E.W. CONRAD, *The Royal Narratives and the Structure of the Book of Isaiah*, in *JSOT* 41 (1988) 67-81, ajoute encore trois éléments communs: la terreur du roi (7,2;

La parenté entre l'«histoire d'Achaz» et l'«histoire d'Ézéchias» est bien réelle. En fait, les deux figures – encore une fois, il s'agit d'un père et de son fils – sont opposées comme type et antitype: là même où Achaz a manqué de foi (cf. 7,9b et 10-13), Ézéchias réagit d'une manière exemplaire: dès qu'il a entendu le message de l'échanson, le roi déchire ses vêtements et se rend au Temple, puis il sollicite la prière du prophète Isaïe. Là où le père s'est opposé au prophète, le fils à fait appel au même prophète. Jusqu'ici, cependant, le phénomène peut être considéré comme assez banal, puisque le système se situe à l'intérieur d'un seul et même livre biblique.

Ce qui est plus étonnant, c'est que ce système est connecté à celui dont j'ai parlé plus haut, entre les livres des Rois et celui de Jérémie. En effet, Achaz, rebelle à la parole prophétique et son fils Ézéchias qui sollicite cette même parole correspondent à Yoyaqim, qui détruit le rouleau des paroles prophétiques et à son père Josias, le roi réformateur qui consulte la prophétesse Hulda. L'analogie générale est renforcée par une série d'éléments plus précis.

- La mention d'Èlyaqim fils de Hilqiyyahu, de Shebna et de Yoah fils d'Asaph en Is 36,3.11.22 est parallèle à celle des princes du temps de Josias[28] et du temps de Yoyaqim[29].
- Comme en 2 R 22–23 et Jr 36, le message – oral, cette fois – est transmis à trois auditoires: les princes, puis le peuple (assis sur les remparts, et qui comprend![30]), et enfin le roi; l'ordre des auditoires est

37,1), le signe (*'ôt*), destiné à confirmer l'accomplissement de l'oracle (7,10-16; 37,30-32), et enfin le salut de Jérusalem, avec l'annonce d'une nouvelle catastrophe (7,15-17.20; 39,6-7). En fait, je crois que 37,30-32 et 39,6-7 sont des passages qui relèvent de rédactions postérieures; quant à la réaction de frayeur du roi, elle se situe à des moments différents du récit, et 37,1 exprime le deuil plutôt que la terreur.

28. Le prêtre Hilqiyyahu, le secrétaire Shaphan, ainsi que Ahiqam, Akbor et Asaya (2 R 22,8-14).

29. Mikayehu fils de Gemaryahu fils de Shaphan, Élishama, Delayahu fils de Semayahu, Elnatan fils d'Akbor, etc. (Jr 36,11-12). Dans le cas d'Is 36, il est probable que le narrateur ne disposait pas d'information sur les fonctionnaires d'Ézéchias en dehors du chap. 22 du même livre, où l'on voit Shebna destitué comme maître du palais et remplacé par Élyaqim. Au chap. 36, Élyaqim est toujours maître du palais, mais Shebna est devenu secrétaire, ce qui est historiquement assez invraisemblable: s'il est tombé en disgrâce, ce n'était pas pour recevoir un poste de cette importance. Le nom de Yoah fils d'Asaph est inconnu par ailleurs dans la Bible hébraïque, mais on observe qu'un autre Yoah (fils de Yoahaz le héraut) est mentionné dans le récit chroniste de la réforme de Josias (2 Ch 34,8), en association avec un autre Hilqiyyahu, grand prêtre (voir aussi 2 R 22,4). Nous avons donc ici un nouveau contact, indirect, avec l'histoire de Josias. Il n'est guère utilisable, cependant: peut-être est-il dû au seul hasard.

30. Il est historiquement peu vraisemblable que le grand échanson de Sennachérib ait été capable de tenir un discours en langue judéenne, comme le dit pourtant 36,13. Ce motif appartient plutôt aux stéréotypes deutéronomistes de la parole reçue aux différents niveaux de pouvoir, et notamment par le roi (voir aussi Jr 26).

différent dans chaque texte, mais les groupes sont les mêmes et, chaque fois, l'instance décisive est celle du souverain.

- Comme Josias, le roi déchire ses vêtements (37,1), puis il envoie les princes auprès du prophète (v. 2).
- Le parallèle avec Josias est encore souligné en 36,7: le grand échanson explique qu'Ézéchias «a supprimé les hauts lieux et les autels en disant aux gens de Juda et de Jérusalem: 'C'est devant cet autel que vous vous prosternerez'»; le roi aurait donc ordonné une réforme religieuse qui anticipe celle de l'an 622 (cf. 2 R 23,4-14)[31].

Pour l'auteur du récit B1, Ézéchias agit comme le pieux roi Josias, mais à l'inverse des rois impies Achaz et Yoyaqim. Cet ensemble de parallélismes est tellement important à ses yeux, qu'il commande les modifications apportées au scénario du récit plus ancien (récit B2, 37,9b-21.33-35) et interprète celui-ci dans la ligne morale de l'école deutéronomiste[32]. La pierre de touche du jugement, c'est l'attitude de confiance envers YHWH, par opposition aux dieux des nations (36,18-20). Et cette confiance s'exprime par le recours au prophète. En l'an 701, Ézéchias est resté fidèle à son Dieu, et YHWH a délivré Jérusalem: c'est ce qui se serait passé en 587 si Sédécias et ses prédécesseurs avaient eu la même attitude.

Le système que nous avons repéré entre 2 R 22–23 et Jr 19–20; 26 et 36 s'étend donc aussi au livre d'Isaïe, avec les chap. 7 et 36–37, où nous constatons la même opposition entre deux générations à l'intérieur de la dynastie davidique. Cela correspond aux préoccupations essentielles de Dtr560. Et même si l'hypothèse de Smelik s'avérait erronée et qu'il fallait s'en tenir à l'opinion classique de la priorité de 2 R 18–20 sur Is 36–39, nous aurions également un système qui relie des grands blocs littéraires tenus jusqu'ici pour indépendants.

III. Ex 19–24 et le livre du Deutéronome

Un deuxième système, indépendant du premier, concerne l'Exode et le Deutéronome. Il est probable que ce dernier livre a d'abord servi d'in-

---

31. H. WILDBERGER, *Die Rede des Rabsake vor Jerusalem*, in *TZ* 35 (1979) 35-47, pp. 38-39, explique que le v. 7b ne correspond pas à la réforme d'Ézéchias comme 2 R 18,4-5 la présente et n'a sans doute aucun fondement historique. De cette observation, il tire cependant une conclusion indue: le v. 7b formerait une addition dans le discours.

32. F. GONÇALVES, *L'expédition*, pp. 449 et 479, a montré que B1 et B2 ont la même structure, utilisent une série d'éléments communs et ne peuvent être tenus pour indépendants l'un de l'autre. Je pense cependant que B1 s'appuie sur B2, et non l'inverse, comme je l'ai montré dans *Hypothèses*, pp. 112-113.

troduction à l'Histoire deutéronomiste[33], et qu'il n'en a été détaché qu'à l'époque perse. Nous serions donc à nouveau en présence d'un réseau dépassant les frontières entre les grands blocs littéraires. Comme j'ai déjà exposé ailleurs[34] les rapports que je crois pouvoir déceler entre ces textes, je me contenterai ici d'un bref résumé.

G. Braulik[35] a montré une correspondance étonnante entre l'ordre des lois du Décalogue (Dt 5) et du Code deutéronomique (Dt 12–26): tout fonctionne comme si le Code interprétait le Décalogue et l'appliquait à diverses situations particulières. Il y a donc la «loi fondamentale» et les «prescriptions particulières», et cette dualité correspond à la structure des traités proche-orientaux dits «de vassalité», modèle littéraire des théologiens deutéronomistes de l'Alliance.

Le rapport entre le Décalogue du livre de l'Exode (20,2-17) et le Code de l'Alliance (20,22–23,33) est analogue. Cette fois, l'ordre est différent, mais on peut constater que chacun des commandements du Décalogue trouve son correspondant dans le *Bundesbuch*. Parmi les prescriptions qui correspondent au Décalogue, les éléments de forme participiale (21,15-17; 22,19) et les commandements apodictiques explicitement religieux (23,12.13)[36] ont vraisemblablement été introduits par un rédacteur deutéronomiste. Ce dernier a donc compris le Code comme une illustration ou une application pratique du Décalogue; sans doute est-ce lui qui a introduit le Code dans son contexte actuel, à la suite presque immédiate du Décalogue. La scène de la ratification de l'Alliance par Israël, au chap. 24, témoigne de cette interprétation du rapport entre les deux recueils législatifs. Dans le texte le plus ancien, on lit: «Ils dirent: 'Toutes les paroles (*d^ebārîm*) que YHWH a prononcées, nous les mettrons en pratique'» (v. 3b). La phrase, qui figurait déjà dans le récit utilisé par le narrateur principal de Dt 5–11* (voir Dt 5,27b), vise le Déca-

33. Telle était déjà l'opinion défendue par M. NOTH, *Überlieferungsgeschichtliche Studien: Die sammelnden und bearbeitenden Geschichtswerke im Alten Testament*, Halle, Niemeyer, 1943; voir encore récemment M. ROSE, *Idéologie deutéronomiste*, pp. 447-448. Pour un aperçu des discussions postérieures à Noth, voir H.-D. PREUSS, *Deuteronomium* (EdF, 164), Darmstadt, Wissenschaftliche Buchgesellschaft, 1982, pp. 20-26. Le système formé par Dt 11,29; 27,4-8 et Jos 8,30-35 (ordre et mise en œuvre) se situe à l'intérieur du même bloc littéraire s'étendant du Deutéronome à 2 R.

34. J. VERMEYLEN, *Un programme pour la restauration d'Israël*, pp. 52-57.

35. G. BRAULIK, *Die Abfolge der Gesetze in Deuteronomium 12–26 und der Dekalog*, in N. LOHFINK (ed.), *Das Deuteronomium. Entstehung, Gestalt und Botschaft* (BETL, 68), Leuven, Leuven University Press-Peeters, pp. 252-272 = ID., *Studien zur Theologie des Deuteronomiums* (SBAAT, 2), Stuttgart, Verlag Katholisches Bibelwerk, 1988, pp. 213-255; ID., *Die deuteronomistischen Gesetze und der Dekalog. Studien zum Aufbau von Deuteronomium 12–26* (SBS, 145), Stuttgart, Katholisches Bibelwerk, 1991.

36. On remarquera que la justification du sabbat (v. 12) correspond à l'interprétation du Décalogue en Dt 5,14-15, et non à celle de Ex 20,11. De même, le v. 13 trouve un parallèle proche en Jos 23,7 Dtr.

logue (cf. *dᵉbārîm*, 20,1), et lui seul. Elle est interprétée et complétée par le rite du sang, qui solennise la promesse d'Israël et l'interprète comme promesse de fidélité à l'Alliance (v. 8). Dans ce nouveau cadre littéraire, où l'on reconnaît la main de Dtr[37], le v. 3a utilise cette fois deux expressions: «toutes les paroles (*dᵉbārîm*) de YHWH» (= le Décalogue) et «toutes les prescriptions (*mišpatîm*)» (= le Code de l'Alliance, cf. 23,1)[38]. Cette juxtaposition se comprend bien si le Code concrétise les Dix Paroles.

Le Décalogue du livre de l'Exode et celui du Deutéronome sont l'un et l'autre flanqués d'un Code plus détaillé, qui en fait l'application concrète. Le premier est donné au début de la marche au désert, et il sera trahi par Israël; le second est donné à la veille d'entrer dans la Terre promise (pour la génération de Josué, qui suit celle de Moïse). Tout cela fait système, d'autant plus que le rapprochement entre Décalogue et Code est, dans les deux cas, l'œuvre de la même école deutéronomiste. Et, comme pour le vaste système réunissant l'Histoire deutéronomiste, Isaïe et Jérémie, il semble bien que l'apport de Dtr560 soit ici décisif. En effet, ce nouveau système concerne, encore une fois, deux générations successives. Surtout, le Code deutéronomique, entouré et truffé de parénèses, est donné comme programme concret de restauration d'Israël, une fois qu'il sera rentré dans le pays du bonheur, afin que ce séjour soit durable (cf. Dt 11,8-9). Cela correspond à la préoccupation de Dtr560, écrite du point de vue de la nouvelle génération: pour elle, il importe moins de montrer les causes du grand malheur provoqué par la faute des pères que de prendre de bonnes résolutions afin qu'un avenir durable puisse être assuré à Israël après le temps du châtiment.

IV. UN PROJET DE «CANON DES ÉCRITURES» AVANT LA LETTRE?

On peut considérer que l'école deutéronomiste a édité ou réédité toute la littérature religieuse israélite connue au début de l'époque exilique: les récits et les lois formant ce qui deviendra l'ensemble Genèse-Nombres[39]; la grande fresque historique s'étendant du Deutéronome au se-

---

37. L'origine du texte est discutée, la plupart des auteurs parlant soit de Dtr, soit d'une tradition indépendante, soit encore de plusieurs strates littéraires. On trouvera un bon exposé de la question dans B. RENAUD, *La théophanie du Sinaï. Ex 19–24. Exégèse et théologie* (CRB, 30), Paris, Gabalda, 1991, pp. 69-75.

38. Le mot *mišpāṭîm*, fréquent dans les passages récents du Deutéronome, ne connaît que ces deux occurrences dans l'Exode, ce qui renforce évidemment le lien. Notons aussi que, les vv. 1-2 étant plus récents (P), Ex 24,3 suivait immédiatement le *Bundesbuch*.

39. Le verdict négatif de J. VAN SETERS, *The Deuteronomistic Redactions of the Pentateuch. The Case against It*, in M. VERVENNE – J. LUST (eds.), *Deuteronomy and*

cond livre des Rois; les recueils prophétiques (au moins Isaïe, Jérémie, Amos, Osée et Michée)[40]. Cette entreprise a été conçue, au moins par Dtr560, comme un immense ensemble de trois groupes de textes interconnectés, un réseau où les éléments communiquent d'un groupe à l'autre[41]. Avec deux objectifs: expliquer le grand malheur et ouvrir un programme d'action pour le temps, considéré comme proche, du bonheur retrouvé. Le tout est placé sous l'autorité des prophètes, à commencer par Jérémie.

Je crois pouvoir affirmer que le projet de cette édition avait une envergure telle, qu'on peut parler en termes de «canon des Écritures»[42]. Le canon n'est pas une simple liste de textes autorisés, qui déterminerait le contenu d'une bibliothèque de tous les livres considérés comme saints, et donc normatifs pour la communauté croyante: c'est aussi la constitution d'un vaste livre, avec sa logique propre et ses articulations, comme avec ses frontières. Pour autant que mes observations soient exactes, le projet de Dtr560 est de cet ordre.

1° L'auteur a rassemblé tous les textes qui lui paraissaient faire autorité en Israël. Cette compilation a sans doute déjà été entreprise par le premier rédacteur deutéronomiste (Dtr575), dans le but de sauver la crédibilité de YHWH après le grand malheur. Tous les textes plus anciens ont alors été réédités, avec des compléments destinés à les mettre au service d'une même vision de l'histoire dominée par la théologie de l'Alliance. Le même rédacteur Dtr575 a probablement déjà rassemblé dans le même but certaines collections – écrites ou orales – d'oracles prophé-

Deuteronomic Literature. FS C.H.W. Brekelmans (BETL, 133), Leuven, Leuven University Press-Peeters, 1997, pp. 301-319, ne concerne que DtrN, la strate deutéronomiste la plus récente selon l'«école de Göttingen».

40. Pour une vue d'ensemble, voir T. RÖMER – A. DE PURY, *L'historiographie deutéronomiste (HD). Histoire de la recherche et enjeux du débat*, in DE PURY et al., *Israël construit son histoire*, pp. 9-120, spéc. 58-71. Je continue à croire que le livre d'Isaïe comporte des éléments deutéronomistes, malgré l'avis de plusieurs auteurs, dont en particulier C.H.W. BREKELMANS, *Deuteronomic Influence in Isaiah 1–12*, in J. VERMEYLEN (ed.), *The Book of Isaiah – Le livre d'Isaïe. Les oracles et leurs relectures. Unité et complexité de l'ouvrage* (BETL, 81), Leuven, Leuven University Press-Peeters, 1989, pp. 167-176.

41. Les systèmes de références croisées observées ci-dessus ne forment qu'un élément de l'interconnexion. Ainsi par exemple, C.H.W. BREKELMANS, *Joshua xxiv: Its Place and Function*, in J.A. EMERTON (ed.), *Congress Volume Leuven 1989* (SVT, 43), Leiden, Brill, 1991, pp. 1-9, a attiré l'attention sur le fait que Jos 24, texte qui porte la marque de l'école deutéronomiste (ce qui n'exclut pas l'usage de sources), fait référence à la fois à l'ensemble de l'Hexateuque et à l'histoire qui suit jusqu'en 1 S 12.

42. «Ainsi se pose la question de savoir dans quelle mesure la formation et la rédaction d'un livre biblique s'inscrivent dans un phénomène d'édition et de canonisation plus vaste»: cette question est posée, à propos du livre de Jérémie et de ses rapports avec la littérature deutéronomiste, par A.H.W. CURTIS – T. RÖMER, *Avant-propos*, in ID., *The Book of Jeremiah and Its Reception*, p. 13.

tiques. À part les oracles d'Ézéchiel, il n'y a guère de texte biblique de l'époque royale qui n'ait fait partie des recueils réécrits par Dtr[43]. Cela permet d'expliquer d'une manière très simple le fait que l'Histoire deutéronomiste ne mentionne pas Jérémie: ce n'était pas nécessaire, parce que le prophète et sa prédication faisaient l'objet d'un recueil spécifique[44]. À lui seul, ce silence témoigne déjà d'un projet d'ensemble, avec une répartition réfléchie des matières entre divers ouvrages.

2° L'édition Dtr575 des textes bibliques était déjà unifiée par son projet théologique: il s'agissait de sauver la foi en YHWH, et donc de donner une explication à la grande catastrophe qui ne remette en cause ni sa justice ni sa bonté envers Israël. Il n'empêche: même si leur édition avait été pensée d'une manière systématique, les grands blocs de textes n'étaient guère reliés entre eux. L'éditeur de la génération suivante (Dtr560) a été beaucoup plus loin dans l'intégration, en établissant des correspondances entre l'Exode et le Deutéronome, ainsi qu'entre le livre des Rois, Isaïe et Jérémie. Le lecteur est renvoyé d'un bloc à l'autre, si bien que toute la littérature deutéronomiste forme désormais un seul réseau de textes, dont aucun n'est isolable des autres. En d'autres termes, le projet était vraiment d'écrire un livre, et non plus de constituer une bibliothèque d'œuvres choisies. Soit dit en passant, cela justifie l'emploi du même sigle pour les différents ensembles littéraires retravaillés dans ce projet unique.

---

43. T. COLLINS, *Deuteronomist Influence on the Prophetical Books*, in CURTIS – RÖMER, *The Book of Jeremiah and Its Reception*, pp. 15-26, observe que l'Histoire deutéronomiste et les livres prophétiques ont connu les mêmes procédés rédactionnels; il ajoute: «It looks very much as if the two bodies of literary material were being submitted to a similar process of composition at roughly the same time» (pp. 16-17). L'absence probable du recueil d'Ézéchiel est logique s'il est vrai que le prophète a au moins achevé sa prédication à Babylone, alors que l'école deutéronomiste doit plutôt être située en Palestine. Cette question est, je le reconnais volontiers, vivement discutée, et il faudrait y consacrer de longs développements. L'origine palestinienne des écrits deutéronomistes me paraît postulée par Dt 16–18: le pays est appelé à être dirigé par une nouvelle dynastie, un nouveau clergé et un nouveau prophétisme; les élites déportées par Nabuchodonosor n'y ont aucune place. Les arguments allégués en sens contraire ne me semblent pas décisifs: 2 R 25,22-26, qui donne l'image d'un pays vidé de tous ses habitants judéens, provient à mon avis d'un rédacteur post-deutéronomiste, qui résume d'une manière tendancieuse Jr 40–41; de même, je pense que la rédaction du livre de Jérémie favorable à la Golah (voir en particulier Jr 24) est postérieure à Dtr. D'autre part, R. ALBERTZ, *Le milieu des Deutéronomistes*, in DE PURY *et al.*, *Israël construit son histoire*, pp. 377-407 (spéc. 394-401), a avancé une série d'arguments en faveur de la localisation des éditeurs deutéronomistes du livre de Jérémie en Palestine.

44. Il en va de même pour les autres prophètes classiques de la seconde partie de l'époque royale. Au-delà des raisons particulières qui pouvaient concerner tel ou tel prophète, il faut s'interroger sur le fait que le silence porte sur l'ensemble d'entre eux. C'est pourquoi je ne puis me contenter des considérations de C.T. BEGG, *A Biblical Mystery: The Absence of Jeremiah in the Deuteronomistic History*, in *IBSt* 7 (1985) 139-164; ID.,

3° S'il est vrai que les renvois d'un bloc à l'autre révèlent, plus que d'autres phénomènes littéraires, l'intention de l'éditeur, le rôle attribué au livre est sans doute significatif. Dans les récits écrits par Dtr560 dans le livre de Jérémie, l'épisode décisif du rejet du prophète et de sa parole ne concerne pas son action prophétique (chap. 19–20), ni son grand discours du Temple (chap. 26), mais le recueil écrit de ses oracles dictés à Baruch (chap. 36); c'est la destruction du livre qui marque la rupture définitive et entraîne ainsi le grand malheur[45]. De même, le récit de 2 R 22–23 insiste sur la découverte d'un Livre de la Loi (*sép^hèr hattôrāh*) dont le contenu doit être aussitôt mis en pratique; comme on le sait, les prescriptions correspondent au contenu de Dt 12–26, c'est-à-dire au livre de la Loi du temps de Moïse dont parle le livre du Deutéronome (30,10; 31,9.24; cf. 29,26)[46] et sans doute celui de Josué (8,34; 23,6; 24,26), loi qui concrétise celle du Décalogue, écrite par YHWH lui-même sur deux tables de pierre (Dt 5,22; 10,4). Le livre constitué par Dtr560 est évidemment beaucoup plus large que ce *sép^hèr hattôrāh*, mais il faut compter avec un phénomène d'homologie: c'est le respect dû à l'écrit donné par Dieu à travers ses prophètes (Moïse, Jérémie) qui commande tout l'avenir du peuple (cf. Dt 11).

4° Alors que Dtr575 proposait avant tout une théodicée et une interprétation du malheur passé, la grande entreprise de Dtr560 donne un véritable programme pour une restauration d'Israël après la fin du malheur (Dt 12–26). Les grands discours parénétiques s'inscrivent dans cette perspective: l'avenir ne pourra être assuré que pour un peuple fidèle à la

The Non-mention of Amos, Hosea and Micah in the Deuteronomistic History, in *BN* 32 (1986) 41-53; ID., *The Non-mention of Zephaniah, Nahum and Habakkuk in the Deuteronomistic History*, in *BN* 38-39 (1987) 19-25. Certains objecteront peut-être que 2 R 18–20 raconte l'histoire des interventions d'Isaïe au temps d'Ézéchias, alors que ce prophète a aussi «son» livre. En fait, contrairement à l'opinion dominante, il semble que ces récits n'ont été introduits dans les livres des Rois qu'à l'époque perse, bien après le travail littéraire des deutéronomistes; voir à ce sujet J. VERMEYLEN, *Hypothèses*, pp. 96-108.

45. Y. HOFFMANN, *Aetiology, Redaction and Historicity in Jeremia XXXVI*, in *VT* 46 (1996) 179-189, relève combien le narrateur de Jr 36 souligne l'écriture du rouleau par Baruch et non par Jérémie lui-même: transmettant la parole prophétique, le livre a la même autorité, quel que soit le scripteur.

46. Déjà le Décalogue, écrit par YHWH lui-même, doit être recopié sur divers supports (Dt 6,8-9; 11,18-21) et le roi doit écrire la loi qui le concerne (17,18). Après le passage du Jourdain, la Loi devra, en outre, être écrite sur des pierres enduites de chaux (27,3.8; cet ordre sera exécuté en Jos 8,32). Sur la signification du passage de l'oral à l'écrit dans le Deutéronome, voir J.-P. SONNET, *Le Deutéronome et la modernité du livre*, in *NRT* 118 (1996) 481-496; ID., *The Book within the Book. Writing in Deuteronomy* (Biblical Interpretation Series, 14), Leiden, Brill, 1997.

Loi d'Alliance écrite dans le livre, imitant en cela la conduite de Moïse, d'Ézéchias et de Josias. C'est au service de cet appel à la fidélité que joue l'opposition entre les figures royales positives et négatives (Achaz, Yoyaqim).

5° Le livre écrit par Dtr560 est revêtu de l'autorité prophétique : non seulement il englobe plusieurs recueils reprenant les oracles des prophètes de l'époque royale, mais il est aussi placé sous le double signe de l'affrontement entre le prophète et le roi (voir le livre de Jérémie, mais aussi l'opposition entre Moïse et Pharaon, Ex 7–11*, ainsi qu'entre Élie et Achab 1 R 17–19*) et de la Loi donnée par le prophète Moïse (Dt 18,18)[47]. L'autorité du «livre Dtr560» est telle, que celui-ci sera reconnu et adopté par les Sionistes, alors que cette œuvre a été produite par les gens restés au pays[48]. Le plus étonnant, c'est qu'elle n'a pas été conservée par les gens de Samarie : les Samaritains ne reconnaissent comme Écriture sainte que le Pentateuque, sans doute imposé par Esdras.

6° Le seul élément qui fasse obstacle à l'hypothèse de l'œuvre Dtr560 comme premier canon des Écritures est son ouverture à des réécritures ultérieures. Le texte n'est pas encore considéré comme sacré au point qu'on ne puisse plus le retravailler. Ce n'est donc pas le canon définitif. Rien ne prouve cependant que l'auteur avait conscience de ce statut provisoire. De plus, les éditions ultérieures témoignent à leur manière de l'autorité du texte : les rédacteurs se contenteront d'expliquer et de compléter, sans que l'on puisse jamais les surprendre à l'amputer d'éléments gênants.

La formation du canon doit se comprendre comme un processus s'étendant sur une longue période, depuis la formation des premières traditions jusqu'à la fixation définitive du texte. Dans le cadre de cette réflexion, l'apport de Dtr560 me paraît être décisif, car les références croi-

---

47. R.P. CARROLL, *Manuscripts Don't Burn – Inscribing the Prophetic Tradition. Reflections on Jeremiah 36*, in M.A. AUGUSTIN – K.D. SCHUNCK (eds.), *«Dort ziehen Schiffe dahin...». Collected Communications to the xivth Congress of the International Organization for the Study of the Old Testament, Paris 1992* (BEAT, 28), Frankfurt/M., Lang, 1996, pp. 31-42, insiste sur le fait que l'écrit n'est nécessaire qu'en cas d'absence du prophète. C'est quand le prophète a disparu que le livre porteur de son autorité en est comme le prolongement. Cela explique l'importance d'un personnage comme le scribe Baruch; selon le texte de la LXX, qui paraît refléter un texte hébreu antérieur au TM, le livre de Jérémie s'achève précisément par la promesse de Jérémie à son scribe (chap. 45 TM). J.-P. SONNET, *Le Deutéronome et la modernité du livre*, p. 486, souligne, dans le même sens, que le message de Moïse ne pourra être transmis sur la terre d'Israël que par l'écriture. Le prophète meurt, mais sa parole survit dans le livre.

48. Voir la note 43.

sées témoignent de la volonté de concevoir une œuvre littéraire unique:
non plus une bibliothèque, mais un livre[49].

Avenue Henri Conscience 156   Jacques VERMEYLEN
B-1140 Bruxelles

49. Cet ensemble intégré sera ensuite refragmenté et connaîtra encore une longue histoire. On peut l'imaginer ainsi: 1° Pendant l'exil à Babylone ou – plus probablement – au début de l'époque perse, les apports de P ne concerneront que le Tétrateuque; une rédaction à tendance eschatologique des recueils prophétiques présente plusieurs points communs avec P, mais on ne trouve aucune trace comparable dans le Deutéronome ou l'Histoire deutéronomiste, sinon peut-être dans la première partie du livre de Josué. 2° L'«école de Néhémie» va retravailler les recueils prophétiques seulement. En dehors de l'œuvre Dtr560, elle écrit les premières formes des livres des Proverbes, de Job et sans doute du Psautier. 3° L' «école d'Esdras» réédite toute la littérature connue à ce moment: Pentateuque (le Deutéronome lui est incorporé, et le livre est isolé comme Torah), Histoire deutéronomiste, Psautier, Proverbes, Job, recueils prophétiques. Le Chroniqueur écrit plus tard, mais dans une ligne assez proche. Dès ce moment, la Torah reçoit son statut pleinement canonique, et le texte de l'Histoire deutéronomiste est fixé définitivement. Peut-être ces deux ensembles sont-ils compris dès ce moment comme «la Loi et les Prophètes». 4° L'«école du Siracide» va faire accéder un nouveau bloc de texte au statut canonique définitif en adjoignant les «prophètes postérieurs» aux «prophètes antérieurs». Cette même école est encore responsable du texte définitif de différents livres, dont il est difficile de savoir dans quelle mesure ils étaient associés les uns aux autres: le Psautier, les Proverbes, Job, les Chroniques, Esdras et Néhémie. 5° La dernière étape de ce processus sera celle du Judaïsme postérieur à la fin du second Temple, avec l'assemblée de Yamnia.

ABBREVIATIONS

AASF B	Annales Academiae Scientiarum Fennicae. Series B
AB	Anchor Bible
ACEBT	Amsterdamse cahiers voor exegese en bijbelse theologie
ADPV	Abhandlungen des Deutschen Palästina-Vereins. Wiesbaden, O. Harassowitz, 1969 -
AnBib	Analecta Biblica
ANET	Ancient Near Eastern Texts Relating to the Old Testament. J.B. Pritchard (ed.), Princeton, Princeton University Press, 1950; 1969^3
ATANT	Abhandlungen zur Theologie des Alten und Neuen Testaments
ATD	Das Alte Testament Deutsch
ATD E	Das Alte Testament Deutsch. Ergänzungsband
ATSAT	Arbeiten zu Text und Sprache im Alten Testament
BASOR	Bulletin of the American Schools of Oriental Research
BBB	Bonner biblische Beiträge
BEAT	Beiträge zur Erforschung des Alten Testaments und des antiken Judentums
BETL	Bibliotheca Ephemeridum Theologicarum Lovaniensium
BEvT	Beiträge zur evangelischen Theologie
Bib	Biblica
BiKi	Bibel und Kirche
BiLiSe	Bible and Literature Series
BN	Biblische Notizen
BN.B	Biblische Notizen. Beiheft
BTSt	Biblisch-theologische Studien
BWANT	Beiträge zur Wissenschaft vom Alten und Neuen Testament
BZ	Biblische Zeitschrift
BZ (NF)	Biblische Zeitschrift (Neue Folge)
BZAW	Beihefte zur Zeitschrift für die alttestamentliche Wissenschaft
CBQ	Catholic Biblical Quarterly
CBQ MS	Catholic Biblical Quarterly. Monograph Series
CE	Cahiers Évangile
CNEB	Cambridge Bible Commentary on the New English Bible
CB OT	Coniectanea biblica. Old Testament Series
CRB	Cahiers de la Revue biblique
CR:BS	Currents in Research: Biblical Studies
CTM	Calwer theologische Monographien
DBAT	Dielheimer Blätter zum Alten Testament
EdF	Erträge der Forschung
ETL	Ephemerides Theologicae Lovanienses

EurHS	Europäische Hochschulschriften. Reihe XXIII: Theologie
EvT	Evangelische Theologie
FAT	Forschungen zum Alten Testament
FOTL	The Forms of the Old Testament Literature
FRLANT	Forschungen zur Religion und Literatur des Alten und Neuen Testaments
FTSt	Freiburger theologische Studien
FzB	Forschung zur Bibel
GAT	Grundriße zum Alten Testament
GTA	Göttinger theologische Arbeiten
HAR	Hebrew Annual Review
HAT	Handbuch zum Alten Testament
HBS	Herders biblische Studien
HSM	Harvard Semitic Monographs
HTR	Harvard Theological Review
IBSt	Irish Biblical Studies
ICC	The International Critical Commentary
IEJ	Israel Exploration Journal
Int	Interpretation: A Journal of Bible and Theology
JAOS	Journal of the American Oriental Society
JBL	Journal of Biblical Literature
JSNT SS	Journal for the Study of the New Testament. Supplement Series
JSOT	Journal for the Study of the Old Testament
JSOT SS	Journal for the Study of the Old Testament. Supplement Series
JTS	Journal of Theological Studies
KAT	Kommentar zum Alten Testament
KHAT	Kurzer Hand-Kommentar zum Alten Testament
LD	Lectio Divina
MtA	Münsteraner theologische Abhandlungen
NAC	The New American Commentary. An Exegetical and Theological Exposition of Holy Scripture
NCBC	New Century Bible Commentary
NCeB	New Century Bible
NEB	Neue Echter Bibel
NRT	Nouvelle revue théologique
NSKAT	Neuer Stuttgarter Kommentar. Altes Testament
NTOA	Novum Testamentum et orbis antiquus
OBO	Orbis biblicus et orientalis
OTG	Old Testament Guides
OTL	Old Testament Library
OTS	Oudtestamentische Studiën
QD	Quaestiones Disputatae

RB	Revue biblique
RS	Religion and Society
RTP	Revue de théologie et de philosophie
SBAAT	Stuttgarter biblische Aufsatzbände. Altes Testament
SBB	Stuttgarter Biblische Beiträge
SBL DS	Society of Biblical Literature. Dissertation Series
SBS	Stuttgarter Bibelstudien
ScrHie	Scripta Hierosolymitana
SHANE	Studies in the History of the Ancient Near East
SJOT	Scandinavian Journal of the Old Testament
SSN	Studia Semitica Neerlandica
ST	Studienbücher Theologie
SVT	Supplements to Vetus Testamentum
TB	Theologische Bücherei
TECC	Textos y Estudios "Cardinal Cisneros"
TGI	Textbuch zur Geschichte Israels. K. Galling (ed.), Tübingen, Mohr (Siebeck), 1950; 1968²
TBAT	Theologische Bücherei. Altes Testament
THAT	Theologisches Handwörterbuch zum Alten Testament. E. JENNI et al. (eds.), 2 vols., München, Kaiser; Zürich, Theologischer Verlag, 1971 (1984⁴), 1976 (1984³)
TR	Theologische Rundschau. Tübingen
Trans	Transeuphratène
TRE	Theologische Realenzyklopädie. Berlin - New York, W. de Gruyter, 1977-
TUAT	Texte aus der Umwelt des Alten Testaments. O. KAISER (ed.), Gütersloh, G. Mohn, 1982-
TW	Theologische Wissenschaft
TWAT	Theologisches Wörterbuch zum Alten Testament. G.J. BOTTERWECK, H. RINGGREN, H.-J. FABRY (eds.), 10 vols., Stuttgart-Berlin, W. Kohlhammer, 1973-1997
TZ	Theologische Zeitschrift
TLZ	Theologische Literaturzeitung
VT	Vetus Testamentum
WBC	Word Biblical Commentary
WMANT	Wissenschaftliche Monographien zum Alten und Neuen Testament
ZAW	Zeitschrift für die alttestamentliche Wissenschaft
ZBK AT	Zürcher Bibelkommentare. Altes Testament
ZEE	Zeitschrift für evangelische Ethik
ZTK	Zeitschrift für Theologie und Kirche

INDEX OF AUTHORS

INDEX OF BIBLICAL REFERENCES

16,5	23		5	17 n. 57	
16,7	27		6	17 n. 57	
16,8	27		8,9	74 n. 9	
16,10	27		9	191, 192	
18	19, 23				
18,1	23		**NEHEMIAH**		
18,2	23				
18,3-34	23		3,34	73	
18,3	23		5,13	24	
18,5	21, 23		9,8	24	
18,11	21		10	191, 192	
18,12-27	26				
18,14	21, 23		**ESTHER**		
18,19	23				
18,22	21		5,5	24	
19,2	28				
20,20	27		**JOB**		
21,7	21				
23,13	25		1-2	22	
24,19	27		1,5	22	
24,20-22	27		1,7	22	
26,22	27		1,9	21	
27	27		1,22	22	
28,25	25		2,2	22	
31,2	215 n. 11		2,3	21, 22	
32,15	27		2,10	22	
32,20-22	22				
34	19		**PSALMS**		
34,8	232 n. 29				
34,19	25		44,2-4	110 n. 39	
34,20-28	24		44,10-23	110 n. 39	
34,20	24		60,2	75	
34,21	24		78	192	
34,23-28	22		89	192	
34,23	26				
34,24	25		**PROVERBS**		
34,25	25				
34,26	26		1-9	96, 97	
34,27	25				
34,31	24		**ISAIAH**		
35,25	4 n. 18				
36,12	4 n. 18		1-39	181	
36,20	226-27 n. 9		1,10	95	
36,21	27		1,26	53	
			6,9-10	52	
EZRA			7-8	21	
			7	1, 230, 231, 233	
1-6	11		7,1-9	53	
2,6	74 n. 9		7,1-2	231	
4,1-5	226-27 n. 9				

7,2	231-32 n. 27
7,3	231
7,4-9	231
7,9	27, 232
7,10-16	231-32 n. 27
7,10-13	232
7,15-17	231-32 n. 27
7,20	231-32 n. 27
8,16	95 + n. 23
8,20	95 n. 23
9,1-6	6 n. 26
10,5-15	53
10,20	27
11,2	90
22	231 n. 25, 232 n. 29
22,15-23	231
22,15	77, 231 n. 25
22,20	231 n. 25
36ff.	187 n. 36
36-39	227 n. 10, 231 + n. 25, 233
36-38	187 n. 36
36-37	230, 231, 233
36	232 n. 29
36,1	231
36,2-37,9	230
36,2	231
36,3	231 + n. 25, 232
36,7	233 + n. 31
36,11	231 n. 25, 232
36,13	232 n. 30
36,17	231 n. 26
36,18-20	233
36,22	232
37,1	231-32 n. 27, 233
37,2	233
37,6-7	231
37,9-21	233
37,9-20	231
37,30-32	231-32 n. 27
37,33-35	231, 233
37,37-38	230
39,6-7	231-32 n. 27
40ff.	189
42,14	189
44,3	190
45,1	117 n. 70

BIBLIOTHECA EPHEMERIDUM THEOLOGICARUM LOVANIENSIUM

SERIES I

* = Out of print

*1. *Miscellanea dogmatica in honorem Eximii Domini J. Bittremieux*, 1947.
*2-3. *Miscellanea moralia in honorem Eximii Domini A. Janssen*, 1948.
*4. G. PHILIPS, *La grâce des justes de l'Ancien Testament*, 1948.
*5. G. PHILIPS, *De ratione instituendi tractatum de gratia nostrae sanctificationis*, 1953.
6-7. *Recueil Lucien Cerfaux. Études d'exégèse et d'histoire religieuse*, 1954. 504 et 577 p. FB 1000 par tome. Cf. *infra*, n°s 18 et 71 (t. III).
8. G. THILS, *Histoire doctrinale du mouvement œcuménique*, 1955. Nouvelle édition, 1963. 338 p. FB 135.
*9. *Études sur l'Immaculée Conception*, 1955.
*10. J.A. O'DONOHOE, *Tridentine Seminary Legislation*, 1957.
*11. G. THILS, *Orientations de la théologie*, 1958.
*12-13. J. COPPENS, A. DESCAMPS, É. MASSAUX (ed.), *Sacra Pagina. Miscellanea Biblica Congressus Internationalis Catholici de Re Biblica*, 1959.
*14. *Adrien VI, le premier Pape de la contre-réforme*, 1959.
*15. F. CLAEYS BOUUAERT, *Les déclarations et serments imposés par la loi civile aux membres du clergé belge sous le Directoire (1795-1801)*, 1960.
*16. G. THILS, *La «Théologie œcuménique». Notion-Formes-Démarches*, 1960.
17. G. THILS, *Primauté pontificale et prérogatives épiscopales. «Potestas ordinaria» au Concile du Vatican*, 1961. 103 p. FB 50.
*18. *Recueil Lucien Cerfaux*, t. III, 1962. Cf. *infra*, n° 71.
*19. *Foi et réflexion philosophique. Mélanges F. Grégoire*, 1961.
*20. *Mélanges G. Ryckmans*, 1963.
21. G. THILS, *L'infaillibilité du peuple chrétien «in credendo»*, 1963. 67 p. FB 50.
*22. J. FÉRIN & L. JANSSENS, *Progestogènes et morale conjugale*, 1963.
*23. *Collectanea Moralia in honorem Eximii Domini A. Janssen*, 1964.
24. H. CAZELLES (ed.), *De Mari à Qumrân. L'Ancien Testament. Son milieu. Ses écrits. Ses relectures juives* (Hommage J. Coppens, I), 1969. 158*-370 p. FB 900.
*25. I. DE LA POTTERIE (ed.), *De Jésus aux évangiles. Tradition et rédaction dans les évangiles synoptiques* (Hommage J. Coppens, II), 1967.
26. G. THILS & R.E. BROWN (ed.), *Exégèse et théologie* (Hommage J. Coppens, III), 1968. 328 p. FB 700.
27. J. COPPENS (ed.), *Ecclesia a Spiritu sancto edocta. Hommage à Mgr G. Philips*, 1970. 640 p. FB 1000.
28. J. COPPENS (ed.), *Sacerdoce et célibat. Études historiques et théologiques*, 1971. 740 p. FB 700.

29. M. DIDIER (ed.), *L'évangile selon Matthieu. Rédaction et théologie*, 1972. 432 p. FB 1000.
*30. J. KEMPENEERS, *Le Cardinal van Roey en son temps*, 1971.

SERIES II

31. F. NEIRYNCK, *Duality in Mark. Contributions to the Study of the Markan Redaction*, 1972. Revised edition with Supplementary Notes, 1988. 252 p. FB 1200.
32. F. NEIRYNCK (ed.), *L'évangile de Luc. Problèmes littéraires et théologiques*, 1973. *L'évangile de Luc – The Gospel of Luke*. Revised and enlarged edition, 1989. x-590 p. FB 2200.
33. C. BREKELMANS (ed.), *Questions disputées d'Ancien Testament. Méthode et théologie*, 1974. *Continuing Questions in Old Testament Method and Theology*. Revised and enlarged edition by M. VERVENNE, 1989. 245 p. FB 1200.
34. M. SABBE (ed.), *L'évangile selon Marc. Tradition et rédaction*, 1974. Nouvelle édition augmentée, 1988. 601 p. FB 2400.
35. B. WILLAERT (ed.), *Philosophie de la religion – Godsdienstfilosofie. Miscellanea Albert Dondeyne*, 1974. Nouvelle édition, 1987. 458 p. FB 1600.
36. G. PHILIPS, *L'union personnelle avec le Dieu vivant. Essai sur l'origine et le sens de la grâce créée*, 1974. Édition révisée, 1989. 299 p. FB 1000.
37. F. NEIRYNCK, in collaboration with T. HANSEN and F. VAN SEGBROECK, *The Minor Agreements of Matthew and Luke against Mark with a Cumulative List*, 1974. 330 p. FB 900.
38. J. COPPENS, *Le messianisme et sa relève prophétique. Les anticipations vétérotestamentaires. Leur accomplissement en Jésus*, 1974. Édition révisée, 1989. XIII-265 p. FB 1000.
39. D. SENIOR, *The Passion Narrative according to Matthew. A Redactional Study*, 1975. New impression, 1982. 440 p. FB 1000.
40. J. DUPONT (ed.), *Jésus aux origines de la christologie*, 1975. Nouvelle édition augmentée, 1989. 458 p. FB 1500.
41. J. COPPENS (ed.), *La notion biblique de Dieu*, 1976. Réimpression, 1985. 519 p. FB 1600.
42. J. LINDEMANS & H. DEMEESTER (ed.), *Liber Amicorum Monseigneur W. Onclin*, 1976. XXII-396 p. FB 1000.
43. R.E. HOECKMAN (ed.), *Pluralisme et œcuménisme en recherches théologiques. Mélanges offerts au R.P. Dockx, O.P.*, 1976. 316 p. FB 1000.
44. M. DE JONGE (ed.), *L'évangile de Jean. Sources, rédaction, théologie*, 1977. Réimpression, 1987. 416 p. FB 1500.
45. E.J.M. VAN EIJL (ed.), *Facultas S. Theologiae Lovaniensis 1432-1797. Bijdragen tot haar geschiedenis. Contributions to its History. Contributions à son histoire*, 1977. 570 p. FB 1700.
46. M. DELCOR (ed.), *Qumrân. Sa piété, sa théologie et son milieu*, 1978. 432 p. FB 1700.
47. M. CAUDRON (ed.), *Faith and Society. Foi et société. Geloof en maatschappij. Acta Congressus Internationalis Theologici Lovaniensis 1976*, 1978. 304 p. FB 1150.

48. J. KREMER (ed.), *Les Actes des Apôtres. Traditions, rédaction, théologie,* 1979. 590 p. FB 1700.
49. F. NEIRYNCK, avec la collaboration de J. DELOBEL, T. SNOY, G. VAN BELLE, F. VAN SEGBROECK, *Jean et les Synoptiques. Examen critique de l'exégèse de M.-É. Boismard,* 1979. XII-428 p. FB 1000.
50. J. COPPENS, *La relève apocalyptique du messianisme royal. I. La royauté – Le règne – Le royaume de Dieu. Cadre de la relève apocalyptique,* 1979. 325 p. FB 1000.
51. M. GILBERT (ed.), *La Sagesse de l'Ancien Testament,* 1979. Nouvelle édition mise à jour, 1990. 455 p. FB 1500.
52. B. DEHANDSCHUTTER, *Martyrium Polycarpi. Een literair-kritische studie,* 1979. 296 p. FB 1000.
53. J. LAMBRECHT (ed.), *L'Apocalypse johannique et l'Apocalyptique dans le Nouveau Testament,* 1980. 458 p. FB 1400.
54. P.-M. BOGAERT (ed.), *Le livre de Jérémie. Le prophète et son milieu. Les oracles et leur transmission,* 1981. *Nouvelle édition mise à jour,* 1997. 448 p. FB 1800.
55. J. COPPENS, *La relève apocalyptique du messianisme royal. III. Le Fils de l'homme néotestamentaire.* Édition posthume par F. NEIRYNCK, 1981. XIV-192 p. FB 800.
56. J. VAN BAVEL & M. SCHRAMA (ed.), *Jansénius et le Jansénisme dans les Pays-Bas. Mélanges Lucien Ceyssens,* 1982. 247 p. FB 1000.
57. J.H. WALGRAVE, *Selected Writings – Thematische geschriften. Thomas Aquinas, J.H. Newman, Theologia Fundamentalis.* Edited by G. DE SCHRIJVER & J.J. KELLY, 1982. XLIII-425 p. FB 1000.
58. F. NEIRYNCK & F. VAN SEGBROECK, avec la collaboration de E. MANNING, *Ephemerides Theologicae Lovanienses 1924-1981. Tables générales. (Bibliotheca Ephemeridum Theologicarum Lovaniensium 1947-1981),* 1982. 400 p. FB 1600.
59. J. DELOBEL (ed.), *Logia. Les paroles de Jésus – The Sayings of Jesus. Mémorial Joseph Coppens,* 1982. 647 p. FB 2000.
60. F. NEIRYNCK, *Evangelica. Gospel Studies – Études d'évangile. Collected Essays.* Edited by F. VAN SEGBROECK, 1982. XIX-1036 p. FB 2000.
61. J. COPPENS, *La relève apocalyptique du messianisme royal. II. Le Fils d'homme vétéro- et intertestamentaire.* Édition posthume par J. LUST, 1983. XVII-272 p. FB 1000.
62. J.J. KELLY, *Baron Friedrich von Hügel's Philosophy of Religion,* 1983. 232 p. FB 1500.
63. G. DE SCHRIJVER, *Le merveilleux accord de l'homme et de Dieu. Étude de l'analogie de l'être chez Hans Urs von Balthasar,* 1983. 344 p. FB 1500.
64. J. GROOTAERS & J.A. SELLING, *The 1980 Synod of Bishops: «On the Role of the Family». An Exposition of the Event and an Analysis of its Texts.* Preface by Prof. emeritus L. JANSSENS, 1983. 375 p. FB 1500.
65. F. NEIRYNCK & F. VAN SEGBROECK, *New Testament Vocabulary. A Companion Volume to the Concordance,* 1984. XVI-494 p. FB 2000.
66. R.F. COLLINS, *Studies on the First Letter to the Thessalonians,* 1984. XI-415 p. FB 1500.
67. A. PLUMMER, *Conversations with Dr. Döllinger 1870-1890.* Edited with Introduction and Notes by R. BOUDENS, with the collaboration of L. KENIS, 1985. LIV-360 p. FB 1800.

68. N. LOHFINK (ed.), *Das Deuteronomium. Entstehung, Gestalt und Botschaft /
    Deuteronomy: Origin, Form and Message,* 1985. XI-382 p. FB 2000.
69. P.F. FRANSEN, *Hermeneutics of the Councils and Other Studies.* Collected
    by H.E. MERTENS & F. DE GRAEVE, 1985. 543 p. FB 1800.
70. J. DUPONT, *Études sur les Évangiles synoptiques.* Présentées par F.
    NEIRYNCK, 1985. 2 tomes, XXI-IX-1210 p. FB 2800.
71. *Recueil Lucien Cerfaux,* t. III, 1962. Nouvelle édition revue et complétée,
    1985. LXXX-458 p. FB 1600.
72. J. GROOTAERS, *Primauté et collégialité. Le dossier de Gérard Philips sur
    la Nota Explicativa Praevia (Lumen gentium, Chap. III).* Présenté avec
    introduction historique, annotations et annexes. Préface de G. THILS,
    1986. 222 p. FB 1000.
73. A. VANHOYE (ed.), *L'apôtre Paul. Personnalité, style et conception du
    ministère,* 1986. XIII-470 p. FB 2600.
74. J. LUST (ed.), *Ezekiel and His Book. Textual and Literary Criticism and
    their Interrelation,* 1986. X-387 p. FB 2700.
75. É. MASSAUX, *Influence de l'Évangile de saint Matthieu sur la littérature
    chrétienne avant saint Irénée.* Réimpression anastatique présentée par
    F. NEIRYNCK. *Supplément: Bibliographie 1950-1985,* par B. DEHAND-
    SCHUTTER, 1986. XXVII-850 p. FB 2500.
76. L. CEYSSENS & J.A.G. TANS, *Autour de l'Unigenitus. Recherches sur la
    genèse de la Constitution,* 1987. XXVI-845 p. FB 2500.
77. A. DESCAMPS, *Jésus et l'Église. Études d'exégèse et de théologie.* Préface
    de Mgr A. HOUSSIAU, 1987. XLV-641 p. FB 2500.
78. J. DUPLACY, *Études de critique textuelle du Nouveau Testament.* Présentées
    par J. DELOBEL, 1987. XXVII-431 p. FB 1800.
79. E.J.M. VAN EIJL (ed.), *L'image de C. Jansénius jusqu'à la fin du XVIIIᵉ
    siècle,* 1987. 258 p. FB 1250.
80. E. BRITO, *La Création selon Schelling. Universum,* 1987. XXXV-646 p.
    FB 2980.
81. J. VERMEYLEN (ed.), *The Book of Isaiah – Le livre d'Isaïe. Les oracles
    et leurs relectures. Unité et complexité de l'ouvrage,* 1989. X-472 p.
    FB 2700.
82. G. VAN BELLE, *Johannine Bibliography 1966-1985. A Cumulative Biblio-
    graphy on the Fourth Gospel,* 1988. XVII-563 p. FB 2700.
83. J.A. SELLING (ed.), *Personalist Morals. Essays in Honor of Professor
    Louis Janssens,* 1988. VIII-344 p. FB 1200.
84. M.-É. BOISMARD, *Moïse ou Jésus. Essai de christologie johannique,* 1988.
    XVI-241 p. FB 1000.
84ᴬ. M.-É. BOISMARD, *Moses or Jesus: An Essay in Johannine Christology.*
    Translated by B.T. VIVIANO, 1993, XVI-144 p. FB 1000.
85. J.A. DICK, *The Malines Conversations Revisited,* 1989. 278 p. FB 1500.
86. J.-M. SEVRIN (ed.), *The New Testament in Early Christianity – La récep-
    tion des écrits néotestamentaires dans le christianisme primitif,* 1989.
    XVI-406 p. FB 2500.
87. R.F. COLLINS (ed.), *The Thessalonian Correspondence,* 1990. XV-546 p.
    FB 3000.
88. F. VAN SEGBROECK, *The Gospel of Luke. A Cumulative Bibliography
    1973-1988,* 1989. 241 p. FB 1200.

89. G. THILS, *Primauté et infaillibilité du Pontife Romain à Vatican I et autres études d'ecclésiologie*, 1989. XI-422 p. FB 1850.
90. A. VERGOTE, *Explorations de l'espace théologique. Études de théologie et de philosophie de la religion*, 1990. XVI-709 p. FB 2000.
91. J.C. DE MOOR, *The Rise of Yahwism: The Roots of Israelite Monotheism*, 1990. *Revised and Enlarged Edition*, 1997. XV-445 p. FB 1400.
92. B. BRUNING, M. LAMBERIGTS & J. VAN HOUTEM (eds.), *Collectanea Augustiniana. Mélanges T.J. van Bavel*, 1990. 2 tomes, XXXVIII-VIII-1074 p. FB 3000.
93. A. DE HALLEUX, *Patrologie et œcuménisme. Recueil d'études*, 1990. XVI-887 p. FB 3000.
94. C. BREKELMANS & J. LUST (eds.), *Pentateuchal and Deuteronomistic Studies: Papers Read at the XIIIth IOSOT Congress Leuven 1989*, 1990. 307 p. FB 1500.
95. D.L. DUNGAN (ed.), *The Interrelations of the Gospels. A Symposium Led by M.-É. Boismard – W.R. Farmer – F. Neirynck, Jerusalem 1984*, 1990. XXXI-672 p. FB 3000.
96. G.D. KILPATRICK, *The Principles and Practice of New Testament Textual Criticism. Collected Essays*. Edited by J.K. ELLIOTT, 1990. XXXVIII-489 p. FB 3000.
97. G. ALBERIGO (ed.), *Christian Unity. The Council of Ferrara-Florence: 1438/39 – 1989*, 1991. x-681 p. FB 3000.
98. M. SABBE, *Studia Neotestamentica. Collected Essays*, 1991. XVI-573 p. FB 2000.
99. F. NEIRYNCK, *Evangelica II: 1982-1991. Collected Essays*. Edited by F. VAN SEGBROECK, 1991. XIX-874 p. FB 2800.
100. F. VAN SEGBROECK, C.M. TUCKETT, G. VAN BELLE & J. VERHEYDEN (eds.), *The Four Gospels 1992. Festschrift Frans Neirynck*, 1992. 3 volumes, XVII-X-X-2668 p. FB 5000.

SERIES III

101. A. DENAUX (ed.), *John and the Synoptics*, 1992. XXII-696 p. FB 3000.
102. F. NEIRYNCK, J. VERHEYDEN, F. VAN SEGBROECK, G. VAN OYEN & R. CORSTJENS, *The Gospel of Mark. A Cumulative Bibliography: 1950-1990*, 1992. XII-717 p. FB 2700.
103. M. SIMON, *Un catéchisme universel pour l'Église catholique. Du Concile de Trente à nos jours*, 1992. XIV-461 p. FB 2200.
104. L. CEYSSENS, *Le sort de la bulle Unigenitus. Recueil d'études offert à Lucien Ceyssens à l'occasion de son 90e anniversaire*. Présenté par M. LAMBERIGTS, 1992. XXVI-641 p. FB 2000.
105. R.J. DALY (ed.), *Origeniana Quinta. Papers of the 5th International Origen Congress, Boston College, 14-18 August 1989*, 1992. XVII-635 p. FB 2700.
106. A.S. VAN DER WOUDE (ed.), *The Book of Daniel in the Light of New Findings*, 1993. XVIII-574 p. FB 3000.
107. J. FAMERÉE, *L'ecclésiologie d'Yves Congar avant Vatican II: Histoire et Église. Analyse et reprise critique*, 1992. 497 p. FB 2600.

108. C. BEGG, *Josephus' Account of the Early Divided Monarchy (AJ 8, 212-420). Rewriting the Bible*, 1993. IX-377 p. FB 2400.
109. J. BULCKENS & H. LOMBAERTS (eds.), *L'enseignement de la religion catholique à l'école secondaire. Enjeux pour la nouvelle Europe*, 1993. XII-264 p. FB 1250.
110. C. FOCANT (ed.), *The Synoptic Gospels. Source Criticism and the New Literary Criticism*, 1993. XXXIX-670 p. FB 3000.
111. M. LAMBERIGTS (ed.), avec la collaboration de L. KENIS, *L'augustinisme à l'ancienne Faculté de théologie de Louvain*, 1994. VII-455 p. FB 2400.
112. R. BIERINGER & J. LAMBRECHT, *Studies on 2 Corinthians*, 1994. XX-632 p. FB 3000.
113. E. BRITO, *La pneumatologie de Schleiermacher*, 1994. XII-649 p. FB 3000.
114. W.A.M. BEUKEN (ed.), *The Book of Job*, 1994. X-462 p. FB 2400.
115. J. LAMBRECHT, *Pauline Studies: Collected Essays*, 1994. XIV-465 p. FB 2500.
116. G. VAN BELLE, *The Signs Source in the Fourth Gospel: Historical Survey and Critical Evaluation of the Semeia Hypothesis*, 1994. XIV-503 p. FB 2500.
117. M. LAMBERIGTS & P. VAN DEUN (eds.), *Martyrium in Multidisciplinary Perspective. Memorial L. Reekmans*, 1995. X-435 p. FB 3000.
118. G. DORIVAL & A. LE BOULLUEC (eds.), *Origeniana Sexta. Origène et la Bible / Origen and the Bible. Actes du Colloquium Origenianum Sextum, Chantilly, 30 août – 3 septembre 1993*, 1995. XII-865 p. FB 3900.
119. É. GAZIAUX, *Morale de la foi et morale autonome. Confrontation entre P. Delhaye et J. Fuchs*, 1995. XXII-545 p. FB 2700.
120. T.A. SALZMAN, *Deontology and Teleology: An Investigation of the Normative Debate in Roman Catholic Moral Theology*, 1995. XVII-555 p. FB 2700.
121. G.R. EVANS & M. GOURGUES (eds.), *Communion et Réunion. Mélanges Jean-Marie Roger Tillard*, 1995. XI-431 p. FB 2400.
122. H.T. FLEDDERMANN, *Mark and Q: A Study of the Overlap Texts*. With an *Assessment* by F. NEIRYNCK, 1995. XI-307 p. FB 1800.
123. R. BOUDENS, *Two Cardinals: John Henry Newman, Désiré-Joseph Mercier*. Edited by L. GEVERS with the collaboration of B. DOYLE, 1995. 362 p. FB 1800.
124. A. THOMASSET, *Paul Ricœur. Une poétique de la morale. Aux fondements d'une éthique herméneutique et narrative dans une perspective chrétienne*, 1996. XVI-706 p. FB 3000.
125. R. BIERINGER (ed.), *The Corinthian Correspondence*, 1996. XXVII-793 p. FB 2400.
126. M. VERVENNE (ed.), *Studies in the Book of Exodus: Redaction – Reception – Interpretation*, 1996. XI-660 p. FB 2400.
127. A. VANNESTE, *Nature et grâce dans la théologie occidentale. Dialogue avec H. de Lubac*, 1996. 312 p. FB 1800.
128. A. CURTIS & T. RÖMER (eds.), *The Book of Jeremiah and its Reception – Le livre de Jérémie et sa réception*, 1997. 332 p. FB 2400.
129. E. LANNE, *Tradition et Communion des Églises. Recueil d'études*, 1997. XXV-703 p. FB 3000.

130. A. DENAUX & J.A. DICK (eds.), *From Malines to ARCIC. The Malines Conversations Commemorated*, 1997. IX-317 p. FB 1800.

131. C.M. TUCKETT (ed.), *The Scriptures in the Gospels*, 1997. XXIV-721 p. FB 2400.

132. J. VAN RUITEN & M. VERVENNE (eds.), *Studies in the Book of Isaiah. Festschrift Willem A.M. Beuken*, 1997. XX-540 p. FB 3000.

133. M. VERVENNE & J. LUST (eds.), *Deuteronomy and Deuteronomic Literature. Festschrift C.H.W. Brekelmans*, 1997. XI-637 p. FB 3000.

134. G. VAN BELLE (ed.), *Index Generalis ETL / BETL 1982-1997*, 1999. IX-337 p. FB 1600.

135. G. DE SCHRIJVER, *Liberation Theologies on Shifting Grounds. A Clash of Socio-Economic and Cultural Paradigms*, 1998. XI-453 p. FB 2100.

136. A. SCHOORS (ed.), *Qohelet in the Context of Wisdom*, 1998. XI-528 p. FB 2400.

137. W.A. BIENERT & U. KÜHNEWEG (eds.), *Origeniana Septima. Origenes in den Auseinandersetzungen des 4. Jahrhunderts,* 1999. XXV-848 p. FB 3800.

138. É. GAZIAUX, *L'autonomie en morale: au croisement de la philosophie et de la théologie*, 1998. XVI-739 p. FB 3000.

139. J. GROOTAERS, *Actes et acteurs à Vatican II*, 1998. XXIV-602 p. FB 3000.

140. F. NEIRYNCK, J. VERHEYDEN & R. CORSTJENS, *The Gospel of Matthew and the Sayings Source Q: A Cumulative Bibliography 1950-1995*, 1998. 2 vols., VII-1000-420* p. FB 3800.

141. E. BRITO, *Heidegger et l'hymne du sacré*, 1999. XV-800 p. FB 3600.

142. J. VERHEYDEN (ed.), *The Unity of Luke-Acts*, 1999. XXV-828 p. FB 2400.

143. N. CALDUCH-BENAGES & J. VERMEYLEN (eds.), *Treasures of Wisdom. Studies in Ben Sira and the Book of Wisdom. Festschrift M. Gilbert*, 1999. XXVII-463 p. FB 3000.

144. J.-M. AUWERS & A. WÉNIN (eds.), *Lectures et relectures de la Bible. Festschrift P.-M. Bogaert*, 1999. XLII-482 p. FB 2400.

145. C. BEGG, *Josephus' Story of the Later Monarchy (AJ 9,1–10,185)*, 2000. X-650 p. FB 3000.

146. J.M. ASGEIRSSON, K. DE TROYER & M.W. MEYER (eds.), *From Quest to Q. Festschrift James M. Robinson*, 2000. XLIV-346 p. FB 2400.

147. T. RÖMER (ed.), *The Future of the Deuteronomistic History*, 2000. XII-265 p. FB 3000.

148. F.D. VANSINA, *Paul Ricœur: Bibliographie primaire et secondaire - Primary and Secondary Bibliography 1935-2000*, 2000. XXVI-544 p. FB 3000.

149. G.J. BROOKE & J.D. KAESTLI (eds.), *Narrativity in Biblical and Related Texts*, 2000. XXII-307 p. FB 3000.

150. F. NEIRYNCK, *Evangelica III: 1992-2000. Collected Essays*. Forthcoming.

151. B. DOYLE, *The Apocalypse of Isaiah Metaphorically Speaking. A Study of the Use, Function and Significance of Metaphors in Isaiah 24-27*, 2000. XII-453 p. FB 3000.

152. T. MERRIGAN & J. HAERS (eds.), *The Myriad Christ. Plurality and the Quest for Unity in Contemporary Christology*, 2000. XIV-593 p. FB 3000.

153. M. SIMON, *Le catéchisme de Jean-Paul II. Genèse et évaluation de son commentaire du Symbole des apôtres*, 2000. XVI-688 p. FB 3000.

154. J. VERMEYLEN, *La loi du plus fort. Histoire de la rédaction des récits davidiques de 1 Samuel 8 à 1 Rois 2*, 2000. XII-746 p.

155. A. WÉNIN, *Studies in the Book of Genesis. Literature, Redaction and History*. Forthcoming.
156. F. LEDEGANG, *Mysterium Ecclesisiae. Images of the Church and its Members in Origen*. Forthcoming.
157. J.S. BOSWELL, F.P. MCHUGH & J. VERSTRAETEN, *Catholic Social Thought: Twilight of Renaissance?*, 2000. XXII-307 p.

PRINTED ON PERMANENT PAPER • IMPRIME SUR PAPIER PERMANENT • GEDRUKT OP DUURZAAM PAPIER - ISO 9706

ORIENTALISTE, KLEIN DALENSTRAAT 42, B-3020 HERENT